MIRAGE IN THE DESERT?

REPORTING THE 'ARAB SPRING'

EDITED BY
JOHN MAIR
RICHARD LANCE KEEBLE

Published 2011 by Abramis academic publishing

www.abramis.co.uk

ISBN 978 1 84549 514 5

Printed and bound in the United Kingdom

Typeset in Garamond 12pt

Abramis is an imprint of arima publishing.

arima publishing
ASK House, Northgate Avenue
Bury St Edmunds, Suffolk IP32 6BB
t: (+44) 01284 700321

www.arimapublishing.com

Contents

Acknowledgements

The editors would like to thank:

The authors – especially the frontline correspondents who, literally in some cases, wrote as they descended from the aircraft steps. Their courage and stamina is outstanding.

The other contributors to the June 2011 conference and to this book who worked *pro bono* (as did the editors).

The Vice Chancellor of Coventry University, Professor Madeleine Atkins, who has been unstinting in her support of the series and the Coventry Conversations over six years.

Pro Vice Chancellor David Pilsbury and Professor Martin Woolley, also of Coventry University, who provided some seed money for the conference.

Our colleagues David Hayward and his Events team at the BBC College of Journalism who provided editorial and technical support for the conference and the book.

Our publisher Richard Franklin at Abramis for his sterling support and for being so efficient.

Finally, our families who have had to live through commissioning, writing and editing at a very non-academic speed in order to achieve our greatest aims – timeliness and impact.

In our last book (published in September 2011) we promised: "One day we will not wake up at the crack of dawn. One day."

Don't worry: that day come soon.

The editors

John Mair is Senior Lecturer in Broadcasting at Coventry University. He has won the Cecil Angel Cup for enhancing the prestige of Coventry University in 2009 and 2010. He invented and produces the weekly Coventry Conversations. He is a former BBC, ITV and Channel Four producer/director on a wide range of programmes from daily news to investigative documentaries on *World in Action* to more considered pieces on *Bookmark*. A Royal Television Society Journalism Award winner, he publishes widely in the media and journalism press including the *Guardian*, bbc.co.uk/journalism and journalism.co.uk. This is his seventh co-written or edited book. For the BBC, he co-wrote *Marx in London*, with Asa Briggs, in 1981.With Richard Lance Keeble, he edited *Beyond Trust* (2008) *Playing Footsie with the FTSE? The Great Crash of 2008 and the Crisis in Journalism (2009)*, *Afghanistan, War and the Media: Deadlines and Frontlines* (2010), *Face the Future: Tools for the Modern Media Age* (2011), *and Investigative Journalism: Dead Or Alive? (2011)*, all published by Arima, of Bury St. Edmunds. He is on the editorial board of *Ethical Space* and chairs the Institute of Communication Ethics. He is also a judge for the RTS Journalism Awards, the Muslim Young Writers and the Society of Editors Press Awards.

Richard Lance Keeble has been Professor of Journalism at the University of Lincoln since 2003. Before that he was the executive editor of the *Teacher*, the weekly newspaper of the National Union of Teachers and he lectured at City University, London, for 19 years. He has written and edited 20 publications including *Secret State, Silent Press: New Militarism, the Gulf and the Modern Image of Warfare* (John Libbey, Luton, 1997); *The Newspapers Handbook* (Routledge, 2005, fourth edition); *Ethics for Journalists* (Routledge, 2008, second edition); *The Journalistic Imagination: Literary Journalists from Defoe to Capote and Carter* (Routledge, 2007, with Sharon Wheeler) and *Communicating War: Memory, Media and Military* (Arima, Bury St Edmunds, 2007, with Sarah Maltby). He is also the joint editor of *Ethical Space: The International Journal of Communication Ethics*. He is the winner of a National Teacher Fellowship in 2011 – the highest prize for teachers in higher education.

Foreword

Why the Job of the Journalist Remains So Vital Today

Justin Webb argues that the coverage of the "Arab Spring" has shown that "good, old-fashioned reporting" plays a part that no amount of social media can. Reporters, once again, he concludes, count for something

At a vital moment during the tense negotiations that led up to the UN Security Council resolution on Libya, a friend of mine who is a senior US diplomat received a text on his secure office phone. Excusing himself from the table, he found a place where he could not be overlooked and brought the message on to the screen. "We need more rinse aid," it said. It was his wife hoping he might be able to concentrate on two things at once.

You will not be surprised to hear that the rinse aid was not bought that day. At times of great international stress normal life, for many people in many professions, has to go by the wayside. Diplomats, military planners, pilots, politicians and, of course, journalists have to be ready to drop everything and embrace changes over which they have no control.

I am not suggesting for a minute that we should feel sorry for them. They all went into these lines of work at least in part because they fancied the thrill of the unknown. But when the unknown arrives – as it has done with some force in the Arab world in recent times – the mark of the true professional is to be found in his or her ability to rise to the challenge of truly fast-moving events.

And what do we discover about journalists in these interesting times? First, and foremost, it seems to me, is our discovery that the profession of news reporting, sometimes thought moribund because of the rise of social media and the decline in the sums available to spend, is actually as important today as it has ever been. Social media outlets are vital and have very obviously played a huge role in the Arab world in recent days, and it is a role explored in this book, but good, old-fashioned reporting, performed by good, old-fashioned reporters, plays a part that no amount of social media can. Reporters, once again, count for something.

Some are crackpots. I know this from my own time "on the road" with wild-eyed photojournalists and publicity-seeking TV people. But the best of them are the least deranged. They are people who take bigger risks than most of us would consider wise – flying into places when everyone is trying to get out – but not just for the sake of it and not without some deeply understood sense of why this work is important.

My aim here is not simply to pat these folk on the back: they would be the first to point out that the real suffering in war zones is visited on local people who have nowhere to go, no flight home to admiring bosses to look forward to, and no audience to hear their tales of near misses and daring journeys.

Bearing Witness to Events

But what these reporters do is terribly important. They are bearing witness to events in a way that cannot be replaced or seriously challenged by social media and "citizen journalists" or, indeed, by television pictures spewed out by an agency and voiced over in the comfort of a London edit suite. They are the eyes and ears of all of us as we decide what we think about war and suffering, what should be done and what should be left undone. Their vision is imperfect and often too local, too focused on this burning tank or this devastated family, but the best reporters, some of whom write in the pages that follow, can open your eyes with a line that everyone else has missed.

After the attack on the convoy of tanks near Benghazi at the beginning of the Libya conflict Antony Loyd, of *The Times*, picked through the bodies and found one still in a support truck. The man had been handcuffed to the wheel. Not everyone in that convoy was bent on harming civilians. Not everyone wanted to be there. Not everyone deserved to die. That is war and that is war reporting.

In her wonderful novel, *The Postmistress*, Sarah Blake recreates the world of Europe in 1940, and has as one of the central characters an American journalist frustrated at the failure of the US to join the war. In the end she travels round Europe recording voices – witnessing the unfolding tragedy as the Nazis extend their grip and using the voices to communicate directly and forcefully to folks sitting at home in peaceful and distant places. The book is in part about the power and the limitations of reportage but its central message is that communicating suffering across thousands of miles is a subtle art but a vital one.

It is as vital today as it was then.

Section 1. One Pair of Eyes: Reporting from the Frontlines

John Mair

Mirage in the Desert? is published less than two months after the symbolic and effective end of the Gaddafi regime with the taking of Green Square in Tripoli on Sunday, 21 August. There are still ten weeks to the first anniversary of the event which launched the Spring – the self-immolation by fruit seller Mohamed Bouazizi in Tunisia on 17 December 2010 .This is the first draft of journalistic history but a thoughtful, and more importantly, a very thorough, one.

Speed does not mean any loss of intellectual rigour. Too many "academics" are used to the glacial pace of traditional publishing and go with the slow flow. Their work is out of date and irrelevant when it appears. To achieve this comprehensive result as quickly as Richard Lance Keeble and I have done, needs niftiness and hard work. Niftiness in setting up a conference where the two sides can initially meet, and exchange ideas, niftiness in widening the commission net to include others (who are not always academics) with something to say and hard work in cajoling and guiding the pieces to publication.

At the heart of our series of books – on the Great Crash of 2008, the reporting of Afghanistan, journalism's future in the Internet Age, the state of investigative journalism and the "Arab Spring" lies an engagement with and an interest in real events and real stories. It is where journalism is, or should, be. Academia too. This is a new book genre – the "hackademic" contemporary tome – as Professor Tim Luckhurst acknowledges in his generous afterword to this volume.

As the legendary James Cameron put it, the best journalism comes from "one pair of eyes". Fresh off their planes from the frontline in Libya, we have persuaded many of the biggest and best names in the British foreign correspondents corps to think aloud and tell their stories on paper. The current cream of the Corp – Alex Crawford of Sky News who scooped the world on 21 August – conveys the sheer adrenalin (and luck) of delivering that exclusive.

> I could barely hear myself talk over the cacophony of gunfire and shouting but I could still make out the sound of jaws dropping in the (Sky News) studio gallery in Osterley. I could sense the excitement in Sky presenter's voice and soon afterwards realised everyone was watching our pictures as the incredulity spread around the world.

Crawford is a three times Royal Television Society Television Journalist of the Year. This is her calling card for the fourth. Her (too often overlooked) Sky News colleague Stuart Ramsay also gets to places where others can only dream of being. In Libya, he was one side of the Gaddafi's Bab al Aziziya compound as it fell to the rebels on Tuesday 23 August, Crawford on the other. Here he tells his remarkable story.

Sky's direct opponents in the British 24 hour news war are the mighty BBC. There's was not a good end to the media war; they were caught out slow and flat-footed as Tripoli fell. Their campaign had been better. Veteran correspondent Jon Leyne, who rarely ventures into print, was in there from the off in Libya in February and reported the largely bloodless Egyptian revolution in January/February.

For me, the most exciting moments were at the start. After six months in Egypt, six years in the Middle East, the ground-breaking demonstration in Cairo on 25 January was a breath-taking revelation. In a few short hours it became clear that the people had lost their fear, and their government had no answer.

His fellow BBC correspondent, Wyre Davies, is an equally experienced and hardened hand in the theatre of the Middle East. He has travelled to Libya five times in six months reporting that civil war from both sides. No trip has been without danger: "I have often compared spending several days and weeks on the front line in eastern Libya to being on the set of *Mad Max*. With their souped-up Toyota pick-ups, onto which they had welded anti-aircraft guns or helicopter rocket pods, the rebels would charge up to the front line. Usually, when confronted by Gaddafi's better-trained and (then) better-equipped troops, the rebels would speed back to the relative safety of Ajdabia or Benghazi, enthusiastically firing their weapons in no particular direction as they went."

Lindsey Hilsum, of Channel Four News, has no live continuous news outlet for her work. She has to craft packages for the built programme at 7pm each night. Not for her the luxury of the live hit as news. Lindsey, the deserved winner of the Charles Wheeler Award for 2011, has been the long distance runner on this story. She has reported from Egypt, Bahrain and Libya where she too was there at the start as at the end rebels entered Bab al Aziziya, the centre of Gaddafi's power, a compound regarded with such fear that previously people would avert their eyes when they drove past. Mukhtar Nagasa, who in a previous incarnation had worked as a dentist in Bath, was one of the first in. "'We met no resistance,' he said, as he showed us video he and friends had taken of them posing in front of murals in the house of Saadi, one of Gaddafi's sons."

John Mair, a "hackademic", TV professional and viewer watched much of their output. In his piece he assesses how the competing television companies fared in their coverage. The BBC admits it was "creamed" by Sky News (especially Alex Crawford) at the end. It was, firmly. Why did this happen – luck, happenstance or design?

One country, Syria, caught up in the "Spring" has been on the margins of the Libya story: most of the news emerging has been of demonstrations and deaths (2,200 according to the UN as of late August). The dictator there – Hereditary President Bashar al-Assad – has simply put up a news curtain around his country. Journalists are not allowed in, news not allowed out. Few have lifted this Information Iron Curtain. The BBC's Sue Lloyd Roberts is an honourable exception. Christine Sylva Hamieh in this section is another. She is a Middle Eastern national living and working in the USA but has been able to use her extensive (and necessarily anonymous) contacts in Syria to build up a picture of the terror there. She reports:

> On one hand, the protesters continue to demonstrate on the streets despite the violent response from the regime claiming that the new reforms proclaimed by President Assad are not for real. On the other hand, the regime maintains its iron fist disregarding regional and international condemnations and calls for the president to step down insisting that there is a foreign conspiracy and that armed gangs and thugs are driving the violence, that they are not true reform-seekers.

That "Spring" could end in very cold "Winter".

The Libyan civil war may have all but ended in triumph but it nearly ended six months earlier for the rebels in a massacre in Benghazi. Nato jets saved the day there. Oliver Poole, a veteran of the Iraq war, was in Eastern Libya as disaster loomed. His first person reporting of the rebel "army" is at the same time moving startling and frightening:

> I even found a Libyan student from London who had abandoned his dentistry studies to fight for a change in his country. In his top pocket he still carried his Oyster card as he went into battle to remind him of the capital, and life, he had left behind. Together this ragtag force went into battle in cars or in pick-up trucks holding mounted machine-guns. Some wore cast-off military clothes. Most were dressed like civilians in motley jeans, hoodies and T-shirts. They had weapons liberated from army depots but weapons alone do not make a fighting force. It requires discipline, command and the knowledge of how not only to take, but to hold, ground. The rebel army had little of any of these. Zeal, they had in spades. But the rest was sadly lacking.

All wars have casualties. Some of them journalistic. Eamonn O'Neill salutes one – his friend the photojournalist and Oscar nominated film maker Tim Hetherington who perished in Misrata on 20 April. "The final images of Hetherington show him being helped by rebels in Misrata descending a ladder, dressed in jeans and wearing his usual light-green field-jacket. ...He is not wearing a flak-jacket and his head is bare." Frontline journalism comes with glory but it can come with a heavy cost.

Finally, James Rodgers, a former BBC correspondent who reported from the cauldron of Chechnya and has now entered the safer groves of the academy, counsels against the fog of propaganda surrounding war and journalists. The "Rixos Hotel syndrome" was alive and well in Tripoli for far too long even to the bitter end and Saif Gaddafi's appearance on 22 August defying gravity and reality. Rodgers' advice:

> So what can journalists do to try to guard against attempts, crude or clever, to influence them? The answer is the best of the old, and the best of the new. By the best of the old, I mean the need to check sources, and check information, as far as possible. That involves not only recognising the enduring value of eyewitness reporting, but also placing renewed emphasis on standing stories up properly. This is where the best of the new comes in. As Andy Carvin (of NPR, USA) has demonstrated with his extensive network of followers on Twitter, new technology does offer new possibilities. Carvin has facilitated extensive coverage of the "Arab Spring" without being based in the region. Only by combining these two approaches – rigorous research and fact-checking, and networks of sources – can journalists hope to generate enough bright rays to burn off the fog of propaganda.

How Sky News secured the world exclusive – entering Green Square as Tripoli fell to the rebel forces

Sky News Special Correspondent Alex Crawford (with camera operators Garwen McLuckie and Jim Foster, and producer Andy Marsh) beat the world's media to report bravely on the collapse of Col. Gaddafi's empire in Tripoli. In this exclusive report, she tells how she secured the scoop: "We felt we were at the heart of a massive story – a Berlin-wall-type moment – powered by Libyan people, albeit helped by Nato jets"

There was a crackle of gunfire – far too close – and the man next to Jim fell down dead, shot through the head. His blood and brains splattered over Jim's neck and shoulder. Jim was covered so much at first I thought *he'd* been hit. Some of it sprayed over Garwen's camera. I was shaking and thought I was going to be sick. But I got out a tissue and wiped Jim's shoulder and then Garwen's lens. Incredibly, it wasn't the worst we'd seen all week. But it was certainly the closest.

It was Tuesday, August 23, and we were outside Gaddafi's compound watching the fighters pounding the exterior wall. We didn't know it then but they were just a couple of hours away from breaking it down and entering the heart of the Gaddafi empire.

We stood in the same clothes we had been wearing all week, clothes which seemed to be permanently wet from perspiration. It was baking hot and we were all sweating – through exertion – and, in my case, not a little fear. Garwen was angry. Now this is unusual. Garwen never gets angry. But he was now. "That was so unnecessary," he said. He had seen it all.

One of the fighters with an AK-47 had just run into the street and fired – aimlessly and without care – and one of the bullets had hit the man rubbing shoulders with Jim and just in front of Garwen and me. He had been killed by one of the fighters on his side. We moved further back along the wall together and all caught our breath. No-one said very much. Like so much that happened that week, events were moving so quickly we didn't have time to dwell. That would come later.

Only Journalists Travelling with the Fighters into the Heart of the Gaddafi empire

A few days earlier we were the only journalists who travelled with the fighters into the heart of Tripoli and Green Square. How did we do it? Why were we the only ones? I have no idea where everyone else was or how it happened. But to us it seemed like the most natural thing in the world. It was still light, we were with people we knew, they were heading forward. There seemed to be little resistance from Gaddafi loyalists or soldiers. Simple. There was no question we wouldn't go with them.

The day (Sunday, 21 August) had begun in Zawiya. I remember thinking as the fighters headed off down the road to Tripoli that we would probably end up sleeping in the car somewhere on that road that night, somewhere along the 30 miles between Zawiya and the capital. I am hopelessly disorganised but I had packed a small backpack with toothbrush, spare clean pants, some make-up and a clean t-shirt. I was rather pleased with myself at my forward planning. But somehow it all got left behind in the scramble when we changed cars. We were reunited with our clothes and toiletries only seven days later. Somehow they are always the things which get forgotten. We never go anywhere without our satellite phones (mine was in the leg pocket of my trousers), passport and ID (back pocket), notebook and pen (flak jacket front pocket) and, of course, this time we carried backpacks with the BGAN terminal, laptop and camera kits. Quite enough to carry and run around with anyway. We can manage without toothbrushes and clean clothes but it's all for nothing if we can't get our material out.

That day was Garwen's birthday. Halfway between the villages of Judaim and Maia where the fighters and we were hemmed in by Gaddafi snipers ahead, we had taken shelter down an alleyway next to a house. I filmed while the boys hugged each other and we sang happy birthday to Garwen as the shells landed around us. That's the way with battles: there are often periods when you are just waiting, waiting for the fighters to advance, waiting to see if it's safe to go on, waiting to work out what you are up against. There was a lot of that that day but it was clear the fighters were buoyant and confident and making far quicker progress than they ever imagined. It took everyone by surprise.

During one such lull, we had pulled back to Zawiya to file a report for the evening bulletin. It was still early and I made the boys scrambled eggs in our safe house while they quickly downloaded the material and Garwen edited. We headed out again and ran into a large convoy of vehicles packed with fighters from Misrata. They had just arrived to bolster the advancing forces. Everyone we spoke to was crazy with excitement. "Today we liberate Tripoli," they kept saying. We thought they were hopelessly optimistic but we followed them. "Let's see how far they get," I thought. When we reached the Khamis Brigade headquarters on the outskirts of Tripoli we found opposition fighters ransacking the building. Some were piling their pickups with chairs and televisions looted from the barracks. This was the HQ of the most feared brigade in all of Libya, run by one of the Colonel Gaddafi's sons, the one in charge of internal repression. They had taken it over. And they were still moving forward.

Surreal Conversation on the Back of a Truck

We found a fighter from Bournemouth and he invited us to join him on the back of his pick-up. Everyone we spoke to was very welcoming and friendly. What followed on the back of the truck ranks alongside one of the more surreal conversations we had that week. "Bournemouth is lovely. I love England," said a fighter dressed in combat clothes, holding an AK-47 and demonstrating a beautiful English accent. "The weather is so great in the summer, much nicer than here."

By now it is dark and we are in a huge convoy. The vehicles are gridlocked as we enter the main road into the capital. We are edging along, hardly moving at all. Everyone is a bit tense because no-one knows what is ahead. Then, as the vehicles start moving again, people start coming out of their homes onto the road to greet us. They are carrying children in their arms and they are applauding the convoy as it makes its way into the city. Women are whooping and making a trilling noise with their tongue. More and more people come out until every vehicle is surrounded. Men are crying in relief and thanking the fighters over and over again. They are hugged and kissed like heroes. We are even thanked as if somehow we have been a part of it. The fighters start firing their guns into the air, which attracts more people onto the streets. What started out as a few dozen greeters quickly turns into hundreds.

I ring into the office and go on air but it's clear there's an element of doubt in London as to what I am describing. "So who are these people, Alex?" my colleague, Steve Dixon, asks. "Where is the Gaddafi support?" I tell him I will try to get pictures for him so he can see for himself. Producer Andy Marsh has heard the conversation and agrees only pictures will demonstrate what we are witnessing. He suggests trying to power up the BGAN, the kit which will connect with the satellite and beam the pictures back to London while we are on the pick-up. Now anyone in television will tell you how incredibly hit-and-miss working a BGAN can be.

You can be in the most stable of circumstances, with no wind, a perfect signal, stationary and safe and it *still* won't work – for no fathomable reason other than it is having an off day. I thought that – like the fighters – Andy must be hopelessly deluded. But it was worth a shot. He plonked the BGAN on the driver's cab next to his laptop and attached the BGAN to a charger which plugged into the car's cigarette lighter. Great. No power issues. Problem one solved. Then he found the satellite signal. Problem two sorted. The BGAN emits a noise when it hits the satellite so he knew he was on the right track. Then as we edged our way along the road he gently moved the BGAN so it maintained sight with the satellite. Problem three nailed (coping with movement). Genius and so simple. Sometimes the dice just has to roll your way and that night it did with double sixes. Soon we were transmitting pictures live back to London and the world. (Later my editor told me one of the newspaper headlines read: "Sky scoops the world with a cigarette lighter!")

13

Everyone Was Watching our Pictures as Incredulity Spread Around the World

I could barely hear myself talk over the cacophony of gunfire and shouting but I could still make out the sound of jaws dropping in the studio gallery in Osterley. I could sense the excitement in Sky presenter Steve's voice and soon afterwards realised everyone was watching our pictures as the incredulity spread around the world….first reaction from the US State Department, Downing Street, the UN…it went on. We realised our pictures were having an impact but never anticipated the scale of it. We had no internet, no mobile phone connectivity, no television, minimal contact with the outside world.

It was Ramadan – and Muslims don't touch alcohol anyway – but the crowd was drunk on excitement, relief and joy. We were pretty heady too. We carried on broadcasting hour after hour until it was well into the early hours. When we finally finished we hugged and kissed Andy. "You beauty," said Garwen. "I don't know how you did that. You were Cat Sat." The nickname will probably stick for some time to come: the man who managed the satellite like an agile cat on the hot tin roof of a fighter's pick-up. It was far too late to ring home. I found out later the family had missed it all. It was Sunday night after all and there was school the next morning.

Mostly, my family are far too busy to spend hours or even minutes watching me on television and I battle against not only delirious fighters with guns but also the even more potent personalities of Hannah Montana and Selena Gomez. No contest. But later my youngest child, Flo, apparently watched with my husband Richard and asked him if they were real bullets. "I'm afraid they are baby," he told her. "But she's okay with her bullet-proof vest on isn't she Dad?" she asked. He reassures her and switches channels. He tells me later Flo believes the bullet-proof vest is akin to the invisible cloak which Harry Potter wears – it's all encompassing and gets the boy wizard through many a scrape. Oh for one of those in Libya.

For the Sky team, there was still a lot more to come. We headed into the city and passed by the hospital. An ambulance was just pulling up and Garwen and Andy jumped off to film it. Jim and I stayed outside with the pick-up, which, by now, was our only transport and we didn't want to lose it.

Within minutes there was shooting outside the hospital. A man was shot in front of us as he was trying to run away. We ran inside the hospital. The pick-up truck disappeared and we were inside our new home – at least home for the next few days.

The Generosity of the Libyan People

Everywhere we went in Libya it struck us just how generous and selfless people were towards us. There was no power in the city, no running water, with rubbish piling up on the streets, fuel and food shortages, but people still gave up what little they had for us. But for the generosity of some Libyans we would have had nowhere to sleep, nothing to eat and drink and no transport. We were taken to one shop by a Tripoli resident who drove us in his car. It had opened briefly, its shutters still half down. "Take what you need," the owner said. We liberally stacked up the car with tins of tuna, dried pasta, bottles of fizzy drink and water. The boot was soon filled, as was the back seat. We were quicker than looters. When we came to pay, he refused. "No, no, no," he said, "This is not right. You are *sahafi* (journalists), we need you.' A row ensued until we literally begged him to take our dollars and give it to his mosque if it so suited him. He finally relented.

We thought the Green Square moment was a turning point. Maybe it was but there were a few more corners to go around yet. Monday night was another twist. Saif Gaddafi turned up at the Rixos Hotel that night, bold as brass, saying the Gaddafis were still in control. It seemed to fill the opposition fighters with fresh impetus and from then on the Bab al Azizaya compound was their focus. They spent Tuesday (23 August) pounding at the exterior walls of the Colonel's vast compound from a number of different directions. It was outside the south gate where we witnessed the poor man mentioned earlier being shot through the head by a fellow "rebel".

Sections of the city were still terribly insecure. A road might be safe to travel down one minute, but return 15 minutes later and there would be firing. When the fighters told us they had broken down the north gate, frankly I didn't believe them. We had to see for ourselves. We raced round there, chaperoned by an English-speaking fighter who insisted he took us every step of the way. He continually stopped and asked the risks ahead? Who is there? Where are they? Is it safe? I think being a woman makes those who are helping us *extra* cautious. In the Arab culture, if anything happens to you while you are in their care, it is a terrible dishonour – and more so if the person you are looking after is female.

We made our way toward's Gaddafi's giant model of a fist crunching an American fighter jet. Tents were already on fire and people seemed to be running in all directions. We set up the BGAN just in time for the top of the *Six O'Clock News*. I could hear the executive producer Jamie Woods talking to me down my earpiece saying: "Hi Crawf, good to see you. We're coming to you soon. Ramsay (Sky News' Chief Correspondent Stuart Ramsay) is also in the compound."

No-one else around the world had live pictures inside Gaddafi's compound and Sky News had *two* reporters in different areas giving a unique perspective. I felt a surge of pride. Sky News is still the baby of the British TV news industry, tiny in comparison to the giant BBC, with all its staff and all its money, and small compared with the powerful ITV. It's partly this smallness which, I like to think, makes us more agile and quick on our feet. But there's also a feeling we have to run faster, run longer, run harder than the others.

Criticisms that we were Gung-Ho or Reckless: All Rubbish

I have heard the subtle criticisms which hint at us being gung-ho or reckless. All rubbish. In my team alone, we are all parents. We have 11 children between the four of us whom we love very much. We spent our time in Libya snatching calls with them by satellite phone, telling stories down the phone to them, promising we'd be back soon. They replied that that was all well and good but Hannah Montana was still on. The idea that we would take unnecessary risks when we have so much to live for is utterly ridiculous.

The criticisms emanate from people who clearly haven't been at the end of the phone line to John Ryley (Sky Head of News) or Sarah Whitehead (Sky Foreign Editor) when they are going through our tactics and operations and exit-plans. Sky has some of the toughest safety procedures in the business and instigated many of them way ahead of our counterparts.

But as well as safety being on our minds (how can it not when you are surrounded by men firing guns) we felt we were at the heart of a massive story – a Berlin-wall-type moment – powered by Libyan people, albeit helped by Nato jets. But not on this day. Time and again the fighters asked us – as if we had a direct line to Nato – "Where is Nato? We need them to bomb the gates."

The fighters around us were deranged with excitement. They had done it and they had done it themselves. Around 16 hours after Gaddafi's son had shown reporters round this same complex and boasted of the family's enduring power, his empire was literally being trampled on by hundreds of opposition fighters and civilians. I spotted a man wearing a Gaddafi-style hat, a gold chain around his neck and carrying an elaborate fly-swatter. He looked, walked and acted a bit like a Libyan Kenny Everett. I asked him where he got the hat. "Oh my god," he said, "I was in Gaddafi's room!" My children tell me later there's a rap song on YouTube where that conversation is set to music and edited very amusingly. It's doing the rounds at their school and suddenly I am not quite so embarrassing to them. It won't last.

Note on the author

Alex Crawford is a Sky News Special Correspondent based in South Africa. She is the current holder of the Royal Television Society's Journalist of the Year, an award she also won three years ago. Last year she was nominated for a BAFTA for her coverage in Pakistan and has been recognised at the Foreign Press Association awards for three years running for her work in India, Afghanistan and Pakistan. She won a Golden Nymph at the Monte Carlo Film Festival for her coverage of the Mumbai terror attacks in 2008. She has been also been recognised in the Bayeaux War Correspondents awards. She has covered wars, conflicts and hostile environments in Iraq, Afghanistan, India, Pakistan and Sri Lanka, Thailand and Burma as well as Africa and Europe including Northern Ireland. She has been embedded with the British, American, Sri Lankan and Pakistani militaries but usually operates in a small team independently.

The Good Guys Were For Once Saved. The Bad Guys Beaten

In this dramatic, eye-witness account, Oliver Poole describes the attacks on Benghazi, eastern Libya, by the forces of President Colonel Gaddafi – and the sudden shift in fortunes for the rebels once the international community intervened. He concludes: "What will happen next we do not know, but a massacre was averted"

The first time I drove into Benghazi there was no government, bureaucracy, police nor army. The Libyan city's inhabitants had risen up against the forces of Colonel Gaddafi and the government's soldiers not killed nor captured had fled from a nearby airfield, al-Bayda, four days earlier.

Those who kept the city functional disappeared with them. The governor ran and the city's police officers cast off their uniforms in case they were lynched. Civil servants were no longer turning up for work. This was partly as there was no one left to pay them to do so and partly as many governmental buildings were torched. Even the grave-diggers had disappeared. Bodies from the recent fighting were starting to pile up in the local mortuary. No one knew what to do with them, not least as there was no one left in a position of authority to ask.

My previous 48 hours had been spent travelling overland from Cairo. It was 22 February and the Egyptian President, Hosni Mubarak, had only been ousted a fortnight ago. Tahrir Square still thronged with celebrating protestors. The singing and chanting could be heard from the balcony of my room at the nearby Holiday Inn. Walking down to see for myself, I found the plaza covered by banners. A youth thrust an Egyptian flag into my hand as I reached its western edge. Children were everywhere, brought by their parents to witness what a better future might look like. Even the watching soldiers were part of the excitement, handing out water and sweets and smiling happily as pretty girls lined up to have their photographs taken with them.

A Town Filled with Refugees Fleeing the Revolution
The border crossing with Libya was at Salum, a four-street town squeezed between the Mediterranean and the desert. It was already filled with refugees escaping the revolution further west. Almost all were African not Arabs and the situation was chaotic as many had been in Libya without a passport.

For some this was because they were brought in by labour gangs instructed by Gaddafi or his henchmen to find cheap workers and their passports had been seized to stop them leaving when they were subsequently not paid on time. For others, it was because they entered the country illegally when seeking a route to the coast, where they had hoped to then get passage with a people smuggler into Europe. As a result, the Egyptians were not letting anyone without official documentation cross the border. They remained, in their hundreds, stuck in the de-nationalised limbo that was the gap between the two border crossings, living off Red Crescent foods hand-outs and wrapping themselves in blankets to escape the freezing nights.

The Libyan revolution was in its infancy then and phone lines and internet connections had been cut so there was little way for the wider world to know what was going on. The first reporters to have entered were still making their tentative way to Benghazi, the eastern city in ancient Cyrenaica that, in the coming weeks, was to become the revolutionaries' *de-facto* capital. That meant there were still few reports about what the situation on the ground actually was. Entering was therefore a leap of faith.

To pass across the border you simply walked, bags in hand, towards the Libyan checkpoint on the eastern side. There, two boys, aged no more than their late teens, stood with AK-47s and welcomed new arrivals with cries of "Libya free" and "Gaddafi bad". There were no stamps nor requests for visas, which was good since the authorities in Tripoli were not issuing them at that time so I – like all the reporters taking that route – did not have one. The boys simply waved me through and towards a line of cars waiting on the main road. Seeing me, the driver of the front vehicle, a battered blue Opel hatchback, jumped out and waved me forward.

"Press?" he asked, the word almost lost in his heavily-accented English. I nodded. "In," he instructed as he opened the front passenger door. "Tell the world of our revolution."

The Lesson to be Learnt about Libya at a Checkpoint
In retrospect nearly all there was to learn about Libya at that time could be gleaned at that checkpoint. The boys in their civilian jeans and T-shirts with the weapons they held in the show-off manner they had seen in Hollywood films; the total absence of anything that might resemble an operating state; the atmosphere of excitement and joy; and above all the cars waiting to pick up those who could publicise what they had done before the regime's forces moved to snuff it out.

My driver would not take money, even though I tried. Nor had he been sent by anyone. It was his idea to come to the border after he heard journalists were getting stuck there with no way to travel further along the coast. "I am doing it for my country," he told me in his broken English. "The world must see before Gaddafi tries to stop us." As he said that he turned his head towards me and pulled a stubby finger across his throat. "Gaddafi is a very bad man. He will not like what we have done."

There was clearly already fear too, besides the excitement and joy. The fear that came from the knowledge that a step had been taken that could not be undone. Fear about what it would mean. Fear of this new unknown.

Benghazi was the same mixture of elation and terror. Rumours were spreading about Gaddafi-supporting "fifth columnists" present in the city and everyone was warned not to walk the streets at night because of snipers. With mercenaries flooding in from Chad to assist Gaddafi's attempt to suppress the revolt, local suspicion focused on anyone with negro rather than Arab features. I heard disturbing reports of people being attacked purely because of the darkness of their skin. There was at least one claim of a summary execution. When a group of local revolutionaries invited television news crews to witness some "mercenaries" they claimed to have captured, a British correspondent asked one why he was in Libya. Visibly shaking with terror, he answered that he had come to work as a cook at a local Benghazi restaurant and had been seized from his apartment the previous night.

When a Hotel became my Home

Home for me was the Ouzo Hotel, an usual name in an alcohol-dry country. It was a 20th century tower block located by a roundabout on the south side of town and was soon the international media centre for the city. Like my driver, the hotel would not at first take money for the room or the food it provided. The people of Benghazi wanted journalists there to report on what was happening. From the early morning volunteers would drift into the lobby offering their services for free as translators and drivers. It was they who ferried me to the military complex at the end of Jamal Abdulnasar Street that had been at the heart of Gaddafi's operation in the city. It was a sprawling base, almost medieval in appearance with its high walls looming over the surrounding buildings and its watchtowers ringed by fortifications separated by slits wide enough for an AK-47 to poke through.

This was where the main fight to free Benghazi was staged. It had taken three days. Gadaffi's soldiers fired not only machineguns but anti-aircraft weapons at the crowd. The protesters had few weapons, many only stones. Bulldozers from surrounding building sites were driven into the base's walls and then TNT, used by locals for blast fishing, piled into vehicles and detonated at the front gate, killing those at the steering wheel. Once the walls had finally been breached the base exposed its dirty secrets. There was the car filled with six burnt bodies, arms handcuffed behind their backs. And there was the pile of soldiers with their hands cut off; tortured and killed because they had refused to fire on their fellow countrymen gathered on the streets outside.

Now, however, the site had become a local day-out, a Benghazi version of Cairo's Tahrir Square. What had once been visible only to the city's citizens if they had been unfortunate enough to be arrested and detained was now open to everyone. Hence everyone seemed to be coming to have a look, most bringing their entire families. Unlike in Tahrir Square, however, the children were not being shown people chanting and singing. They were being shown the labyrinth of underground passageways and cells stretching the size of two football pitches in which political prisoners had been held. On arrival, I found groups of kids, many barely out of nappies, staring in fascination at the dark stains that now covered the sand-covered courtyard just inside the main gates.

Celebrations as the Rebels Take Over Benghazi

The courthouse on Benghazi's main boulevard bordering the Mediterranean was where the Libyan revolution began when protesters gathered outside its entrance on 15 February after Gaddafi's henchmen arrested a group of dissidents. Two days later the streets were filled with tens of thousands of protesters. By the end of that week the buildings that housed the regime's security apparatus were in flames. Now a constant stream of music and anti-Gaddafi slogans played from the courthouse to the exultant crowd outside. Convoys of cars draped in the old monarchical flag that Gaddafi replaced when he seized power in 1969 drove passed, their horns sounding incessantly and with children hanging out of windows flashing V for victory signs. In an entrance a picture of the former ruler has been placed on the ground for every new arrival to wipe their feet.

"For so long we were not able to say anything at all," cried one of the celebrating demonstrators, waving a cartoon of Gaddafi lampooned as the devil in my face as I pressed through the throng to get inside. "You could not speak of what you felt because of the tyrant who controlled us. Today we can finally speak our hearts. We are free."

Inside the courthouse a new government was trying but failing to establish itself. A leadership committee had formed, primarily a mix of academics and lawyers, and their approach seemed to be to ape that of a student common-room circa 1982. Cartoons and slogans had been scrawled all over the walls, many in luminous green paint, mocking Gaddafi as a monster, or a sexual inadequate, or simply a complete loon.

Everywhere meetings were being staged in which all present were encouraged to contribute. Decisions on anything from what sort of elections should be held to who would direct traffic ended up taking hours, sometimes days, as every voice was heard with equal weight. Gaddafi had carefully ensured that any potential alternative to his regime was snuffed out so Libya had no independent political parties, trade unions nor even NGOs. There was nothing that could step in to fill the void. In the rooms of the courthouse – many of them stripped bare of furniture after being looted only a few days before – the people of Benghazi were seeking to develop that alternative but had little context or understanding of how to do so.

There was a marked schism between the groups of local academics, lawyers and businessmen, many of them US or UK educated, who talked about human rights and the rule of law and the more excitable – and numerous – volunteers who were concerned primarily with expunging any influence of Gaddafi from the city by whatever means necessary. One day, when the press turned up at the media centre, the arguments between the two had reached such a level of vitriol that the desks and chairs of the more urbane liaison officials had been thrown on the street and the entrance door temporarily locked.

Power to the People of Benghazi
In this leadership gap, the people of Benghazi simply took it on themselves to provide the services that were previously the responsibility of the state. In the same way that a stream of English-speakers were turning up at the Ouzo Hotel to help out the arriving reporters, locals were taking turns to direct traffic, drive round picking up rubbish or volunteer at the local hospitals. The most popular job for the volunteers, however, was the checkpoints that people took it upon themselves to set up on almost every street. These were part neighbourhood watch, part civil defence force. All were primarily made up of young men with no military training who had got their hands on some form of weapon, in most cases a gun but for some no more than a machete or kitchen knife. All were excitable and enthusiastic about their self-proclaimed responsibilities.

I never had any problems with them but dark rumours spread about what they got up to if they did not like the look of you. Some told of those with west Libyan accents being dragged from their cars and taken for interrogation just because those at a checkpoint did not trust the sound of their voice. Others of homes being broken into on the tip of some unknown, and often unreliable, informer. Bursts of gunfire echoed throughout the day as gangs sought to find pro-regime elements. No one could say for sure who those being detained were nor even where they were being taken. It was almost certainly these volunteers who had been rounding up the negro-featured men accused of being Chadian mercenaries, including the man who claimed he was nothing worse than a transitory chef. Even those supposedly now running the city admitted they were powerless to control them or their activities.

A solution, however, had finally been found for the grave-digging problem. The local scout troop stepped in to help. Subsequently, the burial services held there were staged against the backdrop of the young scouts in their stripped yellow neckerchiefs held by toggles and with their merit badges sown down their sleeve digging fresh graves. When the Western airstrikes finally came it was they who were responsible for dealing with the pulped and mostly unidentifiable body parts from the regime troops hit by the first wave of French planes. The scouts buried them in a mass grave far from the graveyard's entrance.

"Over there," scout leader Salem el-Dadraf, 21, told me as he pointed to the area of turned-over earth marked not by headstones but a line of breezeblocks. "We could not tell which body parts belonged with which as they were in pieces so we poured them into a trench. I will never forget the smell but I'm proud to be doing what I can to help. Everyone must help the revolution."

Ajdabiya: A Town Where Terror was Ever-Present

One hundred and twenty miles to the south of Benghazi was the town of Ajdabiya. This was now the front line between the revolutionaries and the remains of Gaddafi's forces. In Benghazi, the fear of what might come next was largely repressed, glimpsed in the frenzy of the celebrations of the crowds and the enthusiasm with which the city's self-appointed law-keepers went about their task. Ajdabiya was different. Here the terror was visible and ever-present. Everyone in Ajdabiya knew that if the ebb and flow of the revolutionary uprising started to turn against them, theirs would be one of the first places to suffer retribution. Already reports had reached them of pro-government forces ringing the neighbouring city of

Ras Lanuf, establishing camps in the desert outside and not letting cars in or out.

I arrived shortly after 4pm on last day of February. Shortly before, the people of Ajdabiya had learnt that Gaddafi still had the power to hurt them. The knowledge had come with the roar of a jet engine, the explosion of bombs and the sight of billowing smoke rising into the clear blue sky. A Libyan air force fighter jet had flown overhead at only 2,000 feet. Its target was a nearby army base that was one of the Gaddafi regime's largest weapon depots.

Idris Kadiki had just left home to attend afternoon prayers when he heard the explosions. Dressed in a flowing brown robe and with a straggly beard that hung to the base of his neck, he looked – like most Libyans – far older than his 32 years, his face etched with lines and skin leathered by the years of dust and heat. Hearing the air strike explode, he raced back to his house where his heavily pregnant wife had been resting. "She was very upset and frightened and I worried about the baby," he later told me. "I tried to comfort her but in the end the only way I could was to tell her she was wrong. There was no bomb. Everything was safe." Idris knew that was not true, however. In the city's main square hundreds of people gathered chanting anti-Gaddafi slogans and promising defiance. Some had guns that they fired repeatedly into the air. Like wildfire, the belief spread that pro-Gaddafi troops were only a short distance away.

I arrived at the square as the mob decided to descend on the military base by the arms depot to demand more weapons to defend themselves, and met Idris when he offered to take me in his battered brown saloon car to follow them. At the base a senior official was trying to explain that the weapons had to be rationed as there were not enough for everyone. No one was willing to listen to what he said. To try to restore order, the revolutionary official ordered his militiamen to fire their AK-47s over people's heads. It did nothing to silence the mob's demands. "The problem is that after so many years under Gaddafi people find it difficult to believe that he can be weak," it was explained to me. "They believe he can still come and punish them for what they have done." Suddenly two rocket-propelled grenades were fired from the base's interior. The rockets sped out into a desert, bursting into a puff of smoke that caught the light of the sun setting in the west. That finally succeeded in quietening the crowd.

Rebel Army: Just Civilians Wanting to do their Bit

Benghazi may have been chaotic but it was a place filled with enthusiasm for the new state that the people there believed they were building. Ajdabiya was different: Gaddafi's iron fist was clearly targeted at it but there was no real military force to protect its citizens. The defending army was chronically under-trained. They called themselves the "shabab", or the "youth": amateur soldiers who – like those who now directed traffic or manned checkpoints in Benghazi – were simply civilians wanting to do their bit. I came across taxi drivers, cooks, civil servants, all having been issued with a weapon and pledging their determination to fight.

I even found a Libyan student from London who had abandoned his dentistry studies to fight for a change in his country. In his top pocket he still carried his Oyster card as he went into battle to remind him of the capital, and life, he had left behind. Together this ragtag force went into battle in cars or in pick-up trucks holding mounted machine-guns. Some wore cast-off military clothes. Most were dressed like civilians in motley jeans, hoodies and T-shirts. They had weapons liberated from army depots but weapons alone do not make a fighting force. It requires discipline, command and the knowledge of how not only to take, but to hold, ground. The rebel army had little of any of these. Zeal, they had in spades. But the rest was sadly lacking.

The staff at Africa Hotel on the outskirts of town – the only one in Ajdabiya which showed CNN and BBC World and, therefore, the one favoured by the press – seemed to judge how perilous their situation was by the number of journalists staying. The fuller the place the happier they were, presuming this meant that the Western media was confident they were not all about to be stormed by Gaddafi's soldiers that night. By the time I checked in, however, there were very few of us, primarily me, a couple of Associated Press reporters and a BBC crew which included its famed World Affairs Editor John Simpson.

Since there were so few of us, the staff became jumpy, those at the reception desk asking each day what we knew about the location of Gaddafi's forces. The fact we knew even less than them made them just more pasty faced and sunken eyed. Even the presence of one of the world's most recognisable foreign correspondents in Simpson was not enough to reassure them. Indeed, the front desk manager, a small slight-featured man who had learnt his English while living in Brighton, found his presence particularly disconcerting. "But he only goes to the very worst places," he said to me one morning. "When John Simpson is at a place that means things are looking very, very bad."

The regime's army was getting closer. Ras Lanuf, a short distance west of Ajdabiya, was now reported to be totally back under their control. In the west of the country rebel cities were being subdued one-by-one. Then, on 2 March, it became obvious that Gaddafi was determined to cling to power, no matter how much blood had to be shed. With each day he was regaining control of his country. And on 2 March, Gaddafi's soldiers began their attempt to regain control of Ajdabiya itself.

Out of Bed and Packed within Five Minutes

For me, the day started with one of the Associated Press reporters running down the corridor knocking on rooms telling anyone there that they had to flee the town as Gaddafi's men were approaching its outskirts. The subsequent adrenalin shot meant I was up out of bed and packed within five minutes, although the news did not particularly surprise me. The previous afternoon I had finally managed to persuade a former member of the Libyan army's special forces to take me to where the regime's troops were massing at a checkpoint outside Ras Lanuf. Every car that was going either into or out of the town was being searched and mobile phones seized from those travelling into Gaddafi territory in case they might be used to inform those in the east of the military preparations ahead of their planned assault. The regime soldiers I interviewed had been notably confident in their upcoming success. Most were from Gaddafi's own tribe. All were well equipped with modern automatic weapons and rocket-propelled grenades. The pick-ups with machine guns at the back were being moved into position at a fortified checkpoint, which at that stage was the regime's furthest point east it still controlled.

Most notable of all, however, was their fury at the revolutionaries in the east who they believed threatened to cast the country into anarchy and potential religious fundamentalism. "For 41 years this country has been safe," said a senior officer called Moftar Omar, belts of ammunition hanging over his left shoulder. "For 41 years it has been kept from the hands of the Americans, British and Israelis. Now they throw it all away and start burning Libyan buildings and killing Libyan soldiers. Is this their gratitude? Is this their gratitude for what our leader has done for them?

What do these troubles bring? Is there law and order? These people will make us like Iraq where everyone fears for their life, there is no business and we go back to like medieval people. Now we will come for them. How will they stop us? We are soldiers. We are trained. They are just a rabble with guns they do not know how to use."

By the time of my sudden wake-up call, Moftar Omar and his men had reached the oil refinery at Marsa El Brega, which was despite the histrionics of the Associated Press reporters still 30 miles or so outside Ajdabiya itself. Incredibly, considering how Gaddafi's war planes controlled the air and his army had the most modern of military equipment, the people of Ajdabiya had gathered at the town's western gate to stop them getting any further. I found them filling Coca-Cola and Fanta bottles with rags and petrol as makeshift Molotov cocktails. A number carried AK-47s and hunting rifles, with one man running past holding rocket-propelled grenades. Others had only limited weaponry, in some cases not even Kalashnikovs but kitchen knives and, in one instance, a barbecue skewer. As far as I could see most of the 7,000-strong crowd massing at the gate did not have even that level of basic weaponry and were, in fact, totally unarmed. That did not stop them racing towards Brega in any vehicle they could find. By mid-morning they were joined by forces from Benghazi who brought anti-aircraft guns and rocket launchers. Three antiquated Russian-built tanks rolled forward, taken from a liberated arms dump earlier that week.

By 11am the anti-government forces had taken control of the sand dunes that border the oil refinery. There were no officers, no instructions, no plans. Gaddafi's men shelled them with mortar rounds and a fighter jet dropped bombs. Groups of women set up a makeshift kitchen a short distance behind the fighters, ferrying forward water, tea and rice and chicken. By mid-afternoon the number of anti-Gaddafi fighters was sizeable. Working in groups, the fighters slowly surrounded the government troops on three sides, penning them into Brega's university. Anti-aircraft guns which had ineffectually targeted the planes were now pointed ground ward, inflicting devastating barrages.

A Scene of Total Anarchy
It was a totally anarchic scene. The level of casualties on both sides was not large – this being more of a skirmish than a battle – but the amount of firepower being expanded phenomenal. And amid that noise and terror

the remarkable thing, the truly amazing thing, was how these people – these shopkeepers and students and taxi drivers and accountants – were willing to risk everything to hold onto what they had gained. An army of barely armed volunteers was going toe-to-toe with the regime's forces. Throughout the day car after car after car raced down the desert road to deposit fresh fighters to replace those wavering under the machinegun fire, mortar shells and aircraft bombs rained down on them by Gaddafi's military. The whole thing may have been amateurish but it was unquestionably brave. In fact, it was heroically brave. These people were willing to die rather than lose what they had gained and so willing were they to die that an absence of weaponry or tactics apparently did nothing to deter them.

By 5.30pm the Gaddafi forces were in retreat, pulling back to a safe haven 30 miles to the west, closer to the pro-government city of Surte. The people of Ajdabiya had, almost miraculously, won. That prompted utter jubilation, the sky lit up by tracer fire as guns were fired into the air and the road filled with fighters chanting their hatred of their country's despot.

I watched as they later gathered in Ajdabiya's main square to celebrate. I think that was the moment I realised how strong my support for what these people were doing had become, and how desperately I wanted them to succeed. I had spent most of the previous decade in Iraq. There I had spent many, many years hating all sides as they inflicted ever worsening horrors on each other: the Shia militias dragging Sunni civilians into basement dungeons to be tortured by electric drills; the Sunni jihadists and their seeming love of blowing themselves up in markets filled with families; the Americans and their priority on protecting their own soldiers whatever the damage done to the country around them. But that day in Ajdabiya I had seen people go and fight modern machine-guns with a barbecue skewer. The Gaddafi soldier I had talked to the previous day had been right to an extent. There clearly was no gratitude towards Gaddafi. Indeed, these people were willing to risk all they had and all they could be to stop him having any further say over their lives and country.

There was only one conclusion you could draw from that. As I stood in Ajdabiya and watched a people celebrate a victory which, however small, had seemed that morning so very unlikely, I felt that good had for once triumphed over bad. That the little guy – the normal guy, the everyday guy like you and me – had stood up to and beaten the bully who wanted to control him. For once might had not meant right. You don't often have a chance to see that, especially if you do what I do for a living. You certainly never saw it in Iraq. Things, I told myself, might end up different here. It was, I cannot deny, a welcome thought.

Libya Forced Away from the Front Pages

Even though Libya's future hung in the balance, events elsewhere in the world were to force it from the front pages. A devastating earthquake struck Japan, unleashing a series of disasters of near-biblical proportions as first it was struck by a tsunami and then the threat of one of its nuclear power stations experiencing total meltdown. I was pulled out but, even as I tried to make sense of the scale of the disaster that had struck in the Far East, I kept a close eye on how fortune was treating the people I had seen in and around Benghazi.

Little I read was good. Gaddafi had reinforced his men pushing east and that had proved too much for the enthusiastic but untrained *shabab* in their pick-up trucks and civilian cars who tried to stop them. Gradually the front line drew closer and closer to Benghazi itself. Brega fell. Then Ajdabiya itself. The reports from there were grim. Pockets of revolutionaries continued to hold out against the regime's forces but they were being hunted house-to-house. Shops in Benghazi were reportedly shuttered and the streets largely empty amid fears that an assault by government soldiers was imminent. Gaddafi himself appeared in public to warn of the retribution he would reap on all those who had opposed him. A screen text on the state-run al-Libya television channel told people in the eastern stronghold that the army was coming. The message promised that the troops would "cleanse your city". Ibrahim Dabbashi, Libya's deputy UN ambassador who has joined the anti-Gaddafi movement, warned that the international community had only 10 hours to act to stop "genocide" in the east of the country. Might, it seemed, was about to prove right once again.

I found myself back in Cairo, then on the day-long drive to the border. There were no guards at all this time on the Libyan side or cars waiting to pack up journalists. Instead, the only way I could get to the near-by town of Tobruk was to hail one of the taxis that had been among the stream of cars heading the other way, out of the country, as those who could fled the expected murderous rampage by Gaddafi's men and sought sanctuary in Egypt. As I tried to secure a ride, one of the cars heading east stopped ten yards down from me to deposit its passengers. As men, women and children emerged from it, one of the men suddenly collapsed, pawing at his chest in agony. Those around him started giving him CPR but none knew what they were doing, me even less. As I watched he died of his heart attack, the sudden relief at having reached the border safely too much for his body to take.

Tobruk has only one international hotel. When I was deposited at it on the evening of Saturday, 19 March, the place was almost empty. Within an hour it was full as convoys of journalists fleeing Benghazi suddenly arrived. The stories they had showed how close the city was to complete disaster. Two days earlier the international community had finally acted as the United Nations imposed a no-fly zone over Libya and authorised the use of military power to protect civilians. But it now seemed that they acted too late to stop the catastrophe everyone feared.

I know Dan Murphy of the *Christian Science Monitor* from Baghdad. He was one of those who like me was there for years and chronicled how the brief optimism that followed the 2003 invasion was followed by a descent into sectarian violence and then civil war that destroyed what had once been a functional country and reduced it to a level of anarchy from which it is yet to fully recover. We had stayed in the same hotel, drunk together, exchanged horror stories, had friends and colleagues killed or kidnapped. I had rarely, however, seen him as wired as he was when he arrived in Tobruk.

First Sign that the End for Benghazi was Approaching

It was clear that Benghazi was on the brink of going the way of Ajdabiya. The first sign that the end could be approaching came on Friday. Throughout the previous days the people of Benghazi had followed nervously the news of how their earlier victories were being unravelled. Then, on Friday, rumours spread that Gaddafi's troops were approaching the outskirts of Benghazi itself. As the sun started to set, the first explosions could be heard, shelling coming in once or twice an hour into the outskirts of the city. It was around 3am that the attack started in earnest. Dan described how the explosions were now almost rhythmic in their intensity and how many were of such power the sound shook buildings across the city. Light brought the revelation that Gaddafi's troops were now in Benghazi itself. Tanks and soldiers were reported deep into the south-eastern districts, news that spread panic and caused the militiamen who made up most of the rebels amateur army to fall back.

At 8.20 the rebel commanders unleashed the most potent weapon in their armoury: a Russian-made fighter jet seized at the start of the uprising. Such was the confusion that it was shot down almost immediately by their own men, the pilot ejecting but too low to get his parachute to open. By mid-morning Gaddafi's troops had seized a military base and the university. Thick smoke covered much of the city's southern parts and the rebels were struggling to hold a line beyond the city's zoo and one of its main hospitals. The mosques wailed a call to arms. Thousands of families fled, the roads heading north and west filled with vehicles. Along these roads amazing demonstrations of solidarity and support were witnessed. People in villages and towns outside Benghazi lined them with signs inviting anyone who needed somewhere to stay to sleep in their homes. Others handed out water or meals of bread and fruit. Some simply thrust money into the hands of any who needed it.

Such was the seriousness of the situation – and such the pessimism about what would come next – that it was at that point that much of the world's media left too. For Dan the moment came when he went to witness where the rebel Libyan plane had gone down. He had managed to reach within a few blocks of it when he was stopped by one of the volunteer checkpoints so prevalent in the city. The youths, teenagers basically, who manned it warned them to stop. When he got out to talk to them to find out the situation, bullets started ricocheting off the street around them. Looking down an ally he saw the dark green uniform of Gaddafi's soldiers and ran. He ran until his lungs could no longer take it and then hitched a lift back to the Ouzu Hotel with a family escaping the violence. There he found the doors locked and the staff fled. A back-door was still open and he grabbed his computer and kit before hitching another lift towards Tobruk, one on which the driver insisted on playing a cassette by the American rapper 50 Cent for the entire journey. Much of the rest of the media had left just before him. Unable to find vehicles many climbed into the back of a lorry, standing room only for some, to be ferried out of the city.

No one knew exactly what was happening in Benghazi. There were reports of fighting. Some of French airstrikes hitting Gaddafi's armour. Others that tanks had been reported leaving Ajdabiyah and making direct for Tobruk to surround the rebel enclave and stop anyone else escaping for the border. At dawn, Dan and I hired a car and headed west to find out for ourselves. We skirted the coast, believing that was the safest route as the Jebel Akhdar mountains that separate the coastal areas of east Libya from its desert hinterland would slow down any of Gaddafi's track vehicles. All along the route we passed cars heading the other way. In the city of al-Bayda, located part way between Tobruk and Benghazi, people were discussing establishing defences on the outskirts of town, fearful of an attack on them too.

Victory Celebrations Return to Benghazi

But when we reached the outskirts of Benghazi and the first units of shabab we found them celebrating. Indeed, everywhere we found people celebrating. Cars were honking horns and people running through the street waving Libyan independence flags. One group had even dressed up a donkey in a mask of Gaddafi that they were then parading through the streets for others to ridicule.

Benghazi had been saved. By the tightest possible margin. Just when things had appeared at their very worst – when Gaddafi's troops were fighting in the city and people fleeing, when everyone I subsequently talked to expected nothing else to happen to their city than a "bloody massacre" – the international community had stepped up. It was almost dusk and the battle had been feared almost lost when suddenly French fighter jets were reported overhead. Invigorated, the rebels held back the attack and then pushed forward and started to catch tanks and prisoners. As night fell, Gaddafi's men pulled back to what they thought was a safe haven south of the city ahead of the expected resumption of hostilities the following day. That night British and American missiles rained on Libya and French jets attacked the tanks and heavy weaponry gathered south of Benghazi. Now Gaddafi's army in Libya's east was in full retreat.

It had been a very close run thing. The fact is the rebels had neither the organisation nor the leadership nor the military power to stop the retribution being directed at them. So late did the international community leave its decision to act that if they had waited even a few more hours Gaddafi's forces would have got a foothold in the city and, therefore, been almost impossible to displace through air support. So close was it that Gaddafi had even bussed in a group of supporters to stage a rally in Benghazi's outskirts welcoming his soldiers. This was to be broadcast on state TV so as to show that the rebellion would be crushed, and his survival assured. The Libyan revolution had been on the brink of extinction.

It did not happen. It did not happen because the international community acted in time to stop it. If those planes had not come then thousands of people would have likely died and all the jubilation and hope that the prospect of freedom from Gaddafi's rule released in the revolutionary areas destroyed. We only have to see the stories from Misrata and other areas into which Gaddafi's forces advanced to get an indication of what was awaiting the people of Benghazi if the international community had not intervened. The reports of rape, of snipers shooting civilians, of mass arrests, of shells pounding civilian areas.

Where the Air Strikes had done their Worst Damage
That evening I drove to where the air strikes had done their worst damage. The place was a field outside Tarria village, 15 miles south. It was here that French fighter jets had directed their precision weaponry directly on Gaddafi's armoured might. Across the entire area were the twisted, blackened shells of what had been tanks and troop carriers. Three of the tank turrets had been blown clear, now lying yards from the husk of their vehicles with their barrel tips part-buried in the rocky soil. Blood was smeared at one spot, bandages scattered on the floor. Around them a people who had feared disaster revelled in the joy of their survival, the victory marked by cries to God and Libya's future and the sound of machineguns fired into the air.

Children climbed onto the debris to be photographed by their parents. Youths waving Libyan independence flags sat on the barrels of the tanks that still had turrets. A car had its windscreen wipers bent to perch a charred army boot that it paraded in triumph. "It's a miracle," said Mohammed Ahmed, who had come with his two brothers to view the devastation and was staring in a mixture of delight and awe at the crumpled frame of a pick-up truck. "They were killing us. Everything was feared lost. Now it's Gaddafi who is running."

Dozens came up to demand I recorded their gratitude, many shaking with the emotion of their relief. "I love United Kingdom. I love Sarkozy. I love United States," cried one, Ali Aboudata, his fingers formed in V-for-victory signs that punched the air. "My heart is theirs. We are friends forever. You saved our city. You saved our lives."

There were selfish reasons, both internal and external, why the Western countries who acted did what they did. There are questions about what will happen next to Libya and about what the consequences of that intervention are. I saw for myself in Benghazi the ambiguities about what was being created there: the attacks on negros, the volunteers at checkpoints at times bordering on vigilante behaviour. In the coming weeks I witnessed again and again the inability of the Libyan rebels to take full advantage of the opportunities the Western air strikes gave them, not least because Libya remains a deeply tribal society. The Gaddafi solider I talked to may be right to fear anarchy and fundamentalism, particularly if the international community's state-building rather than military response is as disconnected and ham-fisted as it was in Iraq. We have seen since, in Syria, just such massacres allowed to occur elsewhere. Who knows if the chaotic, disorganised, imperfect but ultimately optimistic, democratic and largely religiously-moderate revolutionary movement I witnessed in eastern Libya can survive if it gets control of the country itself.

But that is not the point. That was not Benghazi's issue. Not at that time. Not at that place. Its issue was that there at least a city was protected from disaster. The good guys were for once saved. The bad guys beaten. It may in the end have been might that stopped might. But at least what was done was right. What will happen next we do not know, but a massacre was averted. I have no doubt about that and, like I said, you don't see that very often, especially if you do what I do for a living.

Note on the author

Oliver Poole is an award-winning writer and foreign correspondent who is presently responsible for Special Projects at the *Independent* and *Evening Standard*. He was previously Baghdad bureau chief for the *Daily Telegraph* and has written two books, *Black Knights: On the Bloody Road to Baghdad* and *Red Zone: Five Bloody Years in Baghdad*.

No-one Knew How Many had Laid Down their Lives for this Revolution. People Prayed, Danced and Sang

Lindsey Hilsum, International Editor, Channel 4 News, and her team found themselves in the middle of a gun battle as they covered the collapse of Gaddafi's rule in Libya. No-one was hurt and, in this exclusive account, she describes the extraordinary events they witnessed in Tripoli

We careered into Tripoli with a convoy of rebels touting anti-aircraft guns and mortars on the back of pick-ups. As they honked horns and shouted anti-Gaddafi slogans, women and children stood on balconies cheering and waving. An old man, in a long white robe, watching from the side of the street, said: "They are all my sons."

He looked around him. "This is my street," he said. "This is my house. This is my country. We are free." Another held his grandson up to kiss the fighters, and then knelt on the road weeping and giving thanks to God.

It was August 21. The previous night, rebels from the Nafousa Mountains, west of the capital, had entered Green Square, powering past the remnants of Gaddafi's military, and joining up with those who had started an insurrection in the Libyan capital the night before.

For a brief few hours that night, Gaddafi's people fought back. His son, Seif al-Islam, once regarded as a reformer, but by then his father's most rabid supporter, had appeared in the early hours at their Bab al Aziziya compound to declare that nothing had changed, but then he slipped away. The 42-year Gaddafi era was over, even though the Brother Leader – as he liked to call himself – had not been captured. An old woman, her wrinkled face covered in blue tattoos, spoke for many when she spat out his name and made the sign of throat slitting.

"Bye bye, Gaddafi. Gaddafi, ciao," shouted two young fighters as they drove by, giving V for victory with their fingers. One man, asked where was Gaddafi, replied "Gone with the wind."

The Dangers had not Diminished
But in amongst the celebrations, danger had not diminished. The Channel 4 News team found ourselves in a middle of a gun battle as three snipers fired in our direction. Rebels fired back with AK-47s and a rocket-propelled grenade. Bullets cracked past our heads and struck a lamp-post near where we were taking cover.

"We have caught eight or nine mercenaries," said Salam al Ghadi, a medical student who was brought up in Ireland, as the sound of heavy weapons further down the road drowned out his words. By evening, battles were still raging across Tripoli as the remnants of Gaddafi's army, including mercenary fighters from Africa, attacked rebel checkpoints. At the National Oil building, rebels were marching ten white men into a room with their hands on their heads. "Ukrainian mercenaries," said the commander.

The next day, rebels entered Bab al Aziziya, the centre of Gaddafi's power, a compound regarded with such fear that previously people would avert their eyes when they drove past. Mukhtar Nagasa, who in a previous incarnation had worked as a dentist in Bath, was one of the first in. "We met no resistence," he said, as he showed us video he and friends had taken of them posing in front of murals in the house of Saadi, one of Gaddafi's sons.

Destroying the Ugly Monuments to Gaddafi's Rule

Libya's revolution had started on 17 February in the east of the country. The initial shaky, amateur footage which emerged was breath-taking. In Tobruk, Libya's eastern-most city, young men were using pick-axes to destroy the concrete statues of the Green Book, the ugly monuments to Gaddafi's rule displayed prominently in every town. A crowd of onlookers was cheering: "The people demand the fall of the regime," a slogan they had picked up from Egypt's uprising a few weeks earlier.

In Benghazi, the capital of the east, the revolt was led by the families of 1,200 men who had been killed at Abu Salim prison in 1996, in the worst atrocity of Gaddafi's rule. All political prisoners, some had been lined up against the prison walls while others were loaded into buses before being machine-gunned down. The families had been demonstrating every Saturday for four years, but this time others – inspired by Tunisia to the west and Egypt to the east – joined in. Such was the hatred of Gaddafi in the east, his forces quickly crumbled and people stormed the *katiba*, the central barracks, driving bull-dozers through the walls.

In the west, the revolution was equally decisive from the start. In the Nafousa Mountains, the Berber – correctly known as Amazigh – and other groups had long resented Gaddafi. His forces continued to shell towns such as Zintan and Nalut from the plains, but the fighters swiftly took the towns and held them. The port of Misrata held out through weeks of siege, enduring many casualties.

Nato's Crucial Role

But in Tripoli it was a different story. Those who came out on the streets of the capital to protest in February were brutally suppressed. By the time Nato entered the conflict, preventing Gaddafi's forces from hunting down those who had risen against him in the east, Tripoli had been locked down. Under the surface, there was no calm. As a young woman who escaped the capital said: "In Tripoli, there is no silence in the night."

Men went for training in Tunisia. Women collected money and sent it to fighters in the Nafousa Mountains. Weapons were smuggled in. In some neighbourhoods people shouted anti-Gaddafi slogans and *Allah Akbar* from their rooftops. And all the time, Nato airstrikes were weakening Colonel Gaddafi's defences.

On Saturday 20 August, in a carefully coordinated secret plan, imams called for insurrection from the Tripoli mosques at the break of the Ramadan fast in the evening. On cue, tens of thousands of men came out onto the streets and started attacking Gaddafi's soldiers and police.

"I thought I was the only one in my neighbourhood with a gun," said Mustapha Kraza, a telecoms engineer. "But that night I found at least fifty had weapons. Many got them in secret from the army, from colonels and above." Other weapons were smuggled in by sea from the rebel stronghold of Misrata. Prison guards deserted and men jailed since February's anti Gaddafi demonstrations escaped. State television stopped showing its normal pictures of ecstatic crowds dressed in Gaddafi's favourite green, dancing and cheering for the Brother Leader, broadcasting children's programmes instead.

On 31 August, one day before the 42nd anniversary of the coup which brought Gaddafi to power, Libyans celebrated *Eid*. The old Green Square, backing on to the Medina, was now called Martyrs Square, its pre-Gaddafi name but with new meaning. No-one knew how many had laid down their lives for this revolution. People prayed, danced and sang.

"I need a hundred, a thousand, a million words to say what I feel," exclaimed a middle-aged woman in a pale blue headscarf. The new ban on shooting into the air was ignored as the boys from Misrata let off whatever weapons they had in a cacophony of joy and exhilaration.

Within a few days, it would be time to start rebuilding the country. The infrastructure was crumbling, and oil production – the country's prime earner – had ground to a halt. There would be instability and political infighting. There might yet be guerrilla war as the Gaddafi family and their supporters were still fighting in the deserts south and east of the capital. But for this one day at the end of Ramadan 2011, the Libyan capital was celebrating as never before.

Note on the author
Lindsey Hilsum is International Editor of Channel 4 News. She is writing a book on Libya.

The Reverberating Echo Chamber –
Beyond the Spectacle

As the effects of the Libyan uprising reverberate around the Middle East and Northern Africa, Jon Leyne argues that the provision of intelligent analysis and explanation has remained crucial throughout the coverage of the "Arab Spring". Without it "the viewers, listeners and readers would soon grow bored of the spectacle"

Our Libyan friend and fixer took us to the airbase in Benghazi. The commander there had probably never faced a journalist in his life, certainly never a Western journalist. Senior air force officers never spoke to the Western media under Col. Gaddafi, and we were the first to arrive since the base had been "liberated" by the Libyan opposition a few days earlier.

I knew that there was a great story about the role the base had played in Benghazi's fight against Col. Gaddafi's forces. But the Libyan officer was understandably nervous about this new ordeal of speaking on camera. After some prolonged and delicate negotiations, he finally said the Arabic equivalent of "what the ********, let's just do it." We walked outside. He straightened up his uniform and the interview began.

As it drew to a close, we became aware something was happening behind us. Someone had taken the framed photograph of Col. Gaddafi from its former place of honour on the wall. It was propped up against a chair. Then one of the airmen took aim with his AK-47 and machine-gunned the photograph, to delirious cries of joy and shouts of *Allahu Akhbar*, God is Great.

Over on the airfield we spoke with the crew of a menacing Hind attack helicopter, who told us of how they had been ordered to attack the crowds protesting in Benghazi just a few days earlier. They managed to play for time, pretending to repair a broken fuel line, until it was too dark to fly. By the next day their masters had fled.

On the way back to our hotel we saw the burnt out ruins of the internal security headquarters. In one corner were the tiny, dark cells, into which dissidents, or often just people picked off the street at random, were crammed in, and tortured. Some of the former prisoners were standing around, on hand to relate their terrible experiences. At the front of the building, some other Libyans were loading into their car the secret files they had found in the offices, ready, they said, to prepare for future prosecutions.

Moments of Crazy Exhilaration

That is what it has been like reporting events in Libya and the Middle East these last few months. Often, it has been a news theme park, with stories round every corner, and moments of crazy exhilaration, from which it has been impossible to be immune.

For anyone used to the frustrations of reporting the Middle East, the feeling of liberation has been almost as intense as for the peoples of Tunisia, Libya and Egypt. For years I have developed my patience, spending weeks or months persuading someone to give an interview, only to have them back out at the last minute. Now suddenly we were fending them off, as people were desperate to tell us about their experiences. Where there were no English speakers, suddenly, mysteriously, almost everyone spoke enough English to perform on the BBC.

For me, the most exciting moments were at the start. After six months in Egypt, six years in the Middle East, the ground-breaking demonstration in Cairo on 25 January was a breath-taking revelation. In a few short hours it became clear that the people had lost their fear, and their government had no answer.

As one of the first journalists to arrive in Libya at the start of their revolution, there was another moment of giddy elation as we crossed into the border from Egypt. Long forgotten were those months and years of waiting for a visa. Now the opposition were in control. Or at least so far as anyone was in control of the border post, as there was no serious passport check. The only uniforms were an eccentric collection of hats that almost everyone had donned. We just walked straight into the country, to meet a group of Libyans almost crazy with happiness that they had kicked out Col. Gaddafi's security forces.

Thanks to Libya's close-knit tribal and family system, we soon discovered that the road to Tobruk was safe. Our taxi driver offered us his sofas to sleep on. We broadcast for the *Ten O'Clock News* from his roof, doing a live two-way by torchlight.

Witnessing history

At the back of my mind, always, has been the sense that we are witnessing history, in a way few people are lucky enough to do in their lifetimes. I firmly believe this is a period of change in the Middle East as significant as the break-up of the Ottoman Empire a century ago. And like it or not, we journalists are more than just witnesses, we are playing our part. If no journalists had made it into eastern Libya, then surely the pressure would never have built up for a no-fly zone and the subsequent Nato-led military intervention.

For all the excitement, it's not just a question of journalists scripting a live-action Hollywood action movie. Without intelligent analysis and explanation, the viewers, listeners and readers would soon grow bored of the spectacle.

And for all the talk of the Twitter revolution, and the importance of social media, this has actually been a moment for the good old-fashioned foreign correspondent. Almost all the journalists who have broken the news have done it the traditional way, by being there long term, by making contacts and by knowing their subject.

When I crossed the same border into Libya six months later, the military had uniforms, name tags even. Our passports were closely scrutinised. In Benghazi, an opposition military spokesman was giving regular media briefings. Libya was edging towards becoming a normal country. But the effect of the revolution here would echo round the Middle East, reinforcing change in Egypt and Tunisia, and giving hope to the opposition in Syria and who knows where else.

That echo chamber will continue to reverberate for years to come, and we need to be there to report it, day in day out.

Note on the author

Jon Leyne has been based in the Middle East for the BBC for six of the last seven years. Since June 2010 he has been the Middle East Correspondent based in Cairo. He reported from Cairo throughout the Egyptian revolution. He was one of the first foreign correspondents into Libya to report on the revolution there, and he has also reported on the development of the "Arab Spring" across the region. From 2007 until he was expelled in 2009, he was the BBC Tehran correspondent, reporting on the tumultuous events surrounding President Ahmadinejad's re-election. From 2004 to 2007 he was based in Amman, Jordan, travelling across the region. He has also been based at the State Department in Washington, the United Nations in New York, and in the Balkans.

"This was a moment. We won't forget. We shouldn't have lived. But we did. Get in!"

Stuart Ramsay, Chief Correspondent for Sky News, was part of their reporting double act in Libya with Alex Crawford that secured the world exclusive – entering Tripoli as it fell to the anti-Gaddafi forces. Here, he describes the raw emotion of being first, beating the BBC, ITV – but nor Crawford

OK you have to understand something – this is totally raw and emotional so forgive me. My friend of 20 years Alex Crawford has been f**king lucky and I have been chasing and working harder. For six months I have been chasing – actually my whole life. It is all about timing and Alex was bang on it. It is hot; I am f**ked and my team is f**ked but I AM heading to Bab al Aziziya. Two days, no sleep – determined. When the first tank round came OUT of the compound and flew over our heads I shouted: "Keep f**king driving man – this is a f**king good day – they missed!" It's total war. Impossible to describe. Keep up. It WAR. Proper war.

I meet my mate Miles Amore (*Sunday Times*): "Stu, it's f**king amazing, man, get in – where you been man – f**k!" "F**king Ibiza – what up with your lid?"

(helmet) it has a tear. His body armour is ropey. "Hit man – knocked to ground – f**k," he said. "F**king right. Thank fuck you had it on," I replied. Most of my newspaper mates wear nothing. I go nowhere without. "Now f**k off and live - go." We met two days later and he asked to borrow a hat!

"Dick head – just who the fuck is now going to lend YOU a hat?!"

Bab al Aziziya! You can't imagine the feeling. Those lying Gaddafi f**ks had used that as a barrier for so long and the Misrata Brigade had smashed it in a day. We climbed in. Rounds in and out – non stop. Deaf deaf deaf. Shout stop and indicate "live" to Ed (cam), Tom (prod) and John (security). I am a bit rusty but in element. Team very worried but well on it.

I wanted to be there. I had worked to be there. I wanted to be live as the walls fell. I was – but f**king Crawford was there before me. Our Sat phones banged in to London at the same time. Two lines – we both took the right one – total chance. The newsroom cheered – I could hear it in my ear piece. Two live shots and two reporters from inside the HQ of Gaddafi for an hour.

I did not cry but did later – when you crack something like that it is like winning the world cup or your first under 11's goal and your dad cries. Get It – now keep with this because it is hectic and emotional and I am writing straight from memory – so sorry.

We left – total total chaos. Looting and in-coming. A 50 Cal opens on us from 50 meters. Fly to cover but he following – right right on us. Tracers smash past – that about every third frigging round, inches away. Alex legs it with this nutter bloke in a bloody Gaddafi hat and sword! We follow. Back streets and we in armour. Gun men jumpy hold us up – Sky Fucking NEWS MAN – "Sky News best – welcome to Libya." – You couldn't make it up.

John Simpson, a brilliant brilliant reporter wrote a book about Kabul and its relief. In it he described the brilliance of the Beeb and how it could never be surpassed. Sky News has done the Beeb over so many times since then it's daft – all it shows is that everyone keeps evolving and getting better. The Beeb trained nearly everyone at Sky who is any good and now I hear the BBC training course doesn't exist – what!!????

"Hectic: It was Mega."

The teams meet. Very emotional. We are ALL very good friends. The Crawford team had been on the go for days of fighting. We took them to our rented house miles away and had the most fab few hours ever. We filed four "live" reports. An "as live" I filmed at the compound. A piece for the morning from me. An

Alex VT and a "live" and three on-line pieces. Hectic but we now do this. It was mega. We were writing and reporting history. John our security advisor talked to me after. "Stuart – I didn't know how important this is to you guys. The quiet concentration while you worked and the determination to tell the truth. I thought you all made it up. I am proud of you son." Can you even start to imagine how that feels in this year.

Alex's team – Jim Foster (camera) and Garwen McLuckie (camera) are two of my best friends. Andy Marsh (producer) great friend but also the best friend of my old producer Nick Ludlam soon to be Alex's. They made Alex the phenom she is. Understand the simpatico relevance? This IS the key.

Next day we drove to the hospital Alex had been in. We continued with "lives" from the hospital. Alex's team was exhausted and slept while we went out. Within a couple of hours it went nuts across town. Both teams moved and set up shop under fire. Not just a bit of fire.

You have to move from your fixed live position but you just HAVE to find the firing point. Years of working with the best army in world (Brits) have taught me what to look for and two hours with the most mobile army in the world (Misrata boys) helped me sort that.

While they smashed the Gaddafi forces I was live with Kay (Burley) for an hour. She was great – but when she said if I needed to take cover or leave then I should; I just had to laugh. "Kay I am stuck man." I think it covered it. Foreign Ed Sarah Whitehead rang. "Stuart what the exit plan?" "Sarah there fucking isn't one I am fucked if I move. However, I am not moving coz Paul (Danahar, BBC) has an armoured car and it saving my arse – oh and he sends his love."

"Fine," she said. "I will put you back to sound."

Now all really tired. No food little water. Us two hours sleep in four days. Alex team five in five max. We did "lives" under fire and continuous packages but inevitably the Alex team would leave. All of us utterly utterly gutted. Can't explain feelings. We had to go on. It took a while but they left. It was ours now. Shit YES – get in.

War restarted as we headed south. New compounds. Super hostile. Charred murdered bodies. Massive story. BBC and ITN utterly beaten. Nothing like it. Total smash up.

The bodies very important and big. I rang desk after huge fire fight.

"We have fantastic stuff But mate the bodies are massive man – proper story son – Andy ring Ryley this is a proper story." As Andy Gales the Foreign Ed of the day took this in, the locals surrounded me and started shouting – "Andy Man it fooking massive," how the fuck did they know he was a Geordie?

Massive and important. As I held the hand of a doctor who had taken over the makeshift investigation I was shaking.

"Stuart I will help. But bring the ICC here. Sky News can do this – YOU can do this."

My heart is crying out man – I don't know if we can I will try. But I am strung out to fuck. The war isn't over and I can sense we really really on fire but this is why I am here maybe – I don't know; I have been in wars so often I have forgotten the times I have asked - is this why I am here? To tell this story. Maybe this is it. Maybe they all are. Shit I just don't know.

Next day ICC launches enquiry. I puked. First time I have told anyone. Is that me? Understand? Is that my job done? Over?

Filthy stinking. Walk into live-feed hotel. BBC reporters ignore me – others, some of their most senior, have left.

I, Sky, Alex, none of us care but they needed to dig in and accept that Alex had done them over and I had done my bit to keep it going.

We have worked hard and tried to bring the truth. Tunisia, Egypt, Bahrain, Yemen, Syria and loads more. Sky has been in all – Alex and me and Emma and Dom, JT, Wilson and loads of others have been in. But this was a moment we won't forget. Perhaps we shouldn't have lived. But we did. Get in!

Note on the author
Stuart Ramsay is Sky News' Chief Correspondent and firefighter-in-chief. He has reported for them during the "Arab Spring" from Tunisia, Egypt, Bahrain and most recently Libya where he delivered several world exclusives to the station. Ramsay has received many awards including a 2010 Emmy for *Pakistan, Terror's Frontline*; the London Press Club's Broadcast Journalist of the Year 2009, the Royal Television Society's prestigious Foreign Affairs Award for work in Pakistan's Swat Valley, the Monte Carlo Golden Nymph in 2006 for his coverage of the Pakistan earthquake and, in 2005, Gold from New York Festival for his coverage of the Sudan crisis. In 2004, he was an Emmy Finalist for his coverage of the Liberia war and was nominated for a BAFTA last year. Ramsay has covered wars from Chechnya, through Africa and the Middle East to Afghanistan and Iraq. Since 2003, he has covered Iran and Afghanistan, both as an embedded and independent reporter.

"Covering the 'Arab Spring' has been dangerous, exciting and unpredictable"

Wyre Davies, BBC Middle East Correspondent, recalls dozens of tales of stupidity, horror and farce from his time reporting the Arab uprisings – as well as the many acts of bravery by correspondents

As unique and as different each of the individual Arab uprisings were, Tunisia, Egypt, Libya and others have all presented their own particular reporting challenges. Few people could have predicted that when several thousand young people took to the streets in one of the Arab world's least populous and, arguably, less important nations it would trigger a landslide that has engulfed the entire region in the space of six months.

The irony is that one person could, indeed, see, even in the early days of January, what was coming his way – Colonel Muammar Gaddafi.

As students, state employees and the generally disaffected people of Tunisia took to the streets of Tunis, Sfax and Djerba, it was the leader of neighbouring Libya who sensed what would eventually penetrate his own borders. Gaddafi warned against the "madness" and destabilising events erupting on his doorstep. President Zine al Abedine ben Ali was, according to his fellow dictator, a "strong and good leader". Ultimately there was nothing Col. Gaddafi could do to stop the first tremor that became known as the "Arab Spring".

Tunisia was a relative pushover and perhaps the one place where the term "internet revolution" rang true. Educated, computer-savvy young Tunisians were at the forefront of their rebellion. On Facebook, Twitter and through internet blogs they organised simultaneous protests in towns and cities across the country. They were quick to upload grainy but powerful footage showing how the Tunisian police and state security apparatus violently cracked down against peaceful demonstrations.

Tunisian Regime Ignorant of Modern Newsgathering Techniques

The regime of President ben Ali was ill-equipped to deal with a generation of young people who knew how to get around blunt, Soviet-style state restrictions. Crucially, nor did the regime really understand modern newsgathering techniques that enable media teams to gather and broadcast information in increasingly subtle, less obvious ways.

While the international media did not exactly flood into Tunisia as it would later do in Egypt and Libya, many of those teams who arrived at Tunis airport did so with handy-cams, iphones or flip-cameras rather than the standard large video cameras normally used for newsgathering.

The Tunisian authorities did manage to confiscate dozens of BGAN terminals (for sending images and data via satellite) but many more made it into the country. To the untrained eye they look no different to a computer laptop flung into the bottom of a traveller's suitcase.

Covering the Tunisian uprising was, in the first couple of days, dangerous and risky. Brutal, unforgiving Interior Ministry police would regularly wave their guns in the faces of protestors and reporters alike. Some people were killed – often by snipers shooting from the top of government buildings.

Having arrived, officially at least, in Tunisia as a tourist, I had been unable to travel with my body armour (which would later be a welcome and constant companion in Libya) so trying to film in demonstrations and around sensitive government buildings was always tricky. Time and time again, reporting teams covering the "Arab Spring" have ditched the heavy, obtrusive camera gear with which we normally work moving, instead, with light-weight and less obtrusive kit.

Army's Refusal to Back Regime – the Crucial Turning Point

The turning point in Tunisia was the refusal of the army to support a weakened and discredited regime. Soldiers protected government buildings and were a constant presence on the streets but they did not open fire on the protestors. (This of course was to become a critical feature of the subsequent uprising in Egypt – not so in either Libya or Syria.) The military hierarchy, indeed, made it clear to a president holed below the waterline that he had to go. (Go he did on 14 January 2011 – fleeing on a private jet to exile in Saudi Arabia with as much gold bullion as the plane could safely carry.)

So, Tunisia came and went. Surely, though, the much stronger, notoriously brutal Arab regimes would not succumb to the same kind of student-led, unarmed protest movements? Yet across the Middle East, disenfranchised but often educated people had been taking note. Fed up with a ruling elite which kept the best jobs and best opportunities for itself and its cronies, young people rose up. They wanted a say in how their societies would be run and, in some cases, they were prepared to put their lives on the line to achieve that.

I mentioned above how the role of social media in helping to promulgate and promote the Tunisian uprising was critical. Many commentators also credited Facebook, Twitter and other social media for being at the forefront of subsequent revolts. I am not sure that is true reflection of events.

At the end of the day, especially in country such as Egypt which is lagging behind badly in terms of computer use and accessibility, the most powerful and popular medium of information is still television. The growth and popularity of the Arab cable television stations cannot be underestimated. Watching Al Arabia, Al Jazeera and a plethora of other cable channels is how many young Egyptians took their cue from the Tunisian revolution, not by tweeting or fingering their Blackberrys while sipping skinny lattes on the banks of the Nile.

The Egyptian revolution and its central "stage" – Tahrir Square – became a massive global news event. Not only did the BBC significantly increase its presence and effort (compared to how we'd covered Tunisia) but many other major international broadcasters sent large teams to the Egyptian capital. This meant we were able to dispatch reporting teams further afield – to Port Said, Suez and Alexandria, from where I reported for five days.

When Police Tried to Grab our Cameras

As generally up-beat and positive the atmosphere may have been in Cairo, in the provinces it often felt distinctly more edgy and dangerous. There were clearly hundreds of pro-Mubarak supporters determined to disrupt anti-government demonstrations and gatherings. On several occasions, while filming in Alex, people (who I assumed were undercover policemen) tried to grab our cameras, or even physically tried to drag us away from covering demonstrations.

Amid rising tensions in Alex and with credible reports of journalists being detained and beaten up, we resorted to a patient strategy of driving around the city and only getting out to film when it was safe to do so. Even then, some things went wrong. While trying to film a long queue waiting for a bank to open (having first checked with a few people in the queue) it all turned nasty. Proud, frustrated even embarrassed Egyptians turned on us. We eventually made it out of what could have been a dangerous situation but it underlined that, in some parts of Egypt at least, the "Arab Spring" was far from a homogenous, unifying event supported by everyone and destined to "succeed".

(As it happens, three months later I filmed exactly the same scenario in the centre of Tripoli. There, people could not have been more welcoming and willing to speak to foreign reporters even though they had not been paid for days and had been waiting in line in the scorching summer heat for several hours.)

In its dying days the regime resorted to desperate and blunt measures to stop reporters doing their work. A handful of correspondents were expelled. For several days mobile phone networks and the internet were closed down but the lid was off and there was no way the Mubarak acolytes could suppress so many journalists and more importantly so many millions of Egyptians desperate for change.

The ultimate success of the Egyptian revolutionaries and the downfall of Hosni Mubarak was a massive news story. It was rare, perhaps, that a purely "foreign" news event was covered so comprehensively by global television networks. I was broadcasting live, for radio and television, from Tahrir Square on the afternoon that Mubarak finally stood down and will never forget the atmosphere and sense of achievement felt by hundreds of thousands of ordinary Egyptians.

It seemed as if the entire region was in turmoil, citizens desperate for change everywhere. Even for an organisation as large as the BBC and with a team dedicated to Middle East coverage, it was often hard to keep abreast of things. Many of our "core" stories in the region have been put on the back burner, most notably the Israeli/Palestinian conflict, but in a world with an increasing appetite for news (with ironically ever tighter budgets) tough decisions about coverage have had to be made.

Tumultuous Times

In recent months we have had teams in Bahrain, Yemen, Jordan and (frustratingly) on the borders of Syria. These have been tumultuous times but the story of how the people of Libya rose up against one of the world's most notorious dictators is one of the most compelling of all. It has also, arguably, been the most interesting chapter of the "Arab Spring" even though, compared to Egypt and Syria, Libya is a much less strategically important country. It has, without question, been the most dangerous and challenging to cover.

As I write (early September 2011), I have travelled to Libya on five separate occasions – almost uniquely being able to cover the conflict from both sides. The events of Tunisia and Egypt may have been largely peaceful and mostly homogenous social movements but in Libya it has been civil war. The "trick' in Tripoli (when covering events as a "guest" of the Gaddafi government) was to give your minders the slip and try to report from a capital under siege where many people were clearly too afraid to protest.

In the early days, while staying at the luxurious Rixos Hotel (an establishment that would increasingly resemble an, albeit, comfortable prison) there were some, admittedly, interesting government trips. When the regime still felt it had the upper hand (essentially before the Nato attacks tipped the balance in the rebels' favour) I was flown down to

Gaddafi's home town of Sirte and on to the front line, not far in those days from the rebel stronghold of Benghazi.

What we could film and whom we could speak to was closely and increasingly controlled – more so as the tide turned against Colonel Gaddafi. Sometimes the regime's media machine, despite its Western-educated spokesman and ample resources, was laughably amateur and counter-productive. Presenting an unconscious infant, lying on a bed in a Tripoli hospital, as a "victim" of Nato bombing was a particularly crude stunt. It wasn't too long before we found out she had, in fact, been hurt in a car accident.

We met dissidents in Tripoli, contacted through an elaborate system of encrypting emails and other "methods" such were our justifiable concerns that we were being spied on physically and electronically by our minders. What those meetings with underground protest leaders and students told us, again all filmed on flip-cams and iphones, was that there was a significant body of opposition to Gaddafi in his "fortress" capital but at that point, people were too intimidated and wary of speaking out.

That wariness and fear, as it turned out, was completely justified. On my most recent trip to the Libyan capital we found and filmed evidence that the Gaddafi regime was even more brutal, sadistic and murderous than had previously been thought. Since the regime fell, at numerous locations around the capital, hundreds of bodies have been discovered. Many were victims of torture and, it seems, most had been killed in the days before opposition rebel forces eventually overran Tripoli. Questions of taste and decency always have to be considered when filming at such sites but these were important stories to tell.

Unique Challenges

Covering the conflict, over a period of several months, from the rebel side also threw up its unique challenges. Logistics (food, water and methods of physically getting our stories "out") were problematical, to say the least, in the huge expanse of the Libyan desert. But by far the biggest risk and danger, when covering the war from the rebel front, was the sheer unprofessionalism and chaos in the rebel ranks.

I have often compared spending several days and weeks on the front line in eastern Libya to being on the set of *Mad Max*. With their souped-up

Toyota pick-ups, onto which they had welded anti-aircraft guns or helicopter rocket pods, the rebels would charge up to the front line. Usually, when confronted by Gaddafi's better-trained and (then) better-equipped troops, the rebels would speed back to the relative safety of Ajdabiya or Benghazi, enthusiastically firing their weapons in no particular direction as they went.

On one particularly hairy day, what we had identified as a relatively safe position (a couple of kms behind the front line) became a mortar landing zone, thanks to a rebel fighter who had, unannounced, begun firing rockets towards Gaddafi's troops from within the vehicles of the press corps. The return, incoming, fire was bloody close and, thanks to the soft desert sand, many shells failed to detonate on impact.

I could recall dozens of tales of stupidity, horror and farce from my time in Libya. The rebel fighter who killed himself by banging his jammed weapon on the ground (unfortunately, he was standing over it at the time); the father who gave his five-year-old child a live hand-grenade to play with in Tripoli's (newly renamed) "Martyr's Square"; the carnage and grief after a rebel convoy had been obliterated in a Nato "friendly fire" incident because no-one in the rebel military hierarchy had bothered to tell Nato they had acquired some old Gaddafi tanks and were sending them to the front. (Up to that point, Nato pilots were under the assumption that all heavy armour in the desert was offensive government weaponry and, therefore, a legitimate target.)

Reporting on the street fighting in Tripoli, in the days before the capital fell into rebel hands, was particularly challenging. For days many districts remained in the hands of Gaddafi loyalists who seemed prepared to fight until the bitter end. Many BBC teams came under serious gunfire, either driving through streets we thought were safe or while trying to advance into Colonel Gaddafi's fortified and heavily armoured compound. But there were important stories to cover – the bravery of frontline hospital staff or the hospitals, which had to be abandoned because of heavy fighting, but to where dozens of dead and dying people were still being brought.

There were guns everywhere. Again, there was genuine danger of being "accidentally" hit by falling bullets from celebratory gunfire or by a "fighter" who did not really know how to handle his weapon. Persuading people to hand in their weapons will be a critical stage in trying to pacify and normalise what is still a violent, distrustful country.

Covering the "Arab Spring" has been dangerous, exciting and unpredictable. There are places, in particular the horrendous events of Syria, that we have frustratingly only been able to cover from afar. (The availability and sheer amount of mobile phone and other footage smuggled out or filed from Syria has been invaluable in helping to tell the story of thousands of brave protestors there but the Assad regime has largely succeeded in keeping the international media out.)

Much still to Report
It is also not yet over. Regimes have fallen, dictators have fled and others have yet to succumb. There will be elections, attempts by the elite to halt the tide of reform and inevitable disputes between the forces for change.

What role for women or for the Islamic parties in Egypt? Can the 30 million or so Egyptians who live in desperate poverty ever hope to be part of or benefit from the events in Tahrir Square? If Colonel Gaddafi is eventually caught, will a geographically divided nation ever unite under what is regarded as a generally weak rebel political leadership? Will Tunisia, the country that started all of this, use its undoubted advantages, to push on to full, democratic reform?

The interest and knowledge shown by our audiences to what has happened in the Arab world has been encouraging. I hope it lasts because there is much still to report. As for now, I have a family I have seen precious little of in the last year and I'm sure I'll be on the road again before too long.

Note on the author
Currently based in Jerusalem, Wyre Davies has been a full-time Middle East Correspondent for the BBC since March 2010. He has, however, spent much of the last eight years covering the region for BBC News. Working across television, radio and online, Wyre has made several reporting trips across the Middle East to report the "Arab Spring" and was, indeed, one of the first reporters to arrive in Tunis last January. A Welsh-Mancunian, Wyre was previously stationed as Latin America Correspondent, then as Wales Correspondent for the BBC. He is married with four children – the last of whom arrived in the middle of the "Arab Spring" and has seen far too little of his father!

Behind the Sky Scoop: The Libyan Revolution and British TV news

John Mair looks at the *denouement* of the Libyan Civil War: the fall of Tripoli around the weekend of 21 August 2011. Sky News' Alex Crawford got there first with two other women reporters - from CNN and Al Jazeera. Why? Where was the BBC?

Modern warfare is fought as much on the TV screens and living rooms of the nation as it on the battlefields of Iraq, Afghanistan or Libya. Armies win wars and so too do broadcaster armies. In Britain, the now widespread view is that Sky News (and especially Alex Crawford and Stuart Ramsay) well and truly in the words of one of the BBC's own executives "creamed" (i.e. beat badly)[1] BBC News who were too often flat-footed and behind the story, as one leading media commentator, Professor Tim Luckhurst, of Kent University, (and formerly of the BBC) was quick to point out.[2] Why was this not the Corporation's proudest moment?

First the bald facts: On Sunday 21 August, Alex Crawford and her crew were the first British TV crew (in the close company of CNN and Al

Jazeera) in with the rebel army to Tripoli and the symbolic Green Square. She broadcast live to an astonished world as she has relived so vividly earlier in this book.[3] She told an audience at the Edinburgh Television Festival in August that this was "the most exhilarating moment for all of us". Her explanation of that undoubted journalistic coup? "Right people, right place, right time."[4]

Jon Williams, the BBC's World News Editor, admits the swift rebel advance caught the Corporation on the hop. "No one knew it would end as quickly as it did," he has said. "Lots of people were caught by surprise." Williams is gracious in his praise for Crawford: "I take my hat off to Alex Crawford for some brilliant reporting and I promise you this, if Alex wins the prizes she will be entered for I will be the first person to raise my glass and toast her success."[5]

Crawford, a three-times Royal Television Society Television Journalist of the Year winner (and a shoo-in for a fourth on this one piece alone) then topped that by being the first British television reporter into Gaddafi's ransacked headquarters compound at Bab al-Aziziya on Tuesday 23 August. Her memorable interview there with the rebel fighter who purloined Gaddafi's pantomime military hat will stay long in the mind.[6] On the other side of the same compound, her fellow Sky News Correspondent Stuart Ramsay was also broadcasting live. Later in the week he went on to report live some serious and dangerous fighting in the area.

Ramsay's biggest triumph came several days later on Sunday 28 August when he found and reported exclusively on the seeming massacre of 53 people, allegedly by government troops, on the edge of Tripoli.[7] That piece was both extraordinary in the narrative and journalism but also extremely well judged in its tone.[8]

BBC Nowhere in Sight

On all three of these stories the BBC was nowhere in sight or, as their own Radio Four *Media Show* host Steve Hewlett put it: "Not even in the right town."[9] Sky News took to anchoring much of their coverage live from Tripoli with Anna Botting in the days after the "liberation". The BBC presentation team was stuck firmly in a London studio. There had been an edict earlier in 2011 from above that news presenters on location were now to be the exception rather than the rule.[10] This had the effect for the viewer and for BBC coverage of a distancing from the action and an over-reliance on studio analysis whilst Sky was showing it as it happened. Put simply, the BBC was dull.

Crawford puts this down to size and position of her outfit. "It's partly this smallness which, I like to think, makes us more agile and quick on our feet. But there's also a feeling we have to run faster, run longer, run harder than the others."[11] Sky News had 22 staff in Libya at the end, the BBC had "around 30" in response to criticisms in previous conflicts of over manning. In the midst of the battle, the BBC tried to call a ceasefire. Stuart Hughes, BBC World Affairs producer, commented on the BBC College of Journalism's website: "In the fevered and competitive environment of 24 hour news, it is inevitable that comparison will be made between each network's coverage but please let's leave the post-match analysis of which media organisation 'won the war' until all our friends and colleagues working in harm's way are home safely home."[12] This *cri de coeur* did not find widespread acceptance.

The other major news broadcasters in Britain – ITN and Channel 4 News (produced for Channel Four by ITN) – performed admirably if hindered by a lack of a continuous news outlet on their channels. It is only in fluid and moving situations such as wars that 24 hour news comes into its own and provides a true service of changing information rather than a flow of specious stories.

Lindsey Hilsum, the International Editor of Channel Four News, the Martha Gellhorn of this age and the worthy winner of the *British Journalism Review*'s Charles Wheeler Award for 2011[13] was the marathon runner in this race. She was in Libya at the beginning of the uprising in February and still there at the end in August. Always close to the action as she recalls in her piece for this book[14] on liberating Tripoli, she reported:

> "Bye bye, Gaddafi. Gaddafi, ciao," shouted two young fighters as they drove by, giving V for victory with their fingers. One man, when asked where was Gaddafi, replied: "Gone with the wind."

Sterling Journalistic Work
Her colleague, Alex Thomson, is a classic journalist/firefighter – when he sees trouble he walks towards it rather than to safety. He performed sterling journalistic work on the Tunisia/Libya border in the early days

and in post-liberation Tripoli. His reporting is always of the highest quality as is that of his colleague Jonathan Miller.

The main ITN News (on ITV) has lost much influence and kudos in recent years as the flagship *News at Ten* became *News at When?* and was firmly trumped by the BBC. On returning to its eponymous time slot, it has not regained either audience or influence. Bill Neely, their International Editor, though, is the best wordsmith in British TV news. He did not disappoint in Libya. Channel Five News hardly registered on any scale; an internet search produced no entries for original C5 news from Libya in August 2011. Nothing else needs to be said

Which leaves the BBC News – still the Gold Standard in broadcast journalism world wide. Some of their more experienced correspondents put their boots on Libyan soil from the start in February but back in December and again in January, as Nick Springate, a senior BBC World Affairs producer admitted to a Coventry Conversations Conference in June, the boots were flat footed.

> Nobody at all realised what would happen next, and we didn't even get funding for Tunisia because there wasn't a story. We saw the people massing on the streets in Egypt, but again said no – The President will never go now. Again we were wrong, we weren't prepared.[15]

Jon Leyne is a Middle East veteran having been thrown out of Iran where he was the BBC Correspondent in June 2009 for simply doing his job. Leyne was in Libya from the start to end and his metaphor for reporting the events is rather apt: "Often, it has been a news theme park, with stories round every corner, and moments of crazy exhilaration, from which it has been impossible to be immune."[16]

Wyre Davies, another old hand, was in and out on both sides of the conflict-ducking and diving to get the best stories His conclusion: "Covering the 'Arab Spring' has been dangerous, exciting and unpredictable."[17] The BBC reporter roll call goes on: Rupert Wingfield Hayes delivered one stunning piece when caught in gun-fire when Gaddafi's troops were on the run in Tripoli.[18] His dramatic footage was run again and again on the BBC News Channel. But one wonders if he were working for Sky News would he have done an about-turn so readily and so early?

"Rixos Hotel Syndrome"

To this observer the BBC and other broadcasters suffered too much from "Rixos Hotel syndrome" named after the luxury hotel in Tripoli which the Gaddafi regime used to corral the foreign media for many months. There, the increasingly incredulous official spokesman Moussa Ibrahim "briefed" the assembled foreign media on how Gaddafi was winning the civil war right to and beyond the bitter end. Indeed, it was he who arranged the surprise appearance of a defiant Saif Gaddafi at the hotel on the night after much of Tripoli had been liberated to deny the reality.[19] In the five months before the foreign media had been taken on many facility trips by Ibrahim the lie of which James Rodgers[20] and Wyre Davies[21] expose in this book. It may have been better for news organisations to put up a health warning with any material emanating from the Rixos along the lines of "according to Gaddafi sources". They tried to play cat and mouse with their minders. Usually the cat caught the mice. The nadir of this form of sanctioned journalism was the siege of the hotel when BBC correspondent Matthew Price and others were kept virtual hostage in the Rixos, courtesy of guards/gunmen still loyal to the crumbling regime.[22]

The BBC's Middle East Editor Jeremy Bowen and World Affairs Editor John Simpson, gave the appearance of being freelance, even part-time "firefighters", flying in, hosing down some stories and flying out again. Both were subject to what this author calls "the BBC palm tree syndrome". Wherever there is a war, the BBC seems to find a lit palm tree in front of which to stand its superstar correspondents. Maybe even the tree flies in too?

Whilst it is reassuring to see the "BBC Middle East War Tree" this does have the effect of making the coverage one dimensional and again removed from the action behind the tree. Better a Botting on a Tripoli rooftop than a Bowen in front of BBC greenery.

Anonymous Reports of the "Tripoli Witness"

Two female BBC correspondents are, however, worthy of mention: Rana Jawad was the BBC News Tripoli Correspondent before the uprising started. She simply went underground at great personal risk for five months and reported anonymously as "Tripoli witness" until the liberation of the City.[23] Sue Lloyd-Roberts, whose on-screen appearance is more schoolmarm than journalistic terrier, went undercover in the unreported revolt – Syria – with even more danger. Her pieces were startling and deserve some form of industry award.[24]

The BBC itself could be reflective on its performance. At the Edinburgh Television Festival some nabobs opened up: "We have not exactly covered ourselves in glory," one senior BBC executive admitted to the *Guardian*. One of the corporation's executive directors was more explicit, telling colleagues that the broadcaster had been "creamed" by Sky.[25]

Which begs the question: why? Budgets cannot be the reason: all broadcasters throw money at situations such as Libya with almost gay abandon. They know the name of the game is doing it well and thoroughly. The BBC News operation is huge but maybe it is too back-ended; too many people – "suits" in the back office in White City and not enough on the ground in war zones. Lack of local knowledge and preparedness may be another explanation but the BBC has embedded correspondents all over the Middle East, so too does Al Jazeera. Sky News, Channel Four News and ITN depend on their correspondents making it to the fire in time to file. The firemen (and firewomen) picked up the story very quickly and ran with it.

Another possible cause could be over caution on journalism and health and safety. The hostile environment and safety training which mitigates against taking risks. Jon Williams in his tribute to Crawford continued: "I also think that we should raise our glasses to the people who take very difficult decisions and make a judgement that something is not safe. I salute people for making those difficult decisions." Alex Crawford made the judgement that it was safe. The BBC team made the judgement that it was not safe.[26] There were whispers that Crawford had played unsafe in getting her scoops – she firmly rejects this:

> I have heard the subtle criticisms which hint at us being gung-ho or reckless. All rubbish. In my team alone, we are all parents. We have 11 children between the four of us whom we love very much. We spent our time in Libya snatching calls with them by satellite phone, telling stories down the phone to them, promising we'd be back soon. They replied that that was all well and good but Hannah

Montana was still on. The idea that we would take unnecessary risks when we have so much to live for is utterly ridiculous. The criticisms emanate from people who clearly have not been at the end of the phone line to John Ryley [Sky Head of News] or Sarah Whitehead [Sky Foreign Editor] when they are going through our tactics and operations and exit-plans. Sky has some of the toughest safety procedures in the business and instigated many of them way ahead of our counterparts.[27] Point made.

Maverick Swimming Against the Tide

Being a great foreign correspondent clearly needs the element of the maverick swimming against the tide away from the herd. Niftiness and fleet of foot. You make your own luck. Crawford's "luck" in getting into Tripoli with a rebel convoy was made for her five months before when under siege in a mosque in Zawiyah, east of the capital, cheek by jowl with many of the same people. She and they faced death as she told her Edinburgh audience: "I remember feeling that we had to get the news out, we had to show people what was happening, and if we were going to die we should let everyone know that this is what happened.[28]

Whilst the BBC can teach accuracy, style, etc to correspondents can it ever teach sheer journalistic chutzpah or enterprise? That is vital on all assignments, especially frontline ones. There are no prizes in journalism for being behind rather than ahead of the story. The Libyan revolution left the BBC looking firmly flat-footed and behind the curve, and it will be interesting to see what emerges after the inevitable internal inquiry into their coverage of the next theatre of war. After this "creaming", BBC News will have to sharpen its act.

One long emerging truth became more obvious during this war more than any other: television is now king and in many senses the only reporting game in town. Pictures and live action matter above all. Even the built programmes at 6.00 and 10.00 are losing their importance if not yet their audience.

But the biggest casualties have been newspapers and newspaper foreign correspondents. Their day-after dispatches an increasing irrelevance to an audience which has already been sated on the story and the pictures from the day and night before on television. Newspapers have had to re-invent their reporting role and the live blog is a very good expression of this –

following the story and the noise around the story minute-by-minute bringing in live reports, blogs, tweets from all over. Usually they work.[29] The cross fertilisation of this to BBC News online using a live written blog is interesting. The television networks very firmly "creamed" the newspapers on this conflict. Things can only get worse.

Notes

[1] See www.huffingtonpost.com/.../alex-crawfordon-making-hi_b_942908, accessed on 9 September 2011. And
http://www.guardian.co.uk/media/organgrinder/2011/aug/28/sky-libya-bbc-alex-crawford-tripoli

[2] See http://www.bbc.co.uk/podcasts/series/media 24.8.2011, accessed on 8 September 2011

[3] Alex Crawford in *Mirage in the Desert?*

[4] See news.sky.com/home/world-news/article/16058071 quoted in
www.huffingtonpost.com/.../alex-crawfordon-making-hi_b_942908, accessed on 5 September 2011

[5] See http://www.guardian.co.uk/media/2011/aug/24/bbc-foreign-editor-libya-coverage, accessed on 5 September 2011

[6] See sky news.sky.com/home/world-news/article/16055646, accessed on 5 September 2011

[7] See news.sky.com/home/world-news/article/16058092, accessed on 5 September 2011

[8] See Stuart Ramsay in *Mirage in the Desert?*

[9] See http://www.bbc.co.uk/podcasts/series/media, accessed on 5 September 2011

[10] See www.dailymail.co.uk/.../Helen-Boaden-BBC-News-wasted-money-sending, accessed on 5 September 2011

[11] Alex Crawford in *Mirage in the Desert?*

[12] See www.bbc.co.uk/journalism/.../war-reporting-is-not-a-spectat.shtml, accessed on 5 September 2011

[13] See www.channel4.com/news/lindsey-hilsum-wins-charles-wheeler-award, accessed on 5 September 2011
And Lindsey Hilsum, *Mirage in the Desert?*

[14] See Jon Leyne, *Mirage in the Desert?*

[15] See Wyre Davies, *Mirage in the Desert?*

[16] See www.bbc.co.uk/news/world-africa-14646334, accessed on 5 September 2011

[17] Available online at www.reuters.com/article/.../us-libya-saif-idUSTRE77M01S2011082, accessed on 5 September 2011

[18] James Rodgers, *Mirage in the Desert?*

[19] Wyre Davies, *Mirage in the Desert?*

[22] Available online at www.guardian.co.uk/world/gallery/2011/aug/24/libya, accessed on 5 September 2011

[23] See http://www.npr.org/2011/08/31/140079512/bbcs-tripoli-witness-comes-out-of-hiding, accessed on 5 September 2011

[24] Available online at www.bbc.co.uk/journalism/.../undercover-in-syria-how-sue-ll.shtml, accessed on 5 September 2011

[25] See http://www.guardian.co.uk/media/organgrinder/2011/aug/28/sky-libya-bbc-alex-crawford-tripoli, accessed on 5 September 2011

[26] Available online at http://www.guardian.co.uk/media/2011/aug/24/bbc-foreign-editor-libya-coverage, accessed on 5 September 2011

[27] Alex Crawford, *Mirage in the Desert?*

[28] Available online at http://www.guardian.co.uk/media/2011/aug/27/sky-news-alex-crawford plus and www.huffingtonpost.com/.../alex-crawfordon-making-hi_b_942908, accessed on 5 September

[29] See www.guardian.co.uk/.../middle-east-live/.../libya-syria-israel-middle-east, accessed on 5 September

Note on the author

John Mair is a former BBC, ITV and Channel Four current affairs producer. He sat on the judging panels for the 2010 RTS Television Journalist of the Year (which Alex Crawford won) and on the Society of Editors 2010 Young Journalist of the Year.

"Spring" and "Fall" in Syria

Christine Sylva Hamieh examines the impact of the "Arab Spring" on Syria and concludes: "On the one hand, there is the sense that most of the international community wants President Assad to step down; on the other hand, it looks weary of the scenarios that might take place should he resign"

The "Arab Spring", understood as the wave of Arab unrest in the Middle East, has been the bread and butter of nearly every media outlet in the world. Starting with the Tunisian revolution of December 2010, the media moved to cover the "Arab Spring" in Egypt, Yemen, Bahrain, Libya and then, finally, reached Syria in mid-March 2011. It has been almost six months and the unrest in Syria shows no sign of fading, with both sides of the conflict – the regime and the opposition – being adamant and defiant. On one hand the protesters continue to demonstrate on the streets despite the violent response from the regime claiming that the new reforms proclaimed by President Assad are not for real. On the other hand the regime maintains its iron fist disregarding regional and international condemnations and calls for the president to step down insisting that there is a foreign conspiracy and that armed gangs and thugs are driving the violence, that they are not true reform-seekers.

Amid a complete banning of foreign media and a severe restricted local coverage, the regime has not been able to silence the expression of opposition on the net and to prevent the use of new media outlets – the internet, mobile phones, satellite television – that allows the opposition and activists to coordinate and communicate, to mobilise greater public participation, to inform and raise awareness and to have their voices heard. At the same time, banning of the media resulted in negative repercussion since it allowed distortion of information and facts. The question now is: what is really happening in Syria? And how is the media covering the uprising in Syria?

The Syrian Context

The Syrian uprising represented a shock that hit the Syrian society and undermined its long-standing stability that, for many, was based on "corruption, humiliation and repression as well as on a system that relied on the destruction of political life and civil society institutions".[1] Today, it is clear that the struggle in Syria seems to be produced by the huge gaps between the different classes, whereby the power has long been in the hands of the few, who alienated a large section of the population.

Syria's population is estimated at 21 million and is considered religiously diverse: the Sunnis make up around 74 per cent of the population. The other groups considered as minorities account as follows: Christians 12 per cent, Alawi 10 per cent, and Druze 3 per cent. While the Sunnis are concentrated in big cities such as Damascus, Aleppo, Homs and Hama, the minority groups are spread out in different parts of Syria.[2]

Up until the 1963 revolution, the Sunnis have been favoured in the system and institutions while the minority groups mainly the Alawis and Druze were marginalised. In 1963, the Baath party took power allowing minority groups mainly Alawis and Druzes to become part of the political elite. However it was only in the so-called "corrective revolution of 1970" that Hafez al-Assad came to power, ending the tradition of Sunni presidents in Syria, expelling prominent Sunni officers and working on making the armed forces dominated by the Alawis.[3]

Assad made sure to give power to his own family as well as to members of the Alawite community, who wield a disproportionate power in the Syrian government, military and business elite.[4] The government under Hafez el Assad dealt harshly with domestic opposition. For instance, tens of thousands were reported to have been killed in the crackdown on the 1982 uprising of the Muslim Brotherhood in Hama.[5]

In terms of the media sector of Syria, it is state-owned and controlled by the Baath Party through the office of the Ministry of Information. The regime has been functioning under a highly restrictive state of emergency whereby the state is authorised to control newspapers, books, radio and television broadcasting, advertising, and the visual arts, and has the right to confiscate and destroy any work that threatens the security of the state.[6]

Amid this context, it was difficult to imagine that Syria would follow the example of other Arab countries where the revolts took place. Surprisingly, however, motivated by the successful uprisings and revolutions in Tunisia, Egypt, Libya and Yemen, the Syrian uprising began in March 2011 in the southern border town of Daraa demanding freedom and dignity. Several people were killed when security forces opened fire. The unrest in Daraa quickly spread out to other towns such as Homs, Hama, Deir el Zour and Jisr al Shughour. President Bashar al-Assad sent in tanks and troops to restore order and to besiege these towns.

As a result, hundreds were killed when snipers and tanks fired on protesters and thousands of people fled to Turkey where they remain in refugee camps until today (mid- September 2011).[7] The regime justified its retaliation by claiming, through Bouthina Shaaban, one of Bashar al-Assad closest advisors, that armed gangs were responsible for the killing of protesters in Daraa and other towns such as Latakia, Douma and Homs. She claimed that foreign conspirators were trying to stir sectarian conflict across Syria.[8] Similarly, President Assad stated:

> We have to distinguish between those who have legitimate demands and saboteurs (a small group that tried to exploit the kind majority of the Syrian people to carry out their many schemes)...No political solution was possible with people carrying weapons.[9]

Despite the regime's crackdown, the protesters kept pouring into the streets. They used the social media to coordinate, schedule and organise meetings, communicate and raise awareness amid state attempts at repressions and internet censorship.

Three months later and the protesters remained unwilling to retreat or despair, defying a fierce military crackdown. As a result, President Assad pledged reforms stating that a national dialogue would start soon to review new legislation including laws on the media that cancels penalties against journalists and ensures their freedom, he promised parliamentary elections thus allowing political parties other than the Baath Party. He also promised to look at possible changes to the constitution. Nevertheless, activists and analysts dismissed his promises, saying they failed to engage the demands of protesters.[10] On the other hand, tens of thousands of supporters of Assad rallied in the main squares in the latest show of government support, shouting: "The people want Bashar Assad."[11]

In fact, the government launched a "national dialogue" aimed at finding a political solution to the crisis and stated that it had lifted the emergency law, implemented media reforms and new parliamentary laws that allows political groups other than the Baath party to take part in the elections, investigated police brutality and released some of the political prisoners.[12] The opposition criticised these reforms saying that they were "too late", that "the release of some political prisoners is not the release of all political prisoners" and that the announcement about having "lifted the emergency law" did not coincide with action.[13]

International Condemnation

When the uprising took place in Syria, the international community urged Assad to make political reforms. Then, when Assad promised to make political reforms, the international community started pressuring Assad to start a "concrete action" to implement the promised political reforms before "foreign intervention" begins. "I am not saying the words are meaningless but he needs to act upon them," White House spokesman Jay Carney told reporters.[14] And when Assad started implementing the reforms, the international community adopted a harsher tone calling on President Assad to step down and even imposed sanctions.

Despite all condemnation and sanctions, the Syrian regime seems to remain strong with no perceived imminent danger of collapse. In fact, Assad has shrugged off all international condemnation. Here's a look at the international responses:

- The European Union (EU) banned imports of Syrian oil, saying President Bashar al-Assad was massacring his own countrymen.[15] The EU's decision was criticised by Russia, which has been pressing calls for political dialogue with the Assad government.[16]

- US President Obama demanded that Assad step down: "The future of Syria must be determined by its people, but President Bashar al-Assad is standing in their way…For the sake of the Syrian people, the time has come for President Assad to step aside."[17] The U.S. Secretary of State Hillary Clinton called for a global embargo on oil and gas from Syria, and urged the international community to "get on the right side of history".[18] Moreover, the US Treasury Department said it had blacklisted Syrian Foreign Minister Walid Moallem, a former ambassador to Washington, and Bouthaina Shaaban.[19]

- The Saudis found themselves moving towards opposition against the Assad regime in Syria unlike their stands *vis-à-vis* the uprisings in Tunisia, Yemen and Egypt. In fact, the Kingdom played a key role in the GCC (Gulf Cooperation Council) and Arab League statements condemning the Syrian regime's behaviour. The Saudi ambassador was also withdrawn from Damascus. This, in turn, led other Gulf countries, such as Kuwait and Bahrain, to withdraw their respective ambassadors from Syria.[20]

- Turkey's President criticised President Assad, saying that Ankara had "lost confidence" in Assad's ability to lead his country.[21] Turkey's main concern is about the political aspirations of Syria's ethnic Kurdish population concentrated near the Turkish borders. Turkey's fears emerge from the fact that political instability in Syria could lead to renewed calls for a Kurdish state.[22]

- Syria's closest ally, Iran, has also called on the Syrian government to listen to the people's "legitimate demands". These comments were made by Iran's Foreign Minister, Ali Akbar Salehi.[23] Iran's fears stem from the fact that it would loose its only Arab ally if the Assad regime were to topple. It is mainly concerned that a power vacuum in Syria could spark an unprecedented regional crisis.[24] In this respect, Iran is expected to react strongly to any outside military intervention in Syria.

Military Intervention in Syria?

Apart from the condemnations and sanctions as a way of bringing pressure on the Syrian regime, the international community seems unwilling to send forces to Syria or backup the Syrian opposition in the same manner they supported the opposition in Libya. This is mainly due to concerns that a regime change in Syria would look a lot more like Iraq in 2003 than Egypt in 2011 in the sense that the majority Sunni population is likely to take revenge on the country minority groups particularly the Alawites and Christians. Moreover a civil war would almost become a proxy battle fought by regional powers (Saudi Arabia/Iran).[25]

More importantly, both Great Britain and Russia have ruled out military intervention in Syria. Great Britain's Parliamentary Under Secretary of State at the Foreign and Commonwealth office Alistair Burt said the UK had to be "practical about what levers are available".[26] As for Russia, it has been pressing for political dialogue, wanting the opposition to engage in dialogue with the Assad government.[27] In addition, the Russian President stated that his country was "ready to use its veto to block a Western-sponsored resolution on Syria at the United Nations as it could be used as cover for military action".[28]

As for the US, the Secretary of State Hillary Clinton said President Bashar al-Assad's legitimacy had "nearly run out". She said the US had done all it could to exert pressure on Syria, but she lamented the lack of a strong, united international response.[29] At the same time, she expressed her concern about the US potential loss of opportunity in what she called "redrawing the politics in the Middle East". The concern stems from budget pressures.[30] According to Robert Fisk, the Middle East correspondent of the *Independent* newspaper, the reluctance of the international community to intervene militarily in Syria is explained as follows:

Libya has oil, Syria has little and that despite all the roaring from the Arabs-most of the dictators, in Saudi Arabia, in Bahrain, in the rest of the Middle East, would still prefer a reformed Assad to freedom, dignity and liberty for his people.[31]

Role of the Syrian Army

The uprising poses the greatest challenge to four decades of the Assad family and the Baath Party rule in the country. It is obvious that the uprising is expanding and it seems that the regime is unable to stop it. The people on the streets are in a no-return position because they demonstrated only after they ran out of all other options. Day by day the power of the regime is diminishing, its propaganda that sought to instil fear among the people is failing and the economic situation is worsening by the day. The regime in Syria did resort to the use of violence just as in Libya. Defections in the army, though limited, did take place as in Yemen. However, the struggle in Syria did not turn into a war as in Libya and the possibility of the people occupying the streets as in Yemen seems unlikely. Moreover, a change is unlikely to occur without a change in the authority through the army such as Tunisia and Egypt.

In Tunisia and Egypt, the army had a major role in expelling the president and claiming to adopt the demands of the people and to work on achieving these demands. In Yemen, the army did not intervene; thus the people were able to occupy the streets and maintain a sit-in until the fall of the system.

In Syria, the army is an integral part of the regime. Part of the cohesion within the army can be attributed to the command structure. Key positions in the security apparatus are held by relatives of President Assad, including his brother Maher and brother-in-law Assaf Chawkat.[32] The army is an integral part of the regime: "They still hold most of the cards", Louis Delvoie, a retired Canadian diplomat and currently a senior professor at Queens' University, explains.[33]

Syria seems to defy international pressure relying on its armed forces. So far, the army has shown loyalty to the regime giving limited signs of breaking with the ruling elite. Those who did defect from the army are Sunnis and are also close in social and economic terms to the victims of the crackdown, with some coming from the very neighbourhoods they must now attack. According to Haytham Manna, of the Arab

Commission for Human Rights: "The army in Syria is composed of one million and a half. You cannot talk about 20 cases here and 50 cases there,"[34] Their officers, however, are disproportionately Alawite.

Media Influence on the Course of the Uprising

In this new era of globalisation, knowledge about events from around the world became a necessity. As Syria has banned foreign journalists and restricted local coverage, journalists around the world found the alternative in the digital and social media. They started to use the web to hunt for information, access wire stories and images. For instance, activists inside Syria would upload their footage on the social networks such as Facebook, Twitter and YouTube that can be collected by the foreign media, and reported as news while noting that such news and reports cannot be independently verified.[35]

In other words, one cannot verify the death toll or verify the circumstances such as if the images or videos uploaded have been accurately taken in a specific place and specific time as claimed. This is the result of the failure to allow independent media to cover the events in Syria. Moreover, one cannot verify if these sites are used as platforms to incite violence. Many people remain skeptical regarding the news reported as a result of the social media.

In an interview with a civil servant on how the media is portraying the uprising, he explained that most of the media revealed a lack of balance in the coverage and was being used as a tool to convey a certain message rather than showing what was really happening.[36] On the other hand, another interviewee, an activist, suggested that Assad's decision to ban independent media had backfired on the regime because now the West was using its media outlets as platforms to bring about change in Syria.[37]

A third interviewee, a senior public servant, strongly favoured the theory that external factors were influencing the events in Syria. He believed that Assad's policy of banning foreign media had led to a new media approach, that of falsifying facts and relying on false witnesses who were being paid by non-Syrians to give false confessions.[38] In this context, members of a Russian delegation to Syria were reported to have highlighted the involvement of foreign intelligence and Arab and Western mass media in the media war launched against Syria and in inciting the

Syrian opposition to boycott the dialogue and reject the reforms offered by Assad.[39]

A senior public servant commented: "People are either afraid and hesitant to speak up or are not being used to speaking up so freely…they need time."[40]. He explained this factor in terms of "the social pressure" which is observed in every instance in the Syrian daily life even during the uprising. He explains:

> The social pressure factor is even taking place in the areas where the uprising is occurring, mainly Homos, Hama and Deir El Zour…There are many people who do not want to join the uprising or close their shops. However, they do so because of the "social pressure" factor. In other words, they are directly pressured socially to show that they are also opposition, hence they close their shops.[41]

An independent activist interviewed said they believed there was no transparent media channel in Syria; that the Syrian TV conveyed the views of the regime, that there were internet sites that could not be opened nor accessed except through proxies, and that Arab channels lacked professionalism in journalism. Hence people turned to the Western or foreign media.[42] Moreover, in Syria, when searching terms such as "democratic governance" on search engines like Google and Yahoo, the webpage does not open and the same applies to many terms related to democracy.[43]

Throughout the uprising the Baath party maintained its media campaign seeking to assure the people that they could only be protected by the Baath Party and that this was a secure system.[44] Indeed, under the current regime there is a complete lack of civil society life with no organisations allowed except those that belong to or are affiliated with the Baath Party. These range from youth groups to women's organisations.

Conclusion
The outcome of the Syrian uprising remains uncertain. From all the media and news reports that have been covering the uprising in Syria, it is important to note the following:

It seems protestors are mainly focusing their protests against one person – Assad – without looking beyond the demise of his regime. They are getting angrier by the day because they perceive President Assad as being arrogant and in denial.[45]

No alternative regime or system has been called for. So what is the real purpose of the uprising? The uprising did not expose the real problems. None of its slogans called for clear demands that the new system or regime should adopt and provide. The slogan of "freedom" was not enough to define the alternative. There was no reference to civic engagement, improvement of livelihoods or ending corruption. The uprising seems without any clear purpose. At the same time, the opposition seems scattered and unorganised. There is an internal opposition, an external one, independent protestors and armed gangs. Many of the protestors are weary of the external opposition considering it as being backed and supported by foreign powers.

Although we cannot verify the information that reaches international media, however, it did give us a sense of the dynamics of the Syrian uprising. In the face of an unorganised Syrian opposition and a lack of a centralised leadership, the international community seems confused, undecided on what stand to take *vis-à-vis* Syria. On one hand, there is the sense that most of the international community wants President Assad to step down; on the other hand, it looks weary of the scenarios that might take place should he resign. Such scenarios include a civil war similar to that of Lebanon or Iraq, or the Muslim brotherhood taking control. After six months since the start of the Syrian "Spring" uprising, it seems the "Fall" is here and there is no end in sight.

Notes

[1] Ghazzawi, Wahib (alias for a Syrian intellectual and activist based in Damascus), The Syrian Intifada: Reality and Prospects, *Al Akhbar,*7 September 2011. Available online at http://www.al-akhbar.com/node/20591, accessed on 7 September 2011
[2] Syria, US Department of State. Available online at http://www.state.gov/r/pa/ei/bgn/3580.htm, accessed on 4 September 2011
[3] Syria, US Department of State. Available online at http://www.state.gov/r/pa/ei/bgn/3580.htm, accessed on 4 September 2011
[4] Guide: Syria Crisis, BBC News, 23 June 2011. Available online at http://www.bbc.co.uk/news/world-middle-east-13855203, accessed on 2 September 2011
[5] Fisk, Robert, Conspiracy of Silence in the Arab World, *Independent*, 10 February 2007. Available online: at http://www.independent.co.uk/opinion/commentators/fisk/robert-fisk-conspiracy-of-silence-in-the-arab-world-435762.html, accessed on 1 September 2011

[6] Media of Syria, Wikipedia. Available online at http://en.wikipedia.org/wiki/Media_of_Syria#cite_note-cp-0, accessed on 30 August 2011

[7] Guide: Syria Crisis, BBC News, 23 June 2011. Available online at http://www.bbc.co.uk/news/world-middle-east-13855203, accessed on 2 September 2011

[8] Shaaban, Government has no problem with peaceful protests, Syrian Days, 6 August 2011. Available online at http://syriandays.net/?page=show_det&select_page=2&id=743, accessed on 1 September 2011

[9] Karouny, M. & Y. Bayoumy. Assad blames unrest on saboteurs, pledges reforms, Reuters. 20 June 2011. Available online at http://uk.reuters.com/article/2011/06/20/uk-syria-idUKTRE7553JD20110620, accessed on 29 August 2011

[10] Karouny, M. and Y. Bayoumy, Assad blames unrest on saboteurs, pledges reforms, Reuters. 20 June 2011. Available online at http://uk.reuters.com/article/2011/06/20/uk-syria-idUKTRE7553JD20110620, accessed on 29 August 2011

[11] Syria: Thousands of Assad supporters converge on Damascus, *Telegraph*, 21 June 2011. Available online at http://www.telegraph.co.uk/news/worldnews/middleeast/syria/8588957/Syria-thousands-of-Assad-supporters-converge-on-Damascus.html, accessed on 27 August 2011.

[12] In Syria, government's doublespeak infuriates protesters, *Global Post*, 6 June 2011. Available online at http://www.globalpost.com/dispatch/news/regions/middle-east/110605/syria-government-protesters-reforms-assad, accessed on 1 September 2011

[13] In Syria, government's doublespeak infuriates protesters, *Global Post*, 6 June 2011. Available online: at http://www.globalpost.com/dispatch/news/regions/middle-east/110605/syria-government-protesters-reforms-assad, accessed on 1 September 2011

[14] Syria's Assad promises reforms, critics say "not enough", MSNBC. 6 June 2011. Available online at http://www.msnbc.msn.com/id/43460832/ns/world_news-mideast_n_africa/t/syrias-assad-promises-reforms-critics-say-not-enough/#.Tmoht3N5EbU, accessed on 27 August 2011

[15] Oueiss, K.Y. EU agrees oil embargo as Syrians march against Assad, Reuters, 2 September 2011. Available online at http://www.reuters.com/article/2011/09/02/us-syria-idUSTRE77S5IH20110902, accessed on 3 September 2011

[16] French FM accuses Syrian regime of committing "anti-humanity" crimes, Arab News Agency (ANA), 7 September 2011. Available online at http://www.anaonline.net/en/NewsDesc.aspx?NId=2613, accessed on 8 Septembr 2011

[17] Obama: Syrian President Assad Must Step Down, Huffington Post, 18 August 2011. Availabe online: http://www.huffingtonpost.com/2011/08/18/obama-assad_n_930229.html, accessed on 1 September 2011

[18] Kirkup, K., Situation in Syria Poses Challenges: Experts, *Toronto Sun*, 14 August 2011. Available online at http://www.torontosun.com/2011/08/14/situation-in-syria-poses-challenges-experts, accessed on 28 August 2011

[19] US Sanctions Syrian Foreign Minister and Assad Adviser, *Wall Street Journal*, 30 August 2011. Available online at

http://online.wsj.com/article/SB10001424053111903352704576540623693640518.html?mod=googlenews_wsj, accessed on 1 September 2011

[20] Interview: Michael Young on the "Arab Spring", Arabs Think, 15 August 2011. Available online at http://arabsthink.com/2011/08/15/interview-michael-young-on-the-arab-spring/, accessed on 2 September , 2011

[21] Barnard, Ann, Turkish Leader Says He has lost Confidence in Assad, *New York Times,* 28 August 2011. Available online at http://www.nytimes.com/2011/08/29/world/middleeast/29syria.html, accessed on 2 September 2011

[22] Wyler, Grace, Syria's "Arab Spring" Could Unleash Chaos Across the Middle East, Business Insider, 3 May 2011. Available online at http://www.businessinsider.com/syrias-arab-spring-could-unleash-chaos-across-the-middle-east-2011-5, accessed on 3 September 2011

[23] Iran tells Syria: Listen to Protesters, CBS News, 27 August 2011. Available online at http://www.cbsnews.com/stories/2011/08/27/501364/main20098285.shtml, accessed on 30 August 2011

[24] Iran warns of crisis in the Region if Syria Falls, NPR, 29 August 2011. Available online at http://www.npr.org/2011/08/28/140013639/iran-warns-of-crisis-in-the-region-if-syria-falls?sc=emaf, accessed on 1 September 2011

[25] Wyler, Grace. Syria's "Arab Spring" Could Unleash Chaos Across The Middle East, Business Insider, 3 May 2011. Available online at http://www.businessinsider.com/syrias-arab-spring-could-unleash-chaos-across-the-middle-east-2011-5, accessed on 2 September 2011

[26] Government Rules out Military Intervention in Syria, *Telegraph*, 1 August 2011. Available online at http://www.telegraph.co.uk/news/worldnews/middleeast/syria/8675735/Government-rules-out-military-intervention-in-Syria.html, accessed on 29 August 2011

[27] French FM accuses Syrian Regime of committing "anti-humanity" crimes, Arab News Agency (ANA), 7 September 2011. Available online at http://www.anaonline.net/en/NewsDesc.aspx?NId=2613, accessed on 8 September 2011

[28] Russia to veto Syria resolution-Medvedev, *Herald Sun*, 20 June. 2011. Available online at http://www.heraldsun.com.au/news/breaking-news/russia-to-veto-syria-resolution-medvedev/story-e6frf7jx-1226078645141, accessed on 1 September 2011

[29] Syria: "Dozens Killed" as thousands protest in Hama, BBC News, 4 June 2011. Available online at http://www.bbc.co.uk/news/world-middle-east-13642917, accessed on 30 August 2011

[30] The Crisis in America deprives it from drawing the politics in the Middle East, AlJadeed TV. 17 August 2011. Available online at www.aljadeed.tv/wsg/newsprint.aspx?ln=14641, accessed on 17 August 2011

[31] Fisk, Robert, This slaughter will end only when words of condemnation are acted on, *Independent*, 9 August 2011. Available online at http://www.independent.co.uk/news/world/middle-east/robert-fisk-this-slaughter-will-end-only-when-words-of-condemnation-are-acted-on-2334157.html, accessed on 28 August 2011

[32] Syrian Military Loyal so far, Voice of America, 8 August 2011. Available online at http://www.voanews.com/english/news/middle-east/Syrian-Military-Loyal-So-Far--127231783.html, accessed on 29 August 2011

[33] Kirkup, K., Situation in Syria poses challenges: Experts, *Toronto Sun*, 14 August 2011. Available online at http://www.torontosun.com/2011/08/14/situation-in-syria-poses-challenges-experts, accessed on 28 August 2011

[34] Syrian Military Loyal so far, Voice of America, 8 August 2011. Available online http://www.voanews.com/english/news/middle-east/Syrian-Military-Loyal-So-Far--127231783.html, accessed on 29 August 2011

[35] Syria on "International Protection" Friday, Day Press, 9 September 2011. Available online at http://www.dp-news.com/en/detail.aspx?articleid=95978, accessed on 9 September 2011

[36] Interview 1: A Syrian civil servant. Interview conducted on 6 September 2011

[37] Interview 2: Social scientist and activist in Syria. Interview conducted on 7 September 2011

[38] Interview 3: Senior Syrian public servant. Interview conducted on 7 September 2011

[39] Russian Delegation: Some Western Security Apparatus are involved at Syria Protests, Day Press, 4 September 2011. Available online at http://www.dp-news.com/en/detail.aspx?articleid=95349, accessed on 5 September 2011.

[40] Interview 4: Key Informant. Interview conducted on 7 September 2011

[41] Interview 3: Senior Syrian public servant. Interview conducted on 6 September 2011

[42] Interview 5: Independent activist. Interview conducted on 5 September 2011

[43] Interview 4: Key Informant. Interview conducted on 7 September 2011

[44] Interview 2: Social Scientist and activist in Syria. Interview conducted on 7 September 2011

[45] Interview 5: Independent activist. Interview conducted on 5 September 2011

Note on the author

Christine Sylva Hamieh is an independent researcher with extensive professional experience in the UN and NGO sectors. Her PhD, from the University of York in England, was on electoral competition between Hezbollah and Amal in Lebanon. Her broader research interests include the politics of reconstruction and humanitarianism, Middle Eastern politics, conflict transformation and the issue of humanitarianism in Islamic contexts, donorship from Muslim and to Muslim states, and issues of community regeneration in deeply divided societies. She did her BA and MA in Politics and International Relations at the Lebanese American University in Lebanon.

"Am currently in Misrata": The Work and Legacy of Photojournalist Tim Hetherington

Eamonn O'Neill assesses the lasting professional output and legacy of the award-winning British photojournalist Tim Hetherington who died in a mortar attack in the besieged Libyan city of Misrata, on 20 April 2011

Introduction

The final email communiqué from Tim Hetherington came in the 24 hours before his death on 20 April 2011 and stated: "Am currently in Misrata – would have made interesting article with SJ…"

Typically, for this most forward-thinking and innovative of photographers, the 40-year-old Hetherington was already pondering his next assignment for his main employers, the New York-based *Vanity Fair* magazine. His reference to "SJ" was also characteristic of a professional known for his loyalty and collaborative projects, and indicated his desire to work again with renowned American journalist Sebastian Junger with whom he shared an Academy Award nomination for their documentary on the Afghanistan war, *Restrepo*.

He died on a day of terrible battle in Misrata covering the rebel forces' battle with the violent regime – sometimes room-to-room – in the Libyan city which was coming under heavy bombardment from the forces loyal to Col. Gaddafi. And he died on Tripoli Street, a shattered and much-contested location which formed the shifting frontline for clashing forces. Another photojournalist, Chris Hondros from the USA, and at least eight other civilians died during the same day and two other photographers were badly wounded.

This chapter assesses the complex and highly-creative career undertaken by Hetherington since his early days working as a staff photographer for the UK's *Big Issue* magazine in London. It examines his unique work using different digital formats covering conflict zones and hotspots ranging from Afghanistan, Darfur, Liberia and, briefly, Libya. The chapter includes new testimony from colleagues who knew his work intimately – including his close collaborator Sebastian Junger – and first-hand eyewitness testimony from a fellow-photojournalist who was seriously wounded in the same mortar-attack. The chapter is deliberately aimed at being a starting point for a conversation on Hetherington's astonishing output over a relatively short career, rather than a final word on a professional life cut terribly short.

What Happened in Tripoli Street on 20 April 2011?

Hetherington was riding high on the back of the universal success of his film *Restrepo*. An Academy Award nomination for Best Documentary Feature followed, along with other honours, and unprecedented exposure on major international networks. Whilst validating his creative endeavours, his work had also taken a toll on him. A friend met him in 2008 when he returned to New York city from Afghanistan and noted:

> He called in the morning and wanted to have lunch with me. He definitely was not himself: he was extremely nervous, agitated, kept talking and talking, his eyes staring at nothing. After having lunch he had it in mind to buy a new bag, and started to walk so fast with his crutches on Eighth Avenue that I almost had to run to keep up with him. At some point I put him in a cab and sent him home to rest. Tim would tell me later that what he experienced in Afghanistan had been very traumatic. I had the strong impression that day that death had grazed him.[1]

By April 2011, a mere month after walking the red-carpet at the Academy Awards with Sebastian Junger, he was essentially freelancing in Libya as the so-called "Arab Spring" movement gripped the country. Once again, Hetherington told friends he was in pursuit of his central themes of young men and war.

His relatively few images from Libya show young faces staring at his lens – male and female – in marches, festooned in weapons and ammunition belts, innocent childish eyes holding grenades and, chillingly, a stiff corpse of a war victim protruding from a morgue's drawer. Fellow-photographer American Michael Christopher Brown, who was also seriously wounded in the mortar blast on 20 April which ultimately killed Hetherington, told me:

> In Libya he was using a video camera, a Mamiya film camera and an iPhone to get into his story. And I am damn sure his work there would have looked completely different from every other photographer. Again it was his ideas and grasp of literature and this implementation of his own ideas and various others he had read about that set him apart from other photographers.[2]

The final images of Hetherington[3] show him being helped by rebels in Misrata descending a ladder, dressed in jeans and wearing his usual light-green field-jacket. Unlike images from *Restrepo*, he is not wearing a flak-jacket and his head is bare. I asked Sebastian Junger about his friend's demeanour in Libya and whether he was surprised he had died there? He told me:

> No, I wasn't…He didn't have his medical gear, his helmet – he wasn't looking for it [death] but he was transfixed by the possibility. He went out there not as a news photographer but as someone on his own project. I thought he was taking a profound risk. He'd made peace with dying. It didn't surprise me and ultimately it wouldn't have surprised him either. Tim was a funny combination. He wanted to get married and have a family and we had conversations about how it could be done. [But also] he was certainly a restless soul…[4]

Michael Christopher Brown was with Hetherington when the mortar round hit:

Tim was of course someone who was well prepared and knowledgeable. But though he was often on the front lines I don't consider him a front line photographer *per se*. He had balls of steel but that wasn't his point. He was interested in the broader story so the conflict action pictures were just one piece of a larger puzzle.

All this said…I can say that on that day, 20 April, our group did take many risks and it's almost as if all these tiny risks accumulated and affected our next decisions that resulted in the deaths of Tim and Chris. There were little incidents that threw up red flags throughout the day, at least for me. I didn't have a good feeling about Tripoli Street that entire day.[5]

A mortar hit the Tripoli Street area Hetherington was in and, according to Brown, he lost a lot of blood at the scene from a wound to an artery in one of his legs. Despite transportation to a nearby triage-facility, he was pronounced dead. Fellow photographer from the USA, Chris Hondros, also died in the same attack from shrapnel wounds to his head causing fatal brain-trauma and blood loss.

Who was Tim Hetherington?
Timothy Alistair Telemachus Hetherington was born on 5 December 1970 in the Birkenhead area, near Liverpool, England, and attended St. Patrick's RC Primary School in Southport, Sefton. Later, he was to attend Stoneyhurst College, in Lancashire, a renowned institution founded in 1593 by the Roman Catholic Jesuit Order. The motto of the school is *Quant Je Puis* ("All that I can") and underlines the aim of the Jesuits to weave spiritual learning into the everyday academic curriculum, thus exemplifying faith through action and deed, thus creating "men and women for others".

Hetherington's view of this education was apparently mixed. He told Sebastian Junger, for example, that he was sent to the boarding school when he was around eight years old and that "it was hard".[6] In a profile tribute article written for an American publication and published posthumously, Hetherington, who had already won the World Press Photograph of the Year in 2007 and gained an Academy Award nomination in 2011, explained:

When you are working for yourself, it's very liberating, and you can make really interesting work. My mom was a Catholic, and I was brought up through a lot of my life by Jesuits, who are a tough and mean bunch, so I hate any sense of authority. That's my fate. That sense of not conforming, of doing something that other people aren't doing is always fun.[7]

Yet all his work revealed a great concern for human justice leading one published obituary to state he was "fundamentally a humanitarian".[8] Indeed, one could argue that he had fully lived out and exemplified the Stoneyhurst Jesuit motto by the time of his untimely death.

A life in pictures
Hetherington read Classics and English at Lady Margaret Hall, Oxford, and was by all accounts a popular and successful student. After graduation, a gift of £5000 was bequeathed to him by his late-grandmother, allowing him to travel widely an India, China and Tibet. Hetherington explained: "I had the epiphany when I came back [from India] and realised I wanted to make images. I then worked for three to four years, going to night school in photography before eventually going back to college."[9]

Dr. Daniel Meadows, lecturer in photography and participatory media at Cardiff University who taught Hetherington in 1996-7, said: "I always loved it that Tim managed to present his work so successfully for multiple audiences. In this respect he was the first of my students to be truly 'modern'."[10] Upon graduation in 1997, Hetherington started work in London for the *Big Issue* ,a magazine aimed at getting an income for the homeless. He later reflected on his arrival there:

The job started almost immediately after college ended. I was lucky not to be fumbling around trying to find my feet in a merciless market. The job was billed as a traineeship, but without other photographers and a picture editor, I've had to learn things through trial and error on the job. As the only staff photographer, I've had to become as flexible as possible, doing everything from studio work to still life, press conferences to portraiture and reportage to fashion.[11]

One colleague from the *Big Issue* later recalled how Hetherington was intellectually and technologically curious about his work: "He was really ahead of his time. Back then, he recognised the power of the moving image as well as the still. I remember him telling me he simply couldn't understand photographers who didn't want to capture the things they were witness to without a movie camera as well."[12]

Briefly working at the *Independent* as a regular freelance photographer, Hetherington's next joined the Network agency, which facilitated his first assignments in Africa. For the next eight years he would remain in West Africa reporting across the region. It was, and remains, an area ridden with complex internal conflicts, frequently at the terrible expense of the lives of its own populations, engendering wars of the most brutal kind usually ignored by the worldwide media and witnessed over the medium and long-term only by the most committed and brave of journalists.

Witnessing *Liberia – An Uncivil War*

During the Second Liberian Civil War (1999-2003) Hetherington and fellow journalist James Brabazon were the only two foreign journalists to live behind rebel lines as they fought against the government of President Charles Taylor. This resulted in a series of striking still images and also marked his first work on a documentary film as an assistant producer and cameraman.

The latter role exposed Hetherington to combat situations for the first time in that capacity. The subsequent documentary, *Liberia – An Uncivil War,* contains an array of astonishing scenes shot by Hetherington which suggest someone who has earned his calmness through the experience of having lived in the area. There is no sense of journalism-as-tourism but, instead, one immediately feels through watching the footage an intimacy with the physical surroundings, the rebels themselves and the complex daily political and military events covered.

The opening scene, for example, is filled with heavy rain-washed streets and roads, with shots of people going about their daily business – a child standing at a flooded kerbside, a man covered in a plastic head-to-toe plastic transparent poncho and an elegant woman, dry as a bone under the safety of her umbrella. If this is a film about war in an African country, then the cameraman's eye is telling us that these are ordinary people with lives, just like you and me, with the same banal routines and concerns to contend with when the weather turns foul. The audio-track then plays a local radio broadcast of a male announcer reading the names of children separated from parents because of the civil war. This juxtaposition of the day-to-day innocence of existence, with the less-innocent daily-realities, bridged with layers of music, oral-based audio and fused with seductive images, would later become a hallmark of Hetherington's work, revealing a technical ability to link textures into a seductive and powerful whole.

His still images from Liberia are arresting in their intimacy and candour. Lush landscapes, with endless canopies of trees, shrouded in a dense, soaking raincloud, a scene devoid of humans or the hand of mankind it seems, hint at a forgotten promise of a country founded by freed American slaves and built on the principles of a democratic republic based on the political infrastructure of the USA, the country which supported its inception and even acted a template for its single star and stripes national flag.[13] Then another image changes that narrative: a young, weary man – a rebel fighter photographed in 2003 – slumped in a chair, elbow resting on a scarred surface. His only company is a ready-to-use hand-grenade propped beside him like a bottle of beer. In any other nation, that young face might be sitting on a train, or a park-bench outside a college, looking equally fed up, but, we're invited to ask whether only in countries such as Liberia would he have a life-threatening piece of military hardware for company.[14]

Such proximity to the action and witnessing close-quarters combat is also clear in a shot of rebel fighters unpacking rocket propelled grenades, the way that others might unwrap some frozen hamburgers for a weekend barbeque. Only someone who has lived with the rebels, got to know them as individuals and has clearly gained their trust, could deliver such images.[15]

This, in itself, is a departure from the old-school view of foreign correspondent journalist and photographer, since we are not reading or looking at images supplied by someone dropped-in from a developed country. Instead, through Hetherington's eyes, we are being exposed to material obtained by an insider who understands and predicts what our attitudes and ideas already contain *before* we even begin to view his material.

This approach is inextricably linked to advances in digital technology during a time frame when Hetherington was developing and shaping his career. Back home at this time, the news was overwhelmingly bleak in terms of the accepted narrative of the perceived "negative" impact of technology on the printed press and across the media sector as a whole. Yet, at the same time, technical advances and a determined personal commitment and approach by the likes of Hetherington was delivering new and challenging insights into a forgotten African story. It is at this juncture that we can begin to understand why Hetherington balked on numerous occasions from calling himself a "photographer" or "photojournalist", instead preferring the label – if one had to be applied – "storyteller".

Using Technology to Tell a Story

His willingness to utilise technology (e.g. mobile phone cameras) and deliver material gained from a hard-won, poorly-funded and risky strategy of long-term embedding with the rebels was a fresh way to report foreign conflict. He was – wittingly or unwittingly – actually at the forefront of a new way of seeing the world and telling stories about it to consumers of news globally. A recent study echoes this perception:

> There are more reporters around the world writing for an international audience than there have ever been. The quality and depth of coverage are greater than they have ever been. There is a great deal of nostalgia for the newspaper correspondent of yore, but when the *Baltimore Sun* had a single correspondent in Asia and he got to go to Korea or the Philippines for a week having never been before, was he really bringing greater authority and knowledge to his readers? If he was your single source of information about Asia you probably got a pretty skewed version of reality.[16]

Looking at Hetherington's Liberia images, one also gets the sense that this is a photographer who is not in a hurry to get out of the hellish situation he is in. There is no overwhelming sense of panic in the images. We see an image of a decaying orange, for example, beautiful rings of bacteria surrounding it, like gas rings around a far-off planet and a lush, bucolic landscape framed by a shattered and scarred white tiled wall. These are images that can only be captured by someone with access, patience and a sense of the poignant and the sad.

Hetherington does not shirk from capturing images which tell a more conventional story about war, but even these are subverted slightly and told from his unique perspective. War-graffiti on a wall, reminiscent of both children's stick figures and early human cave-paintings, actually shows a helicopter gunship firing rounds, framed by an AK-47 and a grenade dropping like ripe fruit. Another shot shows two African women both carrying everyday loads: one is a child and an ammunition box, the other is an RPG. The notes tell us there is, in the midst of this horror, actual hope, since the women are taking arms and ammunition to an official disarmament location. The weapons of war are the past, the child is the future and the women have chosen the path they wish to take.[17]

One of the most arresting sections of Hetherington's Liberia project is the access he clearly gained to President Charles Taylor, who later reluctantly resigned from power and now sits in the Hague facing the Special Court for Sierra Leone. The pictures reveal gaudy trappings of power: sinister secret security service personnel; the insouciant puffing on a cigarette by Taylor mid-press conference, the shiny shoes and gleaming Presidential motorcade. Hetherington has managed to capture the tacky inner-world of Taylor's crumbling administration, hinting at its fragility and its cut-throat possibilities.

Hetherington's commitment to what he called the "social justice" aspect of his life-work was clear in his decision to act as an investigator for the United Nations Security Council Liberia Sanctions Committee. He saw more to unite the evidence-gathering role he undertook with the UN, than divide it from similar work in journalism.

Hetherington moved back into journalism afterwards during his work on projects in the region including the BBC's *Violent Coast* series in West Africa (2004); *The Devil Came On Horseback* (2007), about attacks against Darfurian refugees by Arab-backed Sudanese militia squads on horseback in Chad along its border area; and as producer/director for Channel 4's *Unreported World – Nigeria: Fire in the Delta* (2006).

The direction Hetherington was moving in is, with hindsight, clear. He was gaining confidence and skill with each new project, refining his personal and professional humanitarian mission, constantly unearthing new stories on the ground, and using an array of technological options to unpack them for an ever-growing audience base. His next assignment in Afghanistan would both challenge and test his abilities and take his output to new creative and emotional levels.

Afghanistan: *Restrepo*

The project which would elevate Hetherington to a global audience was a 93-minute documentary film named *Restrepo* which he co-directed with US journalist Sebastian Junger. This grew out of a *Vanity Fair* assignment which both writers undertook in 2007 and which saw them jointly spend approximately 10 months spread across a full year embedded with the Second Platoon, Bravo Company, 2nd battalion, 503rd Infantry Regiment, 173rd Airborne Brigade Combat Team of the US Army, in the remote Korengal valley. The men build and then rename their Operating Post (OP) "Restrepo" in honour of Private First Class (PFC) Juan Sebastián Restrepo, the platoon medic who died early in their deployment.

This is a glimpse at a microcosm of the war and significantly only features low-to-mid ranking officers: no politicians or high-ranking officers are filmed. The US mission is to engage with locals and gain trust after they have cleared the valley of insurgent activity. The promise of a new highway through the valley – coined the "Valley of Death" and the "most dangerous place on earth" by US troops – is offered to village elders in return for information about insurgent activity.

From its opening scenes of handheld video shots on a train featuring soldiers from the platoon – including PFC Restrepo who will later die – the film clearly establishes the theme of young men and war. Hetherington later spoke about this: "My examination of young men and violence was…also me trying to understand my own fascination with violence. It was as much a journey about my identity as it was about these soldiers."[18]

Hetherington's skills in film and still images made him both an understandable and unusual choice for this production, since his skill-base and continued interest in the themes of young men and masculine images of war meant he brought a special perspective to the project. This was something that was welcomed by co-director Sebastian Junger in an interview with me:

> *Vanity Fair* magazine arranged for me to hire a photographer for Afghanistan and I looked at some and decided on Tim Hetherington. We went out with the platoon in May/June '07 and went back in September '07. The main thing I had to ask was what kind of physical shape he was in. Not all journalists are in good

shape. Tim told me: "Well, I am pretty lean…" He said it in a very British understated way and I thought: "I'll bet he's an Olympic marathoner!" My first impressions of him were that he was tall, lean and *very* charismatic. Everybody at the arrivals gate stopped and stared at him when he walked through at Heathrow. He was later to prove himself to be somebody who could really keep it together in a combat environment.

So what was it about the work of Hetherington that first attracted Junger?

He was a war photographer who wasn't interested in the "bang, bang" images. He was keen to tell stories in images that were not all filled with action. He felt just action shots were very shallow instruments. He also said to me: "I think the only place men can comfortably express themselves is in the war zone." This was, to him, a story of young men showing love for each other. They have nothing to hide. His photos of them sleeping are amazing – they look as if they are children or as if they're dead. I found myself adopting his sensitivity…What he wanted to communicate and we communicated was something profound about young men. They are captivated by war. So we wanted to tell a universally true story about young men.[19]

The focus stays on the young soldiers at the outset of the film as they undergo the ritual of arriving in Afghanistan. Interviews against black-screen show record their retrospective impressions which were, in a nutshell, wide-eyed fear and apprehension. Like his work in Liberia, Hetherington teases an ease and familiarity out of his subjects which news reports conducted on a shorter time-scale often miss. This is especially evident in the sequence where PFC Juan "Doc" Restrepo is fatally wounded after a contact with insurgents and fellow soldiers display an unsettling air of sadness and vulnerability when reacting to his death.

Another sequence shows a US officer explaining to local elders how cooperation with the US' army's work will make them all rich. As the officer delivers his pitch the camera tilts down to reveal one of the elders struggling to understand how a straw works with a sealed foil-drink package he's been provided with, thus making the unmistakable point that what works on paper doesn't always work in reality when clashing cultures are involved. One of the soldiers explains to camera that he grew up on Oregon and that his mother was "a hippy" and that he "wasn't allowed sugar until he was 13 [years old]". The revelation reinforces the oddness of war itself.

The overall structure and pace of the film is reminiscent of earlier Hetherington projects, in particular his work in both Liberia and Chad. He allows the camera to linger and doesn't use fast edits. As a result we are allowed to watch the full story in Afghanistan and follow the exhausting and nerve-wracking patrols through mountainous villages and listen as the young servicemen claim that a fire-fight is "better than crack". Humour – of the greyest kind – occurs when three Afghan elders arrive to negotiate a price for a cow which has been killed (and eaten with some relish – figuratively and literally) by the men at Restrepo. The viewer witnesses the bureaucratic inertia which the predicament causes. The camerawork suggests the elders, whilst deserving benefit of the doubt, may have learned much about the base during their visit, whilst the young soldiers fumbled to work out their liability regarding the cow they have eaten.

The film takes a darker turn when Operation Rock Avalanche begins, a tactical move from OP Restrepo to expand its operations, which lasted six days and created high probability of engagement with the Taliban. The narrative moves from the intimate (first-person interviews by Hetherington with officers explaining their fears), to the wider perspective of the realities of silent dawn-patrols, to the video-game like detachment of footage from supporting airstrikes. The footage shows in detail the results of this air-bombing, when Hetherington's camera picks up dead local men and seriously wounded children in a village which the men enter. "Show me who is the Taliban?" demands an understandably angry elder through a translator.

When a senior officer is brought in to damp down frustrations, the camera lingers on the sceptical expression of a young villager and an elder politely stifling a yawn. Retrospective interviews assist the viewer in understanding the chaos they will shortly witness which consists of incoming 360-degree fire, resulting in one killed-in-action (KIA) US death and several wounded-in-action (WIA). Hetherington films one young officer breaking down and being comforted after witnessing the killing of a comrade in action: it is a naked display of human fear and incomprehension which the film never shrinks from showing. Later it would be explained that Hetherington actually helped carry the body of the KIA victim, Sergeant Larry Rougle, back to safety. The trust between the subjects and the journalists is obvious from the footage. Junger comments:

> On Operation Rock Avalanche Tim broke his leg on the last night's patrol. It was a really bad situation and he trapped his leg, tripped and heard it snap. He had fractured his fibula. But the medic lied that he'd sprained it, simply to keep him moving. Tim said nothing, although he knew it was broken, and walked all night on that injury in sheer agony. When the men found out later he'd done this, they loved him for it.[20]

The sheer passage of time marking the commitment of the filmmakers is underlined when we suddenly see the platoon patrolling in snow, like ghosts from World Two in the Ardennes Forest in 1944, intercut with close-ups of locals wrapped in beautiful coloured blankets watching from their rickety buildings. Underpinning the film is the theme of the evolution of the troops – a non-linear progression it has to be said – into battle-hardened men. So it is with dismay that we witness them regress when they dance to a mobile-phone remixed 1980s Euro-pop track, resulting in a display of exuberance akin to watching infants in a soft-play area. Yet, the gap between innocence and the brutalities of war grows wider as we are given insights into their thinking. "By the end," laments one soldier, "I wish they [the enemy] were closer, so I could see them when I killed them." This is from the same soldier who earlier explained to the documentary he was brought-up by a hippy-mother and not allowed to eat sugar until he was a teenager.

As their deployment ends, they mark the first anniversary of PFC Juan Restrepo's passing by setting off flares, like kids at a party, and telling tall-tales in his memory. A sequence follows which renders the men against black backdrops, an acoustic guitar soundtrack accompanying silent, yet visually emotive footage of them reflecting on their situation at the OP, revealing emotions through their flickering eyes, a twitch of their heads and even flared nostrils. Captions end the film by explaining that the US forces withdrew from the valley in April 2010 and that 50 soldiers died there defending it.

Hetherington subsequently published a critically-acclaimed book *Infadel* – named after the title the soldiers adopted for themselves when they heard locals called them that and tattoos they gave each other – which sold out its first print run. Earlier, in 2009, a triptych immersive video presentation exhibited in New York city called *Sleeping Soldiers* featuring images from the Afghan base, had had a similarly powerful impact. *Restrepo* went on to garner positive reviews and widespread acclaim for its raw, sensitive and revealing footage. According to Junger:

> We were both thrilled with its success. I didn't want to produce a work which only succeeded with a tiny sliver of the literati. Tim felt exactly the same. Being nominated for an Academy Award meant we'd succeeded. Even Hollywood felt that we'd done something worth paying attention to.[21]

Judgement on a Life and Death in Pictures

Hetherington's death led to a wave of tributes in the USA, UK and across the rest of the world. Accolades paid to him came from serving and former soldiers, NGOs, family and friends. He was mourned, in particular, by colleagues in the world of journalism in all its forms. Channel 4 News in the UK broadcast a special report about his work and *Vanity Fair* magazine published extended and thoughtful pieces by its editor, friends and colleagues.

Unusually, these tributes not only celebrated his lifetime's body of work but also almost universally mourned the loss of work which was undoubtedly yet to come. His work, still available at his website www.timhetherington.com, displays a breadth and depth that is truly exceptional. Hetherington was blazing a creative trail at the time of his death in Libya and his loss was mentioned in those terms.

His use of ease with technology – what Junger called his keenness on "the voodoo of digital photography"[22] – and his willingness to be creative with new media in all its forms, meant he almost invented a fresh language to interpret the chaos of war and its place in a globalised world.

One of the most deeply moving and profoundly disturbing examples of this is a short 19-minute film called *Diary* (2010) which connects short images from many aspects of Hetherington's personal and public worlds, in a beautifully polished visual and audio collage which feels both dreamlike and astonishingly hard-edged. It's almost a glimpse into his brain and thought-processes, a diary in the truest sense, of unfinished impressions, thoughts and ideas as he travels the globe from warzones to cityscapes. It is a courageous display of openness from a quietly spoken and gentle man who took his life and work seriously, whilst always retaining a joyful lightness of touch.

Future conflicts covered by photojournalists cannot ignore the fresh approach which Hetherington's work bequeaths them. His adept use of the new, freely-available digital tools and his success at delivering "stories" told in a multi-layered way has shown there is a new way to cover such events. Whether his successors will infuse their projects with the same penetrating intelligence and regard for the complexities of the human state, is another matter. Let Sebastian Junger sum him up:

> He was a complicated person. He could piss me off sometimes. But then he was full of energy and ideas, and different ways of looking at life. His brain was always drumming away. His mind was a restless animal. It was intoxicating to be around. He woke up that part of my brain that had been dormant. I mean the *Restrepo* "sleeping soldiers" images from Afghanistan, for example, came about one afternoon when he spotted them and started running around taking pictures and telling me: "Look at them! Only their mothers get to seem them this way!" He was right and he woke up that interest and curiosity in me. And he had this beautiful smile.[23]

Notes

[1] See interview with Olivier Bercault. Available online at
http://www.vanityfair.com/online/daily/2011/05/remembering-tim-hetherington-a-giant-of-photojournalism, accessed on 4 August 2011
[2] From an email interview with Michael Christopher Brown by Eamonn O'Neill, 9 August 2011
[3] 20 April by AFP/Getty Images
[4] From a telephone interview with Sebastian Junger by Eamonn O'Neill, 4 August 2011
[5] From an email interview with Michael Christopher Brown by Eamonn O'Neill, 9 August 2011
[6] From interview with Sebastian Junger conducted by Eamonn O'Neill, 4 August 2011
[7] From Tim Hetherington interview, by Rob Haggart, *Outside* magazine, July 2011 edition.
[8] See *Guardian*, 21 April. Available online at
http://www.guardian.co.uk/media/2011/apr/21/tim-hetherington-obituary, accessed on 4 August 2011
[9] ibid

[10] See *Vanity Fair* : Remembering Tim Hetherington, A Giant of Photojournalism, 5 May 2011

[11] See article by Tim Hetherington in *Big Issue*: Aavilable online at http://www.source.ie/issues/issues0120/issue15/is15artbigiss.html, accessed on 4 August 2011

[12] See *Guardian*, 21 April. Available online at http://www.guardian.co.uk/media/2011/apr/21/tim-hetherington-obituary, accessed 4 August 2011

[13] See http://www.timhetherington.com/mentalpicture/portfolio/179, accessed on 5 August 2011

[14] ibid

[15] ibid

[16] Interview with Marcus Brauchli of the *Washington Post* by Richard Sambrook in *Are Foreign Correspondents Redundant? The changing face of international news*, Oxford, Reuters Institute for the Study of Journalism

[17] See http://www.timhetherington.com/mentalpicture/portfolio/179, accessed on 5 August 2011

[18] From Tim Hetherington interview by Rob Haggart, *Outside* magazine, July 2011 edition

[19] From a telephone interview with Sebastian Junger by Eamonn O'Neill, 4 August 2011

[20] ibid

[21] ibid

[22] ibid

[23] ibid

Further Reading/Viewing

Hetherington, Tim, (2003) *Tales from a Globalising World*, London: Thames and Hudson

Hetherington, Tim (2009) *Long Story Bit by Bit: Liberia Retold*, New York. Umbrage edition

Hetherington, Tim (2010) *Infadel*, London: Chris Boot Publishing

Junger, Sebastian (2010) *War*, New York: Twelve Publishing (also published by Fourth Estate, London, 2010)

Junger, Sebastian and Hetherington, Tim, *Restrepo*, (2010) New York: Virgil Films and Entertainment (DVD)

Note on the author

Dr Eamonn O'Neill is a Lecturer in Journalism and Course Director of the MSc in Investigative Journalism at the University of Strathclyde, Glasgow. Over a career spanning 22 years, he has been honoured for his investigative journalism in both broadcast and print in the British Press Awards, BAFTAs and the Paul Foot Award. In 2008, he became the first British recipient of an Investigative Reporters and Editors Award (Special category – Tom Renner Award) in one of the USA's premier peer-judged honours for his work investigating miscarriages of justice. In 2010 and 2011 he received honours in the Strathclyde Excellence in Teaching Awards following nominations by students. He is currently producing/presenting a new BBC Radio Scotland series O'Neill Investigates.

The fog of propaganda: Attempts to influence the reporting of the "Arab Spring" and how journalists should see through them

James Rodgers, a former BBC Foreign Correspondent turned "hackademic", examines governments' attempts to manage the media. In response, he suggests journalists need to adopt rigorous research and fact-checking, and develop wide networks of sources in order to break through the fog of propaganda

After a helicopter attack on a village in Francis Ford Coppola's film *Apocalypse Now*, set during the Vietnam War, the US troops who carried out the assault try to convince the village's terrified inhabitants that they are there to help them. A television news director, played by Coppola himself, urges the soldiers to act naturally, despite the presence of the camera crew. It is perhaps fitting that the great filmmaker included this scene, for it is the Vietnam War – a conflict far from the homes of the American soldiers who fought it, and yet which bitterly divided political opinions on their doorsteps – which still echoes through the American wars, and the journalism scholarship, which came later.

Beginning with the work of Edward Herman and Noam Chomsky, and Daniel Hallin, in the 1980s, that scholarship has often focused on the extent to which the news media are influenced by political pressure, and the extent to which the news media have influenced political elites in their decision making. Coppola's television director and his crew are part of an attempt to make the war seem worthwhile, noble even, to audiences far away who are paying for it in tax dollars, and in some cases, with the blood of their sons. Increasingly, governments seem convinced that in wartime media campaigns are not only a wise, but an indispensable, use of their resources. Government propaganda in wartime is nothing new, of course – but the "Arab Spring" has shown us that it continues, and thrives. There are challenges, and lessons, here for journalism. New technology, so often seen as a crucial factor in the way the "Arab Spring" unfolded, and allowed people to challenge their rulers, will not alone shine brightly enough to drive away the fog of propaganda, and allow audiences to see clearly.

Attempts at News Management: The Fairly Subtle, and the Faintly Ridiculous

In March 2011, with the Nato bombing campaign in Libya newly underway, the Ministry of Defence in London put out a story that an air strike on targets in Tripoli had been aborted. The reason: to avoid civilian casualties. The story was duly reported by the Mail Online,[1] ITV News,[2] the BBC,[3] and others. Announcing some days later the convening of a conference on Libya, the British Foreign Secretary, William Hague, made reference to it, again in the context of the length to which the UK and its allies were prepared to go to avoid civilian deaths.[4]

Consider this as a news story in the light of the old saying about "man bites dog" being news. As every trainee reporter or first year journalism undergraduate knows, "man bites dog" is a story precisely because it is out of the ordinary. Sometimes, when weighing up the strength of a story, it can be instructive to consider whether the opposite would be newsworthy. The headline in the Mail Online was: "Mission aborted on orders of SAS: RAF attack is halted after troops spot human shields." The headline of the opposite story would be something like: "RAF attack goes ahead despite human shields."

By any normal news values – leaving aside humanitarian considerations – the second is a much better story. It is much more unusual. It is shocking. One would hope that the RAF always strives to avoid civilian casualties – therefore, the extent to which such an announcement can really be considered newsworthy is highly questionable. In other words, is it really a story? As the press announcement of a government trying to convince an electorate weary of wars in Iraq and Afghanistan that this new offensive in Libya was worthwhile, it clearly served its purpose. It was also, from the perspective of any officials who were seeking to influence and shape the news agenda, delightfully difficult to verify.

So was the presence of the SAS[5] "spotters" to which the Mail Online article referred. This story of the SAS saving civilian lives may well have been true. It is perfectly reasonable to believe that British Special Forces, or their agents, were in Tripoli to assist the targeting of attacks. It is also perfectly impossible for a journalist to check, unless they suddenly came across the SAS in a Tripoli street (highly unlikely, given the restrictions under which international journalists were placed in Libya then). That angle too needed to be considered in the context of the time.

Up to that point in the military campaign against Colonel Gaddafi, the SAS had not had a particularly good press. Their most prominent appearance in the news had been with the word "fiasco" attached to their august initials. "Fiasco" was the conclusion to the rather bizarre tale of SAS personnel landing in Libya, apparently unannounced, in the middle of the night and being "captured by a group of farmers". This James Bond-style story did not end well for those on Her Majesty's Secret Service. They were detained, and then rather shamefully sent back whence they came by those they had come to help. As James Kirkup wrote in the *Daily Telegraph*,[6] the incident was an "embarrassing failure", which left the Foreign Secretary, "drawing laughter from MPs" when he explained to parliament that it "was caused by a 'serious misunderstanding' about their mission". One wonders if the Ministry of Defence communications team, preparing the press release about the raid being aborted, sensed a simultaneous opportunity to polish the public image of Special Forces whose activities had so recently "drawn laughter". If so, they succeeded. The SAS's cool-headed and compassionate role in the story of the aborted raid featured in many accounts.

The fault lies not with government press officers. They cannot be blamed for doing their job, which is to present military personnel, their political masters, and the activities of both, in a favourable light. The fact that they do so by means of a story which is almost impossible to disprove just makes their tactics all the more effective. It is the job of the journalist to try to see through this (unless, as in some cases, a flag-waving editorial line discourages such enquiry). Sometimes, as in the next example I want to consider, they do so very successfully.

Their task is not always terribly difficult. In June 2011, the BBC's Wyre Davies, who was covering the conflict in Libya, reported his experience of being taken by Libyan government minders to see civilians apparently injured in Nato air strikes.[7] It turned out to be nothing of the sort. Perhaps understanding that the suffering of children in wartime can make particularly memorable and heartbreaking television footage, the minders encouraged the international reporters, including Davies, to tell the story of an infant girl, Hanin, who, the Libyan officials said, had been injured in by Nato bombing.

This, of course, was impossible to verify, but reasonable to assume. It was highly likely that there had been civilian casualties as a result of Nato's attacks on Libya. The Libyan authorities seem to have been poorly stage managers, though. As Davies reported: "A member of the hospital staff passed a scrap of paper to the press. It was a hand-written note, in English, saying the girl was, in fact, hurt in a car accident. The hospital scene, it would appear, was a complete sham." The whole effect of clumsy propaganda was subsequently reinforced when a man who had been presented in the hospital as Hanin's uncle reappeared at the site of another supposed air strike. Challenged by reporters, who recognised him from his earlier role, he was unmasked as a Libyan government employee.

This kind of clumsiness is not confined to the Libyans. Reporting for the BBC from Chechnya in 2000, I remember being taken to a village recently "liberated", in the words of our Russian government minders, from rebel control. The village's football field had become a cemetery. A local woman was brought forward to tell the international journalists who had come on the organised trip what had happened. Our minders had assured us that we would hear stories of civilians killed by Chechen fighters. One of the mounds of earth was noticeably larger than the rest. "Was it the grave of a family?" a photographer asked. Apparently, it was not. The woman, to the frustration of our minders, explained that it was the burial place of some bandits killed by the militia, as the Russian police were then called.

Governments, Public Relations, and Propaganda

As the first decade of this century went on, revenues from rising international energy prices made the Russian government richer. They seem to have become wiser, too. Perhaps realising that they were not seeing their story told in the international media in the way they wanted, they hired western PR agencies to help them. As BBC Moscow correspondent from 2006-2009, I frequently dealt with one such company, GPlus Europe, on stories ranging from the 2006 G8 Summit in St Petersburg, to the 2008 war with Georgia. In that conflict, Georgia, whose government since 2003 has been keen to break free from the residual Russian influence which remained after the collapse of Communism, also used Western PR consultants.

While Russian and Georgian soldiers killed and died on the battlefield in the dusty heat of a Caucasus summer, the two squadrons of spin doctors confronted each other over the international airwaves, bombarding journalists around the world with emails and text messages. Countless other countries, including some of those whose rulers came unstuck in the "Arab Spring", have also sought professional help to develop their media strategies. Global news channels such as BBC World News, CNN, Al Jazeera, and their imitators, have created new, international, audiences. They have also created a new propaganda battleground where consultants and public relations executives fight to get their clients' versions of events accepted. It has become such a major industry that, in 2010, the *Guardian* declared London "world capital of reputation laundering".[8]

"It has been increasing for some time now, and I believe it's still on the increase," a source with long-term experience of the industry said of sometimes unsavoury governments' attempts to improve their image by using the services of Western public relations consultants. "We had an approach a couple of weeks ago from a country that has huge reputational problems, that was waving a multi-million dollar contract, and we turned them down. These were not people we would want to represent," the source explained during a conversation in July 2011, before adding: "They'll find someone in London."

That likelihood is worrying for journalism – especially at a time when both journalists and public relations executives know that reporters' time is increasingly short. In an article for the National Union of Journalists' magazine, the *Journalist,* in 2011, Stefan Stern, a former writer for the *Financial Times*, reflected on his new job with the public relations company, Edelman. He addressed journalists' traditional idea of public relations as the "dark side". He shares his first impressions of his new workplace. "Not very dark. In fact, this seemed to be a surprisingly sunny (and well-resourced) world."[9] The phrase "well-resourced" brings to mind Nick Davies' point in *Flat Earth News* about the greater number of people now employed in PR compared to in journalism.[10]

If corrupt regimes are able to "find someone in London" to launder their reputation, there are potentially serious consequences for the kind of reporting our audiences will receive. And while it is true that digital technology has made a massive contribution to the way the events of the "Arab Spring" have been communicated to listeners, viewers, and readers around the world, those events have also demonstrated its limits, and potential pitfalls. The case of Amina, the Syrian lesbian blogger who was not[11] (as discussed elsewhere in this volume by Daniel Bennett) demonstrated both that online material can be highly misleading, and that social networking sites (in this case, National Public Radio's Andy Carvin and his followers on Twitter) can help to expose the deception.

Twitter and Facebook themselves, however, will not be enough to enable journalists and their audiences to see through the fog of propaganda which governments and their hired assistants summon up with the sorcery of their communications strategies. As Piers Robinson and his co-authors write in *Pockets of Resistance*, their study of British news media and the reporting of the 2003 invasion of Iraq: "Even if, over time, new communication technologies have increased the potential power of news media outlets, increasingly professional government media-management techniques may have been effective in countering these developments."[12]

How Can Journalists Respond?
What can journalists do to try to guard against attempts, crude or clever, to influence them? The answer is the best of the old, and the best of the new. By the best of the old, I mean the need to check sources, and check information, as far as possible. That involves not only recognising the enduring value of eyewitness reporting, but also placing renewed emphasis on standing stories up properly. This is where the best of the new comes in. As Andy Carvin has demonstrated with his extensive network of followers on Twitter, new technology does offer new possibilities. Carvin has facilitated extensive coverage of the "Arab Spring" without being based in the region. Only by combining these two approaches – rigorous research and fact-checking, and networks of sources – can journalists hope to generate enough bright rays to burn off the fog of propaganda.

Notes
[1] The Mail Online (2011) Mission aborted on orders of SAS: RAF attack is halted after troops spot human shields. Available online at

http://www.dailymail.co.uk/news/article-1368626/Libya-RAF-abort-attack-SAS-spot-Gaddafi-using-human-shields.html, accessed on 13 July 2011

[2] ITV News (2011) RAF mission aborted. Available online at http://www.itv.com/news/raf-mission-aborted55848/, accessed on 13 July 2011

[3] BBC News (2011) RAF Tornados abort mission in Libya. Available online at http://www.bbc.co.uk/news/uk-12803217, accessed on 26 July 2011

[4] The Ministry of Defence (2011) Foreign Secretary announces London conference on Libya. Available online at http://www.mod.uk/DefenceInternet/DefenceNews/DefencePolicyAndBusiness/ForeignSecretaryAnnouncesLondonConferenceOnLibya.htm, accessed on 13 July 2011

[5] Special Air Service – British special forces

[6] Kirkup, James (2011) Libya: Whitehall blame game begins over SAS fiasco, *Daily Telegraph*. Available online at http://www.telegraph.co.uk/news/politics/8366880/Libya-Whitehall-blame-game-begins-over-SAS-fiasco.html, accessed on 13 July 2011

[7] Davies, Wyre (2011) Libya: Curious incident of the child "air raid victim". Available online at http://www.bbc.co.uk/news/world-middle-east-13676525, accessed on 14 July 2011

[8] Booth, Robert (2010) PR firms make London world capital of reputation laundering, *Guardian*, 3 August. Available online at http://www.guardian.co.uk/media/2010/aug/03/london-public-relations-reputation-laundering?INTCMP=SRCH, accessed on 14 July 2011

[9] Stern, Stefan (2011) Not so much dark but surprisingly sunny, *Journalist*, April/May p. 15

[10] Davies, Nick (2009) *Flat Earth News: An Award-Winning Reporter Exposes Falsehood, Distortion, and Propaganda in the Global Media*, London: Vintage p. 85

[11] McCrum, Robert (2011) Lessons learned from A Gay Girl in Damascus, *Guardian*. Available online at http://www.guardian.co.uk/books/booksblog/2011/jun/15/lessons-learned-gay-girl-damascus?INTCMP=SRCH, accessed on 25 June 2011

[12] Robinson, Piers; Goddard, Peter; Parry, Katy; Murray, Craig with Taylor, Philip M. (2010). *Pockets of Resistance: British News Media, War, and Theory in the 2003 Invasion of Iraq*, Manchester: Manchester University Press p. 29

Note on the author

James Rodgers is Senior Lecturer in International Journalism at London Metropolitan University. He spent twenty years as a journalist: five for Reuters Television, and fifteen for the BBC. For most of his BBC career (1995-2010) he was a foreign correspondent, completing postings in Moscow, Gaza, and Brussels, as well as numerous other assignments. His areas of specialist knowledge as a journalist are Russia and the former Soviet Union, and the Gaza Strip, where, as the BBC's correspondent from 2002-2004, he was the only international journalist permanently based in the territory. He covered all the major stories of post-Soviet Russia, including the election in 1991 of Boris Yeltsin, the breakup of the USSR later that year, the two wars in Chechnya, the presidency of Vladimir Putin, and Russia's war with Georgia in 2008. While based in Gaza, he also reported from Israel and the West Bank. In 2001, he was in New York and Washington to cover the aftermath of the attacks of September 11th. He reported for the BBC from Baghdad and Tikrit at the time of Saddam Hussein's capture in December 2003. His book, *Reporting Conflict*, is due to be published by Palgrave MacMillan in 2012.

Section 2. What do we Mean by the "Arab Spring"?

John Mair

First, as Mrs Beeton might have said, let us define our terms. Western journalism has labelled a series of events throughout the Middle East and North Africa in 2011 the "Arab Spring" (we have deliberately put it in inverted commas throughout this volume). But there are clearly several "Springs" and how do we define a movement still fermenting throughout so many Middle Eastern and North African countries in the autumn?

Will Barton, of Coventry University, uses the *Communist Manifesto* and *Wind in the Willows* as his set texts to explore the origin of the super-narrative phrase and concludes that it "amounts to the appropriation of events into a construction in the service of the Western powers".

Kevin Marsh, one of the deeper thinkers in modern journalism, a former editor of the flagship *Today* on BBC Radio Four, delivers a closely argued piece in which he doubts the very existence of the "Spring". Drawing on the controversial theories of the postmodernist philosopher Jean Baudrillard, he says the Western media have presented not reality but a mythical, hyper-real narrative:

> Since 1914, we journalists have stroked ourselves with the idea that journalism is the first draft of history. Since 1943, we have conceded it is merely a "rough" draft. But for all its roughness, journalism's super narratives tend to survive the revisions of time, in part at least and most usually in their titles. Expect to read the winter and spring of 2011 described as the "Arab Spring" in decades to come. But the "Arab Spring" did not take place. Proof, if any were needed, of Hemingway's maxim: "The first draft of anything is shit."

David Hayward, of the BBC College of Journalism (who co-produced the conference which gave birth to this volume), argues against using another ready-to-wear template – that of the Velvet revolutions in Eastern Europe in 1989. This time round there is no Berlin Wall to pull apart brick by brick, no over-riding issue linking countries and no Soviet imperialist power to evict: "The 'Arab Spring' was not 1989 all over again. Rather, it was the 'Arab Spring': a very different and in some ways far more complicated series of events."

Next, Kate Smith, of Napier University, Edinburgh, and Ben McConville, of Northumbria University, ask if the Western media marginalised the economic roots of the "Arab Spring" which started with food riots in Tunisia. They ask if this narrative has been forgotten in the reporting. Are the underlying causes of the Arab Spring being misunderstood and misinterpreted by the Western media?

Finally in this section, Alexander Kazamias, also of Coventry University, looks back to Lawrence of Arabia a century ago and the work of Edward Said on post-colonialism to find a frame of reference for the coverage. He argues that Said's critique of the "Orientalist" bias of dominant Western representation of Arab cultures is still highly relevant when examining the reporting of the recent uprisings

Whose "Spring" is it Anyway?

Will Barton explores the origins of the phrase "Arab Spring" and concludes that it "amounts to the appropriation of events into a construction in the service of the Western powers"

Taken all in all, the crisis has been burrowing away like the good old mole it is.
(Letter from Karl Marx to Freidrich Engels, 22 February 1858)

The Mole had been working very hard all the morning, spring-cleaning his little home. First with brooms, then with dusters; then on ladders and steps and chairs, with a brush and a pail of whitewash; till he had dust in his throat and eyes, and splashes of whitewash all over his black fur, and an aching back and weary arms. Spring was moving in the air above and in the earth below and around him, penetrating even his dark and lowly little house with its spirit of divine discontent and longing. It was small wonder, then, that he suddenly flung down his brush on the floor, said "Bother!" and "O blow!" and also "Hang spring-cleaning!" and bolted out of the house without even waiting to put on his coat.
(The Wind in the Willows, Kenneth Grahame, Chapter 1)

Where do revolutions come from? What precisely is the spark that causes the explosion? Marx was clear that revolution is always there, *in potentia*, just below the surface. Most of the time, injustice, oppression and exploitation continue unchallenged in their role as the everyday life of human society, but the tensions they create simmer away silently until something, perhaps something in itself very small, opens up a crack in the smooth surface and all the anger and bitterness rush out in a torrent that can sweep away governments and power structures or can be put down only with the use of great force.

There's also something about the "Spring" – a sense of newness, of revival and rebirth that makes it seem a particularly appropriate time for uprisings. Marx was writing to Engels in the aftermath of the great year of European revolutions in 1848, which was referred to at the time as the Spring of Nations and the Springtime of the People.

The wave of revolutions that year swept around the world – not only Europe, but South America too were taken up in the storm – began in France in February. Reactionaries talked of it as one group of fools aping another. Progressives spoke of the Spirit of the Age.

In seeking explanations, we reach for analogies and so journalists writing about the "Arab Spring" of 2011 have cast around for a parallel and found it in the "colour revolutions" of Eastern Europe in the early to mid-2000s (Georgia was Rose, Ukraine was Orange). This suggested that the Arab revolutions, like their Balkan predecessors, stemmed from a shared past – a single underlying motif like the collapse of the Soviet bloc and the implosion of Yugoslavia. That being the case, it was easy for liberal interventionists to see a one-size-fits-all response – Western intervention to support "democratic" rebels against "tyrants". As so often, support for democracy was cashed out in terms of bombing people. The solution to tyranny in the Middle East, it seems, is always more dead Arabs.

No Simple Parallel to be Drawn

The trouble with using one wave of revolutions as a model to explain another is that there is no simple parallel to be drawn. Whatever idiosyncrasies the uprisings of Eastern Europe and the Balkans had, they were all against regimes in which they arising from and created by the authoritarian communism of the old USSR. They were largely characterised by a desire for a polity more like those of the EU and the

US and for a free market economy and an uncritical admiration for both bourgeois representative democracy and consumerism.

The regimes of the Middle East are much more varied. The political structures against which people protested and within which they acted were far more heterogeneous. In Tunisia, where the current wave of insurrection began, government was in the hands of a decadent dictatorship. Ben Ali was vulnerable to pressure from street demonstrations, quickly became isolated and was relatively easily forced from office and fled the country. Whether what has replaced him will be much of an improvement will no doubt become clearer when the constituent assembly elections are conducted this autumn.

Egypt was theoretically led by an elected president but his legitimacy was void. He had governed under a permanent state of emergency and elections were compromised as opposition candidates who might win were not allowed to stand. This left him essentially dependent upon the support of the armed forces, and when they declined to maintain it, he was toast.

Neither the Egyptian nor the Tunisian events can really be considered revolutions in the same sense as the classical models of France 1799 or Russia 1917. The regimes were weak and unable to defend themselves and fell with comparatively little bloodshed. Libya was a different matter.

Gaddafi was a revolutionary leader. He came to power by overthrowing a monarchy and proclaiming a republic. Libya's political system is a kind of Islamic socialist people's republic. It disdains parties and representative democracy in favour of what it claims is a form of direct democracy through councils. The regime while it survived was clearly very unpopular with many of its citizens – perhaps the majority of them – but it was clearly also supported by some of them. The armed forces were largely loyal to the regime. Revolution in Libya was always going to be a riskier and more violent project and so it transpired.

Danger of Simplistic Explanations
Here we can see the danger of simplistic explanations of events, based not on knowledge of the situation but on facile parallels with something that looks similar at first glance. An analogy with a different set of insurrections leads to an assumption that geographical contiguity implies

political similarity. This allows the easy characterisation of all the events as "democratic forces" (people like us – nice people) rebelling against "tyrants" (monsters like Hitler). The assumption that because Ben Ali and Mubarak were open doors that needed only a push, so would be Gaddafi leads to the call to intervene on the side of the good guys. Lisa Anderson[1] stresses the importance of seeing each Arab country as distinct and individual:

> For the United States to fulfil its goals in the region, it will need to understand these distinctions and distance itself from the idea that the Tunisian, Egyptian and Libyan uprisings constitute a cohesive Arab revolt...The young activists in each country have been sharing ideas, tactics and moral support, but they are confronting different opponents and operating within different contexts.

This is surely right, yet in the same issue of the same journal, Goldstone[2] wants to create and offer an analysis that shoehorns all these events into a single model:

> ...1848 and 1989 are not the right analogies for this present winter's events. The revolutions of 1848 sought to overturn monarchies, and those in 1989 were aimed at toppling communist governments. The revolutions of 2011 are fighting something quite different: "sultanistic" dictatorships.

Within this coinage, he subsumes not only Tunisia, Egypt and Libya but also Sudan and Syria.

The tendency of Western commentators to construct overarching models where none is justified by the facts can only obscure what is actually happening and mislead readers about the appropriate response. Not only does this threaten our ability to comprehend and to judge the events, it makes a crucial difference to the events themselves as social constructions. The "Arab Spring" is not something the Arabs invented. It is a construction upon and of the events by others. The very form and existence of the specific actions and activities becomes transformed into something else – a media event. The ownership of the perception of political actions is transferred from the protesters themselves to the commentators, from East to West. Slavoj Zizek[3], commentating on

Badiou's understanding of the mediation of political reality through its theorisation, writes:

> The Event is the truth of the situation that makes visible/legible what the "official" situation had to "repress", but it is also always localised – that is to say the truth is always the truth *of* a specific situation. The French Revolution, for example, is the Event that makes visible/legible the excesses and inconsistencies, the "lie" of the ancient regime, and it is the truth of the ancient regime situation, localized, attached to it. An Event thus involves its own series of determinations: the Event itself; its naming (the designation of "French Revolution" is not an objective categorising but part of the Event itself, the way its followers perceived and symbolized their activity) …

So the representation and characterisation of the actions of revolutionary protesters in Arab lands is expropriated by Western commentators and governments, making them into events within the politics of Western nations.

Devising a "Humanitarian" Intervention

Intervention undisguised is not an option under international law and the United Nations so it becomes necessary to devise a strategy that looks humanitarian, while still effectively taking sides in a civil conflict. This is the demand that we should use armed force to defend the innocent, prevent genocide, war crimes, and so on. Inexorably, we become part of the action and part of the problem. What was at first presented as protection now begins to look more like regime change. France admitted to supplying armaments to anti-Gaddafi forces. Week after week, bombing raids continued. The situation in some of the "rebel strongholds" came close to the situation of the Vietnamese village that had to be destroyed in order to save it.

Once again the simplistic assumptions of liberal humanitarian interventionists ally them with imperialism. In trying to understand why, it is instructive to look at where the rhetoric of an Arab Spring came from. It was not coined this year. Sourcewatch commented:[4]

Arab Spring is a term that was used beginning in March 2005 by numerous media commentators to suggest that a spin-off benefit of the invasion of Iraq would be the flowering of Western-friendly Middle East democracies. The term took on a new meaning in 2011, as democratic uprisings independently arose and spread across the Arab world.

Conspiracy theorists will be pleased to note that the first four uses of the term given by Sourcewatch (El Amrani[5], Jacoby[6], Regan[7] and Youlton[8] – all 2005) appear within four days of each other, all in American publications. Whether that indicates a common source for the coinage, collusion or simply a small *zeitgeist*, it amounts to the appropriation of events into a construction in the service of the Western powers.

Notes

[1] Anderson, Lisa (2011) Demystiying the Arab Spring: Parsing the Differences between Tunisia, Egypt and Libya, *Foreign Affairs*, Vol. 90, No. 3 May/June pp 2-7

[2] Goldstone, Jack A (2011) Understanding the Revolutions of 2011: Weakness and Resilience in Middle Eastern Autocracies, *Foreign Affairs*, Vol. 90, No. 3 May/June pp 8-16

[3] Zizek, Slavoj (2010) Paul and the Truth Event, Milbank, John and Zizek, Slavoj (eds) *Paul's New Moment*, Michigan: Brazos Press pp 74-99

[4] Sourcewatch (2011) "Arab Spring". Available online at http:// www.sourcewatch.org/index.php?title =Arab Spring, accessed 12 July 2011

[5] El Amrani, Issandr (2005) Egypt, Lebanon, and the "Arab Spring, *Arabist*, 10 March

[6] Jacoby, Jeff (2005) Editorial: The Arab Spring, *Boston Globe*, 10 March; also published 11 March 2005 at townhall.com.

[7] Regan, Tom (2005) Will "Arab Spring" lead to "summer of liberty"? Some experts worry US "triumphalism" masks more complicated issues in push towards Arab democracy, *Christian Science Monitor*, 14 March

[8] Youlton, Michael (2005) Is Spring Banging at the Doors of the Arab World? *Blanket*, 10 March

Note on the author

Will Barton is a Senior Lecturer in Media and Communication, Coventry School of Art and Design. He has published a number of papers on the representation and commodification of war and is co-author, with Andrew Beck, of *Get Set for Communication Studies* (EUP, 2005). He is currently working with Shao Hongsong on a book about the New Confucianism in contemporary China.

The "Arab Spring" Did Not Take Place

Kevin Marsh draws on the controversial theories of the French postmodernist Jean Baudrillard to argue that the media have presented a mythical, hyper-real narrative about the "Arab Spring" – rather than its reality

On 21 November 1935, a former diplomat and soldier Jean Giraudoux opened his new play at the *Théâtre de l'Athénée*, in Paris. Called *La Guerre de Troie n'aura pas lieu (The Trojan War Will Not Take Place)*[1] it imagined and created an eve of conflict debate in which the heroes and heroines of the Trojan War argued to avert the coming catastrophe.

It was typical of its era, surreal and absurd at one and the same time. And it worked on a number of levels. At its simplest, it was a critique of the politics and diplomacy that had failed to avert the Great War and were failing to contain a resurgent, militant Germany. At another level, it was a play about fate and inevitability. The "Trojan War" did take place, at least within the minds of the audience and the confines of the mythological universe Giraudoux was drawing on and reflecting on stage. Arguments to avert it were futile. Strong reasoning, compelling alternatives could not turn aside what was inevitable.

It works on yet another level, too. The Trojan War isn't just any old story about any old war. It might not be as well known today as it was in 1935, but it is one of the defining stories of our culture. And as Giraudoux's audience watched, they were witnessing characters on stage whom they "knew" in most cases better than they "knew" the real people around them. Hector, Helen, Priam, Ulysses and the rest: they "knew" them because of the narrative that defined them and which the characters themselves, paradoxically, created. They were not just locked into an inevitable narrative, they *were* that inevitable narrative. They could not exist without it; it could not exist without them. Irony was folded inside irony. If Hector's arguments to avoid war had been allowed to prevail, he could not exist as the Hector we "know" because the story he exists within, "The Trojan War", would not exist.

Watching Giraudoux's play, the audience were like time-travellers watching our grandparents debate whether or not they should marry.

Existential Irony

It was to this existential irony that, nearly sixty years on, the postmodernist writer and academic Jean Baudrillard referred in his 1991 collection of essays, *The Gulf War Did Not Take Place*,[2] essays originally published in *Libération* and the *Guardian* in the winter and spring of 1991. As "The Gulf War" was about to take place, was taking place, and had taken place. Or rather, as Baudrillard argued, as the events that coalition politicians, military and media portrayed as "The Gulf War", was about to take place, was taking place, and had taken place.

Baudrillard turned Giraudoux's ironies on their head. In his account of a war not taking place, it was the audience that was unwittingly caught in the inevitability authored for them, not the characters on stage.

He did not argue that nothing happened nor that there was no military action, violence and death in Iraq in the first months of 1991. There self-evidently was. His argument was with what we thought it was. And the violence and deaths were not "The Gulf War", except in the minds of coalition politicians, military and media. And audiences. Baudrillard's argument was not as complex as his detractors portray it. For "The Gulf

War" to have taken place, there would have to have been real combat between coalition and Iraqi forces. There was no such combat. No war.

Sure, the coalition was bombing and firing missiles from 30,000 feet. And inviting audiences to whoop at the images from the warhead nose-cams. It cycled and re-cycled images of civilians and conscripts consigned to hell. It was all to establish a narrative called "The Gulf War". A narrative we "knew"'. A narrative nourished by Cent Com and the media in Doha.

Baudrillard argued this was not "The Gulf War". Coalition and Iraqi forces did not actually meet in combat. Each did its belligerent stuff, but each did it as if they were in different universes. Coalition troops were so distant from true combat that fewer died in the "war" than would have died back home in gang-fights, as crime victims or in road accidents. For his part, Saddam did not sacrifice troops and civilians to fight "The Gulf War". The 100,000 dead, according to Baudrillard, were the price he had to pay to stay in power:

> ...the final decoy that Saddam will have sacrificed, the blood money paid in forfeit according to a calculated equivalence, in order to conserve his power.[3]

And conserve his power he did – for a further twelve years. The "victors" did not win and the "vanquished" did not lose. Spring 1991 in Iraq may have been an "atrocity". A bloody series of appalling atrocities – but "The Gulf War" did not take place.

Why a Semioticist's Whimsy May Matter

Baudrillard's essays may appear to be a semioticist's whimsy – worse, a French semioticist's whimsy – or a vaguely interesting academic diversion. Rather like Giraudoux's play may seem, in the end, no more than an intellectually challenging night in the theatre. Except that...what things are and how we journalists portray them matters hugely to us. And to our audiences.

Journalists – especially editors in newspaper and broadcasting newsrooms – find themselves working an ugly trick every day on their audiences. On the one hand, we are about telling them something new, something salient. Something significant that they don't already know. Something they didn't know they don't know and didn't know they need or want to know. Dealing in truth, something close to education. On the other, we have to engage them – with tantalising headlines, with facts and observations that sit at the extreme edge of truth. And with stories. Stories that, by virtue of being well written or well told alone, engage their attention and turn it to matters they never knew they needed to know something about. Dealing in impact.

The tool we know that has the most impact of all is the "super narrative". The huge, over-arching narrative that binds other, minor narratives together. That gives them meaning above what they are in themselves, offering the audience what Aristotle called ἀναγνώρισις – "recognition". The means to recognise and empathise with people culturally, emotionally and socially distant from ourselves. The means to link disparate events. To recollect them at a later date. We often give these super narratives snappy, instantly recognisable, memorable titles. Titles we can use in a blazing strap or an over-the shoulder identifier in a TV news bulletin: "The Moors Murders"; "The Fall of Communism"; "Showdown in the Desert"; "The Credit Crunch".

And, paradoxically, the more that those of us living in digitally hyper-charged cultures are *able* to know – via the web, social media, 24/7 TV channels – the more we *need* these super narratives. To tell us: "Hey …this matters – and here's why" or "Hey…it's that thing again, the one you were interested in last time." Or they even tell us: "Hey…you might not think you know anything about this, but it's a lot like this other thing." At the same time, those technologies that have increased the quantity of what we can know have decreased what we "know" in common.

The Hyper-Reality of the Super Narrative
That, in turn, means that journalism's super narratives have had to become more reductive, more detached from reality, more resembling what Baudrillard called "hyper-reality". They become illusions. Just like "The Gulf War". They become misleading and unpredictable, too. It's harder and harder for those of us who create these super narratives to know or predict all that the references will excite in our audiences. What references, precisely, the word "Arab" will generate in the minds of those in the audience. Yet we persist in it.

It's easy to see how and why we reached for the super narrative that we called "The Arab Spring". We knew that something was happening and sensed that it was out of the ordinary. People were on the move, politically on the move. For the most part, it was the Arabic speaking countries we were most interested in. And by the time we realised we needed to name it, it was early spring. And spring carries overtones of new life. New growth. Re-birth after a long, dark winter. It was ideal.

Journalists assumed, probably quite rightly, that few in their audiences would be hugely engaged by a tragic row over property rights in a country most thought of only as a holiday destination. Or in yet *another* Sunni/Shiite religious squabble in a country that was almost never in the news and to which most people could not point on the map. Or in an elite in the Arab world's only democracy as it debated the merits and demerits of its confessional constitution.

Create a super-narrative, a hyper-reality called "The Arab Spring" and you might have a chance. Any expression of popular discontent in any Arabic speaking monarchy or despotism was a signifier of "The Arab Spring". It felt real. It felt energetic. It was full of movement. And terrific TV pictures.

But "The Arab Spring" did not take place.

The Reality of the Tunisian Uprising

Think back to the event that in most of us in the Western media identify as the beginning. 17 December 2010 when Mohamed Bouazizi, a Tunisian street trader in Sidi Bouzid, set himself on fire, protesting at the arbitrary exercise of power by the police and local government officials. A petty abuse of authority that prevented him exercising his property rights, his right to trade, his right to earn a living. The police had continually harassed him. Confiscated his goods, even the barrow from which he sold fruit and vegetables. Officials kept revoking his trading permits, seeking ever bigger bribes. Basboosa, as he was known to family and friends, suffered 90 per cent burns. Within hours of his self-immolation, there were local, then regional then national street protests. He died on 4 January 2011 and by the end of that month, President Zine El Abidine Ben Ali had gone. The revolution had begun.

And that might have been that. The Tunisian January.

Except, Egypt seemed to follow where Tunisia had led. Like Tunisia, it was an Arabic-speaking pseudo-democracy. There were self-immolations. Growing street protests. And no less a figure than Mohammed el-Baradei, international diplomat and the man who the opposition wanted to challenge President Mubarak, warned that change was "inevitable" in his native, estranged Egypt following revolution in Tunisia.

Egypt was big. Egypt mattered in a away that Tunisia didn't, so it was time for the super narrative. Finally, the story went, the Arab world was emerging from its despotism to join the only true political faith; Western liberalism. Populations will rise spontaneously, thirsting for freedom and justice. Like Giraudoux, we placed characters we "knew" – the masses in Arabic speaking countries – inside a super narrative that we "knew" – all nations' remorseless progression to democracy.

And that super narrative, the "hyper-reality" if you like, drove what we looked for and reported. What we headlined. And, just as importantly, what we didn't. "The Arab Spring" was a "domino" story, we decided. One Arabic despotism after another would fall to Western ideas of liberal democracy. The people would, at last, build Stockholm in the sand, celebrating plurality, embracing the rule of law.

And before long, we journalists became familiar with the modalities. There would be a "Day of Rage", linked often to Friday prayers – so we made sure the cameras were there. Articulate young men and women would find the TV cameras, or the cameras would find them, and they would speak in polished Harvard English about freedom and democracy and law and the burning desire for justice. And we would show how Facebook and Twitter and SMS were their communication tools of choice.

And because we knew these were Muslims we looked for the hidden hand of the Muslim Brotherhood in Egypt and the machinations of Islamic fundamentalists elsewhere. We speculated on whether "The Arab Spring" would weaken or strengthen al Qaeda.

Just as Baudrillard argued, the pictures and themes and interviews we selected were all images of the hyper reality we called "The Arab Spring".

114

We collected and shared them as if to confirm that what *must* be taking place really was taking place.

What the Media Missed

There was much the media overlooked, much that was inconsistent with the super narrative that declared this was "The Arab Spring". At the mundane level, the millions in every country who did *not* become involved in the popular uprisings, either out of fear, lack of interest, distance or because they sustained in themselves a weary cynicism that nothing was changing, nothing would change. We overlooked the images of daily trade and schooling and bureaucracy and traffic and and and…anything that was happening just as before, untouched by the super narrative.

At the symbolic level, we overlooked the near total absence of Arab nationalism in "The Arab Spring". We overlooked the presence of non-Arab actors; the Berbers in Morocco – non-Arabs – Kurds in Iraq. Jews in Tunisia and even Coptic Christians in Egypt.

And we overlooked the role of tribalism, personal fear, vengeance, familial loathing. "The Arab Spring" was a political movement. We could not include non-political dynamics.

That's not to say we ignored the complexities. We didn't. But, with few exceptions, we were oblivious to the obvious. That the causes and characteristics of each uprising were different from any other – and that once journalists had listed them all, they became meaningless as signifiers. They were not unique features that identified "The Arab Spring" and only "The Arab Spring".

That list of causes and characteristics – in one constellation or another – would have defined and explained any and every political movement and popular rising throughout history. Here it was poverty and cronyism, there the frustrations of an educated, ambitious middle class. Here there was benevolent monarchy, there cruel dynastic autocracy, there a personal fiefdom of a tribal strong man. Here there was sectarian division, there generational animosities. In some places it was all or most of the causes, in others one or two.

Going Beyond the Super-Narrative to the Essential Truth

One of the few journalists who "got" this essential truth was the BBC *Newsnight* Economics Editor Paul Mason. When he tried to account for "what's going on", he eschewed the super narrative "The Arab Spring". He found, instead, twenty deep factors that applied as much to the *banlieues* of Paris and the suburbs of Dublin as it did to any Arabic speaking autocracy. Mason spoke instead about a "...protest meme ... sweeping the world" that did not seek a total overturn but sought "a moderation of excesses".[4]

But those journalists who preferred to stick with the super narrative had much to draw on from the lines the narrative's characters wrote for themselves. Take the ubiquitous slogan, chanted and scrawled on the walls of public buildings: الشعب يريد إسقاط النظام (ash-shab yurīd isqāṭ an-nizām): "The people want to end the regime." We heard it first in Tunis. And then in Tahrir Square in Egypt. And in Bahrain, Yemen, Syria, Beirut and Jordan. It validated the grand narrative, provided the motivation for it. Gave an explanation for thinking the way we did. "Ash-shab yurīd isqāṭ an-nizām" had the virtue of sounding like the historical inevitability journalists "knew" was being played out on the Arab street. We "knew" it had only ever been a matter of time before the Arabs succumbed to the inevitable history of liberal democracy and threw off the despots. This was how history progressed. The media turned "historical" inevitability into narrative inevitability and "ash-shab yurīd isqāṭ an-nizām" proved they were right.

Phew. It *was* "The Arab Spring".

Yet this slogan, though ubiquitous, meant different things to different people in different places. In imperfectly democratic Lebanon, it was little to do with despotism or poverty. It was a call for the end of its confessional constitution – a constitution that placed religious and sectarian differences at the heart of the state. Differences that kept the country weak, permanently in thrall to its despotic neighbour, Syria, and a permanent threat to its powerful southern neighbour, Israel.

In Tunisia, it demanded an end to cronyism, corruption and economic suffocation. In Egypt, it was the susurration of a discontented middle-class – professionals, small businessmen, a bourgeoisie frustrated at the limitations an ageing military ruler placed on their political aspirations.

116

While in the Palestinian territories, where the alienation of Hamas and Fatah from Israel continued to guarantee the impossibility of a two-state settlement in the region – the slogan was tweaked toالشعب يريد انهاء الانقسام – "the people want to end the division".

Arab academics and Western students of the Arab world seemed to endorse our choice of super narrative, too. Much as Mohammed el-Baradei had done. We were seeing "a people [moving] as a whole, into spontaneous protests" wrote one[5]. Young Arabs "will no longer tolerate...the contempt and disrespect their governments have shown them" said another, adding that they do not just mean their own "corrupt governments; they also mean the old regime that has prevailed for decades in the entire Arab world, from the Atlantic to the Gulf"[6]. It was a "youthquake"[7]. There was "social cohesion and unity in the project"[8] most agreed. It was "The Arab Spring". Except it did not take place.

How the Tumultuous Events in Tunisia took us by Surprise

The Tunisian revolution that followed the demonstrations surprised us – none more so than President Zine El Abidine Ben Ali, who scuttled away from power in the dead of night. The demonstrations in Tahrir Square, Cairo, were a surprise too. We might just be forgiven for seeing the seeds of the Egyptian 'revolution' in the earlier events in Tunisia, especially when President Mubarak was forced to step down. Except, there will be autumn elections in one, Tunisia, while the army still clings on to power in the other, Egypt.

Though we wanted, expected and predicted that "The Arab Spring" would follow the super narrative, we now find it did no such thing. Arabic-speaking populations have not emerged into the broad, sunlit uplands of Western, liberal democracy. The old regimes have made the least possible concessions to respond to political demands. Or have thrown handfuls of petrodollars at those demanding social reform – better healthcare, education, reduced poverty. The political and economic dispensation in Algeria, Bahrain, Jordan, Kuwait, Lebanon, Morocco, Oman and Saudi Arabia has shifted not one millimetre.

The civil war in Libya followed a different course, as did the cycle of demonstration and repression in Syria – and in both cases, events slid over into new super narrative – "The Libyan Civil War" and "The Syrian

117

Repression". They were no longer "The Arab Spring" and most audiences no longer make that association.

For the rest, though, if you were to go out into the streets of Britain a year on from Basboosa's suicidal protest and ask readers, listeners and viewers: "What happened in 'The Arab Spring'?" you would almost certainly have reflected back to you the super narrative journalists created for them.

The people speak, spontaneous protests – hurrah. Democracy, justice, freedom – hurrah. An end to repression and corruption – hurrah. Arab dictators forced to listen to their people. The Arab world finally following in the West's historical footsteps. Hurrah. Except, "The Arab Spring" did not take place.

How Real People Shaped the Events

There was irony here, too. Just as much as in *The Trojan War Will Not Take Place* ... except that this time it was the journalists, the creators of our hyper-reality who could not see outside their super narrative and were defined by it. Unlike Giraudoux's characters, the real people of those Arabic speaking states – those on the streets and those in power alike – were able to shape events and were not delimited and defined by our account of those events.

None of this would matter if it were not for the simple truth that this model, this creation of super narratives, is increasingly the one the media follow, especially in the way it reports world news. For we journalists, now believe we cannot explain and our audiences cannot understand the world unless we fold it inside a super narrative, a hyper-reality.

It has always been the case, of course, that journalism has had an existential need to create narrative entities outside events themselves. To place on top of reality a story or stories, narrative entities without which it could not exist. There is too much information in the world, too much of the world.

As long ago as 1922, the American magazine publisher and author Walter Lippman wrote in *Public Opinion*[9] that journalism is a limited, reductive activity. It cannot report all of reality and to exist it has to be the product of a "standardised routine" that selects and presents. A routine that makes use of "watchers stationed at certain places" – journalists, reporters – to spot a "manifestation". Not reality. Not a complex truth. But a "manifestation", an event that "signalises" that there is a reality, that that there is a truth. And to be news:

> The course of events must assume a certain definable shape, and until it is in a phase where some aspect is an accomplished fact, news does not separate itself from the ocean of possible truth.

From "Manifestation" to "Definable Shape"

Ninety years on, that "ocean of possible truth" is many times squared greater than anything Lippmann had in mind. The journey from "manifestation: to "definable shape" has to be very much quicker, too, in a world of 24/7 live and continuous news and the instantaneous web. And it is cross-cultural and trans-global.

Where it was once about merely recognising those "definable" shapes – a news sense, a nose for news – now it is about creating them. Creating those super narratives. Such as "The Arab Spring".

So we journalists have to think harder about how and why we create these super narratives. Something we now do almost instantaneously with events themselves and as a matter of routine. We need to think harder about the kind of super narratives we create, too.

"The Arab Spring" bulged with Western liberal political assumptions and associations. It was a narrative certainty. But those certainties were built on ideas which, to those who do not share the Western view of mankind's inevitable "progress", look like, feel like and are intellectual imperialism.

Our inevitabilities were not realised and may never be realised. And, in an inversion of Giraudoux's irony, it is we – the Western authors and Western audience – who are locked into an inevitable narrative.

Since 1914, we journalists have stroked ourselves with the idea that journalism is the first draft of history. Since 1943, we have conceded it is merely a "rough" draft. But for all its roughness, journalism's super narratives tend to survive the revisions of time, in part at least and most usually in their titles. Expect to read the winter and spring of 2011 described as "The Arab Spring" in decades to come.

But "The Arab Spring" did not take place. Proof, if any were needed, of Hemingway's maxim: "The first draft of anything is shit."

Notes

[1] Giraudoux Jean (1935), *La Guerre de Troie n'aura pas lieu* Available online at http://www.wikilivres.info/wiki/La_guerre_de_Troie_n%E2%80%99aura_pas_lieu, accessed on 1 August 2011. See also Fry Christopher (1983) *The Trojan War Will Not Take Place*, London: Methuen

[2] Baudrillard, Jean (1991) *La Guerre du Golfe n'a pas eu lieu*, Paris: Galilée

[3] Baudrillard, Jean (1995) *The Gulf War Did Not Take Place*, Bloomington: Indiana University Press

[4] Mason, Paul (2011) Twenty Reasons Why It's Kicking Off, BBC *Newsnight* blog. Available online at http://www.bbc.co.uk/blogs/newsnight/paulmason/2011/02/twenty_reasons_why_its _kicking.html, accessed on 1 August 2011

[5] Challand, Benoit (2011) The Counter-Power of Civil Society in the Middle East, Deliberately Considered. Available online at online http://www.deliberatelyconsidered.com/2011/03/the-counter-power-of-civil-society-in-the-middle-east-2/, accessed on 1 August 2011

[6] Khalidi, Rashid (2011) Reflections on the Revolutions in Tunisia and Egypt, *Foreign Policy*. Available online at http://mideast.foreignpolicy.com/posts/2011/02/24/reflections_on_the_revolutions_i n_tunisia_and_egypt, accessed on 1 August 2011

[7] Ghosh, Bobby (2011) Rage, Rap and Revolution: Inside the Arab Youth Quake, *Time* Magazine. Available online at http://www.time.com/time/magazine/article/0,9171,2050022,00.html, accessed on 1 August 2011

[8] Khalidi, Rashid op cit

[9] Lippman, Walter (1922) *Public Opinion*, London: MacMillan. Available online at http://xroads.virginia.edu/~Hyper/lippman/header.html, accessed on 1 August 2011

Note on the author

Kevin Marsh is Director of OffspinMedia (www.offspinmedia.co.uk) and a host/facilitator at Coventry Conversations/BBC College of Journalism events. He was formerly Executive Editor of the BBC College of Journalism and Editor of *Today*. He produced investigations into the Brighton Bomb, the Cyprus Spy Trial, the Ponting Trial and is currently an executive producing a new investigation into the Nazi's Treblinka camp. His latest book, *Stumbling Upon the Truth*, about Lord Hutton, New Labour and the BBC, will be published by Biteback in September 2012.

The "Arab Spring": 1989 and All That?

David Hayward argues that it is misleading to lump all the extraordinary events occurring in countries such as Tunisia, Libya, Egypt, Syria, Yemen and Bahrain under one, simplifying title – the "Arab Spring". All of them are very distinct. As he concludes: "In contrast to the events which led to the fall of the Berlin Wall, there was no single overriding issue to fight against during the so-called 'Arab Spring'"

To watch, read and listen to the coverage of what is now universally known as the "Arab Spring", three things seemed to have become accepted facts in the reporting. Firstly, these were to be the first successful revolutions driven by social media. Secondly, "corrupt" governments and leaders of the Arab states were set to topple in a swift domino effect. The very nature of the phrase "Arab Spring" suggested this would be over in a very neat and contained period of time. And thirdly, what we were seeing in the Maghreb, North Africa and the Middle East, was the same as the collapse of communism in eastern Europe in 1989.

The issue of the social media revolution is being dealt with in other chapters of the book and at the time of writing (August 2011) the domino is yet to fall past Tunisia, Egypt and Libya. There is widespread unrest in Syria and unease throughout the rest of the region, but the speed of collapse inferred in late January and February 2011 has far from come true.

The issues I am going to explore in this chapter are the similarities, correlations and contrasts of the Arab Spring with the decline of communism in Warsaw Pact countries more than two decade previously.

Equating a Current Story with Events of the Past

It is always convenient, for both the journalist and audience, to equate a current story with events of the past. It's easier for the reader, listener and viewer to understand if you put it in this context. Look at the riots in the UK in the summer of 2011, they were like the riots of 1981, 2001 etc etc etc all over again.

However, reality can have a frustrating habit of getting in the way of this known and accepted trend. The social dynamic which caused the race riots in Brixton in 1981 has nothing to do with gangs of youths in 2011, looting in Salford, setting fire to furniture stores in Croydon and attacking Poundland in Leicester.

The same applies to 1989 and the Arab Spring. Tim Marshall, Sky's Foreign Affairs Editor, illustrates this fact of journalism in a blog he wrote on 17 March 2011:

> There's an old journalist joke about events which appear similar, it goes: "One, two….trend." Thus to some sections of the media did Tunisia and Egypt become a trend that would sweep the Arab world. The template for this "Arab Spring" was Europe 1989 and the domino effect. That appeared to make it easy to understand for Europeans. The problem was – it was the wrong analogy.[1]

But this comparison is so easy for journalists and politicians alike to make. As late as July 2011 the Russian President, Dmitry Medvedev, was likening the two. In a speech to Foreign Ambassadors at the Kremlin he stated the revolts in North Africa and the Middle East were of a historic character and could "pave the way for transformations similar to those taking place in Central Europe after the fall of the Berlin Wall".[2]

However, as Tim Marshall points out, the two are not the same. It is wrong to place the template of one series of events over another when, in reality, the context and circumstances are very different.

Gorbachev's *Perestroika*

The events in eastern Europe of 1989 became inevitable when Mikhail Gorbachev introduced *perestroika* and *glasnost*. The policies, which literally translate as openness and restructuring, spelt the end of Soviet control over countries behind the Iron Curtain. It meant that the suppression of the Hungarian Revolution in 1956 and the intervention such as the Prague Spring in 1968 would never happen again.

This was shown in the weeks which led to the fall of the Berlin Wall in November 1989. In a reported telephone call between Erich Honecker, the soon-to-be-deposed leader of the German Democratic Republic (East Germany) and Mikhail Gorbachev, Honecker was told in no uncertain terms that he could not rely on the support of Soviet troops to put down any protests against the state. By the time the Berlin Wall fell, the domino effect was well and truly underway. The end of communist rule in Poland was soon followed by Hungary, the Velvet Revolution in Czechoslovakia, East Germany and Romania.

The fall of President Nicolae Ceausescu in Romania, in December 1989, was to provoke the only truly violent uprising. In the final few days of the decade, more than a thousand people were killed. Violence began in the western Romanian city of Timisoara, sparked by the sacking of a priest, Laszlo Tokes, who had been critical of Ceausescu's government. It spread throughout the country to the cities of Sibiu and Arad, and the capital Bucharest.

Ceausescu and his wife, Elena, were arrested after dramatically fleeing Bucharest in a helicopter when a crowd he was addressing turned against him. They were executed on Christmas Day 1989. Ironically, the most violent revolution of 1989 also proved to be the one which saw the least change in senior members of the government. Ion Iliescu, the new President, and Petre Roman, the new Prime Minister, were both influential members of Ceausescu's ruling party.

The Factors Behind the 1989 Revolutions

It is naïve to say that all the revolutions in east Europe were caused by exactly the same issues, but strong factors in each were economic pressures and growing demand for a more open and free democratic society. Combine this with the new openness, communication and awareness of the life in the West and the end of communism in central and eastern Europe became a foregone conclusion. The issues of nationalism were to emerge later, especially in the states making up the Soviet Union and Yugoslavia. But in the late summer and autumn of 1989 the causes were similar. To put it simply, the revolutions whether violent or peaceful were all about overthrowing communism.

This was also made easier in many respects by the existence of established and structured opposition movements. Lech Walesa and the Solidarity movement in Poland, Vaclav Havel in Czechoslovakia and the emergence of leading reformers such as Imre Pozsgay in Hungary. Speaking to the BBC's then-Diplomatic Editor, the late Brian Hanrahan, in 2009, Pozsgay said:

> For a long time…I believed in communism. But from the early '80s I realised it was unreformable - and the only thing to do was to change that system…I came to the conclusion that I could do more for my country from the inside, in a position of power than as a marginalised opposition figure.[3]

In contrast to the events which led up to the fall of the Berlin Wall, there was no single overriding issue to fight against during the so-called "Arab Spring". The catalyst for what was to become an astonishing series of events came in the form of a street vendor from the provincial Tunisian town of Sidi Bouzid. Mohammed Bouazizi set himself on fire on 17 December 2010 in protest at local corruption – and died in a hospital near Tunis on 4 January 2011. In his suicidal act of protest, Bouazizi set in place a series of events which led to the fall of the President of Tunisia, Zine El Abibine Ben Ali. The so-called Jasmine Revolution was underway.

It is still very interesting to look at articles written at the time. On 28 December 2010, writing on the *Guardian* "Comments is Free" pages, Brian Whitaker, the former Middle East editor for the Guardian wrote of the similarities to the fall of Ceausescu 22 years before:

Watching events in Tunisia over the past few days, I have been increasingly reminded of an event in 1989: the fall of the Romanian dictator Nicolae Ceausescu. Is the Tunisian dictator, Zine El Abidine Ben Ali, about to meet a similar fate?[4]

Tunisian President Flies – and the Protest Multiply
Just over two week later, on 14 January 2011, Ben Ali fled to Saudi Arabia via Malta, ending a 24-year rule of the country. The protests over food prices, unemployment and the economy now began to spread through neighbouring countries in the Maghreb and further across North African and the Middle East.

Protests and demonstrations begin in Algeria at the start of the year. On 13 January, Mohsen Bouterfif set himself on fire in an apparent copycat suicide of Mohammed Bouazizi. He had failed to find himself a job or house. The economic pressure of the region was translating into action.

Three days later a man set himself on fire in Egypt, another suspected copycat action. At the end of January, the revolution in Egypt was in full swing. Tahrir Square in Cairo become the focus of the world as President Hosni Mubarak fought, as it turned out fruitlessly to hold on to power. He resigned on 11 February, leading to mass celebrations across the country.

By the end of January unrest was spreading to Bahrain, Jordan, Yemen, Palestine, Morocco and the Lebanon. Syria and Libya the two countries which at time of writing (August 2011) continue to dominate the coverage.

Libya has been the scene of a bitter civil war since February 2011 with Nato to all intents and purposes providing air support of the rebel forces. Syria continues to see mass protests throughout the country, with thousands of protestors killed in clashes with the security services.

2011: Not a Uniform Series of Revolutions
There is no doubt that the early events of the "Arab Spring" were sparked by genuine decent and opposition to the corrupt dictatorships, a real demand for change. But it is wrong to use this template across the whole region. This not a uniform series of revolutions against a common ill – as Tim Marshall goes on to argue in his March 2011 article:

In Tunisia there was a genuine uprising which appeared to have popular support across the country. The people succeeded in getting rid of the President and his kleptomaniac family when the army decided it was time for him to go. Now the country is being pulled in several directions. The democratic opposition parties are trying to organise in order to win elections, the military cares more about stability than anything else, and the newly legalised Islamists have seen the gap and are now trying to drive through it...

In Egypt, we have a situation where the military was in charge, and the military is still in charge. The army wanted Mubarak and his son, Gamal, out of the picture anyway. The uprising gave them the opportunity and they used it to good effect...What has happened in Libya gives many Arabs pause for thought. How far do they want to push this? Elsewhere, Morocco, Saudi Arabia, Jordan, Oman, the UAE [United Arab Emirates], Algeria and Syria do not seem to be dominoes about to fall. Yemen is, was, and will be a basket case. Bahrain is a Shia-Sunni struggle and a proxy war for the Saudis and Iranians.[5]

And these complexities have been evident in the make-up of the Libyan rebel forces – as highlighted in a BBC College of Journalism Seminar held on 24 August 2011 at BBC Television Centre.[6] Professor Fawaz Gerges, Director of the Middle East Centre at the London School of Economics, the BBC's International Development Correspondent, David Loyn, and BBC World Affairs Correspondent, Mark Doyle, had all been to Libya and had spent time with the opposition forces. They each described the different factions they encountered, regionally, culturally and economically. This is not one coordinated well established party fighting to take over power. Rather, it is a collaboration of many different groups, tribes and parties all fighting with the aim of overthrowing a dictatorship which has controlled the people of Libya for four decades.

Related in Action: Not the Cause
When you begin to look at each of the individual revolutions, uprisings, demonstrations and protest movements which make up the so-called "Arab Spring", the diversity amongst them is particularly striking. You can argue that a catalyst did spark a series of related events. But they were related in the action, not the cause. Egypt is not Tunisia, which in turn is not Bahrain. It is absolutely wrong to lump the revolutions in one neat

category. It can be argued that this was the case in eastern Europe in 1989 but it was not in the Middle East and North Africa in 2011.

It is the duty of any reporter, journalist and commentator covering the story to make this clear. The background and context of this story are hugely important to tell, especially if journalism is to considered the first draft of history. The rule of assuming "one, two – trend" needs to guarded against as does the habit of placing one neat historical context over another. The "Arab Spring" was not 1989 all over again. Rather, it was the "Arab Spring": a very different and in some ways far more complicated series of events.

Notes

[1] Tim Marshall, Sky News, Foreign Matters, What Arab Spring? 17 March 2011. Available online at http://blogs.news.sky.com/foreignmatters/Post:8a603f66-2227-4279-91e5-2af07b7690bd, accessed on 20 August 2011

[2] See http://eng.kremlin.ru/, accessed on 1 August 2011

[3] Hungary's role in the 1989 revolutions, BBC News, Brian Hanrahan, 9 May 2009. Available online at http://news.bbc.co.uk/1/hi/8036685.stm, accessed on 3 August 2011

[4] How a man setting fire to himself sparked an uprising in Tunisia, Brian Whitaker, *Guardian*, Comment is Free, 28 December 2010. Available online at http://www.guardian.co.uk/commentisfree/2010/dec/28/tunisia-ben-ali, accessed on 2 August

[5] Tim Marshall, Sky Foreign Matters, What Arab Spring? 17 March 2011. Available online at http://blogs.news.sky.com/foreignmatters/Post:8a603f66-2227-4279-91e5-2af07b7690bd, accessed on 1 August 2011

[6] What Now for Libya? BBC College of Journalism blog, David Hayward. 24 August 2011. http://www.bbc.co.uk/journalism/blog/2011/08/video-what-now-for-libya.shtml, accessed on 25 August 2011

Note on the author

David Hayward is head of the events for the BBC College of Journalism. He has been a BBC journalist for 16 years, working as a reporter, producer and editor in local and network radio, regional TV and for the World Service Trust. He lived and worked in eastern Europe in the late 1990s running projects in Romania, Bosnia, and Albania.

How the Media Marginalised the Economic Roots of the "Arab Spring"

The "Arab Spring" started with food riots in Tunisia. Kate Smith and Ben McConville ask if this narrative has been forgotten in the media reporting. Are the underlying causes of the "Arab Spring" being misunderstood and misinterpreted by the Western media?

If we understand food riots as purposeful and organised political actions but with an aim of relieving food scarcity and precipitating relief measures[1] rather than necessarily obtaining more political freedoms then it is clear that there is an economic claim at the heart of food riots: not only for food entitlement and better distribution but for social justice.[2,3] Using media and politics this chapter explores the underlying reasons for the way media narratives unfolded in the "Arab Spring".

With many of the causes of food crises emanating from international situations and practices in trade and finance, agriculture and the environment, then it can also be argued that food riots are effectively repeated claims for global food security, made on a local level. In each case they are protests against hunger and a call for action. The degrading food security situation is a global political issue. As the most salient and deadly of the 2011 food riots so far, heightened perceptions of injustice over food rights, the recourse to violence and the state-sanctioned violent response are manifest in the Tunisian violence. It offers an opportunity not only for contemporary analysis of the causes and triggers for an unfolding international situation but asks if the media coverage has accurately reflected this.

As the "Arab Spring" moved from Tunisia through North Africa and into Syria the narrative trajectory of the story and agenda moved from acts of civil disobedience to acts with wider political consequences. Have the Western media misrepresented events or did the political agenda change? If misrepresented, is this due to normative newsroom behaviour or political agendas in the West?

News, Stories and Media Narratives

The detachment of news narratives from reality has been explored by a number of scholars. As Golding and Elliott state,[4] news stories are, as the term suggests, "stories as well as news". In the UK and the US the dominant type of journalism is the Anglo-American or liberal model which is characterised by a predetermined set of norms or world view in which journalists seek to reconcile news narratives. This liberal world view influences the viewing, gathering, interpreting and disseminating news within the context of democracy, freedom of expression and support for market economies. The mainstream media in both the UK and US reported the "Arab Spring" in the context of the Anglo-American model and so as the narratives of the events unfolded, the rioters or rebels and their governments were characterised by the Western media within a framework of oppressed and oppressor in a struggle for political power that spread through the region. Perhaps this compulsion to explain the "Arab Spring" within the terms of liberal Western media is one of the reasons why food security was not widely prevalent in the UK and US coverage. What if the UK and US media viewed the "Arab Spring" through another lens? The journalist and writer Philip Seib offered an alternative to the Anglo-American model in the form of "global journalism" which asserts the need for reporters to understand how the interconnected or "shared commonalities" of different countries affect one another in terms of politics, economics, social and ecological practices.[5] In the face of global changes Seib suggests that correspondents in the field should "master" new information, understand the substance of new issues and be fearless in acquiring new sources. In other words, if we apply Seib to the "Arab Spring", journalists on the ground opted for information and sources, and therefore a narrative, which they knew and understood and may have avoided using facts and sources of which they were unfamiliar. These sources could have included NGOs, aid agencies, activists and rebel or government officials who may have understood the Tunisian rebellion, for example, in terms of food security.

For Guy Berger global journalism is not only about the professional journalist becoming savvy about the world beyond the confines of Anglo-American introspection. In assessing the possibilities brought by the rise of online media Berger identifies "a new species of unintentional foreign correspondents" in the shape of local reporters whose work is accessed on the web.[6] Within the context of hyperlocalism the local can become global as outputs are disseminated on the internet. However, the idea of a leap from local to international reporting perhaps continues to make assumptions about press freedom and global or universal cultural understanding of interpreting and transmitting ideas. In countries of the antipodes, North America and Europe the phenomenon of the local report going global may be possible, but it may not apply to all countries. Some rebels and brave bystanders within each uprising of the "Arab Spring" became "citizen journalists" by using social media to transmit images and actions around the world, including Tweets and images posted on sites such as YouTube. However, in Libya for example, the state controlled media continued to broadcast pro-Gadaffi propaganda even after the fall of Tripoli. While in state hands the Libyan media could not perform the functions of hyperlocal to global journalism. So, some of the challenges around reporting in the "Arab Spring" may revolve around structural and organisational issues.

In the transmission model vs. ritual model of news making, Carey states that ritual is about "the maintenance of society in time; not the act of imparting information but the representation of shared beliefs" while transmission is about delivery "truth" or facts.[7] Carey says that under the ritual model the news becomes not information, but drama. However, the food riots were dramatic *per se*, so the ritual theory cannot account for how the "Arab Spring" was reported. The media chose to produce a narrative around civil unrest due to lack of grain or food.

Schlesinger, in his case study of the BBC, demonstrated the contradictory nature of how many Western media organisations worked.[8] He explored how ritual or the processes of news gathering and dissemination were constructed via cultural and working practices and to some degree predetermined despite the BBC's official position of being neutral and factual. This construction imposed meaning on news not only by way of selection "but also their angling and mode of presentation".[9]

The Routinisation of News

This routinisation of news means that judgment about what is newsworthy are based on value judgments around meaning, timing and cost. A major variable that has changed since Schlesinger's assessment of the BBC is the cost of reporting from areas of conflict. Digital technology means that the need for a costly full crew is not always necessary. In fast-moving news stories international journalists now use video links, mobile telephones and social media to convey stories. As rebels converged on Green Square in Tripoli in August 2011, Sky News transmitted poor quality mobile telephone pictures based on the journalistic maxim that if it is the best picture available, it is the best picture.

Nevertheless, ease of access is also a factor associated with cost. The post-World War II period had witnessed a significant decline in the number of foreign correspondents active in the field, but changes in technology and cost constraints had also led to new practices in the field for international journalists.[10] While the post 9/11 period led to a resurgence in the status and need for foreign correspondents, the practices of the international journalist had changed in line with technological changes such as the internet, satellite links and social media. From the wars in Iraq and Afghanistan, a new breed of star conflict reporters had emerged, whose presence seemed to grade the severity of the conflict they were covering.

Christine Amanpour, of CNN, or John Simpson and Orla Guerin of the BBC, were highly mobile and able war reporters who became symbolic markers of the seriousness of conflicts for the news organisations they worked for. The reporters' coverage of conflict was often characterised by first person reportage and to-camera reports. On occasion they became part of the story, such as Simpson's entry into Kabul at the falling of the Taliban regime. So, their very presence would signal the gravity of the conflict. However, at the time of the uprising in Tunisia the typical foreign correspondent was sent into a country of which they knew little and were made to make "instant assessments" and quick reports about what was going on without full knowledge of the background, history or culture of the place being reported upon.[11] A new vocabulary and set of values around conflict had emerged including phrases such as "our boys" and the post-9/11 use of "rogue states" and "terrorist threat". The journalists had arrived in North Africa for what would become the "Arab Spring" with a value set around the post-9/11 narrative of the "Axis of Evil" and US President George Bush Sr's "New World Order".[12]

"Cheerleader Journalism" Emerges

Some American networks such as Fox News and some British newspapers such as the *Sun* and the *Daily Mail* were now practising "patriotic journalism" or cheerleader journalism. To lesser and varying degrees other, but not all, Western media fell into line with this. Indeed, the British tabloid the *Mirror*, took an anti-war stance in the run up to the invasion of Iraq, but performed a volte face and fell into line with the rest of the media when it realised it was losing circulation because of its position. Journalists covering the "Arab Spring" now had a set of values, or frames, around the meaning and outcomes of conflict and of religious and social issues within Arab countries. As there was no direct military intervention in most of the conflicts, except Nato air strikes in Libya, the journalists took on the role of bystander rather than cheerleader in the "Arab Spring" conflicts.

Nevertheless, they made comparisons with Iraq and Afghanistan in terms of al-Qaeda threats, terrorism, counterinsurgency and a lack of civil society, based on recent experiences, sometimes personal experiences, in the wars in Afghanistan and Iraq. They derived questions around failed states, political vacuums, tribal conflict, religious fundamentalism and international terrorism. For example, when Tunisian president Zine al-Abidine Ben Ali fled to Saudi Arabia in January 2011 reports from the BBC (Tunisia: Ex-President Ben Ali Flees to Saudi Arabia) while acknowledging the economic issues at the heart of the revolt, concentrated on "abandoning power" and focused on the security situation in the capital Tunis as Prime Minister Mohammed Ghannouchi took control. The AFP news agency also reported on the security situation mentioning "looting in several suburbs" of Tunis in reports on 15 January. With the collapse of the Mubarak regime in Egypt, journalists on the ground and in newsrooms drew comparisons with the immediate era after Saddam Hussein in Iraq or the Taliban in Afghanistan were removed from power. Sometimes drawing on their own experiences of reporting Afghanistan and Iraq, journalists speculated on the role of the Egyptian army and police in maintaining law and order and the risk of allowing foreign insurgents into the country to direct dissent along extremist lines. Similarly in Libya, soon after the fall of Tripoli journalists speculated on the possibility of internecine or sectarian conflict within the country while drawing parallels with Iraq. On 31 August a BBC report warned of the potentially unstable situation as rebels delivered an ultimatum to Gaddafi loyalists in Sirte. Noting the large number of weapons circulating in the country, one report emphasised that the rebels were not a unified force and may even turn on each other. So, fears of social and political unrest became the narratives of the "Arab Spring" because the journalists sought meaning from the most recent experience of tumult within other countries even though the "Arab Spring" was brought about by civil and political unrest, rather than foreign intervention. Fallen regimes were often characterised as kleptocracies. Reports looked at the Ben Ali regimes in terms of vanished riches, including one from the BBC (Tracking down the Ben ali and Trabelsi fortune – 31 January 2011) and also reports by various media in Gaddafi's luxury jet liner and numerous houses in and around Tripoli (Inside Col Gaddafi's luxury airplane – rebels give tour of captured luxury airplane, *Daily Telegraph*, 28 August 2011).

Newsroom practice is also a determinant of the narrative deployed by news media and so the issue of conformity and professional behaviour in the newsroom should also be considered. The world view of the journalists and the commissioning editors become entwined in the drive to get published or broadcast. Shared reality in the newsroom, according to Donsbach has "crucial functions in the building and maintaining of stereotypes and for the socialisation of individuals. Therefore 'truth' is not reached in every instance, but it is 'the best the individual can get in order to validate his/her own perception of reality".[13] This is manifest in pack journalism in which journalists reporting on a story confirm facts and quotes between each other before contacting the news desk. It leads to the homogeneity of news in terms of newsgathering and outputs. The need to conform and the imperative to not miss any part of the story clouds the objective need to report the story as seen.

Add to this the inherent dangers of reporting from a conflict zone and the reasons why journalists would want to physically work together, finding strength in numbers, can be seen. This need to conform extends beyond the journalist on the ground. Executives constantly compare and evaluate outputs and processes with competitors. Despite the obvious rivalries between reporters and news organisations, they are competing for the same shared reality or for the same information or interpretation. The question most likely on the lips of an executive is "Why did you miss?" this aspect of a story rather than "Why did you not find something different from your competitors?"

Framing the "Arab Spring"

Donsbach says the journalist's predisposition to certain stories can affect their judgment on the newsworthiness of a controversial story.[14] Entman points out that framing will lead to the selection of a "perceived reality" and make it more salient in ways which promote a particular problem definition, interpretation or evaluation.[15] Couple this with the perception of a shared reality then the news production processes become about conformity to established views of what is important, what is the stereotype and what is the narrative within a story. Meikle defines framing of the news as "newspaper narratives define reality through their plot structures. News images define reality by selecting and framing".[16] This selection is not only of which images to or ideas to choose from, but a selection of which ones count in the first place. So the value judgments become about much more than a justification of cost, they become about the meaning and value of stories.

Cultural and religious stereotyping may also have played a part in the framing of the news out of Tunisia, Egypt, Syria and Libya. Post 9/11 coverage of Islamic countries in some Western media tended to focus on a "menacing image of Islam", according to Vultee.[17] Since 9/11, Ibrahim stated, Muslims had been "mostly framed" as "fanatic, irrational, American-hating and violent oppressors of women' by the US network news channels".[18] With the "Arab Spring" came a new narrative about Islam, one of the oppressed shaking off the oppressor. But the Western media may have reverted to pre-9/11 stereotypes, based on a series of crises such as the OPEC oil crisis and the Iranian revolution which characterised the "Arab Spring" as a moment of instability as demonstrated by its impact on crude oil prices and the potential for the 'return of Islam'.[19] The National Transitional Council's commander in

Tripoli, Abdel Hakim Belhadj, was characterised as an Islamic fundamentalist for his role in anti-Gaddafi movement the Libyan Islamic Fighting Group and alleged contacts with al-Qaeda and Osama Bin Laden.

Couple these stereotypes with the perceived technical imperative to keep the narrative simple and the ability to create challenging journalism starts to diminish. The television routine of keeping questions simple or the written routine of the inverted pyramid style of journalism means the consumer need only consume the essence of a story, say the top three paragraphs or headlines, but this may discourage the consumer from reading in depth analysis and coverage of a major story. Furthermore, while the rate of access to technology can often be overstated, social media, news apps, smart phones and even bite-sized news TV and radio bulletins can encourage this style of top line news to be created and consumed.

Studies suggest that the use of blogs, wikis and other forms of citizen journalism means the incessantly active audience is constantly moving, picking up stories and passing them on, then dropping interest in them as they move on to the next click.[20] In the case of the Arab Spring, this may have manifested itself in the consumer only knowing that there was civil unrest in these countries and not the underlying causes, or reasons for the unrest. The phrase "Arab Spring" has become shorthand for a more complex international situations and may well be a mirage in the desert.

Framing, according to Gitlin is "a way to organise the world both for journalists who report it and, in some important degree, for us who rely on their reports".[21] This might suggest the narrative in coverage of the "Arab Spring" had moved to suit a world view. As Zelizer points out, framing is often viewed by scholars in "conjunction with scholarship on agenda setting and priming, framing research focused on story presentation as a way of explaining the news".[22] Once civil unrest started to spread out of Tunisia and into Egypt and other Arab states the agenda began to move and to focus on the unrest and its geopolitical consequences. For example, the media focused on the implications of unrest and potential regime change within each country in terms of its meaning to the region and how that might impact on world politics. As Gitlin noted of framing, "news concerns the *event*, not the underlying condition; the *person*, not the group, *conflict*, not consensus; the fact that '*advances the story*', not the one that explains it".[23] Implicit in the idea of advancement is the idea that stories have velocity, in other words they must move on in order to be considered new news.

Drawing on the experiences of Iraq and Afghanistan, Western news outlets focused on a call for democracy and a warning about spreading Islamic fundamentalism as regimes fell in the "Arab Spring". According to Entman, "to frame is to select some aspects of a perceived reality and make them more salient".[24] So, in terms of coverage of the revolts the underlying themes may have become lost in the attempt to make the consequences more salient. While the theories of framing drew upon tools such as language and visual images, McCombs et al also point out that framing performed "a second level agenda setting in linking salient characteristics of journalistic stories with the audiences' interpretations of them".[25]

Was the complex truth about the food riots and growing global food crisis so unpalatable that the media had decided to move the narrative on to the political consequences of the riots and its impact on geopolitics and instability in the nations? Was it an easier story to tell about the undoing of despots and civil unrest in terms of a fight between good and evil against a backdrop of the threat of extremist infiltration on the ground in these countries? When other questions about global resources, consumption and responsibilities could be ignored?

Political economists such as Mattelart take an international perspective on media production, which includes the exchange of cultural goods and flow of information.[26] They posited that flows of information driven by international news agencies – in line with music, film, TV and other cultural outputs – are "strongly influenced" by American mores, rationale, interests and standards. According to Guyot, they draw on Latin America's desire for cultural independence from the cultural hegemony of American or Anglo-American sensibilities.[27] Meanwhile, the decade since the 9/11 attacks had been characterised by the rise of blogging and social media. Guyot points out that in many Western countries including Italy, France and the UK, there has been a concentration of media in the hands of fewer and fewer owners. The personal pressure on the journalist in an environment of fierce competition, short term contracts and a lack of job security drives media professionals "to self-censorship, shallow investigation and infotainment".[28] So, on a personal basis the individual journalist on the ground can be self-censoring. He or she is producing the narrative that will stick within the wider narratives, contexts and understanding of owners and editors. They know what "works" and what does not work and are rarely able to convince superiors otherwise.

Conclusion

In terms of the "Arab Spring" the journalists on the ground, while aware of the causes of the uprising in Tunisia, may have self-censored and decided to go with the narrative of the riots being political rather than economic. A simplified narrative which framed it as good vs. evil or tyranny vs. liberation rather than a more complicated idea about globalisation, demographic time bomb and the interconnectedness of the struggle over scarce and diminishing resources. This latter narrative might ask too many questions about consumption in the West and its impact on others around the globe. In this case the political economy of the reporting of the "Arab Spring" may not have been about direct instruction to ignore the causes, more the rituals and self-censorship of newsroom cultures.

As Kevin Williams states: "The motif within which the world is reported is shaped by news values and practices rooted in the cultural understandings journalists and their audiences bring to the part of the world being reported."[29] In this sense the journalist is self censoring not only in terms of his/her job, or because of the constraints of reporting, but also because of the perceived tolerance of the audience. There is an inherent understanding by journalists in the Anglo-American tradition of what interests the audience and what reinforces their prejudices about a country, race, religion or economic or political situation.

Notes

[1] Berazneva, J. and Lee, D. (2011) Explaining the African Food Riots of 2007-2008: An empirical analysis, CSAE Annual Conference, Oxford

[2] Sen, A. (1981) *Poverty. and Famines: An. Essay on Entitlement and. Deprivation*, Clarendon Press: Oxford

[3] Walton, J. and Seddon, D. (1994) *Free Markets and Food Riots: The Politics of Global Adjustment*, Oxford: Blackwell

[4] Golding, P. and Elliott, P. (1979) *Making the News*, London: Longman p. 115

[5] Seib, P. (2002) *The Global Journalist: News and Conscience in a World of Conflict*, Lanahm MD: Rowman & Littlefield

[6] Berger, G. (2009) 'How the internet impacts on international news: exploring paradoxes of the most global medium in a time of "hyperlocalism"'. *The International Communication Gazette*, Vol. 71, No. 5 p. 366

[7] Carey, J. (1989) *Communication as Culture*, London: Unwin Hyman p. 18

[8] Schlesinger, P. (1987) *Putting Reality Together: BBC News*, London: Taylor and Francis p. 135. This study is somewhat dated but its conclusions are still relevant for media analysts today

[9] ibid p. 135

[10] Williams, K. (2011) *International Journalism*, London: Sage p. 5

[11] Harrison, P. and Palmer, R. (1986) *News Out of Africa*. London: Hilary Shipman. p. 76, cited in Williams, K. (2011) *International Journalism*, London: Sage p. 5

[12] ibid: 8

[13] Donsbach, W. Loffelholz, M. and Weaver, D. (eds) (2008) *Global Journalism Research: Theories, Methods, Findings, Future*, Oxford: Blackwell Publishing p. 67

[14] ibid: 72

[15] Entman, R. (1993) Framing: Towards Clarification of a Fractured Paradigm, *Journal of Communication*, Vol. 43, No. 3 1 pp 51-58 p. 52

[16] Meikle, G. (2009) *Interpreting News*, Basingstoke, Palgrave MacMillan p. 68

[17] Vultee, F. (2009) Jump back Jack, Mohammed's here: Fox News and the construction of Islamic peril, *Journalism Studies*, Vol. 10, No. 5 pp 623-638

[18] Ibrahim, D. (2010) The framing of Islam on network news following the September 11 attacks, *International Communication Gazette*, Vol. 72, No. 1 pp 111-125

[19] Said, E. (1981) *Covering Islam: How the Media and Experts Determine How We See the World*, London: Routledge & Kegan Paul, cited in Williams, K. (2011) *International Journalism*, London: Sage p. 154

[20] Singer, J. Journalism Research in the United States, Loffelholz, M. and Weaver, D. (eds) (2008) *Global Journalism Research: Theories, Methods, Findings, Future*, Oxford, Blackwell Publishing p. 152

[21] Gitlin, T. (1980) *The Whole World is Watching*, Berkeley: University of California Press p. 7

[22] Zelizer, B. (2004) *Taking Journalism Seriously*, London: Sage p. 141

[23] Gitlin, T. (1980) p. 28

[24] Entman, R. (1993) op cit: 52

[25] Zelizer, B. op cit: 141 McCombs, M., Shaw, D. and Weaver, D. (eds) (1997) *Communication and Democracy: Exploring the Intellectual Frontiers in Agenda-Setting Theory*, Mahwah, NJ: Lawrence Erlbaum

[26] Mattelart, A. (1994) *Mapping World Communication: War, Progress and Culture*, Minneapolis: University of Minneapolis Press

[27] Guyot, J. (2009) Political-economic factors shaping news culture, Preston, P. (ed.) *Making the News: Journalism and news cultures in Europe*, London: Routledge p. 96

[28] ibid: 105

[29] Williams, K. op cit: 113

Notes on the authors

Kate Smith is Programme Leader of the BA Journalism at Edinburgh Napier University and is a working journalist. Ben McConville is a Principal Lecturer in Journalism at Northumbria University. He is a regular contributor to the Associated Press news agency, former New York correspondent for the *Scotsman* and former Foreign Editor of *Scotland on Sunday*.

Covering the "Arab Spring": Oriental Revolutionaries in the Mainstream Western Media

Alexander Kazamias argues that Edward Said's critique of the "Orientalist" bias of dominant Western representations of Arab cultures is still highly relevant when examining the reporting of the recent uprisings

In 1916, T. E. Lawrence travelled to the Hijjaz to investigate the causes of an unexpected Arab rebellion. In his account of the journey, Lawrence explains how the purpose of his visit increasingly became to "find the yet unknown master-spirit of the affair", a person he instantly recognised as soon as he met Feisal Hussein (later to become one of the organisers of the Arab revolt against the Ottoman Empire and King of Iraq 1921-1933): "I felt at first glance that this was the man I had come to Arabia to seek – the leader who would bring the Arab revolt to full glory," he wrote.[1]

Nearly a century later, a much greater and more remarkable uprising has swept across the Middle East causing thousands of Western journalists to travel to the region to report on it. Yet almost nowhere in the ceaseless and jam-packed coverage of what they called the "Arab Spring" was there a place for any of its young radical leaders. Of course, much has been said about Mohamed Bouazizi, the 26-year-old Tunisian itinerant vendor who started the Tunisian Revolution when he immolated himself in front of Sidi Bouzid town hall on 17 December 2010. However, Bouazizi's story is not so much about the underground activity that triggered the Jasmine Revolution as about the desperate state of Tunisian youth under Ben Ali's autocratic rule. As for the hundreds of Arab leaders who played a decisive role in making of the "Arab Spring" happen, there is hardly a name or a face for Western audiences to remember. After months of incessant reporting, these figures are still unknown to most people in the Western world.

The Relevance of Postcolonial Criticism

In his groundbreaking study, *Orientalism* (1978), the Palestinian scholar Edward Said showed how colonial officials such as T. E. Lawrence, despite their admiration for the Orient, still thought about its people as essentially primitive, inferior and unfit for self-government.[2] In a sequel to the book, *Covering Islam* (1981), Said broadened the scope of his argument to suggest that old colonial prejudices extended into the postcolonial era, where they continue to play a dominant role, particularly in contemporary portrayals of Islamic societies by the US media. For some critics, such as the broadcaster and former editor of the *New Statesman*, Anthony Howard, the central thesis of *Orientalism* might be acceptable, but the contention that in the 1980s the US media still maintained the same colonial bias in its portrayal of Middle Eastern people was seen as pushing the argument too far.[3] Still, in the revised edition of the book in 1997, Said not only stood by his original analysis, but went on to say that "a serious deterioration in the situation [he] described in the original edition of *Covering Islam*" had taken place.[4]

What I intend to show in this chapter is that in 2011, much of the reporting on the so-called "Arab Spring" across the mainstream Western media continues to rely heavily on Orientalist prejudices and symbols in the way analysed by Said in *Covering Islam*. Especially pronounced in this regard is the extensive use of stereotypes portraying the Arabs as "ignorant of self-government" – a notion deployed to justify their colonisation during the nineteenth century[5] – but also as incapable of independent thought and modernising without the help of Western technology and guidance.

Of course, there are striking disparities between the "positive" news coming out of the Middle East today and the "negative" stories about the region which, as Said's analysis revealed, prevailed in the Western media until the eve of the "Arab Spring".

In place of the old headlines about "Islamic terrorism", Shiite "jihadism", Iraqi WMDs and Saudi public executions, the main news story about the region in 2011 is the victory of "democracy" and "freedom".

Nevertheless, stereotypical portrayal is less about the story one tells and more about the assumptions hidden in its narration. Even colonial rulers often told good stories about their subjects. Lord Cromer, for example, admired Sheikh Mohamed Abdu, a man who led the revivalist Islamist movement in the late nineteenth century, but this did not make the British Proconsul any less Orientalist in his portrayal of the Egyptian scholar's views.[6]

Consequently, in getting a significantly better press after the recent uprisings, what changed in the dominant Western representation of the Arabs is mainly confined to its form. This is precisely the shift which the recently overused (and often misused) media sound bite about the alleged return of "Arab dignity"[7] actually seeks to achieve: to reconstruct the image of the Arab after the revolutions of 2010-2011 from that of an undignified religious fanatic and supporter of terrorism to that of an "honourable" and "modernising" oriental. In either case, however, the fundamental stereotypes remain. Even with their dignity regained, the Arabs are still considered to be incapable of independent thinking and unable to progress without the support of the West.

Taught by Gene Sharp
Five days after Hosni Mubarak's removal from power, an article by Sheryl Stolberg in *The New York Times* claimed that a retired US academic named Gene Sharp was the main intellectual force behind the Egyptian Revolution.[8] Sharp is the author of numerous books on nonviolent resistance, including the widely translated *From Dictatorship to Democracy* (1993). According to the article, some of the leaders of Egypt's "6 April Movement" had read Sharp's *198 Methods of Nonviolent Action*, and one blogger, Dalia Ziada, discussed it in her workshops, which were also attended by Tunisian trainees. On the basis of this evidence, Stolberg

titled her article "Shy U.S. Intellectual Created Playbook Used in a Revolution" and went on to make the exaggerated claim that Sharp was the mastermind of the Egyptian revolution.

Interestingly, the headline also stresses that Sharp is a "shy" person. Emphasis on this character attribute, in this particular context, carries profound implications. In an earlier radio interview, which Stolberg quotes in her article, the retired US academic had refused to take credit for the Egyptian revolution saying "the people of Egypt did that – not me". In fact, Sharp has repeatedly stated that he did "not feel responsible" for what had happened in Egypt.[9] But in calling him "shy", Stolberg's report subtly implies that, because of his humility, his words must be understood as meaning the opposite of what they said. What she was telling us, in effect, was to read Sharp's statement as saying: "I did that – not the people of Egypt."

Within less than a week, the Gene Sharp story had made the headlines of other leading Western media, such as CNN, the *Week* magazine, the BBC and the Canadian *Now* magazine, while the journalist Ruaridh Arrow began to direct a documentary film titled *Gene Sharp – How to Start a Revolution*.[10] Meanwhile, newspapers such as the *Boston Globe*, without citing further evidence, ran editorials which claimed that, besides Egypt, Sharp had also inspired the revolution in Tunisia. From the article's headline, however, one was led to conclude that the man's influence was certainly much greater. "Sharp: The Man Who Changed the World," it said![11]

Egyptian Objections do not Matter

What is particularly worrying, of course, is that at no stage throughout this hype did any mainstream American, British or Canadian journalist seriously question the strikingly thin evidence on which such cosmic generalisations were based. With the same range of sources used to produce Stolberg's report, anyone could easily start attributing the Egyptian and Tunisian revolutions to a host of other writers with arguably greater influence among young Arab revolutionaries, such as Trotsky, Lenin, Chris Harman, Sayyid Qutb or Ayatollah Khomeini. More shocking, however, is the ongoing pretence that the Gene Sharp story has not been subjected to widespread criticism across the Arab world. Stolberg's article is probably the only one that mentions the objections of a Lebanese writer, but in typically Orientalist fashion, these were presented as the solitary view of an obsessed fanatic: "Not everyone is impressed. As'ad Abu Khalil, a Lebanese political scientist and founder of the Angry Arab News Service blog, was outraged by a passing mention of Mr. Sharp."[12]

What was not and probably never will be reported by the mainstream Western media is that leading Egyptian activists, such as Hossam El-Hamalawi, As'ad Abu Khalil and others have publicly stated that they had never heard of the American professor's name until *The New York Times* article mentioned it. As Hamalawi writes in his blog, for him and other Egyptian revolutionaries, the Palestinian activists were "the major source of inspiration, not Gene Sharp, whose name I first heard in my life only in February after we toppled Mubarak…and whom the clueless *NYT* moronically gives credit for our uprising".[13]

On 15 April, Hamalawi and Hana Selim decided to voice their objections on a wider scale and set up a Twitter hashtag which they satirically titled "Gene Sharp taught me". Among the numerous tweets they received, there was one which said "GeneSharpTaughtMe that backward brown & black people need the permission of white man to revolt against his puppets", while another remarked: "I hope the *NYTimes* is paying attention to the #GeneSharpTaughtMe hashtag".[14] Although no leading Western media ever paid attention to the hashtag, a professor at the American University in Cairo, Rabab El-Mahdi, was quick to analyse the Gene Sharp saga as part of an emerging Western grand narrative aiming to "Orientalise" the Egyptian revolution.[15]

Led by Mark Zuckerberg

An equally important element of this narrative is the ongoing dissemination of the myth about the essentially technological character of the Arab revolutions. The subversive role of online social networks had been originally discussed during the Moldovan and Iranian protests of 2009 and the coining of the terms "Facebook" and "Twitter revolution" dates back to these and not to the Arab uprisings. However, with the Tunisian revolution, what had been up to that point an intellectual debate about the possibilities and limits of cyber-utopianism, suddenly turned into a discourse with clear Orientalist connotations. For, unlike Moldova and Iran, Tunisia was a successful revolution and this raised new questions about who should take the credit for its success.

To resolve this issue, an article by Roger Cohen in *The New York Times* on 24 January 2011 argued that Tunisia was "perhaps the world's first revolution without a leader. Or rather, its leader was far away: Mark Zuckerberg, the founder of Facebook". In an even more shocking statement, the article went on to describe the Tunisians who faced the bullets of Ben Ali's security police with their defenceless bodies as a mere "vehicle" of the online network – a remarkable confusion of humans and machines. "Its vehicle [i.e. of Facebook] was the youth of Tunisia, able to use Facebook for instant communication and cyber-inspire their parents," it said.[16] These views were mainly criticised at the time for their crude technological determinism, by both critics who were friendly to Cohen, such as *Guardian* columnist Timothy Garton Ash, and by others, like myself, who clearly saw them as insulting to the young revolutionaries who led the Arab uprisings.[17]

A Leading Dissident Without a Name

What is more remarkable, however, is that when Cohen wrote that the Tunisian youth were a "vehicle", he was not sitting in a quiet New York office battling with abstract ideas. His report was written from Tunisia and, as one would expect, it claimed to be providing first-hand information gathered from conversations with local people. Yet, one wonders how many Tunisians could have possibly told Cohen that their revolution was "without a leader". His article, moreover, mentions "the new youth minister, a 33-year-old former dissident blogger [who] tweets from cabinet meetings", but this individual is neither given a name nor a face. For Cohen, the striking image of a shorn Slim Amamou as he was accepting his cabinet post shortly after his release from prison did not suffice to suggest that, perhaps, there stood one of the revolution's leading figures. Amamou was important only insofar as he was able to carry his laptop and link the Tunisian cabinet to Twitter.

For all his colonial prejudices, T. E. Lawrence would have certainly been impressed by Amamou and would have tried to paint his profile through an inspired, albeit arrogant description. In Roger Cohen's journalism, however, things are somewhat different. There is an interesting passage in Said's *Orientalism* which contrasts the European stereotype of the Arab in the colonial era as a "faintly outlined camel-riding nomad" with his post-Second World War image in the United States as "a shadow that dogs the Jew".[18] If we compare the portrayal of Arab leaders in T. E. Lawrence's account of the 1916-18 revolt with their dominant representation in the

Western media during the "Arab Spring" of 2010-2011, we are bound to conclude that, unfortunately, Said's critique has not yet lost any of its relevance.

Notes

[1] T.E. Lawrence, *Seven Pillars of Wisdom – A triumph*, London: Jonathan Cape, 1942 pp 68, 92

[2] Edward W. Said, *Orientalism: Western Conceptions of the Orient*, London: Penguin, revised edition, 1995 p. 228

[3] Anthony Howard, Reporters and the Critic. Review of Edward W. Said, *Covering Islam*, *New York Times*, 26 July 1981 p. 7

[4] Edward W. Said, *Covering Islam: How the Media and the Experts Determine How we See the Rest of the World*, revised edition, London: Vintage, 1997 p. .xxvi

[5] Edward W. Said, *Orientalism*, op cit p. 228

[6] Evelyn Baring (Earl of Cromer), *Modern Egypt*, London: Macmillan, 1908, Vol. 2 pp 179-180

[7] Among others, Roger Hardy has written after the Tunisian revolution that "there is a dignity deficit" throughout the Middle East; see Could other Arab countries follow Tunisia's example?' BBC, 15 January 2011. Available online at http://www.bbc.co.uk/news/world-africa-12198039, accessed on 1 September 2011

[8] Sheryl Gay Stolberg, Shy U.S. Intellectual Created Playbook Used in a Revolution, *New York Times*, 16 February 2011

[9] Jay Kernis, Gene Sharp: How to Overthrow a Tyrant, *CNN*, 17 February 2011. Available online at http://inthearena.blogs.cnn.com/2011/02/17/gene-sharp-how-to-overthrow-a-tyrant/, accessed on 1 September 2011

[10] ibid.; David Cairns, The 83-year-old Academic who Inspired the Egyptians: Gene Sharp's how-to guide on Non-violent Revolution Helped Boot out Mubarak, the *Week*, 20 February 2011; Ellie Kirzner, Revolution in 198 steps, *Now Magazine*, 17-24 February 2011; BBC Radio 4, Gene Sharp: The US scholar who inspires Middle East uprisings, 20 February 2011. Available online at http://www.bbc.co.uk/news/world-us-canada-12518436., accessed on 1 September 2011

[11] Ruaridh Arrow, Gene Sharp: Author of the Nonviolent Revolution Rulebook, BBC, 21 February 2011. Available online at http://www.bbc.co.uk/news/world-middle-east-12522848, accessed on 1 September 2011; Editorial, Sharp: The Man who Changed the World, *Boston Globe*, 22 February 2011

[12] Sheryl Gay Stolberg op cit

[13] Hossam El-Hamalawi, Nabil Fahmy: This Revolution Actually Serves Israel as well, *arabawi*, 17 April 2011. Available online at http://www.arabawy.org/2011/04/17/fm-nabil-fahmy-this-revolution-actually-serves-israel-as-well, accessed on 1 September 2011

[14] Tarek Amr, Egypt: Gene Sharp Taught us How to Revolt, *Global Voices*, 15 April 2011. Available online at http://globalvoicesonline.org/2011/04/15/egypt-gene-sharp-taught-us-how-to-revolt/, accessed on 1 September 2011

[15] Rabab El-Mahdi, Orientalising the Egyptian Revolution, *Jadaliyya*, 11 April 2011

[16] Roger Cohen, Facebook and Arab Dignity, *New York Times/International Herald Tribune*, 24 January 2011

[17] Timothy Garton Ash, Not 1989. Not 1789. But Egyptians can learn from other revolutions, *Guardian*, 9 February 2011; Alexander Kazamias, The Anger Revolutions in

the Middle East: An Answer to Decades of Failed Reform, *Journal of Balkan and Near Eastern Studies*, Vol. 13, No. 2 June 2011 pp 146-148

[18] Edward W. Said, *Orientalism*, op.cit pp 285-286

Note on the author

Dr Alexander Kazamias is Senior Lecturer in Politics at Coventry University. He has written several articles and book chapters on the modern history of Egypt, the politics of Greece and Greek-Turkish relations. He is author of The "Anger Revolutions" in the Middle East: An Answer to Decades of Failed Reform, *Journal of Balkan and Near Eastern Studies*, Vol. 13, No. 2, June 2011. He is currently Visiting Research Fellow at the Centre for the Study of the Arab World (CASAW), University of Edinburgh.

Section 3: Al Jazeera: The Voice of the Arab Street?

John Mair

Much more important and significant in the "Arab Spring" than any Twitter or Facebook feed was the satellite feed from the eleven Arab television news stations. One only has to see the forest of dishes on the rooftops of Tunis or Cairo to see their potency. None is of more importance than the Al Jazeera broadcasting from Doha in Arabic since 1996 and from London and other centres in English since 2006. Al Jazeera would claim to be "the voice of the Arab street" representing and reporting the disenfranchised and dissatisfied living under the yoke of authoritarian regimes. It certainly gets up the noses of many of them. But is that or just the voice of the Emir of Qatar?

Alan Fisher, a veteran "Al Jaz" correspondent, now based in Washington, was party to the station using social media as new platforms for getting the news to and from the masses in the "Spring". He argues that social media were transformative but not determinants. His rationale:

There simply are not enough journalists in the world to cover every event and so we have always relied on eyewitnesses; people who present us with facts, details of what has happened. They have, mainly since the advent of the web, come to be defined as "citizen reporters".

Mashaal Mir has had unique access to some senior Al Jazeera figures in Doha and elsewhere. She asks them the crucial questions about whether in Egypt they were simply reporting or were they campaigning for change especially in Mubarak's Egypt? Focusing particularly on Al Jazeera English, she ends up on the fence:

> On the one hand, it can be argued that during the Egyptian revolution, Al Jazeera was practising good journalism by giving airtime to all sides and trying to explain the extraordinary events. On the other hand, it would be foolish to assume that Al Jazeera did not promote an "activist spirit" against Mubarak's regime

John Mair examines the broadcasting role of Al Jazeera in the "Spring" and asks whether it has come of age and achieved its "CNN Moment". It certainly was omnipresent in the region as gatherer and transmitter and it shows signs of breaking into the US television market. Al Jazeera was always close to the "Spring" action whether or not it was officially in the country. But the jury is out on whether, as they claim, "Al Jaz" has replaced the BBC as the most trustworthy (if not the first) source of news in the region.

With an annual budget in excess of 750 million US dollars, the footprint of Al Jazeera Arabic and English will continue to be huge in the Middle East and the rest of the world. The way in that electronic boot is used will be much more effective and longer lasting than any Twitter feed.

The "Arab Spring", Social Media and Al Jazeera

Alan Fisher, Senior Correspondent at Al Jazeera, argues that the social media are both transforming the media landscape – and playing a crucial role in changing the world. At the same time he stresses: "The changes in Tunisia and Egypt were not driven by technology. These were revolutions driven by the people"

Introduction

The dramatic events of the "Arab Spring", the mobilisation of calls for democratic change across the Middle East and North Africa (MENA) are still unfolding. At the time of writing, summer is almost over and the winter beckons. Yet people are still protesting on the streets of Bahrain, Yemen, Syria and Jordan. In the squares of Cairo, people insist the Egyptian revolution remains unfinished.

Many governments in the West were caught out by the pace of developments in the first months of 2011 and found themselves desperately scrambling to catch up to public opinion. In an effort to provide instant interpretation, much of the media found itself also struggling to explain what appeared to be sudden and dramatic changes. That, as Cottle suggests, is perhaps an acknowledgement of failure. He maintains that the Western media was guilty of refusing to report on the...

> ...everyday suppression of political dissent, human rights abuses and earlier emergent protests whilst uncritically reporting on their own government's trade and arms initiatives and conciliatory diplomatic relations bolstering such regimes in power. If Western media had performed a more independent and critically engaged role, is it conceivable that the Arab uprisings of 2011, though surprising in terms of their speed and scale, could nonetheless have been better understood and contextualised within a preceding narrative of growing political disenchantment and despair? (p. 650)[1]

And so the myth of the social media revolutions was born.

The idea that Facebook or Twitter or similar social media networks operated as the main agent of social change is to adopt a technological determinist position or in Marshall McLuhan's famous phrase to accept "the medium is the message" where technology is considered an independent factor which draws its own consequences.[2] Yet this diminishes the political and social elements at work and overlooks the most fundamental element of the "Arab Spring". The changes in Tunisia and Egypt were not driven by technology. These were revolutions driven by the people.

It is important, therefore, not to overstate the role of social media in the changes that have been achieved, the protests that continue. While Zakaria acknowledges "technology – satellite television, computers, mobile phones and the internet – has played a powerful role in informing, educating and connecting people in the region. Such advances empower individuals and disempower the state",[3] Haseeb believes the technology has gone one step further than empowering by "initiating and igniting these events" (p. 117).[4] The development of new media cultures meant that what had once been done face-to-face has been effectively appropriated and aligned to assist contemporary revolutionary movements, yet the driving force remained an accumulation gathered over several years of disenfranchisement, of impotence to confront and challenge the ruling elites who were considered venal and corrupt.

First e-revolution – in the Philippines

Modern media tools have been used in the past to provoke regime change. The first e-revolution was 20 years ago. Accused of corruption, President Joseph Estrada of the Philippines refused to step down. In a country where text messaging was hugely popular, people took to their phones to begin the fight. Texters urged supporters to "Wear black to mourn the death of democracy" and called for one million people to meet outside the presidency and protest. They did, in an overwhelming and peaceful show of dissent.

In echoes of what was to come in 2011, the President appeared on TV first to announce he would not resign, and then to call fresh elections in which he would not stand. The military and the police sided with the people and withdrew their support. Four days after the first texts were sent, the President bowed to the inevitable and resigned. Estrada himself described the events as a "coup de text".[5] Technology may have marshalled the support, but the anger against Estrada had been simmering for some time.

The anti-Estrada messages were sent from friend to friend and through what would now be called a social network; a reminder that such things existed before the internet was created or widespread. Facebook, Twitter, YouTube and other sites and places are simply effective and efficient tools for connecting geographically and politically disparate groups. In Tunisia and Egypt, the regimes had become discredited and despised. In countries where speaking openly and critically of the regime was dangerous, the online world provided a place for people to vent their fury. Social media sites were employed to support a common cause and helped break the barrier of fear, allowing people to see that their thoughts and hopes of change were not restricted to the few but to the many. The social network sites became the biggest echo chamber in human history. And soon events in Tunis and Cairo and Alexandria were motivating and empowering protesters in Libya, Syria and Yemen.

Throughout periods of the "Arab Spring", I spent a great deal of time in Doha at the headquarters of my employer, Al Jazeera English. Several news organisations used social media as a significant factor in their coverage of events in the Middle East. It was used to source and corroborate stories and, in return, gave people a feeling of involvement and engagement in the news gathering process, a system described by

Rosen[6] as horizontal news gathering, but is perhaps more circular in nature as news was consistently shared and exchanged between people using new media and traditional outlets. I can only speak with any certainty on the processes employed and developed by Al Jazeera English, my employer and will do so below.

Social Media, Al Jazeera and the "Arab Spring"

With the first signs of unrest in Tunisia, Al Jazeera had to rely on a network of bloggers to provide clear and accurate information from inside the country. They had been sourced in the days and weeks before, established as credible and reliable and provided a vital link in a country where Al Jazeera was banned. Slowly the channel managed to get people into the country under normal travel visa conditions. Precautions were taken; the most obvious was no-one travelled if they had a journalist's visa in their passport. No-one carried the normal kit you would expect from a journalist or a TV crew. Once in country, they operated undercover, remained unnamed on air – often titled simply "our special correspondent" – and so were able to provide dramatic first-hand accounts of the dying hours of a dying regime. When Tunisian President Zine El Abadine Bin Ali finally fled, one of the first acts of the authorities was lift the ban on Al Jazeera and allow it to open an office and operate freely in the country.

In June 2010, the death of a young man, Khaled Said, after an altercation with a number of police officers in Alexandria, Egypt, led to the creation of a Facebook page "We are all Khalid Said". By mid-June the page had 130,000 followers and was the biggest centre of dissident opinion in Egypt. In the immediate aftermath of events in Tunisia, it became the successful rallying point for the on-line community to air their anger and frustration against the Mubarak regime.

The page was administered by Wael Ghonim, under the name El Shaheed. He created an event inviting people to join a protest on 25 January. Fifty thousand people answered the call and took to the streets as the protests moved from online to the physical world. The Egyptian security services managed to track down Ghonim and arrest him but many people had rights to administer the site and continued to post. Social media continued to stoke the anger of revolution, even with the arrest of its leaders.

Worried by the threat the protests posed, the Egyptian government put political pressure on providers to shut down general access to the internet, thus acknowledging the role it was playing in the political battle with the protestors. While they could do little about the growing content in cyberspace or exert control over anything they disliked, they could block the avenues accessing it. Yet again protesters inventively found a way around the restrictions. They discovered the computer lines through the Cairo stock exchange were still operating and so managed to hack in to use some of the capacity there to maintain and publish the website. They called friends abroad and asked them to tweet on their behalf. The information flow may have been restricted, but the authorities failed to shut it off completely.

Obama and the "Right to Peaceful Assembly"

The decision to shut down access to the internet became a major story which brought global attention to the protests in Egypt and even provoked US President Barack Obama to appeal to the Egyptian government to restore access saying social media was protected under "the right to peaceful assembly".[7]

President Hosni Mubarak's antipathy for Al Jazeera has been well documented. Touring the Arabic channel's headquarters in Doha in 2001, he is said to have remarked: "This matchbox. All this noise is coming out of this matchbox."[8] Realising that closing down avenues to internet content was not enough to re-establish complete control; he took aim at what he perceived to be an old enemy. First, the channel's Cairo office was closed down and the accreditation of the journalists was suspended. People on the streets were expressing frustration at state media and believed there was a more complete picture on the satellite channels. This clearly worried the authorities. The network then found its signals blocked. Quickly, a new satellite carrier was found and social media were used to get the message out about where the channel could now be located. Many homes across Egypt continued to be lit by the pictures from Al Jazeera. In defiance of the ban, the channel's reporters continued to work, gathering material and broadcasting reports on air, but it was increasingly dangerous. One reporter who works for a UK broadcaster confided in me that it was the first time he was happy to admit in a Middle East country he was not from Al Jazeera when confronted with an angry crowd.

153

State media openly criticised Al Jazeera, not surprisingly, portraying its coverage in a negative light, making wild and unfounded accusations about the motivation of its coverage. For those with no access to alternative news sources, it appeared to be a compelling and damning argument, and further increased the risks to those undertaking the role of newsgathering on the ground.

This became apparent when Al Jazeera teams ventured out on to the streets. They found themselves clearly targeted by the regime's supporters. Equipment was confiscated and smashed. Journalists and camera operators were arrested, threatened or beaten up; angry knife wielding mobs pursued our news teams in Alexandria. When correspondent Ayman Mohyeldin, the most prominent face of Al Jazeera English's coverage in Egypt, was detained by the army for more than seven hours, social media were used to raise an alert and pressure the authorities into releasing him.

Twitter Campaign Secures Release of Journalist for Detention

A Twitter campaign began with the hash tag #freeayman. In less than forty minutes from the first tweet from a desk in Doha, it was trending worldwide; with many people demanding, as Ayman holds an American passport, that the US authorities intervene. The US State Department was informed, contact with senior regime figures was reportedly made and a short time later Ayman was released.

Despite all the difficulties, the bravery of the teams on the ground and accessing the resources of social media meant that Al Jazeera could continue to cover events in Egypt. A camera attached to a satellite phone in a building overlooking the square meant there was coverage from Tahrir Square, 24 hours a day. The picture was not of the best quality, often grainy or blurred and sometime it distorted considerably, but people on Facebook and Twitter contacted the channel urging it not to switch it off. One tweet said if the screen goes blank, "the world will no longer be watching and they will kill us".

Given the restrictions in accessing material on the ground, social media became an important source of material. Again, a network of trusted bloggers and tweeters kept us informed of what was happening in the communities. It was decided early on to establish a desk in the newsroom to deal exclusively with social media. A small team was assigned to monitor Twitter, Facebook, Flickr, YouTube and similar sites. They studied the conversations and trends, looked for interesting updates and then would highlight them to the news desk before organising them into a news narrative for hourly broadcast from "the web-desk"as part of the on-going coverage. The best of the pictures, the most dramatic or those which clarified something which was regarded as significant was flagged to the correspondent working on the main report of the hour, which for logistical reasons was being pulled together in Doha, and would be included alongside Al Jazeera's own material and video sourced from news agencies.

Al Jazeera and "Crowdsourcing"

Al Jazeera was being sent dozens of videos and links to still pictures every day. Each one had to be viewed, assessed and then analysed to find the best images and weed out the fakes. It was a long, demanding job but absolutely necessary. For example, we were sent pictures that claimed to be a protest in a suburb of Cairo but we quickly established that it was actually a demonstration from Iraq in 2005. Those pictures never went to air. It helped to have Egyptians in the office, who knew the places, could identify the accents and could establish authenticity, but we could also send the material back out to social media for corroboration in a process which has come to be known as "crowdsourcing".

One of the most dramatic sequences broadcast on Al Jazeera was a protestor arguing with police in Alexandria. The scene was filmed on a telephone from a balcony several storeys up. As the man shouts at the police, a single shot is heard and he drops to the ground dead. The anguished screams of the person filming, the immediate human reaction to turn away and then return to the scene is all there. A person using Twitter, who lived in Alexandria, alerted me to the footage on YouTube a short time after it was posted and urged we use it, which we did. Rosen (2011)[9] argues this demonstrates that people are connected to others as effectively as they are linked up to big media. As well as creating wider participation in the media, this personal connectivity with the news, this link to the finished product gives the public investment in the story, empowering them as part of the conversation in significant events, as participants rather than observers. Added to the pictures provided from Egypt by established news agencies, for broadcasters such as Al Jazeera it makes the coverage more human, more connected to the experiences of those on the ground.

People contacted the channel saying they wanted to let the world know what was happening in their areas and with their communities, so Flip video cameras were distributed. There has been some criticism of this on a number of points. Firstly, there is the suggestion that it puts people are risk. The recipients of the camera were warned not to do anything that would put themselves or their families in danger but most were living in areas where unrest was already widespread and they wanted to capture it and give it a wide audience. Secondly, there is the argument that this changes the dynamic of reporting. Due to the inherent risks, journalism in areas of conflict has always been about providing a snapshot, grabbing a micro moment of a macro event. Social media allow us as journalists to have more pieces of the picture.

There simply are not enough journalists in the world to cover every event and so we have always relied on eyewitnesses; people who present us with facts, details of what has happened. They have, mainly since the advent of the web, come to be defined as "citizen reporters". It is a title which sits uncomfortably with some of my colleagues, inferring that somehow their efforts equate to those of trained, experienced journalists. Yet in its rawest form, the material provided is simply a commodity. As Doull points out,[10] it gains value when context is added. Real journalism is committed when the facts are gathered, fashioned into a clear narrative and explained in the proper contextual framework as part of a larger conversation.

And so for Al Jazeera English, as social media tools were helping to feed the coverage, the internet also became an increasingly useful tool in getting the news to a much wider audience. Online viewing, through live streaming on the Al Jazeera's website and through providers such as Livestation, grew massively. Of those watching around the world, about half were from the USA[11] where access to Al Jazeera English has been restricted. Social media became an invaluable tool for many news organisations. It was a way around restriction and censorship; it increased the breadth and scope of the coverage. It engaged the immediate audience as participants and left the wider audience much better informed about unfolding events.

Future Challenges
The media are still being denied access to many areas where there are continuing reports of unrest and revolution, such as Syria and Bahrain

and to a lesser extent, Yemen. Social media are again filling the void, providing pictures and eye witness reports which allow organisations such as Al Jazeera to tell important stories which could have slipped by, ignored and unnoticed because access for traditional media was impossible.

Yet as Morozov[12] has highlighted, the internet is not populated solely by those demanding change. Numerous governments including those who would be regarded as repressive are now monitoring what is posted on line and reacting either by challenging directly at the point of contact or in more sinister ways. As TV and radio stations have been blocked and banned in the past for similar reasons, he argues that if sites such as Twitter and Facebook are regarded as significant drivers of political change, as facilitators of revolutions, then some authoritarian governments may "declare that internet-search services are a 'strategic industry' like energy and transport and move to block foreign companies in this area" (pp 67-68).[13]

Certainly governments such as Bahrain, in a very short period of time, have grown more accomplished in engaging through social media. The government there has a strong presence on Facebook. There are a number of proxies who will promptly challenge journalists – sometimes aggressively and occasionally abusively – if they post anything there or on Twitter that could be perceived as critical of the establishment. They are well organised and their responses are – in the main – thorough and targeted and speak with an authority which suggests these are in some way officially supported or sanctioned. Certainly they are less likely to run into the problems highlighted by Morozov above. And state controlled media, be it newspapers, television and radio will continue to discredit those who stray from the official line, acting as a propaganda tool for those who oppose change.

Social media will come under pressure in such circumstances but will inevitably find ways to adapt and adjust, to remain the voice of dissent and opposition. Cottle[14] says this is an inevitable challenge, part of the continuing battle of political communication and of control.

Conclusion

Traditional media have been quick to seize upon the potential of social networks and websites as a significant source of information and as a platform to engage with the audience. For many organisations it also becomes a less expensive way of continuing coverage. In the MENA revolutions, by using and broadcasting pictures and stories highlighted on social media, traditional media helped confer an early legitimacy to the demonstrations by highlighting and providing recognition of the protesters' aims, sense of grievance and cause. This was often ahead of the position taken by governments around the world. Only as the extent of the protests was grasped and with it the realisation that regimes such as Mubarak's in Egypt would not survive did official announcements move from calls for greater accountability to a more supportive stance for those on the streets.

Cottle believes this allowed traditional media "to adopt a more independent and critically informed news stance"[15] than normal marking a perceptible shift from the views being expressed by the political elite. Cottle also maintains that the coverage of channels such as Al Jazeera English helped inform the views taken of the protest by other news organisations and agencies on how significant the protests were, leading to a "more independent and sympathetic" view.[16]

In return social media has weakened the mainstream media's role as gatekeepers. No longer do they have exclusive control over what is covered and what is ignored, what is important and newsworthy and what is regarded as insignificant. There are now many avenues for people to get their pictures, stories, movies, tweets out. Sambrook suggests this is "increasingly helping countries to develop a public space for debate"[17] and these tools have altered the dynamics of the public sphere moving towards the ideal of something truly dialogic and interactive.

As Al Jazeera and the "Arab Spring" have established, the days have gone of governments believing that by closing off transmitters or taking over radio and TV stations; of blocking mobile phone signals or satellite TV signals; or shutting down the internet they will somehow win the propaganda battle. There is still the risk that they will turn their guns on their own people as has been seen in a number of places in the past two years. The state only prevails only when it reacts to citizens' ability to be more publicly vocal and to coordinate more rapidly on a larger scale than before these tools existed. Social media have clearly changed the media landscape – and is playing a part in changing the world.

Notes

[1] Cottle, S. (2011) Media and the Arab uprisings of 2011: Research notes, *Journalism*, Vol. 12 pp 647 -659

[2] See McLuhan, M. (1964) *Understanding Media*, London: Routledge

[3] Zakari, F. (2011) Why There's No Turning Back in the Middle East. *Time Magazine*, Vol. 177, No. 6. Available online at http://www.time.com/time/world/article/0,8599,2049804,00.html, accessed on 5 July 2011

[4] Haseeb, K. El-D. (2011) On the Arab "Democratic Spring": Lessons Derived, *Contemporary Arab Affairs*, Vol. 4, No.2 pp 113-122

[5] Quoted in Kalil, T. (2008) *Harnessing the Mobile Revolution* The New Policy Institute, University of California, Berkeley p. 13

[6] Rosen, J. (2011) Media 140 Frontiers Conference : Innovation in Journalism. '*The Great Horizontal*' Keynote Address 13/4/2011 Barcelona. Quoted in http://www.journalism.co.uk/news/-media140-jay-rosen-on-a-golden-age-of-press-freedom/s2/a543689, accessed on 31 August 2011

[7] Obama, B. President (2011) Statements made on 28 January 2011. Available on line at http://www.time.com/time/world/article/0,8599,2045085,00.html accessed 1 September 2011

[8] Quoted in Friedman, T. (2001) *Glasnost in the Gulf. New York Times*, 27 February

[9] See Rosen op cit

[10] Doull, M. (1997) Journalism into the 21st Century, *Journalism: A Reader* M. Bromley & T O'Malley (eds) London: Routledge pp 273-280

[11] Elder, M. (2011) Al Jazeera English vs. Russia Today, Global Post, 13 February. Available online at http://www.globalpost.com/dispatch/egypt/110210/russia-today-al-jazeera-english, accessed on 31 August

[12] Morozov, E. (2011) *The Net Delusion: How not to Liberate the World*, London: Allen Lane

[13] Morozov, E. (2011) Whether Internet Control? *Journal of Democracy*, Vol. 22, No. 2, April pp 62-74

[14] Cottle op cit

[15] ibid: 654

[16] ibid

[17] Sambrook, R. (2010) *Are Foreign Correspondents Redundant?* Report by the Reuters Foundation for the University of Oxford p. 101

Note on the author

Alan Fisher has been a journalist for almost thirty years and has reported from more than 60 countries. He joined Al Jazeera English before the channel's launch in 2006, based in the London News Centre. He has recently taken up the position of Senior Correspondent based in Washington DC. He is closely involved in the training of journalists across the Al Jazeera network. He has spoken at many international conferences on the role of the media, the coverage of breaking news and Al Jazeera and has been a guest lecturer at the London School of Economics Summer School. He holds a Master of Arts (MA) in Mass Communications from the University of Leicester.

Was Al Jazeera English's Coverage of the 2011 Egyptian Revolution "campaigning journalism"?

Mashaal Mir has had access to the Al Jazeera journalists and executives who reported the Egyptian "revolution" which ignited the "Arab Spring". Were they reporting or campaigning for change – or was their journalism some combination of the two?

As the historic events of the 2011 "Arab Spring" unfolded from Tunisia and Egypt, the world sat glued to television and laptop screens. But it wasn't CNN or BBC that was bringing the best, up-to-date developments in Egypt. It was Al Jazeera.[1] The Qatari based news channel's reportage of Egypt gained worldwide recognition for its outstanding coverage of the revolutionary events.

However, there are questions about whether Al Jazeera helped create and, ultimately, fuel the Egyptian revolution by slanting its reportage in favour of the anti-Mubarak protesters and thus practised campaigning journalism. I will, therefore, analyse Al Jazeera's coverage of the Egyptian revolution and ask whether the channel was practising campaigning journalism? This will be done by examining their broadcast and online material. I will look into the type of stories that Al Jazeera covered, the images and footage they used, as well as the tone of their reporting. Interviewing Al Jazeera journalists who were either reporting from Egypt or involved in other ways in its coverage, I will also ask whether Al Jazeera was promoting campaigning journalism through its wide usage of citizen journalism and social media.

"Campaigning Journalism": Giving a "Voice to the Voiceless"

Campaigning journalism is perhaps best described as a practice of reporting a story from a certain angle or for a specific cause. There is often a spirit of activism in campaigning journalism. In the case of Al Jazeera, the term "campaigning journalism" might apply to their coverage of the Egyptian revolution: did the channel overtly back the cause of the anti-Mubarak protesters in Tahrir Square, Cairo?

While CNN had "experts" in their studio talking about what was happening in Egypt and what impact it might have on the US, Al Jazeera was on the ground talking to people who were a part of the movement.[2]

However, Al Jazeera's unique street-level approach to covering the revolution brought criticism, especially from the Egyptian government which cracked down on the channel in the midst of the protests.[3] Egyptian government officials accused the channel of fuelling anger and distorting the truth in Egypt by repeating images and by giving airtime to activists, anti-Mubarak protesters and especially the opposition.[4] Similarly, Bill O'Reilly, a celebrated Fox News host, accused Al Jazeera of inciting riots across the Muslim world.[5] Gregg Carlstorm, an online journalist for Al Jazeera, reported and interviewed protesters from Tahrir Square. Why had Al Jazeera decided to give valuable airtime to protesters and the opposition?

> One reason is that they don't have many other outlets. They don't get that airtime. We were definitely sympathetic to the protestors. I wouldn't argue with that. I think frankly it was hard not to be. So it's a case where it doesn't really bother me personally that we were sympathetic and frankly they deserved it.

Abdullah Mussa, an Al Jazeera producer and journalist, was reporting from Egypt during the revolution when he was badly beaten by pro-Mubarak thugs and almost lost his life. He questions the lack of airtime for activists and protesters on other networks, saying that it was crucial to tell their side of the story. "The protesters were a part of the story. Actually, they were a very, very big part of the story. How can you not ask them or question them or even interrogate them?" he added "How can you not do that?"

Blogging the Revolution?

One way of analysing how Al Jazeera treated opposition groups is by considering its Live Blog of Egypt.[6] The Live Blog was a supplement to the live broadcast coverage and was constantly updated with videos, interviews, statements and eye-witness reports.

Al Jazeera had interviews and statements from senior Egyptian ruling party member Mustafa al-Fiqi, the opposition party, the National Association for Change and its leader Mohamed ElBaradei, and fellow opposition leader Amin Iskander. While the majority of the Western media speculated on the role of the Muslim Brotherhood, Al Jazeera featured comments and interviews from the organisation both on their blog and on their live coverage. For example, the channel interviewed Ramey, a protester in Tahrir square.[7] Al-Jazeera gave Ramey seven minutes on air and introduced him, saying: "It's very cold out there [Tahrir Square] but Ramey is still out there, still defiant and determined to stay." The choice of words is interesting here; notice how the reporter builds up a sympathetic opinion of the protester even before the interview has begun.

Likewise, Al-Jazeera aired a special feature (and uploaded it on its website) during the revolution called "Voices from Cairo's Tahrir Square". The feature was entirely dedicated to the anti-Mubarak protesters, including interviews, comments and reactions from them.

The tone and language used while reporting and interviewing has a determining effect on how the reader (or listener) views the individual in question. For example, Al-Jazeera interviewed protesters describing Mubarak's regime as a "useless" and "military government" and responsible for "killing people" at Tahrir Square.[8]

Al-Jazeera's coverage of the revolution cannot be classified as "campaigning journalism" unless it is compared with the Egyptian state media. Significantly during the revolution, Al-Jazeera had its cameras on the demonstrations in Tahrir Square while the Egyptian state TV had its cameras on a bridge showing cars driving by. Let one of their correspondents on the spot, Abdullah Mussa, pick up the story: "I don't know if you saw, but we even broadcast two pictures: the picture that Al Jazeera was showing, and another picture of what the Egyptian state TV was showing. In this way, we were showing two sides of the same story. We were showing the free media and the not-so free media." Clearly Al-Jazeera was making an effort to underline the difference in how the story was being reported inside and outside Egypt and was, in effect, saying to the Egyptian people and everyone else around the world: "The regime is trying to lie, to cover up, to silence the people. We are telling you the truth, listen to us."

Ayman Mohyeldin, an Arab-American journalist based in the Middle East, said that Al Jazeera had been a "microphone and a conduit for ordinary citizens in the Arab world who want to express themselves, express their dissatisfaction with the government and express their demands".[9]

Using Citizen Journalism and Social Media

Al Jazeera also provided a free live stream of its coverage through YouTube and saw a 2,500 per cent increase in traffic to its website.[10] Bilal Randree, online journalist and producer for Al-Jazeera, commented: "Traffic to our website increased incredibly during our coverage of Tunisia, but especially during Egypt. Also, our presence on social media, like YouTube, Facebook and Twitter, was boosted with links to our website being shared thousands of times." The website's Live Blog, in fact, drew in up to ten times as much traffic as the lead story of the website. Randree continued:

> During the Tunisian revolution and from the beginning of the Egyptian uprising we started running Live Blogs and they became very popular. Those who were following the story closely didn't want to come to the website and read a new story with much of the old context – they wanted breaking news as and when it happened…The format of our new Live Blog allowed us to post updates, including text, images and video, constantly on a 24/7 basis. The Live Blogs have now become a permanent feature of our website.

Another interesting tool that Al Jazeera used in its coverage was citizen journalism. There is a difficulty in assessing the overall impact of citizen journalism. Gregg Carlstorm, an online journalist with Al Jazeera, commented: "When I was down in Tahrir Square, everyone would have a mobile with either pictures of the protests on it, or videos to show me, so some of that we were able to take and use it as a part of our coverage." And according to Riyaad Minty, head of the social media at Al Jazeera:

> When the protests started in Egypt, we were still running with our Palestine Papers.[11] That was our story. But online, I had many people telling me that something unexpected was happening in Egypt and why Al Jazeera wasn't there. So we were able to take that information and take it to our newsroom and say: "Guys, something is happening in Egypt, and it's big." So not only did citizen journalism help Al Jazeera cover the revolution; it was actually the reason why Al Jazeera started reporting on Egypt in the first place.

Abdullah Mussa said citizen journalism played a "significant role" in their coverage and helped Al Jazeera shape a narrative of what was going on in Egypt. "Al Jazeera couldn't be everywhere. Citizen journalism helped the revolution itself, because citizens were spreading information. And by spreading information they are telling the story. It helped shape a narrative." Al Jazeera did not shy away from using graphic images or horrific footage of injuries to anti-Mubarak protesters. The video footage was raw, unedited and predominantly sent in from the protesters.

Al Jazeera controversially broadcast a video on 4 Febrary 2011 which showed, what seemed, a government car intentionally drive through a crowd of peaceful protesters.[12] Another video of a government van running over protesters was uploaded on Al Jazeera's Live Blog.[13] The video was shared on Facebook and Twitter, and several copies of the video were uploaded under different accounts on YouTube. Consequently, both video caused outrage and disgust towards the Mubarak regime, as expressed through the many comments on both videos.[14]

Another example was the iconic video of a young man walking up to a tank and just standing in front of it. The footage was not aired on Egyptian state television and only aired on other foreign networks after Al Jazeera showed it.[15] Abdullah Mussa said the video footage of the tank confrontation that Al Jazeera broadcast helped break the psychological barrier of fear and bring Egyptians out on to the streets.

> The psychological barrier of fear, especially in a country like Egypt, breaks when you see the protests. Seeing is believing. Egyptians couldn't see anything like those protests before; they've never seen anything like that. They could never imagine. Once they saw it, they could imagine it. So, when you see that, you see people unite. The tank footage was simple, yet powerful. The tank became useless. That image was a part of breaking that fear barrier and we broadcast that.

Riyaad Minty, who leads Al Jazeera Network's social media initiatives, said that the channel got in touch with key bloggers, activists and protesters before the government eventually cracked down on the internet. "We usually identify key bloggers, activists and get our correspondents in touch with them so there is always a line of communication open, even after the internet shuts down," he said. Does this then create an in-built bias in the coverage? Riyaad Minty responded: "We use citizen journalism to help deepen our coverage, but it cannot be used, and never is, used on its own. It's a great supplement, but we need journalists on the ground who can give it context and meaning."

"I prefer to use the term 'citizen-submitted content' as the role of the journalist was still vital in the process," said Bilal Randree. "For us as journalists, receiving content from citizens in various areas that we build good relationships with, who understand in what format and with what details to submit content – this is important for enhancing our coverage "Citizen journalism required journalistic input rather than being a story on its own. "Citizen-submitted content is never the story – rather it is used to enhance the stories that we are already telling. For example, if someone sent me a powerful video, I would never make that the news," said Bilal Randree. "Rather, having researched a specific incident, gathering details and information from as many sources as possible and then verifying this again as much as possible, I would construct a story for online. Anything that is submitted to us is then used as part of that story. Submitted material is never the story, but rather enhances a story that was already being told." Abdullah Mussa said that those who criticise Al Jazeera for showing too citizen journalism content do not understand how journalism works.

One big argument against Al Jazeera is that we fuel the fire [revolution] by showing pictures repetitively. My answer is: It's news bulletins. We show the best pictures in one hour. That news bulletin is repeated again and again and again. We don't assume people sit and watch Al Jazeera 24/7. We assume they watch Al Jazeera for a couple of minutes, an hour maximum, and that's it. That's how news broadcast works.

Activist-Inspired News Values?

The idea of Al Jazeera's coverage being a campaigning force in Egypt was discussed by Nabil Echchabi, a blogger for Huffington Post. According to Nabil Echchabi, Al Jazeera operated in a "general climate of political profiteering and impunity of leaders"[16] while the lack of people's representation in Egypt helped Al Jazeera's "spirited coverage". "Al Jazeera is a network on a mission, not only to report but to restore Arab dignity and replace muzzled politics with a new culture of civil dialogue." Al Jazeera, according to Nabil Echchabi, goes beyond just incorporating campaigning journalism in its coverage; it becomes a force for political change. The channel speaks on behalf of the ordinary people; it becomes the " voice of the people". It helps the people ask questions and most importantly, get answers. Similarly, Tony Harden argued in the *Telegraph* that Al Jazeera's coverage of Egypt was not limited to just reflecting the events, but also creating and securing the revolution through its tireless campaigning and journalistic work.[17]

Abdullah Mussa disagreed. "Our aim, or editorial perspective, isn't to motivate, fuel or encourage. Our job is to tell the story. So when that canon shot happened it was natural for us to broadcast that and said: 'This is what is happening.' We are just telling the story. If that has a bigger effect, then that is not what we want or our objective, or our problem."

"Our Aim is to Tell Both Sides of the Story"

Abdullah Mussa insisted that Al Jazeera was not campaigning for a specific cause in Egypt.

If you truly want to tell the story, you have to tell both sides. It's as simple as that. You can't just give government official and experts airtime. You have to give all sides of the story. So in Egypt, when the government said something, we said: "The government has said this", so we were giving them a voice, giving them airtime. When Mubarak spoke, we aired it. When any government official spoke, we aired it. We even aired criticisms against us. But you have to because you are telling the story. It's very hypocritical if you don't.

Bilal Randree suggested that Al Jazeera gave viewers the opportunity to experience the events unfold in Egypt simply by broadcasting what was happening on the ground. "I would say we did the opposite [of campaigning journalism]. We just showed our audience what was really happening on the ground. For example, when Egyptian state television was reporting that there was a curfew and things were calm, and they were showing images of empty streets around the Nile, we showed the protesters that were camped out in Tahrir Square and others places on a split screen. We didn't even need to say anything – we left it for the audience to see and understand for themselves."

When asked to give their opinions on Nabil Echchabi's statement about Al Jazeera trying to restore Arab dignity and become a sort of political movement, most of the Al Jazeera journalists I interviewed not surprisingly disagreed. For instance, Gregg Carlstorm commented: "I think I would separate Al Jazeera Arabic from Al Jazeera English. I think it's definitely true on the Arabic side, I think clearly it's a pan-Arab broadcast, it doesn't take a lot to create a pan-Arab narrative. And so I think that statement fits for to the Arabic channel. I think the English tries to be a little more or an international broadcaster, it tries to do a little less of that."

Indeed, though Al Jazeera English is the sister channel to the Al Jazeera Arabic, editorially the channels have different outlooks. "We are not out to restore dignity to the Arabs. Al Jazeera Arabic is broadcast to the Arabic speaking world and that's their audience," said Abdullah Mussa. "So they will take stories that concern Arabs because that's their market. Now, for Al Jazeera English, our audience is the English-speaking world, which is wider. Even the angles that we take to tell the story are different because of our audience…We are a Middle East channel after all, and this is our strength."

Soraya Agaoglu was in charge of producing "Egypt Burning"; a three part series about the fall of Mubarak. "There have been many disagreements and debates among Al Jazeera journalists on our position in Egypt. There are some who believe that Al Jazeera did act like in an activist manner by pushing so relentlessly and just not willing to give up. We were covering stories that other networks were not, we were giving a voice to people other networks were not. We were simply putting ourselves out there for the sake of the story," she said. "Then there are others who think that by doing what Al Jazeera did in Egypt, the way we covered Egypt, that is not campaigning journalism. That is simply good reporting."

Al Jazeera had certainly difficulties reporting freely in Egypt because the government viewed Al Jazeera as a tool for the people. Arguably, oppressive regimes (such as the Egyptian one) are not fond of foreign media highlighting issues or even simply reporting on stories that do not fit their own agenda. Inevitably, oppressive regimes see Al Jazeera as on the side of the people. Reuters journalist Regan E. Doherty[18] suggests that Al Jazeera's reportage reflects a sharp cultural shift in a region where oppressive regimes are capable of silencing stories they do not want aired or published. Consequently, once Al Jazeera does publish or air a story that the government wishes to silence, the drive to keep the story on the air gets mistaken for campaigning journalism.

Al-Jazeera English v Al-Jazeera Arabic

Faisal J. Abbas, former media editor of the daily newspaper *Asharq Al Awsat* and currently blogger and analyst for the Huffington Post, summed up the views of many when he commented: "Quite frankly, in the Arab region, Al Jazeera English had very little influence in Egypt and has very little influence in the Arab world. Al Jazeera Arabic is what helps push these revolutions and any effect that had come from Al Jazeera network on Egypt; it is certainly from the Arabic channel, not the English."

It has, in fact, been Al-Jazeera Arabic, not Al Jazeera English, that has helped shape a narrative of rage against not only the Egyptian regime but oppressive regimes for the past fifteen years since it was founded in 1996. "Al Jazeera English is, with all due respect, irrelevant. It is absolutely irrelevant in the Arab world," says Abbas. "It is influential in London, Washington, the English speaking countries, in decision-making countries like US in the language they understand. In an accent that they understand, in a tone that is not very loud as Al Jazeera Arabic because Al Jazeera Arabic is known for loud, shouting, screaming reporters. Al Jazeera English is a mutation of Al Jazeera Arabic, but a good looking mutation."

So Al Jazeera Arabic probably had a far greater influence on the Egyptian revolution than Al Jazeera English. "As you know [Al Jazeera Arabic] has competition in Al Arabiya, so observers say that while Al Arabiya was trying its best to portray Mubarak in a favourable light, Al Jazeera Arabic was hard on Mubarak," says Abbas. "So I think there was a sympathetic light shed on anti-Mubarak protesters, from the Al Jazeera network in general. But if I did have to compare, I think Al Jazeera English doesn't have the level of activism that Al Jazeera Arabic has."

Broadcaster, Reporter, Campaigner, Political Pressure Group?

On the one hand, it can be argued that during the Egyptian revolution, Al Jazeera was practising *good journalism* by giving airtime to all sides and trying to explain the extraordinary events. On the other hand, it would be foolish to assume that Al Jazeera did not promote an "activist spirit" against Mubarak's regime. Significantly, the Director General of Al Jazeera, Wadah Khanfar, said at the 2011 TED conference[19] that the Tunisian people "were our reporters feeding our newsroom with pictures, with videos and news". "We are the voice of these voiceless people; we are going to spread the message. Al Jazeera took the voice from these people and we amplified it, we put it in every sitting-room in the Arab world and internationally and globally through our English channel and then people started to feel that there's something new happening."

Bilal Randree's said that Al Jazeera "amplifies the voice of the people". It did not speak for the people, nor did it tell the people what to say. On the contrary: "What we do is give them the platform to give their side of the story," he said. "This is exceptionally important for those that have not been given the right to tell their stories before."

Let the final word go to Abdullah Mussa: "We hope to be the voice for the voiceless. If we are, then it is an honour. If we aren't, then that is what we strive to be. We want to be telling the story as honest as possible, to tell the story of the individual. And in this way, yes, we do become the voice of the people."

Interviewees

Abdullah Mussa – Al Jazeera producer and journalist, 17 April 2011
Gregg Carlstorm – Al Jazeera online journalist, 18 April 2011
Bilal Randree—Al Jazeera online journalist and producer, 17 April 2011
Ramsey Zarifeh- Deputy head for Newsgathering at Al Jazeera, 17 April 2011
Riyaad Minty – Head of Social Media at Al Jazeera, 18 April 2011

Bilal Randree – Al Jazeera producer and online journalist, 1 May 2011
Faisal J. Abbas – Former media editor of daily newspaper *Asharq Al Awsat*, now blogger and media analyst for the Huffington Post, 14 April 2011

Notes

[1] In this chapter "Al Jazeera" specifically refers to Al Jazeera English. When mentioning Al Jazeera Arabic, this will be done clearly

[2] See http://www.siskiyoudaily.com/opinions/columnists/x1802976205/Brian-Mackey-Al-Jazeera-English-in-Middle-East-has-CNN-moment, accessed on 31 August 2011

[3] See http://www.foreignpolicy.com/articles/2011/02/08/the_al_jazeera_effect, accessed on 15 May 2011

[4] See http://www.foreignpolicy.com/articles/2011/02/08/the_al_jazeera_effect, accessed on 15 May 2011

[5] See http://www.foreignpolicy.com/articles/2011/02/08/the_al_jazeera_effect, accessed on 15 May 2011

[6] See http://blogs.aljazeera.net/middle-east/2011/01/28/live-blog-281-egypt-protests, accessed on 1 August 2011

[7] See http://www.rawstory.com/rawreplay/2011/02/al-jazeera-speaks-to-an-egyptian-activist/, accessed on 1 August 2011

[8] See http://english.aljazeera.net/news/middleeast/2011/02/2011212597913527.html, accessed on 10 May 2011

[9] See http://www.cpj.org/blog/2011/03/q-ayman-mohyeldin-al-jazeera-english-correspondent.php, accessed: on 15 May 2011

[10] See http://techcrunch.com/2011/02/13/al-jazeeras-social-revolution-in-realtime/, accessed on 13 May 2011

[11] Al Jazeera obtained more than 1,600 internal documents from a decade of Israeli-Palestinian negotiations. See http://english.aljazeera.net/palestinepapers/, accessed on 18 August 2010

[12] See http://www.youtube.com/watch?v=KZec3vCttkw, accessed on 10 May 2011

[13] See http://www.nowpublic.com/world/egypt-police-van-hit-run-video-police-run-over-protesters-2754164.html, accessed on 10 May 2011

[14] See http://www.youtube.com/watch?v=KZec3vCttkw, accessed on 1 August 2011

[15] See http://www.youtube.com/watch?v=_-R5876zbKo, accessed on 1 August 2011

[16] See http://www.huffingtonpost.com/nabil-echchaibi/al-jazeera-and-the-promis_b_821105.html, accessed: on 12 May 2011

[17] See http://www.telegraph.co.uk/news/worldnews/northamerica/usa/8439736/The-Arab-Spring-uprisings-of-2011-are-being-hailed-in-Washington-as-the-Al-Jazeera-moment.html accessed on 09 May 2011

[18] See http://in.reuters.com/article/2011/02/17/industry-us-aljazeera-idINTRE71G0WC20110217, accessed on 10 May 2011

[19] See
http://www.ted.com/talks/wadah_khanfar_a_historic_moment_in_the_arab_world.html, accessed on 31 August 2011

Note on the author

Mashaal Mir is a Danish-Pakistani journalist who moved to London in 2009. She is currently in her final year at Kingston University, London, studying Journalism with Politics BA programme. Passionate about documentary-making, politics and religion-related issues, she hopes to work in broadcast journalism. Mashaal Mir's published work can be found online at www.mashaalmir.com.

Reporter or Provocateur? The "Arab Spring" and Al Jazeera's "CNN Moment"

John Mair looks at how the Arabic television news channel Al Jazeera has come of age in the "Arab Spring". It has been close to all the action, some say too close. Is the "Arab Spring" the channel's "CNN Moment" and if so why?

As the hopes and optimism of the glory days in Tunisia and Egypt end in an autumn of hand-to-hand fighting and claim/counter-claim on the streets of Tripoli and Damascus, the role of Al Jazeera in the whole process has come in for praise and for some questioning. Al Jazeera was there at all the key moments[1] but was it simply too close to the action? Was it a reporter or provocateur?

Those who work for Al Jazeera are keen to come forward with explanations and praise of their work. This author conducted a public talk session at Coventry University (in an acclaimed series known as the "Coventry Conversations") with senior Al Jazeera London anchor Stephen Cole in March 2011. That, and the podcast from it,[2] have proved a rich seam for this chapter. Likewise, Salah Negm, Al Jazeera's Director of News in Doha, was equally forthcoming in his interview with Jonathan Gornall for the *National* in June 2011.[3] That, also, provided a rich seam of the Al Jazeera view.

Negm is a veteran of Arab Public Service broadcasting for "Al Jaz", the BBC and MBC. He knows his onions when it comes to the Arab world and political unrest/upset. He does not readily accept the simple term "Spring", preferring to see the events as an "Awakening": "What do you think is more representative [of] what's happening? Isn't it an awakening? Spring is happening every year."[4]

Cole, also a veteran of reporting and presenting for the BBC, SkyNews and CNN before helping to found Al Jazeera English in 2006, told his Coventry audience: "The revolutions were led by young people who had just had enough. Tunisia is the most secure and progressive country in the Islamic world. 80 per cent of population belonged to the middle class. The 'Spring' began with a human story: young market trader slapped by a female inspector set himself on fire. People saw pictures of it on TV, tweeted and read blogs."[5]

On a Mission to Inform

For both of them, Al Jazeera is on a mission to inform and educate its audience. Long gone are the days where authoritarian regimes could keep uncomfortable news and events from the eyes and ears of their people. Cole commented: "We cannot live in a world where a story like Egypt which has consequences for the whole world without the audience knowing anything about it."[6] Informing, though, can lead to trouble.

During the Egyptian Uprising in January and Febraury 2011, Al Jazeera became deeply distrusted and unpopular with the then Egyptian authorities fighting as they were for hegemony. News from Tahrir (or Freedom) Square going global via "Al Jaz" was far from welcome. They simply closed down (or tried to) the Al Jazeera operation in the country on 30 January. Cole stressed: "The Egyptian government systematically targeted Al Jazeera. The police targeted people carrying the Al Jazeera logo. All our offices were ordered to be shut down."[7] But down is never out with Al Jazeera; they simply went underground and secured the news and pictures in other ways from citizen journalists and their own people. Negm added: "The easiest step a government can take is to deny accreditation to Al Jazeera's news teams, but then you can go undercover and we can send our correspondents to get the story."[8] Which the station did in Egypt to the fury of impotent authorities.

There is a history to Al Jazeera's relationship with many Arab governments. Since the founding of Al Jazeera Arabic in 1996, the station has been a thorn in the side of most authoritarian regimes in the region with the notable and obvious exception of Qatar, who are the paymasters. Hugh Miles has provided an excellent history of the first ten years in his 2005 (updated 2009) book *Al Jazeera: How Arab TV Challenged the World*.[9] In it, he chronicles well how the Arab regimes resented the reporting of "Al Jaz" and, where they could, did their best to stymie it. The very same President Hosni Mubarak, who was fighting for his political life in January 2011, had asked to see Al Jazeera's HQ when on a trip to Qatar in 2000.

On Al Jazeera's coverage of the Uprising, Mubarak is reported to have thundered: "All this trouble from a matchbox like this!"[10] Arab Ambassadors were regularly sent to the Emir in Doha, the financier of AJ, to register their government's disapproval (and their secret praise). As Hugh Miles puts it: "Arab ambassadors in Doha said they spent so much time complaining about Al Jazeera that they felt more like ambassadors to a TV channel than ambassadors to a country. Occasionally, after an ambassador had launched an official complaint, he would add, off the record, that he thought Al Jazeera was doing a great job."[11]

So in Tunisia, Egypt, Libya, Syria, Bahrain and Yemen, Al Jazeera did not simply go in to report the "Spring" from a neutral starting position. Because of their fifteen year history they had "form" and maybe an agenda of their own

The Voice of the Middle East? Reporters, Cheerleaders or the Voice of Doha?

Opinion is divided as to whether AJ is the voice of the Arab street. There are now many broadcasters competing for supremacy on Middle Eastern airwaves especially at a time of crisis and significant news such as the "Spring". The BBC, here as elsewhere in the world, used to hold sway as the voice of record. No more, according to Cole: "We have overtaken the BBC...we are a lot better than the BBC."[12] And the reason for that? "Al Jazeera gets people talking to people."

But the rainbow around Al Jazeera and its broadcasting position is not universal. Critics point to its partiality. Marc Ginsberg, the former US Ambassador to Morocco, in a very strong piece for the Huffington Post in January 2011, commented: "Stoking anger and hostility has become Al Jazeera's mantra, and its producers have taken to heart the axiom 'If it bleeds it leads' to such a degree that baton-swinging policeman clubbing Tunisian demonstrators literally took up the entire first ten minutes of one news broadcast as the emotional reporter cried into his microphone about the unjustness of Arab autocrats."[13]

Ginsberg went on to condemn the channel's "favourite political pastime of disgorging its anti-authoritarian editorial bias across all of its media platforms...Through internet and Twitter feeds, Al Jazeera sees itself less and less as exclusively a news gathering organisation and more and more like a 'Wizard of Oz'-type instrument for social upheaval in the region."[14]

In this, Ginsberg is repeating long-standing criticisms of Al Jazeera though these criticisms had abated in recent years as it "went respectable", particularly after the founding of Al Jazeera English in 2006 and the expensive hiring of British journalistic talent of the calibre of David Frost, Rageh Omaar, Stephen Cole and Alan Fisher. The mother station, Al Jazeera Arabic, may have been misunderstood simply because too many in the West simply did not speak Arabic. Cole, in a previous Coventry Conversation in 2010, said: "I think the reason people didn't like Al Qaeda/Al Jazeera television was because the allegation was that we'd shown beheadings which we have never done. But nobody knew the channel anyway. None of you had watched it, you'd only seen a headline saying Al Jazeera Arabic or Al Jazeera, so nobody had seen it but everybody had a view, which is the worst kind of ignorance."[15]

As we saw in Egypt, Al Jazeera is adept at getting round reporting restrictions wherever they are put in their way. Much use is now made of user generated content and during the "Arab Spring" the station handed out flip video cameras for their citizen reporters to use. To what extent were these citizens simple reporters or cheerleaders subject to the "Heisenberg effect" of changing behaviour by the very nature of being there with an "Al Jazeera camera" in hand? Ambassador Ginsberg is in no doubt: "Americans should not underestimate the role that the ever popular Arab news channel Al Jazeera plays in challenging the Arab world's status quo, using events in Tunisia to fuel its favourite political pastime of disgorging its anti-authoritarian editorial bias across all of its media platforms – much to the anger and hostility of most Arab rulers, particularly those Al Jazeera views as too pro-Western.[16]

Certainly, the station as a whole has an effect wherever it is viewed in the region. Positive according to Cole who talks of the "transformative impetus to make information available to those who should be the source of all power – the people. We are now playing a role no different to responsible media in developing or developed countries: extracting info from the powerful to pass on to the people".[17] In February, AFP transmitted a photograph around the world of a slogan spray-painted on a wall in Tobruk, eastern Libya: "Freedom = Aljazeera."[18] The big question, though, remains open whether Al Jazeera in all its forms is acting as observer and objective reporter or something more agenda-driven.

"Getting the Net": Using New Platforms to Get the Message out

One huge advantage of having the Emir of Qatar's deep pocket as your banker is that Al Jazeera has been able to afford to move into the digital and internet sphere without fear of the cost. Before the "Arab Spring", and especially during it, the station has used live streaming, live blogs, live tweets as a way of enhancing their journalism with first person "reports". The citizen journalists use their Twitter, Facebook accounts and blogs to get their message out from the Uprising frontline to Al Jazeera and the world. Al Jazeera uses social media to access audiences who would normally be difficult or impossible to reach. At the start of the "Arab Spring/Awakening", there very few carriage agreements for AJE in the United States. Cable station owners were simply too prejudiced or afraid to offer a platform to "al Qaeda TV". The way round that roadblock has proved very simple – stream the output live on the web via aljazeera.net, help the audience to find it via Twitter to the website and watch it grow.

On screens of any size, the "Arab Spring/Awakening" has been Al Jazeera's "CNN Moment". That Atlanta-based news station – previously derisorily called "Chicken Noodle News" – came of age with its live reporting of Operation Desert Storm in Kuwait and Iraq in January 1991. American and world viewers were able to watch live American "smart bombs" hitting targets in Iraq and the Allied troops intercepting Saddam Hussein's Scud missiles with Patriot missiles. It made for good television and made CNN. From then on, CNN was taken seriously by fellow professionals and, more importantly, by the audience.[19] It had arrived.

Likewise, Al Jazeera English in 2011 found its range. "Al Jazeera English's coverage left other TV news outfits standing and the channel experienced what the *Miami Herald* called 'its CNN moment', squeezing its way into the US consciousness, predominantly through the narrow portals of live internet streaming and Twitter," reported the *National*.[20] As Stephen Cole stressed: "There's a new eco system-traditional and new media not competing but complimentary. Seven million watched it via the web in the USA, two million of them watching the video stream."[21]

Al Jazeera English's online head, Mohamed Nanabhay, added: "At any given time there were three times more people on the live blog than on the main story [on Al Jazeera's homepage]. Your editor usually invests [so much time] in the lead story...but if you look at the numbers, people were on the live blog hitting refresh. [So] we threw more resources into that."[22]

On 13 February 2011, US technology media website TechCrunch analysed what it called "Al Jazeera's social revolution (in real time)" and concluded that "where once people tuned into CNN to watch governments collapse, this time around they tuned into Al Jazeera on the web".[23]

Two days earlier, when Egypt's President Hosni Mubarak had resigned, "everyone wanted to watch and they flooded to Al Jazeera's English website. Concurrent real time visits spiked from about 50,000 right before noon ET to 135, 371". The number of people on Al Jazeera's website at any moment – driven to it primarily by the station's Twitter feeds – rose to 200,000 and that, reported TechCrunch, "translated into millions of people watching on the Web. And what was the biggest source of social media traffic? It wasn't Facebook. It was Twitter When it comes to spreading real time news, the social revolution is very real and Twitter is in the vanguard".[24]

But "getting" the internet and the power of new media to find new audiences did not come out of the blue. They needed investment in hard and software but content and immediacy are still the kings on and off the internet. Al Jazeera's online chief commented Nanabhay commented: "What's behind [our social media success] is excellence in world-class journalism. The social media campaigns have been methods to get people to watch that content and make up their minds. Once you see it, you'll be hooked and come back for more."[25]

Getting into the Biggest Market of them all – the USA

The "Arab Spring" and Al Jazeera's reporting of it, has helped the station start to crack the biggest English speaking market – the USA. According to Cole: "Something strange is starting to happen. American viewers are starting to demand to see us. America has woken up. Our coverage has been referred to as our 'CNN moment'. We now have 230 million viewers – which is not bad without marketing and public relations. *The New York Times* praised our 'total immersion coverage'."[26] The channel found itself with some unlikely allies such as the new media guru Jeff Jarvis, of the City University, New York. He ran a Twitter campaign to get Al Jazeera on to US screens It worked. The station became available to some cable subscribers in New York in August 2011, having previously been available only as an option for some viewers in Washington DC, Ohio and Los Angeles.[27]

Respectability followed. In May 2011, Columbia University's Graduate School of Journalism in New York named Al Jazeera English as the recipient of its Columbia Journalism Award, given in recognition of "singular journalism in the public interest". CSJ Dean Nicholas Lemann, in his citation, said: "Al Jazeera English has performed a great service in bringing the English speaking world in-depth coverage of the turmoil in the Middle East...We salute its determination to get to the heart of a complicated story unfolding in countries where news has historically been difficult to cover."[28]

So the chink in the US audience armour is starting to show light. Stephen Cole sees another continent as the next step towards AJ's march on the world news stage: "Africa is important to us. We want to take centre stage as a channel, the fastest growing news channel in the world."[29]

The Competition for the Arab Audience

Media used to be fairly straightforward in the Middle East. It comprised simply television and radio stations – state-owned and state-controlled – and the BBC Arabic Service. Al Jazeera Arabic came along in 1996 and since then the skies and screens have become crowded. A simple internet search produced the following channels broadcasting today in the region – Al Arabiya, Abu Dhabi TV, Al Manar, Ana Radio, Arab Radio and

Television, Lebanon Future Television, LBCSAT TV, MTV Lebanon, Orbit Satellite TV and Syria Satellite. All competing with al Jazeera for the Arab audience.

It has meant they have sharpened their act and maybe made them more radical in the process in order to stand out.

Building the Foundations in a "Pillbox" in Doha

The Emir of Qatar, Sheikh Hamad bin Khalifa, founded Al Jazeera Arabic in 1996 to bolster his liberal domestic and foreign policies. It proved to be an oasis in a desert of little information in the Arab world. Stephen Cole: "Middle East viewers were used to state-controlled media. They flocked to Al Jazeera which became compulsive viewing. Unelected leaders used to maintain the monopoly of information, Over the past fifteen years free media has been successful in breaking the official grip. It came at a price-continuous closure of our bureaux and sponsorship of smears to damage our credibility."[30]

The refugees from the BBC Arabic Service, a joint BBC/Saudi government venture which had imploded the year before in arguments over censorship, provided the backbone of the infant Doha station. They brought many "BBC/public service values" with them such as "objectivity", "balance" and never taking "No" for an answer! Salah Negm, now Director of News, commented: "At the time, it was a new style of journalism coming to the Middle East and, of course, officials, governments and people were not used to that kind of journalism. If we ask a question, we want an answer, and you are going to have a follow-up question, and the next follow-up question, saying: 'What do you think about that?' and he says a word and that's it. But we don't take this for an answer."[31]

Newness and brashness and truth-telling are never values at a premium in closed authoritarian societies. Al Jazeera Arabic was quick to find foes. The Saudi Interior Minister Prince Nay in 1999 alleged: "That channel is a distinguished high quality product but it serves up poison on a silver platter."[32] The Arab oligarchs put pressure on the channel directly through their diplomats but also, more subtly, through simply not putting advertising on the supposedly "commercial" channel. Fortunately, the deep pockets of Sheikh Hamad bin Khalifa kept them broadcasting, as Miles points out: "The Emir has continued to shape domestic policy to sustain the channel. Without his continued political and financial benevolence it would have ceased transmitting long ago."[33]

In many senses, Al Jazeera Arabic and Al Jazeera English are this rich man's toy. Cole revealed to his Coventry audience that the Qatar government pays $750 million annually towards the channels. In a flight of fancy, he said the Emir was trying to turn his kingdom into "the Switzerland of the Middle East".

America Blows Hot: "Al Qaeda TV"

America may now be the new audience oyster for Al Jazeera to crack open but it has been a turbulent fifteen year roller coaster ride between the channel and US administrations. The moniker "Al Qaeda TV" came from the station showing video messages from the US Public Enemy No. 1 Osama bin Laden first on 29 October 2004 and later a whole series of audio and video tapes right through to 2010.

The Bush administration was not best pleased to see their post 9/11 nemesis on Arab TV screens. The then-Defense Secretary, Donald Rumsfeld, acted as the hammer calling the channel in April 2004 "a mouthpiece of Al Qaeda" whose journalism was "vicious, inaccurate and inexcusable". Rumsfeld said its decision to air explicit footage of civilian casualties in Fallujah, Iraq, in 2004 was "just outrageous nonsense".[34]

This was echoed seven years later by a contemporary critic, former Ambassador Ginsberg in his Huffington Post tirade: "Al Jazeera has proven worthy in Gaza, in Lebanon, in Iraq and in Iran of its reputation as a fiery instigator of public opinion and less an impartial reporter of it."[35] "Al Jazeera TV=Al Qaeda TV" was some reputation to have.

America Blows Cold: Rapprochement

Nothing lasts forever in the Arab World nor in the Arab broadcasting world. Al Jazeera has come out of the doghouse of the US State Department. Administrations have changed: so, too, Secretaries of State. Likewise the product of Al Jazeera is more understandable and maybe better quality than its Arabic sister station. Moreover, America now needs Al Jazeera. Hillary Clinton, the current US Secretary of State, told the Senate Foreign Relations Committee on 1 March 2011 as the "Arab Spring" was gathering momentum and the US was about to intervene in Libya that America was losing the international information war. Al

Jazeera, she said, was "literally changing people's minds and attitudes" and, like it or hate it, "it is really effective...In fact, viewership of Al Jazeera is going up in the United States because it's real news". Secretary Clinton continued: "You feel like you're getting real news around the clock instead of a million commercials and, you know, arguments between talking heads and the kind of stuff that we do on our news which, you know, is not particularly informative to us, let alone foreigners."[36]

In seven years, Al Jazeera has gone from Public Enemy Number One to an officially sanctioned provider of "real news". "Al Qaeda TV" was dead.

So, is Al Jazeera the messenger or the Message?

If the first function of good journalism is to both tell the truth and create mischief then the output of both Al Jazeera news channels qualifies. For fifteen years it has been part of the political and broadcasting ecology of the Middle East. It has been at the epicentre of change, some say it is the epicentre. According to former Ambassador Ginsberg: "Al Jazeera has proven worthy in Gaza, in Lebanon, in Iraq and in Iran of its reputation as a fiery instigator of public opinion and less an impartial reporter of it."

But in response, Stephen Cole, a loyal *arriviste* on the Al Jazeera scene, is quick to stress: "Basically, I think now we're the dominant channel covering the developing world. In other words, being based in the global south we're trying to reverse the information flow that has traditionally moved from the wealthy north to the poorer countries south of the equator and it sounds a bit pompous but we're trying to be the voice of the voiceless, delivering in-depth journalism from these very under-reported regions of the world."[37]

Somewhere between those two polarities lies the truth. The "Arab Spring" may have proved the coming of age of the Al Jazeera channels but true maturity and trust comes with even more ageing. Time alone will tell that.

Notes

[1] The best chronology of the "Spring", by far, is provided by the *Guardian*. See http://www.guardian.co.uk/world/interactive/2011/mar/22/middle-east-protest-interactive-timeline, accessed on 14 August 2011

[2] See http://coventryuniversity.podbean.com/2011/03/30/stephen-cole-al-jazeera-and-the-recent-arab-revolutions/, accessed on 14 August 2011

[3] See http://www.thenational.ae/news/worldwide/middle-east/arab-spring-brings-al-jazeera-to-full-bloom; Jonathan Gornall, 24 June 2011, accessed on 16 August 2011

[4] ibid

[5] See http://coventryuniversity.podbean.com/2011/03/30/stephen-cole-al-jazeera-and-the-recent-arab-revolutions/, accessed on 14 August 2011

[6] ibid

[7] ibid

[8] See http://www.thenational.ae/news/worldwide/middle-east/arab-spring-brings-al-jazeera-to-full-bloom; Jonathan Gornall, 24 June 2011, accessed on 16 August 2011

[9] Hugh Miles (2009) *Al-Jazeera: How Arab TV News Challenged the World*, London: Abacus

[10] ibid p. 11

[11] ibid p. 58

[12] See http://coventryuniversity.podbean.com/2011/03/30/stephen-cole-al-jazeera-and-the-recent-arab-revolutions/, accessed on 14 August 2011

[13] http://www.huffingtonpost.com/amb-marc-ginsberg/al-jazeera-fueling-tunist_b_811865.html January 20th 2011, accessed on 16 August 2011

[14] ibid

[15] See cutoday.wordpress.com/2010/.../al-jazeera-presenter-comes-to-coventry, accessed on 16 August 2011

[16] See http://www.huffingtonpost.com/amb-marc-ginsberg/al-jazeera-fueling-tunist_b_811865.html January 20th 2011, accessed on 16 August 2011

[17] http://coventryuniversity.podbean.com/2011/03/30/stephen-cole-al-jazeera-and-the-recent-arab-revolutions/, accessed on 14 August 2011

[18] See http://www.thenational.ae/news/worldwide/middle-east/arab-spring-brings-al-jazeera-to-full-bloom; Jonathan Gornall, 24 June 2011, accessed on 16 August 2011

[19] See Piers Robinson (2002) *The CNN Effect: The Myth of News, Foreign Policy and Intervention*, London: Routledge

[20] See http://www.thenational.ae/news/worldwide/middle-east/arab-spring-brings-al-jazeera-to-full-bloom; Jonathan Gornall, 24 June 2011, accessed on 16 August 2011

[21] See http://coventryuniversity.podbean.com/2011/03/30/stephen-cole-al-jazeera-and-the-recent-arab-revolutions/, accessed on 14 August 2011

[22] See http://mashable.com/2011/03/05/al-jazeera-digital/What the Egyptian Revolution Taught Al Jazeera About Digital, 5 March 2011, Adam Ostrow, accessed on 16 August 2011

[23] ibid

[24] ibid

[25] ibid

[26] See http://coventryuniversity.podbean.com/2011/03/30/stephen-cole-al-jazeera-and-the-recent-arab-revolutions/, accessed on 14 August 2011

[27] See Al Jazeera English launches on New York cable. Spy Report, 2 August 2011. Available online at http://www.mediaspy.org/report/2011/08/02/al-jazeera-english-launches-on-new-york-cable/, accessed on 23 August 2011

[28] See http://www.journalism.columbia.edu/news/406, accessed on 16 August 2011

[29] See http://coventryuniversity.podbean.com/2011/03/30/stephen-cole-al-jazeera-and-the-recent-arab-revolutions/, accessed on 14 August 2011

[30] ibid

[31] See http://www.thenational.ae/news/worldwide/middle-east/arab-spring-brings-al-jazeera-to-full-bloom; Jonathan Gornall, 24 June 2011, accessed on 16 August 2011
[32] See http://www.journalism.columbia.edu/news/406, accessed on 16 August 2011
[33] Miles op cit p. 58
[34] ibid p. 29
[35] http://www.huffingtonpost.com/amb-marc-ginsberg/al-jazeera-fueling-tunist_b_811865.html January 20th 2011, accessed on 16 August 2011
[36] See http://www.huffingtonpost.com/2011/03/03/hillary-clinton-calls-al-_n_830890.html, accessed on 16 August 2011
[37] See http://coventryuniversity.podbean.com/2011/03/30/stephen-cole-al-jazeera-and-the-recent-arab-revolutions/, accessed on 14 August 2011

Note on the author

John Mair is a senior lecturer in Journalism at Coventry University. John is a former BBC Current Affairs producer who has also worked for Channel Four and ITV in the UK and for broadcasters abroad. He is a Royal Television Society Journalism Award Winner and has been for the last two years a judge in the RTS National Journalism Awards. He invented the Coventry Conversations, a conference series from which this book emerged.

Section 4. The Problem of the "Twitter Revolutions"

John Mair

The digital fanatics claim the uprisings of the "Arab Spring" as "Twitter" or "Facebook" revolutions. Sadly this is not the case. The internet was blocked in Libya for several months and was still blocked in Syria as the book went to press (September 2011). In the early uprisings in Tunisia and Egypt there is some evidence of Twitter/Facebook as an accelerant but NOT as a cause. But the rebellions culminated years of social and industrial protests in these countries.

People revolt and put themselves in danger because they are hungry, unemployed, fed up in other ways. Not because they are told to do so in 140 characters. There is a confusion of the media and the message. Sometimes deliberate.

Daniel Bennett, a scholar of new media and conflict, discusses the sad and exemplary case of the deceit of "A Gay Girl in Damascus" which purported to be just that and was taken at face value. In fact, it was a heterosexual American post graduate student Tom McMaster in Edinburgh. As "Gay Girl" lived on the internet, so it was exposed on it through the good work of Andy Carvin, of NPR Washington, and his Twitter followers. According to Bennett: "Identifying and reporting authentic voices online was an important way to access the story of the 'Arab Spring', but Tom MacMaster's hoax provided a timely reminder of the challenges of verifying material posted online."

Professor Simon Cottle, of Cardiff University School of Journalism, looks more closely at the role of new media in the early days of the "Spring" and the usage of new media by more traditional journalists and concludes:

> ...both new and old communications captured and circulated images of dissent and collective struggle around the world and through sometimes creative adaptations managed to circumvent attempts by repressive states to contain and control the communication environment and thereby nullify their political charge – both domestically and internationally.

Finally in this section, City University Journalism Masters student Teodora Beleaga (with the help of Paul Lashmar) examines the role of another claimed accelerant of change – the WikiLeaks tranche of diplomatic cables unlocked to the world in November 2010. They laid bare the excesses of the Ben Ali and Mubarak regimes, Beleaga concludes:

> It remains for each of us to judge for ourselves whether WikiLeaks has indeed been a catalyst for the uprisings or not. As for the matter of whether WikiLeaks has played any part in the revolutions, it is doubtful that their contribution (as little or as grandiose as we choose to see it) will go unaccounted for in the history books.

One clear lesson to be learned for journalism from the "Arab Spring" is that new media delivers new sources of information which have to be verified using old and new methods. It widens the palette from which we paint a picture story. Whether it is cause or accelerant or social movement in its own right is open to much discussion and dispute, the jury is still firmly out on that.

A "Gay Girl in Damascus", the Mirage of the "Authentic Voice" – and the Future of Journalism

Daniel Bennett examines the phenomenon of "A Gay Girl in Damascus" fake blog which fooled many journalists during the "Arab Spring". Exposure of the deceit came not from the methods of traditional journalism but through a new form of collaborative investigation facilitated by the internet

Amina Abdallah Araf al Omari regarded herself as the "ultimate outsider". On her blog, "A Gay Girl in Damascus", she claimed to be 35-years-old, female, half-American, half-Syrian and gay.[1] Inspired by the revolutionary fervour of the "Arab Spring", her blog posts compellingly documented her personal life as a gay woman and her involvement in the political protests against the Syrian President, Bashar al-Assad.

In April 2011, a post describing how her father had stopped Syrian security services from arresting her led to coverage in the *Guardian*, CNN, CBS and Global Voices. Amina Araf was a pseudonym which had been adopted to conceal her identity, but based on her blog posts and email correspondence with journalists she was represented in the media as an "authentic voice" for the movement against al-Assad's repressive government. She was "an unlikely hero of revolt in a conservative country".[2]

Too unlikely, as it happened. Several months later Amina Araf was unmasked as a fictional character created by Tom MacMaster – a 40-year-old American studying at Edinburgh University. In an apology to the blog's readers, the postgraduate student maintained that "while the narrative voice may have been fictional", "the facts on this blog" were "true and not misleading as to the situation on the ground". He believed he had created an "important voice" for issues which he "felt strongly about".[3] Members of the gay community in the Middle East, however, claimed that he had put people at risk, while journalists criticised his "offensive",[4] "arrogant" and "Orientalist" fantasy.[5]

MacMaster's fictional blog had spiralled out of control but his experiment had inadvertently exemplified the difficulties of performing journalism in the digital era. By removing the physical body and collapsing the geographic, the internet allows us to alter, switch, conceal and simulate our identities more easily and to a greater extent than we have done in the past.[6] In contexts such as the Syrian uprising, when it was difficult for journalists to access individuals in "real life", many reporters were reliant on the digital representations of individuals as a starting point for their journalism.

The story of "A Gay Girl in Damascus" highlights how journalists and readers alike can be seduced by the mirage of the "authentic voice" online, but it also demonstrates that traditional journalistic fact-checking and verification practices were inadequate despite news organisations' emphasis on them in the aftermath. Uncovering "the truth" of Amina Araf's blog was, instead, made possible by a collaborative investigation and verification process facilitated by online networks.

The Context of the Syrian Uprising

The uprising against the Syrian government did attract media attention as part of the "Arab Spring" – a wave of political unrest sweeping across the Middle East and North Africa. The Syrian protests, which began in March 2011, were fuelled by anger at corruption, rising prices, a lack of job prospects, inadequate concessions and the inflammatory response from Syria's security forces. Demonstrators were arrested and shot, while tanks entered Banyas, Deraa, Homs and the suburbs of Damascus. By September 2011, human rights groups claimed 2,200 civilians had been killed by the Syrian regime in an effort to crush the protests.

Chronicling events in Syria, however, was far from straightforward for media organisations. Foreign journalists were expelled from the country shortly after the first protests. Many reporters were forced to wait for fleeing Syrians to arrive at the Turkish border in order to speak to people in person and hear first-hand accounts. A few journalists remained in Syria operating under pseudonyms, but news emanating from the country often relied on the bravery of those sending emails, uploading YouTube videos and posting to social media sites.

The Lure of Amina Araf

It was understandable, then, that the Western media were drawn to Amina Araf's blog. It was unusual and different, offering an alluring first-person glimpse into life in Damascus. Her blog personalised the potential for political and social change in Syria. Amina Araf appeared to be a perfect example of what Ethan Zuckerman identifies as a "bridgeblogger" – somebody who mediated the concerns of the Syrian people to the English-speaking world through her knowledge and experience of the cultures of both Syria and the United States.[7] Araf painted a picture of life for "them" – the heroic "ordinary" Syrians who were protesting against al-Assad's regime. Yet, at the same time, the blogger spoke to "us" in our Western image, offering a "blend of humour and frankness, frivolity and political nous".[8] As Aditya Chakrabortty noted: "This woman thinks like you, blogs like you and appears to have sex like you. She is foreign only in name."[9]

The man behind Amina Araf, Tom MacMaster, had created an illusion based on the uncertainty of geography online, a photograph of a woman living in London and an awareness of what was happening in Syria which was as informed as many other observers. But we completed the illusion – the "authentic voice" of Amina Araf was one Western readers and journalists alike wanted to believe. She seemed to encapsulate hopes for greater freedom of expression for women, sexual liberation in conservative societies and democratic progress in the Middle East. Her voice also demanded attention: in the words of Global Voices blogger, Jillian York, "it was the sense of courage we saw in her, to tell her story so loudly, that made us believe".[10]

Identifying Authentic Voices Online

The internet opens up the possibility of hearing many more voices than we have done in the past. But we also have a tendency to listen only to those voices we want to believe in. Tom MacMaster appears to have been a lone fantasist whose creative fiction went too far, but there are many more calculated attempts to influence our perception of reality. "Authentic" or "credible" voices are actively sought as conduits for the messages of institutions, authorities, governments, militaries and corporations as they attempt to maintain power and influence in a networked communication environment.

The internet era has also thus far created a plethora of "glocalised journalists" who at once have access to thousands of sources all over the globe but who are, at the same time, tethered to their physical location at their newsroom desk.[11] Verifying and assessing the authenticity of online sources is becoming a daily challenge for these journalists. If our understanding of the "real" is increasingly based on its representation through the "virtual" then we need "journalists" who can act as trusted guides to the voices demanding our attention on the web.

The Journalist's Role Representing Reality

The cultural role of journalists and news organisations in society is dependent on their claim to distinguish between authentic and fake in order to "mediate reality".[12] Ideally, their stories should provide a "truthful" representation of events that actually happened or an "acceptable approximation of the truth".[13] The picture of reality which journalists offer has always been constructed, dependent on a variety of limiting factors and often plain wrong, but the internet has illuminated journalism's fault lines as never before. Although journalists are now far savvier in their use of the web, Tom MacMaster's hoax highlighted the pitfalls of operating as a journalist in the digital era.

It is obvious that journalists and news organisations cannot afford to abandon internet sources altogether. After all, many "authentic voices" adopted digital channels to tell the story of the "Arab Spring". YouTube videos from anonymous users provided snapshots of the uprising in Tunisia. Google Executive Wael Ghonim was just one of a number of Egyptians who communicated the overthrow of President Hosni Mubarak through Facebook and Twitter. Yemeni blogger Afrah Nasser provided updates and pictures from protests in Sana'a, while several active bloggers and Twitter users were arrested for chronicling events in the Gulf kingdom of Bahrain.[14]

Identifying and reporting authentic voices online was an important way to access the story of the "Arab Spring", but Tom MacMaster's hoax provided a timely reminder of the challenges of verifying material posted to the web. An editorial in *The Times* used Tom MacMaster's blog as an illustration of "the impossibility of reliable reporting in a situation where sources cannot be verified".[15] Reflecting on their own mistakes *The Guardian*'s Readers' Editor concluded that in the future the newspaper would "have to redouble its efforts in establishing not just methods of verification, but of signalling to the reader the level of verification we think we can reasonably claim".[16]

Although "professional" techniques and practices were re-emphasised in the aftermath by the traditional media, the story of Amina Araf demonstrated that the future of verification and the maintenance of journalism's role as portraying events that have actually happened will increasingly rest on the cultivation of a network of sources and investigators. The weakness of the internet is that many journalists are forced to verify information without face-to-face access to the subject of their stories, but the network it creates enables journalists to have immediate access to far more sources than in the past and facilitates collaborative investigative projects spanning a number of countries.

Unmasking Tom MacMaster: Collaborative Investigation and Verification

The mirage Tom MacMaster had created began to dissolve when he posted a piece purportedly written by Amina Araf's cousin on 6 June. It delivered the alarming news that Amina had been seized by three armed men. MacMaster later said he had decided that the blog was attracting too much attention and he had been looking for a way to close down the blog, but his chosen method for bringing Amina Araf's adventures to a close was ill-advised. The post triggered a campaign to free the detained blogger. Reporters Without Borders demanded her release, a Facebook group quickly gathered 15,000 supporters and US embassy officials in Syria began their own investigation.

Doubts began to surface about Amina Araf's identity when traditional journalism combined with the power of a network of internet sources.

The *Guardian*, which had led coverage of the blog in the UK, received a call from a Croatian woman living in London called Jelena Lecic who told the paper that a picture of her was being used as Amina Araf's image. The *Guardian* also revealed that their journalist in Syria, "Katherine Marsh", who was operating under a pseudonym, had never managed to meet Amina despite several efforts.

Over in the United States, the *Washington Post* discovered that Sandra Bagaria, a woman in Montreal claiming to be a good friend of the blogger, had only ever corresponded with Amina by email.[17] Liz Henry, a blogger and web developer, was also concerned that nobody seemed to have ever met Amina Araf.[18] Similarly, Andy Carvin, a senior strategist at NPR, was hearing from various Syrian sources communicating with him via Facebook and Twitter. They were not only sceptical about Amina's stories, "they weren't even convinced she existed".[19] Carvin told CNN that the more people he asked the less he learned, "because no one had met her".[20]

On 12 June, the Electronic Intifada website compiled a list of reasons why they felt Amina Araf was linked to an American man called Tom MacMaster, an Edinburgh University postgraduate student.[21] They found that a United States address in Georgia used by Amina Araf on a discussion group matched a property belonging to Tom MacMaster. They matched a photograph in a Picasa album belonging to Britta Froelicher, MacMaster's wife, to a photo appearing on "A Gay Girl in Damascus". Finally, they noted that "Paula Brooks", Chief Executive of LezGetReal.com, had apologised for publishing articles written by Amina Araf on the basis that she had used an Edinburgh University IP address to access the LezGetReal servers. (In another twist, "Paula Brooks" was subsequently revealed to be Bill Graber, a 58-year-old man living in Dayton, Ohio).

Tom MacMaster's mirage was constructed on the basis of an elaborate digital identity, but it was his own engagement online and the rapid accumulation of evidence from several interconnected investigations and dozens of sources which led to the detection of his hoax. This is what the future of investigation and verification looks like in an age when people publish and share first, then gather, filter and verify.[22] Where previously journalists have sought to triangulate information from a few sources, now they are increasingly calling on the "collective intelligence"[23] of "the people formerly known as the audience"[24] and the connections formed between individuals online. Multiple sources accessed immediately online as part of interlocking, collaborative investigations across continents have the power to identify "real" people and 'truthful' stories behind "virtual" representations. Refining these skills and processes is necessary if we are to identify and amplify "authentic voices" calling for political and social change in the Middle East, North Africa and around the world.

Conclusion: The Real, the Virtual and the Future of Journalism

"A Gay Girl in Damascus" was "touted as one of the authentic voices from the uprising against the Assad regime".[25] Journalists have long had to guard against potential hoaxers. Tom MacMaster was not the first person to dupe the media with a fantasy and he will not be the last. But his creation of Amina Araf's blog was emblematic of the more fundamental challenges facing journalists reporting the Arab Spring.

In a digital age, the subjects of journalists' stories "are dwellers on the threshold between the real and virtual", "inventing" themselves as they "go along".[26] In environments where the real and virtual are dissolving, people can easily be who they pretend to be and not who they actually are. 21st century journalists often face situations, such as the one in Syria, where they are unable to witness events in 'real life'. They consequently have to make judgements, usually at speed, about whether to trust the identity of a "real" person through their "virtual" representation in the form of text messages, emails, blogs, Twitter feeds and YouTube videos.

In order to maintain their cultural dominance over the representation of reality and their role in making sense of the world, journalists and news organisations have thus far reiterated their commitment to traditional practices of fact-checking and verification. Traditional journalistic practice, however, was not sufficient to spot the Amina Araf hoax; it was the adoption of a networked approach to journalism that ultimately uncovered Tom MacMaster. Increasingly, understanding and representing reality requires a "mutualistic interaction" between traditional news organisations and the new models of journalism,[27] enabling us to identify, hear and amplify the "authentic voices" calling for political and social change around the world.

Notes

[1] Various formulations of her name appeared in media reports including Amina Arraf and Amina Abdullah. She was also cited as being 25 years old in a number of reports

[2] K. Marsh, A Gay Girl in Damascus becomes the heroine of the Syrian revolt, *Guardian*, 7 May 2011. Available online at http://www.guardian.co.uk/world/2011/may/06/gay-girl-damascus-syria-blog, accessed on 21 July 2011

[3] T. MacMaster, Apology to Readers, A Gay Girl in Damascus, 12 June 2011

[4] *Times*, The Curious Case of Amina Arraf; A stupid internet hoax mocks those who genuinely risk their lives for freedom, 14 June 2011

[5] B. Whitaker, Gay Girl in Damascus was an arrogant fantasy, *Guardian*, 13 June 2011. Available online at http://www.guardian.co.uk/commentisfree/2011/jun/13/gay-girl-in-damascus-hoax-blog, accessed on 26 July 2011

[6] S. Turkle, *Life on the Screen: Identity in the age of the Internet*, London: Weidenfeld and Nicolson, 1999 p. 10

[7] E. Zuckerman, Meet the bridgebloggers, *Public Choice*, No. 134, 2008 pp 47–65

[8] K. Marsh op. cit. 2011

[9] A. Chakrabortty, The geography lesson of Gay Girl in Damascus, *Guardian*, 14 June 2011. Available online at http://www.guardian.co.uk/science/2011/jun/13/geography-off-the-map, accessed on 26 July 2011

[10] J. York, Journalistic verification, Amina Arraf, and Haystack, Jilliancyork.com, 10 June 2011. Available online at http://jilliancyork.com/2011/06/10/journalistic-verification-amina-arraf-and-haystack/, accessed on 21 July 2011

[11] B. Wellman, Little Boxes, Glocalisation and Networked Individualism, Revised papers from the Second Kyoto Workshop on Digital Cities II, Computational and Sociological Approaches, 2001

[12] B. McNair, What is Journalism?, H. De Burgh (ed.) *Making Journalists*, London: Routledge 2005 p. 30

[13] ibid

[14] Reporters Without Borders, Bahraini and Syrian Authorities try to impose news blackout, kidnapping in Yemen. Available online at http://en.rsf.org/bahraini-and-syrian-authorities-04-04-2011,39946.html, accessed on 23 July 2011

[15] *Times* op. cit

[16] C. Elliott, The authentication of anonymous bloggers, *Guardian*, 13 June 2011 Available online at http://www.guardian.co.uk/commentisfree/2011/jun/13/open-door-anonymous-blogger, accessed on 26 July 2011

[17] L. Sly, "Gay Girl in Damascus" may not be real, *Washington Post*, 8 June 2011. Available online at http://www.washingtonpost.com/world/middle-east/gay-girl-in-damascus-may-not-be-real/2011/06/08/AGZwCYMH_story.html, accessed on 21 July 2011

[18] L. Henry, Painful doubts about Amina, Composite, 7 June 2011. Available online at http://bookmaniac.org/painful-doubts-about-amina/, accessed on 21 July 2011

[19] A. Carvin, Andy Carvin on the fake Syrian blogger "Amina", CNN, 13 June 2011, Available online at http://www.youtube.com/watch?v=Uf5NlSGOB4Q, accessed on 26 July 2011

[20] ibid

[21] A. Abunimah, New evidence about Amina, the "Gay Girl in Damascus" hoax, Electronic Intifada, 12 June 2011. Available online at

http://electronicintifada.net/blog/ali-abunimah/new-evidence-about-amina-gay-girl-damascus-hoax, accessed on 13 June 2011

[22] C. Shirky, *Here Comes Everybody: How change happens when people come together*, London: Penguin, 2009 pp 35, 81

[23] P. Lévy, *Collective Intelligence: Mankind's Emerging World in Cyberspace*, tr. Robert Bononno, Cambridge, MA: Perseus Books, 1999

[24] J. Rosen, The people formerly known as the audience, PressThink, 27 June 2006. Available online at http://journalism.nyu.edu/pubzone/weblogs/pressthink/2006/06/27/ppl_frmr.html, accessed on 12 January 2010

[25] A. Christie-Miller, "Lesbian" blogger book plan, *Times*, 14 June 2011

[26] Turkle, op. cit

[27] Y. Benkler, A Free Irresponsible Press, *Harvard Civil Rights-Civil Liberties Law Review*, (forthcoming, 2011). Available online at http://www.benkler.org/Benkler_Wikileaks_current.pdf, accessed on 26 July 2011

Note on the author

Daniel Bennett is a PhD candidate in the War Studies Department at King's College, London. He is writing his thesis on the impact of blogging on the BBC's coverage of war and terrorism (2011). The project is funded by the Arts and Humanities Research Council in conjunction with the BBC College of Journalism. He writes *Reporting War*, a blog for the Frontline Club in London, which explores the use of new media to cover conflict.

Cell phones, Camels and the Global Call for Democracy

Simon Cottle examines the role of the new media during the "Arab Spring", the symbolism of the mass demonstrations and role of correspondents observing and experiencing close-up repressive state violence as well as the collective exhilaration of the protestors struggling for political change

How can we account for the generally sympathetic and humanising coverage evidenced in much of the Western media toward the so-called "Arab Spring" and contrary to established academic and political expectations? Here three principal features of today's media and communication environment are identified that help to explain this democratic framing: 1) the role of new media and interpenetrating communication flows in disseminating voices of dissent and potent images worldwide; 2) the symbolism and dramaturgy of the mass demonstrations themselves that resonated culturally in Western media; and 3) the role of correspondents observing and experiencing close-up repressive state violence as well as the collective exhilaration of the protestors struggling for change in such political crucibles as Tahrir Square.

Introduction

Media and communications, both old and new, performed an inextricable part in the so-called "Arab Spring". They continue to do so in its unfolding political trajectory around the world. Indeed, the very terms "Arab Uprising" and "Arab Spring" have become, courtesy of the Western media, part of the established lexicon for these momentous events, labels that serve to define them in ways that Western audiences can understand and which resonate with images and ideas of democratic struggle. There was not one "Arab Uprising", however, but many "uprisings" across the Middle East and North Africa in the first half of 2011, and each continues to unfold according to its own political dynamics.

The protests, demonstrations and civil insurrections that flowed first through the streets and central squares of Tunisia and Egypt, then Morocco, Algeria, Yemen, Oman and Bahrain, as well as in Iran and Lebanon and, more tentatively, in Saudi Arabia, were all marked by their own preceding histories and contemporary weighting of state, military and oppositional forces. As I write, in August 2011, Libyan rebels, following six months of civil war, have just entered Tripoli and, with the backing of United Nations' airpower, are poised to bring down Muammar Gaddafi's 42-year regime of power.

President Bashar al-Assad of Syria, meanwhile, is subject to international condemnation and sanctions only, and continues to unleash his security forces on his own population who, notwithstanding the mass killings and detentions, show no signs of losing their resolve to remove Assad from power. Earlier in the year, Zine al-Abedine Ben Ali in Tunisia and Hosni Mubarak in Egypt were ousted by popular opposition and mass demonstrations and interim authorities promised elections. Ali Abdullah Saleh in Yemen also agreed to step down in forthcoming elections and King Mohamed VI of Morocco set about implementing constitutional reforms. The ruling al-Khalifa family and King Abdullah of Saudi Arabia, for their part, cynically sought to buy-off discontent at home while sending security forces to help crush non-violent protests in Bahrain.

As these different political trajectories suggest, we are dealing with different autocratic regimes, differing political contexts and contingent processes of change. Importantly, the role(s) of media and communications within and across these different uprisings is also no less complex or differentiated. Though the role of new social media has often been highlighted, with some Western commentators tempted to call such events the "Facebook Revolution" or "Twitter Revolution", the role of media and communications within them is a good deal more complex than this. While certainly granting new social media their due, we need to better understand the overlapping and interpenetrating ways in which media systems and communication networks in complex ways entered into these events and communicated them around the world. As I have argued elsewhere,[1] a number of different media and communication inscriptions can be discerned in these important events and each warrants closer inspection in future academic studies. Such studies will need to attend to:

1) How state controlled Arab media variously served to recognise or ignore calls for social justice and political democracy in the period preceding the 2011 uprisings and how and why Western media also turned a blind eye to these same forces of growing discontent.

2) The wider role of Western media and global communication flows in valorising cultures of consumerism *and* the tenets of democracy inside different Arab societies over recent years.

3) The role of new media in sustaining news forms of social conviviality in everyday life and thereby sustaining, both virtually and physically, pluralised identities and interactions in emergent civil society.

4) How new social media, often in interaction with mainstream media and communication flows, served to coordinate mass protests and disseminate messages of solidarity to potential supporters and graphic images of the human costs of their non-violent struggle to publics worldwide.

5) How these same new media tools were deployed by repressive states to target and debilitate the voices of opposition and deny dissident voices communication channels to the outside world.

6) The role of media in transnationalising protest across the Middle East, North Africa and the Gulf states whilst desisting a "media contagion" thesis based on simplistic ideas of "behaviourism" and a de-politicised view of collective action and struggle.

7) The role of international media and communications in helping to recognise and legitimise the political views and democratic aspirations of the oppositional movements, sometimes in advance of national and international political elites.

8) How the events in questions reverberated in repressive states around the world and how this in turn influenced their own internal forms of media censorship and control directed at future opposition.

9) How the established international human rights regime and, specifically, the United Nations' protocols on the "responsibility to protect" (R2P), informed media representations and public deliberation of the United Nation's interventions in Libya, but not, for example, Syria.

10) How processes of democratic momentum in the post-uprising phase can either become stymied or supported in and through new forms of media and institutional and regulatory frameworks.

In all these different ways, then, media and communications have complex ways entered into the politics of the uprisings both temporally, over time, and spatially, across local, national, regional and international political jurisdictions. Here we explore further how and why media and communications helped to grant these politically tumultuous events a human and sympathetic face around much of the world and thereby helped to legitimise the protesters collective actions in terms of democratic struggle – a definition that could only resonate with wider Western audiences.

Such "democratic" media framing in Western mainstream media could reasonably be taken as unlikely, and for at least two principal reasons. First, in a post-9/11 world marked by the "global war on terrorism" and bloody military interventions in Iraq and Afghanistan, Western media have often been criticised for contributing to a widespread and reductionist view of Arab societies, Islam and Muslims, viewing each through a homogenising lens of suspicion, fear and ignorance.[2] Something of this Western Orientalist outlook certainly surfaced early on in the first wave of protests in Tunisia and then Egypt, with media commentators and others expressing surprise at their secular, non-violent and democratic nature and confounding expectations that radical Islamists would, inevitably, be behind such mass challenges to state power.

Second, according to established research findings, radical protests and demonstrations are unlikely to find balanced much less sympathetic media representation. Past studies document how news frames invariably delegitimise political protests and their political claims, denigrating or even demonising the participants involved, labeling them as deviant, and emptying out "the political" by emphasising violence, drama and spectacle.[3] That said, geopolitical interests and outlooks can also enter the media frame, when reporting on political protests and movements in other countries, especially when the protests concerned are challenging regimes "hostile" to the media's host nation.[4] But this does not easily equate with, for example, Mubarak's Egypt, widely regarded as the most "Westernised" of Arab societies and the most important bastion of Western support in the Middle East. So how can we account for this humanising and generally sympathetic coverage found in much of the Western media and contrary to established political and academic expectations?

The discussion that follows identifies three principal features of today's media and communication environment that together help to explain this democratic framing. Each is signaled in the chapter's title: "cell phones", "camels" and the "global call for democracy". First, we consider the much-talked about role of new social media in the uprisings – YouTube, Facebook, Twitter and the like – and how these interfaced with mobile telephony and established mainstream media in the West to bring information and images to audiences world-wide – often as the events unfolded live on the streets. Second we turn to the symbolic and dramaturgical power of the mass demonstrations and how these resonated culturally and powerfully in Western media. And third we also discuss the role played by experientially "embedded" correspondents who observed, close-up and personal, the threats and dangers of being inside such symbolic centers as Tahrir Square in Egypt as well as the collective enthusiasm and exhilaration for political change exhibited by the protestors when in their midst.

Cell Phones: The Rising Tide of Democratising Communication

New social media – YouTube, Twitter, Facebook – along with online bloggers, mobile telephony and more traditional means of communication media all played their part in communicating, coordinating and channeling the rising tide of opposition. Together they managed to bypass state controlled national media and circumvented attempts at communication control and blanket censorship, propelling images and ideas of mass defiance across the Middle East and North Africa and beyond. Unlike earlier acts of self-destruction, the images of Mohammed Bouazizi self-immolating himself in the Tunisian town of

Sidi Bouzid in December 2010, a desperate act of defiance following his denied attempts to work as a street vendor, were captured on video phones by passersby. When posted on YouTube and Facebook, as were those of the mass protests that followed his funeral and the state repression that ensued, such images proved incendiary. In the simmering political discontent of Tunisia and further afield across the Arab world, these images symbolised not only a desperate act of defiance but also unmet democratic aspirations in the face of growing youth unemployment, social injustice and political corruption and authoritarianism.

With 65 per cent of the population of the Middle East under the age of 30 and many "technology-savvy and adept at using new forms of communication to bypass state controls and mobilise around common issues or grievances" a powerful means of coordinating and communicating mass protests was in their hands and "bloggers in Egypt and Tunisia were instrumental in publicising and spreading accounts of torture and human rights violations by the security services".[5] As protestors came up against state repression and military violence, images and accounts of human rights abuses rapidly coursed through available media channels and networks, often confounding attempts by authorities to censor and control the communications environment. Dubbed the "Global YouTube News Bureau", vivid images bearing witness to human rights abuses circulated widely including those originating from countries where some of the worst state atrocities took place such as Libya and Syria and where authorities banned or tightly corralled foreign correspondents. Graphically documenting nonviolent protests being met by deadly state violence, many of these dramatic images flowed through the world's mainstream news services.

In other words, new social media and mainstream media appear to have often performed in tandem, with social media variously acting as a watchdog of state controlled national media, alerting international news media to growing opposition and mass protests and providing raw images of these for wider dissemination. International news media, in turn, including Al Jazeera, helped to distribute the flood of disturbing scenes and reports of the uprisings easily accessed via Google's YouTube and boomeranged them back into the countries concerned. Mainstream newspapers and news broadcasters in their online variants also increasingly incorporated direct links to new social media, effectively acting as a portal to their updating communication flows and near live-streaming of images coming direct from the protests.

These interpenetrating communication flows do not support exclusive claims about the effects of new social media, but rather point to the complex nature and opportunities of today's enveloping communication environment. As commented in the report *Social Media in the Arab World*: "If content had remained strictly on Facebook, its audience would have been limited to those who are members of certain groups, and would not likely have been disseminated in ways that proved pivotal to the media coverage."[6] The evident and pronounced differences in new social media penetration within and across different Arab societies, further underlines how media and communications played, and continue to play, a powerful but differentiated part in the political coordination and wider communication of the uprisings.

What is clear is that both new and old communications captured and circulated images of dissent and collective struggle around the world and through sometimes creative adaptations activists managed to circumvent attempts by repressive states to contain and control the communication environment and nullify their political charge – both domestically and internationally.

Camels: Symbolism and Dramaturgy *for* Democracy

The democratising impetus of today's interpenetrating communication networks and media systems does not only inhere in the technological capacity to capture and circulate images and ideas speedily and extensively to different places and publics. It also inheres in the nature of those images and ideas and how they came to powerfully resonate with distanced audiences. The fact that some images have political charge resides in their symbolic potency and dramaturgic framing. Societies perceive culturally as well as cognitively and all social collectives draw upon established cultural scripts, symbols and performances to help make sense of new events. The so-called "Arab Spring" is no exception.

In an earlier analysis of movement strategy and dramaturgic framing in the American civil rights movement, Doug McAdam,[7] for example, observes how the movement could deploy and benefit from the deep-seated norms and discourses of democracy:

> By choosing action sites and forms of protest that invite nondemocratic responses by state actors, movements in democratic polities have the ability to transform the greater coercive power of the state from an asset into a liability. Resting as it does on the consent of the governed, legitimate state authority can be delegitimated should it appear that it is attempting to maintain consent through coercive means (p. 117).

In the decidedly undemocratic context of the Arab uprising, of course, the protestors were under no allusion of the likely repressive responses by state authorities when challenging their coercive, illegitimate power. They strategically sought to confront this "democratically" nonetheless by mass demonstrations and, for the most part, nonviolent means. The political possibilities of dramaturgic framing were thereby no less operative in this undemocratic context and when viewed by Western news media, and derived in part from the protestors' performative enactment of democratic aims and actions, including nonviolent tactics. When witnessed by global communication systems such scenes and performances could only resonate with the normative outlooks and democratic sensibilities of Western audiences.

Jeffrey Alexander, in *The Civil Sphere* (2006), also considers Martin Luther King's strategy for civil rights in the US, observing how, "By provoking repression and possibly even violence from the movement's southern opponents, nonviolent tactics could make visible and dramatically powerful the anti-civil domination that characterised southern society." "Instead of submitting to surreptitious cruelty in thousands of dark jail cells and on countless shadowed street corners," Martin Luther King wrote, the movement's nonviolent tactics would force the southern "oppressor to commit his brutality openly – in the light of day – with the rest of world looking on."[8] In the context of today's world media "looking on", now often 24/7 through multiple channels and in real-time, this making "visible and dramatically powerful" was heightened in the global coverage of the mass demonstrations in the "Arab Spring". A few examples of the symbolic and dramaturgical nature of the uprising in Egypt, and its appeal for the world's news media, help make the case.

Some of the most startling and dramatic scenes of the mass demonstrations in Egypt, including the "Day of Anger" (25 January) followed by the "Day of Rage" and then the "March of the Millions" (1

February), that forced Hosni Mubarak's departure, were all set in Tahrir Square. Like other major squares and plazas in capital cities, Tahrir Square (Liberation Square), symbolised an important landmark in the nation's capital and is positioned close to a number of sovereign national institutions. The square had already accrued symbolic meaning as the site of the 1977 Bread Riots and March 2003 demonstration against the Iraq War and, before that, historically, as the site of demonstrations against British occupation in 1919 and nationalist opposition to Kedive Tawfik in 1881. It was through its sustained media coverage, however, that the symbol and drama of Tahrir Square became known worldwide.

The images of the protestors in Tahrir Square beamed across the Western media, showed the good nature and harmonious atmosphere of the assembled crowds, literally "demonstrating" their civility and democratic purpose in and through their actions. Inside the Square people engaged in animated discussions, monitored different media and entertained each other through songs, music and poetry. Flowers were offered to the military overseeing the Square and Coptic Christians formed a protective ring around praying Muslims. It was the generally secular ambition of the demonstration, however, that came to publicly define it in the media, reinforced through political slogans written on placards and posters in English and prominently displayed for Western media by protestors who wore, as is generally the case in the capital city, Western attire.

Images such as these, therefore, carried a symbolic and democratising charge, one that helped to rupture the Western post-9/11 view of Arab societies populated by religious fundamentalists and violent extremists. This symbolism was, inevitably, thrown into sharper relief when juxtaposed against the images of state brutality meted out by armed police and security personnel targeting peaceful demonstrators and the dead and bloodied bodies left in their wake. This binary of symbolism found further political charge when situated in the reporting of live, dramatically unfolding events.

One of the most graphic illustrations of the powerful dramaturgy of Tahrir Square came on 2 February 2011 when armed supporters of President Mubarak mounted horses, camels and chariots and rode at full speed into the amassed crowds, beating them with clubs and sticks as they went. This dramatic moment was captured live by many of the world's

TV media now encamped around the Square. Here's a CNN reporter responding live, as best he can, to these unexpected, unscripted scenes:

CNN Live, Breaking News: Camels and Horses Storm Tahrir Square:

Oh it's absolutely tense, it's even more than tense, there's a really strange scene unfolding there right now. We just saw a group of riders on horseback and we're still seeing it, charging into the crowd, we see guys on horseback with clubs, charging, they're pro-Mubarak protestors, charging into the crowds, right there, up there, outside the Egyptian museum, guys on horseback with clubs, guys on *camelback*, guys on *chariots* who are now charging into the crowd. I would say it's about 50 or 60 horses that are now charging...You can probably see the horses coming back here as well, as it seems both sides are trying to fight for turf there, on Tahrir Square which of course is such an important symbol in this, if you will, this "uprising" which has been going on, and so far occupied solely by anti-Mubarak demonstrators but now these pro-Mubarak demonstrators on the scene and seemingly bringing in any weapon that they can with these people on horseback...Right now I have not yet seen any sort of ambulances on the scene. So it's obviously a very serious situation, where you have these things happen, like when you have an army of rioters on horseback come in (CNN Live, 2 February 2011)

As the presenter struggles to makes sense of the unexpected scenes unfolding in front of his eyes, his impromptu commentary betrays not only a loss of fluency brought on by the drama and excitement of what is being witnessed, but also how blame and culpability becomes infused in the moment of making sense of the unfolding drama and its symbolic forms. Camels, so long the tourist symbol *par excellence* of Egypt, when set alongside chariots and even horses in this violent incursion, here take on a decidedly less benign aspect. In the setting of Tahrir Square and unleashed in such dynamic movement against the established presence of nonviolent crowds, they become not only the symbols of traditional, pre-modern Egyptian society, but anti-symbols visibly pitched against civility and democracy.

No wonder perhaps that the CNN correspondent narrating the scenes stumbles toward the language of "uprising". This was just one notable moment of dramaturgy and symbolism that was likely to have resonated through the Western media's "sense-making" of the Egyptian uprising. There were, of course, many such dramaturgical moments and symbolic performances in the reporting of the "Arab Spring", such is the stuff of social revolutions, and these helped to constitute its democratic framing in the Western news media. Activists and protesters on the ground were also aware of the need for international media recognition and were often seen clamoring to put their case to international audiences and governments in front of mainstream news cameras. How the world's assembled media in Tahrir Square responded to these calls *for* democracy, also played a part, discussed next.

The Global Call for Democracy: Journalism Getting Close Up and Personal

The startling and dramatic scenes from Egypt of the "Day of Anger" (25 January) followed by the "Day of Rage" culminating in the "March of the Millions" (1 February), that forced Hosni Mubarak's departure (announced on 11 February), pulsed through satellite and international news coverage. Foreign correspondents in Tahrir Square not only helped to focus world attention on these momentous events but also granted them a human face. By these means, mass demonstrations on the streets of Egypt became less distanced, less humanly remote. Visceral scenes and emotional testimonies elicited in places such as Tahrir Square brought home to watching millions something of the protestors' everyday despair and democratic aspirations as well as their extraordinary courage in confronting, by non-violent means, repressive state violence. At least 846 Egyptians, we know, were killed during 18 days of protest in Egypt's uprising and countless more wounded.[9]

Whereas Western governments at first seemed to be wrong-footed by the surprise and speed of the Arab revolts and equivocated about their possible causes, demographic composition and legitimacy (especially in respect to their foremost Middle East ally, Egypt), many Western news media appeared to grant early recognition to the protesters' aims, sense of grievance and cause. Only as the political efficacy of the mass protests was grasped and the demise of regimes such as Mubarak's Egypt anticipated, did official pronouncements begin to move towards supporting the demonstrators, their civil rights and calls for regime change.

This finding suggests that mainstream media can, on some occasions, adopt a more independent and critically engaged news stance even when political elites may exhibit a relatively united front in terms of their expressed views on the political contention in question.[10] Part of the explanation for this more independent and sympathetic media representation can be found in today's global media ecology,[11] where 24/7 news channels including CNN, BBC World and Al Jazeera, mobile telephony and new social media all provide in differing permutations new opportunities for communicating the voices of dissent and disseminating images of human rights abuses.

And, we have also heard how the symbolic and dramaturgical framing of these events in the news media has contributed to their public enactment as struggles *for* democracy. Helping to bring this home to distanced viewers was the up-close and personal scenes and testimonies collected by correspondents physically "embedded" in the crowds and experiencing themselves threats and violence from an increasingly desperate regime. The phenomenological dimension of embedding, so acutely observed and consequential in the context of war reporting,[12] it seems can also be at work in other contexts of journalist immersion especially when witnessing human vulnerability and traumatic events, whether humanitarian crises,[13] disasters,[14] or popular uprisings confronting state violence.

The images of state brutality and repressive violence captured via new social media and media monitoring services such as BBC Monitoring, that survey round-the-clock, TV, radio, press, internet and news agency sources worldwide, help to "narrow the distance" between unfolding events and those witnessing them whether geographically dispersed audiences or the news editors and journalists watching and editing them back in the newsroom.

> It is the personal testimony provided by user-generated content that gives the emotional power to the storytelling - unlike much of the professionally shot material, which is one step removed from the events portrayed. It is an emotional power that has an impact on our audience and newsroom journalists alike. But it is not just the graphic images that make up this new frontline. Technology – from mobile phones to Skype – now allows participants and bystanders to share their experiences direct and unmediated (Assistant Editor, BBC Interactivity and Social Media Development).[15]

Countless news reports of correspondents on the ground being subject to harassment, and violent assaults also speak to the journalists' personal immersion into a world of threat and possible violence. The *Guardian* newspaper, for example, recounted numerous instances of violence meted out to journalists in its article "Egypt protests: BBC, CNN and Al Jazeera journalists attacked" of 3 February 2011. Here we read how journalists from the BBC, Al Jazeera, and other Arab news organisations were "facing fresh attacks from pro-government 'thugs'" and how Channel 4 News reported that "Mubarak's 'secret police' were threatening journalists to keep away from the streets of Cairo" while "Jonathan Rugman, Channel 4 News' foreign correspondent, tweeted: 'One journalist punched in face, another stabbed in leg by pro-Mubarak thugs in Cairo this morning. On their way to hospital now.'" And Jon Snow, the broadcaster's chief news anchor was also quoted, amongst many others, saying: "Media hotel [is] suffering Mubarak thugs attacking all our attempts to get out to report."[16] When witnessing violence and themselves experiencing threats and personal attacks, the correspondents' political acuity, understandably enough, becomes contextually heightened and the democratic nature of the protestors' struggle increasingly recognised.

No wonder the scenes and voices emanating from Tahrir Square became reported with a palpable sense of elation. Here's BBC correspondent George Alagiah reporting from the heart of Tahrir Square:

> They came from all over Cairo converging on Liberation Square, hoping it would live up to its name. And some came from much further afield. Now this gentleman has just shown me his British passport and he says he's just flown in to be here. "Why is it important to be here today?" "I wanted to be with my brothers and sisters, the young, the old, the children, the people on the wheelchairs, all the people that have suffered during Mubarak's term, for 30 years." This uprising has given space to those whose voices have not always been heard. "We're all Egyptian," she says, "women, men and children. We all represent the country equally."

> Young and old, rich and poor, they were all here. Even the children have a message for the president. "Go away," they shout. A father who hopes his daughters will remember this day as the one that changed their fortunes. Now you only have to be here for a few

moments and you get that sense of elation, that ability to speak out for the first time in, what, 30 years or so. Look at this: You've got flowers given to the soldiers as a gift probably, and down here you've got a sweet stand. A traditional sweet stand. This is part rebellion, but it's also part festival. This was a show of unity. All want Mubarak to go.[17]

Journalists and correspondents embedded *inside* the physical sites of democratic struggle experience not only the imminent sense of threat and repressive state violence arraigned against the protestors and themselves, but also something of the solidarity of the crowds and their sense of elation when united in their democratic endeavor – and this becomes infused in their reporting.

Conclusion

This discussion has pointed to how a combination of three media and communication factors combined to enhance the public definition and elaboration of the "Arab Uprising" or "Arab Spring" as legitimate movements *for* democracy. Together the role of new social media in combination with established media in disseminating voices of dissent and images of state brutality worldwide, the symbolic and dramaturgical forms of these unfolding events, and also the role of correspondents physically embedded with the protestors confronting threats and violence and experiencing something of their elation in challenging repressive state power *all* played a key part in reporting the "Arab Spring". It was by these means that Western news media accepted early on their democratic claims and represented these momentous political challenges as legitimate struggles *for* democracy.

Notes

[1] Cottle, S. (2011) Reporting the Arab Uprisings: Notes for Research, *Journalism: Theory, Practice and Criticism*, Vol. 12, No. 5 pp 647-659; Cottle, S. (2011) Afterword: Media and the Arab Uprisings of 2011, Cottle, S. and Lester, L. (eds) *Transnational Protests and the Media*, New York: Peter Lang pp 293-304

[2] See, for example, Poole, E. and Richardson, J. (eds) (2006) *Muslims and the News Media*, London: I. B. Tauris; Altheide, D. (2009) *Terror Post 9/11 and the Media*, New York: Peter Lang

[3] For reviews,see Cottle, S. (2008) Reporting Demonstrations: The Changing Media Politics of Dissent, *Media, Culture & Society*, Vol. 30, No. 6 pp 853-872

[4] See Fang, Y-J. (1994) "Riots" and Demonstrations in the Chinese Press: A Case Study of Language and Ideology, *Discourse & Society*, Vol. 5, No. 4 pp 463-81

[5] Ulrichsen, K., Held, D, and Brahimi, A. (2011) The Arab 1989? Open Democracy. Available online at http://www.opendemocracy.net/kristian-coates-ulrichsen-david-held-alia-brahimi/arab-1989, accessed on 1 August 2011

[6] Ghannam, J. (2011) *Social Media in the Arab World: Leading Up to the Uprisings of 2011*, Washington, D.C.: Center for International Media Assistance p. 16

[7] McAdam, D. (2000) Movement Strategy and Dramaturgic Framing in Democratic States: The Case of the American Civil Rights Movement, Chambers, S. and Costan. A. (eds) *Deliberation, Democracy and the Media.* Oxford: Rowman and Littlefield pp 117-134

[8] Alexander, J. (2006) *The Civil Sphere*, Oxford: Oxford University Press p. 339

[9] Figures compiled by Egyptian fact-finding committee, reported in *Wall Street Journal*, 20 April 2011

[10] C,f. Bennett, L. (1990) Toward a Theory of Press-State Relations in the United States, *Journal of Communication*, Vol. 40, No. 2 pp 103-25; Bennett, L., Lawrence, R. and Livingstone, S. (2007) *When the Press Fails: Political Power and the News Media From Iraq to Katrina*, Chicago: Chicago University Press; Hallin, D, (1994) *We Keep America on Top of The World*, London: Routledge

[11] Cottle, S. (2009) *Global Crisis Reporting: Journalism in the Global Age*, Maidenhead: Open University Press

[12] Morrison, D. and Tumber, H. (1988) *Journalists at War: The Dynamics of News Reporting During the Falklands Conflict*, London: Sage; Morrison, D. (1994) Journalists and the Social Construction of War, *Contemporary Record*, Vol. 8, No. 2 pp 305-320

[13] Cottle, S. and Nolan, D. (2007) Global Humanitarianism and the Changing Aid-Media Field: "Everyone was Dying for Footage"', *Journalism Studies*, Vol. 8, No. 6 pp 862-878

[14] Cottle, S. (2013) Journalists Witnessing Disasters: From the Calculus of Death to the Injunction to Care, *Journalism Studies* (forthcoming)

[15] Eltringham, M. (2011) The New Frontline is Inside the Newsroom, BBC College of Journalism. Available online at http://www.bbc.co.uk/journalism/blog/2011/03/how-the-newsroom-handles-confl.shtml, accessed on 1 August 2011

[16] Halliday, J. (2011) Egypt protests: BBC, CNN and al-Jazeera journalists, *MediaGuardian*, 3 February. Available online at http://www.guardian.co.uk/media/2011/feb/03/journalists-attacked-in-egypt-protests, accessed on 1 August 2011

[17] BBC, Cross-section of Egyptian society attend protest 1 February 2011. Available online at http://www.bbc.co.uk/news/world-middle-east-12339344, accessed on 1 August 2011

Note on the author

Simon Cottle is Professor of Media and Communications and Deputy Head of the School of Journalism, Media and Cultural Studies (JOMEC), Cardiff University. His latest books are *Global Crisis Reporting: Journalism in the Global Age* (Open University Press, 2009), with co-editor Libby Lester, *Transnational Protests and the Media* (Peter Lang, 2011), and, with Mervi Pantti and Karin Wahl-Jorgensen, *Disasters and the Media* (Peter Lang, forthcoming). He is the series editor of the Global Crises and the Media series for the publisher Peter Lang.

Leaking, Tweeting and Uprising: WikiLeaks and the "Arab Spring"

Teodora Beleaga discusses whether the content of the WikiLeaks cables released in 2010 were the motor of the "Arab Spring" or something more modest

"Twenty secure phones to assist in staying anonymous: $5,000. Fighting legal cases across five countries: $1,000,000...Donations lost due to banking blockade: $15,000,000...Watching the world change as a result of your work: *priceless. There's some people who don't like change; for everyone else, there's WikiLeaks.*" So runs the voiceover of the latest classic MasterCard advertising campaign spoof starring Julian Assange,[1] the founder of WikiLeaks.

Product placement and sums mentioned aside, perhaps the most intriguing aspect of the video is its implicit suggestion that WikiLeaks has caused the protests in Tahrir Square, Egypt. In response to this, a renowned Egyptian blogger produced a post titled: "Dear Julian, it was not the Wikileaks."[2] But, WikiLeaks is not alone in claiming credit for the Arab uprisings and there's more than one Egyptian blogging that WikiLeaks had little to do with the protests.[3] So which is it?

This chapter aims to explore some of the claims that have been made regarding the involvement of the whistle-blowing organisation, WikiLeaks, in shaping the events taking place in the Middle East. The focus will be set mainly on the Jasmine revolution in Tunisia and partially on the Egyptian revolution, as these countries are not only the pioneering future democracies of the region, but they are also said to have inspired the following uprisings in neighbouring countries,[4] since, to put it in Julian Assange's words: "courage is contagious".[5]

In their annual report on "The state of the world's human rights",[6] Amnesty International argues that "WikiLeaks and the newspapers that pored over previously confidential government files, [acted] as a catalyst in a series of uprisings against repressive regimes, notably the overthrow of Tunisia's long-serving President Zine al-Abidine Ben Ali".[7] In the report, which only covers events from 2010, AI's Secretary General Salil Shetty explains how "in particular, some of the documents made clear that countries around the world were aware of both the political repression and the lack of economic opportunity [in Tunisia], but for the most part were not taking action to urge change [thus following their own interests]".[8] This is a key element to be considered when looking at some of the claims made for WikiLeaks as motor of the revolutions.

Although AI's report also hails the mainstream press, such as the London-based *Guardian*, for having published the WikiLeaks released cables,[9] Julian Assange claims the full credit for his organisation given his statement that "media in general are so bad, we have to question whether the world wouldn't be better off without them altogether".[10] Still, one has to ask how many visitors does the WikiLeaks site get compared to the readership of some mainstream news websites that can rise to well over 30 million users per calendar month?[11]

The WikiLeaks Revelations

The New York Times' Executive Editor, Bill Keller, was also reported to have said that "WikiLeaks revelations have, in part, fuelled the remarkable events in the Middle East".[12] Furthermore, the *Guardian*'s David Leigh and Luke Harding, currently no allies of Asssange, also write in their book on WikiLeaks, *Inside Julian Assange's War on Secrecy*: "One of the most interesting – and subtle – immediate positive outcomes of the WikiLeaks saga was in one of those normally obscure countries. Following publication of excoriating leaked cables from the US mission in Tunisia, about the corruption and excess of the ruling family, tens of thousands of protesters rose up and overthrew the country's hated President, Zine al-Abidine Ben Ali." Nevertheless, in a later paragraph they argue that the Tunisians "already knew their ruling family was debauched; they didn't need Wikileaks for that".[13] Similarly, Assange is quoted in one of the WikiLeaks editorials[14] saying:

> My suspicion is that one of the real differences in the cables about Tunisia came in showing that the United States, if push came to shove, would support the army over Ben Ali. That was a signal, not just to the army, but to the other actors inside Tunisia, as well as to the surrounding states who might have been considering intervening with their intelligence services or military on behalf of Ben Ali (many of these dictators in the Middle East prop each other up).

However, for WikiLeaks to have been a catalyst for the "Arab Spring" it must have caused the revolutions to have happened "suddenly, unexpectedly, or prematurely".[15] Given the scale of the events, it is rather clear that there were more factors both determining, as well as allowing, for the protests to take place. As for the timing of the Jasmine Revolution, it could be argued it was not as sudden or unexpected as one may think. Yasmine Ryan comments for Al Jazeera that there were more Tunisians setting themselves on fire before Mohamed Bouazizi, whose act was massively reported to have triggered the uprisings. Additionally, a relative of Bouazizi, Rochdi Horchani, said to Al Jazeera: "We could protest for two years here, but without videos no one would take any notice of us."[16] Thus what Rochani points to are the social networks, Facebook and Twitter, for having helped the promotion and distribution of the Tunisian Revolution. The same social networks have been deemed the "most appalling spying machine[s] that have ever been invented" by WikiLeaks' mastermind Julian Assange.[17]

Nonetheless, as past events have shown us, so called "Twitter revolutions" are not enough on their own. Take, for example, the Moldavian uprisings in April 2009[18] when the social networks helped gather the thousands of students who took over the House of Parliament while at the same time assisting the secret police gather information about these students for either detaining them or simply forcing them to return home.[19] The Moldavian protests were perhaps the first to be hailed as a "Twitter revolution" in the media, but the revolution did not gain much success. For Russia quickly moved to support the Moldavian Communist Party[20] in blaming the protesters – and this helped stop any other country from interfering (Libya-style) in any way.[21]

Therefore, Assange and Amnesty International are both right in claiming WikiLeaks contributed to the "Arab Spring" since their cables portrayed the situation in both Tunisia and Egypt for the whole world to see. What the Middle East protesters were claiming was backed up by hard evidence, unlike in Moldavia where the students lacked proof of the voting scam they argued had taken place. Assange also believes that "one is either a participant in history or a victim of it, and that there is no other option",[22] but it takes more than one participant to change the world and it certainly takes more than one man to run WikiLeaks. For even WikiLeaks' current life span would have been questionable if it was not for all the support Assange attracted for his organisation, whether it was from the sources providing him the infamous cables, from the mainstream media whose partnership proved invaluable in spreading the word on the leaks or from all the supporters worldwide whom have donated towards the organisation thus ensuring its financial survival.

The Crucial Timeline
The timeline is also essential to look at in this debate.[23] The Jasmine Revolution in Tunisia was reported to have started in Sidi Bouzid with the self-immolation of Mohamed Bouazizi on 17 December 2010. Little over two weeks earlier, on 30 November 2010, WikiLeaks published four leaked cables on Tunisia, two originating from "Embassy Paris"[24] and the other two from "Embassy Tunis".[25] Following the Tunisian uprising, President Ben Ali fled the country on 14 January 2011. Similarly, in Egypt, the protests are said to have been triggered by the bombing of a Coptic Church in Alexandria on 1 January 2011,[26] and culminated with the first organised protest on 25 January 2011 in Tahrir Square, Cairo. President Mubarak stood down on 11 February 2011 handing his powers over to the army. While hundreds of cables appear to have been leaked on 16 February 2011 on Egypt, it is rather complicated to track down the number of cables released either during the revolution or before with servers crashing over internal errors.[27] Yet it was reported in the media that cables released on 28 January 2011 had "fuelled the unrest".[28]

As events unfolded, protesters used social media tools, the sites Twitter and Facebook, to both communicate between themselves and let the world know what was going on. In response, these websites, and others, were constantly being blocked, with profiles erased or hacked into and used for other reasons. Thus, of particular significance is also the reportedly restrictive access both Tunisians and Egyptians had to the leaked WikiLeaks documents.[29] For, blackout aside, the question of whether, how and for what amount of time did Tunisians and Egyptians have access to this documents is crucial to solving this matter. Additionally, a representative number of people needs to have learned of the documents and have spread the word in order for them to have made such a difference as to be regarded as a catalyst to the events that followed.

To conclude with, this is certainly a debate with little prospect of reaching a resolution, and, given the current circumstances in the Arab world (note Libya and Syria), with little prospect of being put to rest too. Which is why, until a full-scale research into all the fundamental questions surrounding the issue is conducted and made available, it remains for each of us to judge for ourselves whether WikiLeaks has indeed been a catalyst for the uprisings or not. As for the matter of whether WikiLeaks has played any part in the revolutions, it is doubtful that their contribution (as little or as grandiose as we choose to see it) will go unaccounted for in the history books.

- **The author thanks Paul Lashmar for his invaluable contribution to this chapter.**

Notes

[1] Video: http://mashable.com/2011/07/01/wikileaks-mastercard-spoof/ and on Tahrir link. Available online at http://www.democracyreview.com/2011/07/wikileaks-priceless-spoof-of-mastercard.html, accessed on 1 August 2011

[2] Full post available online at http://egyptianchronicles.blogspot.com/2011/07/dear-julian-it-was-not-wikileaks.html, accessed on 1 August 2011

[3] Another blogger, among others: http://bikyamasr.com/wordpress/?p=35631

[4] "In no time the upheaval in Tunisia triggered tremors in other countries," reads the Amnesty International report (p. 14)

[5] In conversation with Julian Assange Part II. Available online at http://wikileaks.org/In-Conversation-with-Julian,107.html, accessed on 1 August 2011

[6] Full report available online at http://www.amnesty.org/en/library/asset/POL10/001/2011/en/519da037-1492-4620-9ed5-cac8f1cfd591/pol100012011en.pdf, accessed on 1 August 2011

[7] Amnesty International hails WikiLeaks and *Guardian* as Arab Spring "catalysts", Paul Walker, *Guardian*, 13 May 2011. Available online at

http://www.guardian.co.uk/world/2011/may/13/amnesty-international-wikileaks-arab-spring, accessed on 1 August 2011

[8] Full report available online at http://www.amnesty.org/en/library/asset/POL10/001/2011/en/519da037-1492-4620-9ed5-cac8f1cfd591/pol100012011en.pdf, accessed on 1 August 2011

[9] Amnesty International hails WikiLeaks and *Guardian* as Arab Spring "catalysts", Paul Walker, *Guardian*, 13 May 2011. Available online at http://www.guardian.co.uk/world/2011/may/13/amnesty-international-wikileaks-arab-spring, accessed on 1 August 2011

[10] Comment made by Assange in an interview for RT, video available on YouTube at http://www.youtube.com/watch?v=M27qRXZsIsg, accessed on 1 August 2011

[11] Guardian sets record with 37m online readers, netimperative, 29 January 2010. Available online at http://www.netimperative.com/news/2010/january/guardian-sets-record-with-37m-online-readers, accessed on 1 august 2011

[12] A priest of free speech who wanted to reveal everything except his own story, Easter Addley, *After Wikileaks*, *Guardian* supplement, 5 February 2011

[13] Leigh, D. and Harding, L. (2011) *WikiLeaks: Inside Julian Assange's War on Secrecy*, London: Guardian Books, p. 247

[14] In Conversation with Julian Assange Part I, Hans Ulrich Obrist, Wikileaks, 23 May 2011. Available online at http://wikileaks.org/In-Conversation-with-Julian.html, accessed on 1 August 2011

[15] From the *Oxford Dictionary*. Available online at http://oxforddictionaries.com/definition/catalyst and http://oxforddictionaries.com/definition/precipitate, accessed on 1 August 2011

[16] See How Tunisia's revolution began, Yasmine Ryan, Al Jazeera, 26 January 2011. Available online at http://english.aljazeera.net/indepth/features/2011/01/2011126121815985483.html, accessed on 1 August 2011

[17] Comment made by Assange in an interview for RT, video available on YouTube at http://www.youtube.com/watch?v=M27qRXZsIsg, accessed on 1 August 2011

[18] Election by stealth, Stela Brinzeanu, *Guardian*, 8 April 2009. Available online at http://www.guardian.co.uk/commentisfree/2009/apr/08/moldova-protest, accessed on 1 August 2011

[19] The trouble with Twitter, James Harkin, *Guardian*, 29 December 2009. Available online at http://www.guardian.co.uk/commentisfree/2009/dec/29/trouble-twitter-social-networking-banality?INTCMP=SRCH, accessed on 1 August 2011

[20] Russia furious with EU over Twitter revolution, Shawn Walker, *Independent*, 9 April 2009. Available online at http://www.independent.co.uk/news/world/europe/russia-furious-with-eu-over-twitter-revolution-1666121.html, accessed on 1 August 2011

[21] Dispute hits Europe's gas supplies, BBC News, 7 January 2009. Available online at http://news.bbc.co.uk/2/hi/7814743.stm, accessed on 1 August 2011

[22] In conversation with Julian Assange Part II, Wikileaks. Available online at http://wikileaks.org/In-Conversation-with-Julian,107.html, accessed on 1 August 2011

[23] "Arab Spring": An interactive timeline of Middle East protests, Garry Blight and Sheila Pulham, *Guardian*, 12 July 2011. Available online at http://www.guardian.co.uk/world/interactive/2011/mar/22/middle-east-protest-interactive-timeline, accessed on 1 August 2011

[24] The cables can be found at
http://cablesearch.org/cable/view.php?id=06PARIS2069&hl=tag%3ATS and
http://cablesearch.org/cable/view.php?id=06PARIS2069&hl=tag%3ATS, accessed on
1 August 2011

[25] ibid

[26] Egypt bomb kills New Year churchgoers, David Batty, *Guardian*, 1 January 2011.
Available online at http://www.guardian.co.uk/world/2011/jan/01/egypt-bomb-kills-
new-year-churchgoers, accessed on 1 August 2011

[27] I have attempted several times on different days and at different hours to find the
cables on cablesearch.org, with the website giving a 500 internal error code after the 25th
page. This may be just a coincidence

[28] WikiLeaks cables fuels flames of unrest in Egypt, *Telegraph*, 28 January 2011. Available
online at
http://www.telegraph.co.uk/news/worldnews/africaandindianocean/egypt/8287842/
WikiLeaks-cables-fuel-flames-of-unrest-in-Egypt.html, accessed on 1 August 2011

[29] How Arab governments tried to silence Wikileaks, Ian Black, *Guardian*, 17 December
2010. Available online at http://www.guardian.co.uk/world/2010/dec/17/arab-
governments-silenced-wikileaks, accessed on 1 August 2011

Note on the author

Teodora Beleaga has graduated with a First Class Honours degree in Journalism and
Media from Coventry University in July 2011. Following her studies she was offered a
place at two of the most prestigious journalism schools in the world, Columbia School
of Journalism and City University Journalism. She was also admitted on the Erasmus
Mundus Journalism Programme at both Aarhus University and the University of
Amsterdam. Starting September 2011, she will be studying Interactive Journalism at City
University London.

Section 5. Women on the Media Frontlines and During the "Spring"

John Mair

It is still hotly disputed who got the broadcast scoop of the Libyan rebels entering Green Square in Tripoli on the evening of Sunday, 21 August. One thing is certain:-the reporter was female. Alex Crawford, of Sky News, is felt to have the edge but Sara Sidner, of CNN, and Zeina Khodr, of Al Jazeera English, were not far behind on air.

Jackie Gregory, of Staffordshire University, takes a more global view of the role of women in general during the "Arab Spring". She analyses the emergence of the woman as icon for her country and its struggle. These include Iman al-Obeidi of Libya, the rape victim who burst into the journalists' hotel to tell her story, Israa Abdel-Fattah, the Egyptian activist who became the "Facebook girl", Maryam al-Khawaja, the face of Bahrain, Tawakul Karmen for Yemen as well as Saida Sadouni, of Tunisia. As Gregory argues:

The framework of using women as icons appears to be a quick shorthand for portraying the troubles of entire nation – brave but vulnerable, protesting but often brutally abused, beautiful but bloodied – superficial generalisations which do not get under the true skin of a country. The icon is not male because he would not represent victimhood. Female icons rarely represent a country's power, wellbeing, and success.

Crawford described movingly earlier in this volume how she and her crew were in "the right place at the right time"; Zeina Khodr and Sara Sidner describe how they got to the frontline in Glenda Cooper's excellent contribution. She has interviewed all three plus others such as Lindsay Hilsum, of Channel Four News, who also featured earlier in this volume. Cooper looks at the history of female war correspondents as well as the contemporary and concludes: "Crawford *et al* made clear women can report in the traditional 'macho' way – and do it just as effectively, armed only with a car cigarette lighter."

Julie Tomlin, who organises events for the Frontline Club in London, looks at a different group of frontline women: Arab women in and out of the state media. Shahira Amin, the deputy director and anchor of Egypt's Nile TV, who resigned on principle from her position on 3 February; Reem Haddad, the director of Syria's state television network and spokeswoman for the Ministry of Information and Hala Musrati, a Libyan TV anchor who became known as "Gaddafi's presenter" for her slavish and undying loyalty in the dying days of his regime. And, as Tomlin puts it, "the certainties of the West and its media are also being shaken in many ways, including by the refusal of women in the Arab world to fit its stereotypes".

Both on the streets and on screen in Arab and Western countries, women have had a prominent role during the "Spring". Whether this re-positioning is temporary or permanent, time and the progress of the "revolutions" will tell.

The Iconic Female in the "Arab Spring": Just an Illusion?

Jackie Gregory explores women's role in the "Arab Spring" and the ways in which the Western media have either ignored or stereotyped their experiences

The Arab Spring sprang as a surprise to the Western media. Eyes were focused in a different direction. Foreign correspondents were more likely to be holed up in Jerusalem than Tunis and suddenly they were miles away from the seismic story. In the previous twelve months, the British press had concentrated on the Israel/Palestine issue (Afghanistan/Iraq notwithstanding) with more articles devoted to this than to Tunis, Eqypt and Libya put together. [1] Little wonder they hadn't seen what was coming.

Once the mainstream media hot-footed it to the hotspots, there was a second "surprise" – women who were central to the action. They were a galvanising force on the streets, at home, in the workplace and through social media. This wasn't in the script – the English-speaking one at any rate.

Stereotypes of the Arab Woman Confounded

It was clear that a revision of long-held Western perceptions of all Arab women being without voice and confined to the home was overdue – but tensions arose in reporting this. Some of the first stories highlighting women's involvement were, in fact, analyses of why this fact had not gained more press attention. Once the women's stories started to emerge, so did additional narratives that women were fighting for their own rights and to be free from gender oppression. But the truth, as always, is more complicated.

The women who had taken to the streets in Tunisia, Egypt, Yemen, Syria, Libya, Bahrain had done so to support the popular uprising to overthrow dictatorships. They died, were injured, imprisoned, abused alongside the men. Fighting for their own rights was never the primary aim.[2] However, women are now fearful that once the dust settles, the same old kind of order will return – with men remaining the dominant force in society – and their efforts will go unrewarded.

As women's involvement gained more currency in the media, so did another kind of narrative – the individual female becoming an icon for their country – yet this has attracted virtually no analysis. As new uprisings burst on to the streets, suddenly in the Western media, there sprang on to the page a single woman who was either a catalyst for the protest or who came to represent either the country or the protest.

This woman was depicted as strong but vulnerable, a victim but also a powerful force. It is rarely a man who symbolises a country, always a woman. She is an emotive symbol – used by the media to tell a complicated story. The women themselves did not ask to become icons, they were fighting for a cause they believed in along with thousands of their fellow women and men. To claim they represent a whole country is to negate the differing views, cultural, sociological and political mores within a society, and resort to stereotype. With a Western media consumed by celebrity and picking on a small cast of characters to variously celebrate and humiliate, it appears that the "shortcut" to reporting on a life-threatening, life-changing, serious political upheaval was to project the ambitions and the woes of each country on to one particular woman.

These include Iman al-Obeidi of Libya, the rape victim who burst into the journalists' hotel to tell her story, Maryam al-khawaja – described as the face of Bahrain, and Lara Logan, a South African journalist working for an American TV channel, who was attacked during the Tahrir Square celebrations. These icons are held up as brave but in need of rescue, patronised by the West, admired and pitied in the same breath by a Western audience.

The Female Icon: An Illusion?

In an analysis of print media that is also available online, and commentary taken from blogs, this chapter will contend that the female icon, through no fault of the woman who is held up as one, is there to embody the complexities of a particular state and cloaked with the perceptions and the personality the West throws on them, only to disappear from Western view as the story and the media's flighty concentration moves on to another country. Left behind are the experiences and voices of thousands of other women unheard. For academic writers Shahin Cole and Juan Cole,[3] most of the international media were initially missing the women's story for two reasons: their obsession with other parts of the Arab world, and the mindset that Arab women are oppressed. The Coles said:

> Women couldn't have been more visible in the big demonstrations of early to mid-January in the streets of Tunis, whether accompanying their husbands and children or forming distinct protest lines of their own – and given Western ideas of oppressed Arab women, this should in itself have been news.[4]

Women, they point out, have historically played their part in mass protests such as during the Algerian fight for independence from France from 1954-1962, the campaigns for unions in Tunisia since the 1940s, and the 1979 revolution in Iran, but it was the size of the female crowd which made a difference this time round. They argue:

> The sheer numbers of politically active women in this series of uprisings, however, dwarf their predecessors. That this female element in the "Arab Spring" has drawn so little comment in the West suggests that our own narratives of, and preoccupations with, the Arab world – religion, fundamentalism, oil and Israel – have blinded us to the big social forces that are altering the lives of 300 million people.

To the Egyptians, there was no surprise that the "revolution" finally erupted.[5] There had been industrial unrest in Egypt since 2004, with more than 3,000 strikes taking place, many led by women.[6] When reporters did pick up on the women protesters, their interpretation of what was happening displayed a complete confusion of how this should be framed, reverting quickly to Western paradigms. Laura King, for instance, for the *Los Angeles Times*, wrote:

> Almost from the outset of unrest that erupted nine days ago, women and girls have made up a substantial presence in Tahrir Square, Cairo's central plaza, which quickly became the focal point of the struggle. Gaggles of teenage girls, dignified matrons and white-haired grandmothers have trekked daily to the Square, swelling the crowd at a time when numbers were a crucial gauge of opposition power.[7]

This kind of description, where women are grouped according to stereotype and without any sense that the female protesters had their own individual political will, angers writers from Arab countries and post-colonial feminist writers alike, as we shall see, including Lila Abu-Lughod, of Columbia University, Dr Natana Delong-Bas, of Boston University, and writers from Muslimah Media Watch. They argue the Western media reports from its own standpoint, an outsider looking in and imposing its own values to read the situation and construct a narrative.

Critics of Easy Stereotyping

News articles focusing on a single woman in need of "rescuing" or "being supported" by outsiders – with the West like a gallant knight coming to the "poor" woman's aid – are not new. Post-colonial feminist Gayatri Chakravorty Spivak[8] described this kind of media coverage, in 1998, as "white men saving brown women from brown men". Dr Natana J Delong-Bas, editor in chief of the *Oxford Encyclopaedia of Islam and Women*, reacted to this kind of coverage of the "Arab Spring":

> These women are not waiting for someone to come and rescue them. They are active participants in their own liberation. They are leaders who provide vision, strategy, technological expertise, networks, logistics, determination, courage and sheer numbers. In stark contrast to the image of Arab women in charge of nothing but their homes, these women are picketing outside supermarkets, staging sit-ins with their children, organising demonstrations,

networking with each other, teaching workshops on the tactics of nonviolence, tearing down security fences and marching through checkpoints to connect with people on the other side.[9]

Fatima Outaleb, founding member of the Union for Women's Action in Morocco, notes: "The Western media is shaped according to certain agendas, to certain priorities they have in mind, and policies regarding Arab women. They have ignored the reality that Arab women have always been at the heart of revolutions in the region - whether leading, strategising, raising awareness or mobilising as bloggers, or on Facebook."[10]

Comment is Free...and Fierce

Feminist blogger Megan Kearns[11] was one of the first in January 2011 to highlight the participation of women in the "Spring". She argues that women are also "crucial in the media as commentators, or in political discussions". The Comment is Free section of the *Guardian* website has facilitated some of this debate. Soumaya Ghannoushi,[12] a researcher from the School of Oriental and African Studies, wrote in March, 2011 that the protests have revolutionised how the West views Arab women, and "is shattering stereotypes that they are repressed and submissive victims of a misogynist society". She tells the story through 77-year-old Saida Sadouni who camped out for two weeks in front of the Prime Minister's quarters in Tunis and organising the Kasbah picket which was pivotal in forcing the interim government out of office.

"Saida Sadouni does not conform to the typical image of an Arab revolutionary...She is today widely hailed as the mother of Tunisia's revolution, a living record of her country's modern history and its struggle for emancipation," says Ghannoushi.

Ghannoushi broadly echoes the Coles in saying that the women are rebelling on two fronts: against the conservative Muslim community who demand that women preserve the family's honour through sexual purity and submissiveness and, secondly, against the Western "neo liberals" who view Arab and Muslim women "through the narrow prism of the Taliban model" and believe they need deliverance from the West. But Nesrine Malik,[13] a London-based writer from Sudan, suggests in an April post of Comment is Free that Ghannoushi herself was guilty of perpetuating another widely-used myth – that of a single Arab woman as a figurehead for a whole country. Malik believes women taking part in the 2011 protests are being tokenised to lend legitimacy and "dignity" to a male revolution, which once over, will not improve women's rights and that lip service only is paid to gender rights. "It is the same currency of 'dignity', so emotively useful during the fight, which is used against women once the revolutionary fervour has died down," says Malik, citing how the Eqyptian military imposed "virginity tests" on women after Mubarak's fall.

She concludes that it is not the Western media waking up to dismantle stereotypes which will further the female cause, but by women themselves becoming involved in civic justice and political reform and making changes from within their countries.

It is clear from my trawl of articles from the mainstream print media posted online that Ghannoushi was not alone in using this reductive narrative of telling it through one woman. Perhaps it is the simplest way for Western journalists parachuted in to a country to make sense of what is going on. Some countries have not had a free press, the back catalogue is not immediately there, nor is there a network of local journalist contacts to draw on. If they could tell it through the eyes of one person they have an emotive, simple story, easily filed.

But there could be other reasons. In fact, Chandra Mohanty, in her essay "Under Western Eyes",[14] cites the ubiquitous use of "Third World woman" as a continuum of colonisation. This notion of a "Third World woman" comes to represent everyone without taking into account cultural, religious, political or socio-economic references between countries which are as every bit as diverse as those between France and the United States, for example. Mohanty continues: "This average Third World woman leads an essentially truncated life based on her feminine gender (read sexually constrained) and being Third World (read ignorant, poor, uneducated, victimised etc)." She argues that, while the West continues to assume it is the superior power, then there will forever be images such as "the veiled woman", "the powerful mother" and "the chaste virgin".

The Female Icons of the Arab Spring?

During the "Arab Spring", the women who became icons include Israa Abdel-Fattah, the Egyptian activist who became the "Facebook Girl"[15];

Maryam al-Khawaja, the face of Bahrain[16]; Tawakul Karmen, an icon for Yemen[17] as well as the already-mentioned Saida Sadouni, of Tunisia, and Iman al-Obeidi, of Libya, who will be discussed in more depth in this chapter along with al-Khawaja. There is one exception to these icons, in Syria, the face here is a 13-year-old teenage boy Hamza al Khatib, who was tortured and murdered.[18]

Anthropologist Lila Aby-Lughod[19] warned of the dangers of plastering "neat cultural icons like Muslim women over messy historical dynamics" after the 9/11 terror attack. She advocates the avoidance of the idea of the West trying to "save" the East, arguing instead for the West to take on their responsibilities and address the global injustice which shapes the politics of poorer countries.

False Icons?

There has been one particular story from the "Arab Spring" which illustrates how the Western media imposes its values. It was a story which gained more media coverage in America and Britain both on television and in print than most others. It came to define the uprisings. In February 2011, the British and US media chose to "go large" in their focus on one single woman in particular, who is white, US-based and a journalist – one of their own – and through her experience, the media has sought to disseminate their view of the Arab world.

TV foreign correspondent Lara Logan was attacked on 21 February 2011 and subjected to a sexual assault while reporting for American channel CBS on the celebrations in Tahrir Square. In right-wing press reports there was an implicit undercurrent that this "attractive" woman should have stayed at home, among her own people – it became yet another version of rescuing a damsel in distress. In Britain, the *Daily Mail* became obsessed with the story. It ostensibly played out her "bravery", but then interwove descriptions of her appearance and history of her love life into each article, along with photographs of her being pregnant, and attending glamorous events with her partner and previous partner. The underlying tone was that Tahrir Square was no place for a blonde woman to get mixed up with Muslim men.

Mary Elizabeth Williams,[20] a writer for salon.com, railed against a more extreme version of this view written by Simone Wilson[21]. Wilson, after describing Logan as having shocking good looks, wrote in *LA Weekly*: "In a rush of frenzied excitement, some Egyptian protesters apparently consummated their newfound independence by sexually assaulting the blonde reporter." This quotation and others about Logan's love life, led Williams to accuse Wilson of "a hideously twisted bit of commentary on an assault victim, one that repulsively mingles the woman's attractiveness and sexual history with a violent crime".

In the first and second of their Logan articles, the *Mail* reproduced comments of ITV correspondent Julian Manyon[22] who wrote in the *Spectator* about Logan's "charms". "The considerable physical charms of my travelling companion, the delectable Lara Logan, who exploits her God-given advantages with a skill that Mata Hari might envy", he salivated. What the *Mail* failed to say was that Manyon had made these claims 10 years earlier in 2001 but the paper chose to drag them out from the files for this story. Also embedded in the same report were allegations of anti-semitism. To quote the *Mail*: "The *New York Post* reported that a CBS source claims her attackers shouted 'Jew! Jew!' during the assault."[23] A third-hand quote at best which cannot be verified, but the Mail used it on both 16 and 17 February[24] and again on 21 February 2011.[25]

Later, the *Mail* quotes Logan talking about when she was detained by the Egyptian army days before the attack in Tahrir Square. "We were accused of being Israeli spies," she said. Indeed, in the 21 February article, the Israeli agent line (which Logan said had been adopted before this attack) and the "Jew! Jew!" quote are now merged in the same report and repeated, to give the effect they both happened at the same time.

In this later article, the *Mail* reveals more details of the attack by what it calls a "frenzied" mob. It quotes *The Sunday Times* as saying "sensitive parts of her body were covered in red marks that were originally thought to have been bite marks". It adds these turned out to be wheals from aggressive pinching. Therefore, there had never been any need to include the "bite" line, except to paint a gratuitous picture of alleged "animal" behaviour by Muslim men. Logan was "saved" by a group of women "wearing religious robes".

There is no doubt that Logan suffered a brutal sexual assault but there was a prurience in the *Mail*'s reporting and underlying tone of disapproval that was not unlike the narrative of a Victorian Gothic novel where the heroine "faints" when masculine brutishness becomes too much. This undermines the very real trauma which Logan went through. The Logan incident was hijacked to promote prejudices about Muslim men, about Islam v Judaism, whether a mother should be a war correspondent, or good looking, or even both. It was reductive in that it didn't use this incident to take an in-depth look at the wider experience of Egyptian women. The media coverage of Lara Logan, apart from a few quotes from herself, did little to promote their rights.

Women in Egypt have been subject to sexual harassment over many years. In 2008, a study by the Eqyptian Centre for Women's Rights found that 83 per cent of women had experienced sexual harassment and that the majority of these women were veiled and dressed modestly.[26] This was reported at the time by the BBC, but the issue of harassment only gained wider prominence in Britain and USA when one blonde Western reporter came under attack – and then only as an addendum.

The Libyan Woman whose Plight simply Could not be Ignored

Another story which captured the print media's attention was that of Libyan lawyer Iman al-Obeidi. She burst on to the journalists' radar on 26 March 2011 when she gate-crashed their hotel, the Rixos in Tripoli, blood stained and angry, telling how she had been raped. Jonathan Miller, of Channel 4 News, told the *Daily Mirror* how a fight ensued as military police sought to silence her and journalists tried to stop her being dragged away again. Miller said: "The assembled journalists had been under virtual house arrest at the hotel in March. We had been unable to get a real sense of what life was like for ordinary Libyans. Iman had just changed that."[27]

The Libyan government countered that she was a prostitute, mentally unstable and drunk. After a chaotic few days of not knowing where al-Obeidi had been taken to, she was later given refuge in Qatar. But not before various stories had emerged that she had been saved by the West and given refuge in the US. Headlines such as "Libyan rape victim flees the country with help from defecting soldiers and Western diplomats"[28] were typical.

When in Qatar, al-Obeidi gave an interview saying how important it was that the world knew of her plight. "If they weren't scared of the journalists and cameras and the world watching, then what would stop them killing me? But at least I was satisfied I'd created a scandal. I didn't want to keep silent about what had happened to me," she said.[29]

After her initial outburst in the hotel, Libyan officials announced al-Obeidi had been charged because it is an offence in Libya to accuse someone of a sexual crime. According to Muslimah Media Watch this led to articles and comment in the Western media about "honour", "tribe" and "protection".[30] MMW believe this was a right-wing exploitation of the story to promote hysteria about Sharia law. It ignores the fact, it says, that Col. Gaddafi has a fear of Islam and is no upholder of the faith or Sharia law. The writer, Tasnim,[32] says: "Any story of a Muslim woman being raped necessitates, of course, some outraged rhetorical flourishes on how Muslim men treat Muslim women like chattel, as though rape was some kind of cultural crime restricted to barbaric Middle Eastern countries. It is not."

In the same article, Muslimah Media Watch also contends that Western media, either through ignorance or prejudice, portrays Arab women as "victims" and patronises these women when they do not conform to this stereotype. The organisation says it is problematic that Iman al-Obeidi has become a symbol, not only in the West but in Libya. It quotes Libya's (now defected) Ambassador to the UN Abderrahman Shalgham as saying: "Iman is Libya – Libya the victimised, raped and silenced land" and then MMF adds as comment: "This nationalist fantasy, or more accurately Shalgham's appropriation of it for emotional effect, is problematic and disturbing on multiple levels."

An Icon in Bahrain?

Similar views of frustration followed the publication of an article by Karen Leigh, in the *Atlantic*. Leigh had taken the now familiar framework of portraying one country's revolution through the eyes of one woman. This time is was Maryam al-Khawaja, of Bahrain, "her anecdotes and big brown eyes humanising Bahrain's faltering opposition for a West that did not fully understand it."[31] It is ironic that Leigh writes about the West's lack of understanding while using the literary device of one person being metaphor for a whole country, and so becomes guilty of reduction and generalisations herself. In a subsequent paragraph, al-Khawaja is described as the face of one of the most repressed of "Arab Spring" revolutions. The article highlights the personal abuse and surveillance she undergoes for speaking out. The online version of this article sparked many comments. "I would request the author to focus on the US human rights grave abuses throughout the world," says one.[32] Several other

Bahrainians say that al-Khawaja does not represent them at all. Some feel that al-Khawaja only speaks for Shia people.

It Really was Only an illusion

Then there was the icon who turned out to be the figment of a 40-year-old man's imagination. The blog "A Gay Girl in Damascus" which attracted a worldwide following and garnered much comment from journalists turned out to be a hoax. The blog itself has now been removed from the internet, but left behind are a wealth of comment articles about why we were taken in.

Tom MacMaster, an American studying for a PhD at Edinburgh University, wrote under the pseudonym of Amina Abdallah Aral al Omari, purporting to be a lesbian and talking about her life as a gay person in a Muslim country. Before it was revealed as a hoax, Sara of Muslimah Media Watch wrote: "What is most refreshing about Abdullah's blog is that she does not paint herself as the voice of Syria's revolution. She represents herself as an individual, and speaks honestly about her own lived experiences."[33]

But it was too good to be true; and MacMaster was eventually exposed. As Josephine Tovey comments in *The Sydney Morning Heralds*: "The character constructed was someone many liberal-minded people in the West wanted to believe in: a feminist, a proud lesbian, a representative of a pro-democracy political movement. She was articulate, passionate and brave, a deft writer who filtered a complex event into a palatable, compelling personal story of struggle."[34]

She was a middle-aged man's fantasy but also a Western fantasy too.

So what Holds the Revolutions Together?

The "Arab Spring" uprisings have a myriad of threads, each country having their own political, social, cultural and belief systems. The journalists are not helped by the fact that the national media in each country has often not been free to oppose the party line, and once they are in the country, the journalists' movements are severely restricted. Moreover, pointing to right wing media and far right political parties, the Secretary-General of the Organisation of the Islamic Conference, Dr Ekmeleddin Ihsangola[35] says: "This situation only serves to remind us of the inadequate knowledge among many Europeans of the common roots and historical connections linking the Islamic world and the West. It is also indicative of the need for new relationships based on understanding, tolerance and respect for cultural diversity."

Add to this stereotyping and lack of understanding of the role of women in different countries, and it is clear why it is difficult to gain a balanced view of the true picture through the thousands of words which have been published. The framework of using women as icons appears to be a quick shorthand for portraying the troubles of entire nation – brave but vulnerable, protesting but often brutally abused, beautiful but bloodied – superficial generalisations which do not get under the true skin of a country. The icon is not male because he would not represent victimhood. Female icons rarely represent a country's power, wellbeing, and success.

The challenge now is also for each country to set up a freer press to reflect the views, struggles and triumphs of all from the inside. Chris Doyle, director for the Council of Arab-British Understanding, points out that Al Jazeera was more important than Facebook in motivating the revolutions because they broadcast reports from the Arab perspective which are accessible to the vast majority.[36] The print media needs to adopt a similar attitude, monitoring blogs and using writers based in the countries involved. As Kearns and Malik pointed out, this requires giving women the chance to be commentators and political participants and truly listening to what they are saying.

If this shift does not take place, then new figureheads and icons, lip service and stereotyping will continue to come and go – an illusion of change, masking the daily struggle for human rights, leaving the voices of thousands of other women on mute.

Notes

[1] Gould, C, Preoccupation with Israel in the British media: Reporting of Israel, Egypt, Libya and Tunisia prior to the Arab Spring, Just journalism, May 2011 Available online at http://justjournalism.com/wp-content/uploads/2011/05/Preoccupation-with-Israel-in-the-British-media.pdf, accessed on 1 July 2011

[2] Booth, R; Chrisafis, A; Finn, T; Marsh, K; Rice, X; Sherwood, H, Women have emerged as the key players in the Arab Spring, *Guardian*, 22 April 2011. Available online at http://www.guardian.co.uk/world/2011/apr/22/women-arab-spring?INTCMP=SRCH, accessed on 4 July 2011

[3] Cole J; Cole S, The Women's Movement in the Middle East, TomDispatch.com, 26 April 2011. Available online at

http://www.tomdispatch.com/post/175384/tomgram%3A_shahin_and_juan_cole%2C_the_women%27s_movement_in_the_middle_east_/#more, accessed on 1 July 2011

[4] ibid

[5] DeLong-Bas, N, Strong voices of women of the Arab Spring, *Bali Times*, 20 June 2011. Available online at http://www.thebalitimes.com/2011/06/20/strong-voices-of-women-of-the-arab-spring/, accessed on 5 July 2011

[6] Cole, J and Cole, S, op cit

[7] King L, Protests raise hopes for women's rights in Eqypt, *Los Angeles Times*, 2 February 2011.Available online at http://articles.latimes.com/2011/feb/02/world/la-fg-egypt-women-20110203, accessed on 4 July 2011

[8] Spivak Chakravorty G, Can the Subaltern Speak? Marxism and the Interpretation of Culture, Nelson C; Grossberg L, London: Macmillan, 1998

[9] DeLong-Bas, N, op cit

[10] Russeau, S, Spring Not New to Arab Women, IPS, 18 May 2011. Available online at http://www.ipsnews.net/news.asp?idnews=55680, accessed on 5 July 2011

[11] Kearns M, Taking It To The Streets, The Opinioness of the World, 31 January 2011. Available online at http://opinionessoftheworld.com/2011/01/31/egyptian-women-take-to-the-streets-alongside-the-men-to-protest-the-government/, accessed on 5 July 2011

[12] Ghannoushi, S, Perceptions of Arab women have been revolutionised, Comment is Free, Guardian Online, 11 March 2011. Available online at http://www.guardian.co.uk/commentisfree/2011/mar/11/arab-women-revolutionised-egypt-tunisia-yemen, accessed on 5 July2011

[13] Malik N, Arab Women Protesters – Not free, Just Figureheads, Comment is Free, Guardian Online, 2 April 2011. Available online at http://www.guardian.co.uk/commentisfree/2011/apr/02/arab-women-protesters, accessed on 5 July 2011

[14] Mohanty, C, *Under Western Eyes: Feminist Scholarship and Colonial Discourses*, Durham and London: Duke University Press, 1998

[15] Bohn L, I want a democratic Eqypt, The Cairo Review of Global Affairs. Available online at http://www.aucegypt.edu/GAPP/CairoReview/Pages/articleDetails.aspx?aid=24, accessed on 5 July 2011

[16] Leigh, K, Exiled and 24: The Young Woman Fighting For Bahrain, *Atlantic*, 29 June 2011. Available online at http://www.theatlantic.com/international/archive/2011/06/exiled-and-24-the-young-woman-fighting-for-bahrain/241190/, accessed on 5 July 2011

[17] Coleman, I, A Day In the Life of a Yemeni Revolutionary, Huffington Post, 20 January 2011. Available online at http://www.huffingtonpost.com/isobel-coleman/a-day-in-the-life-of-a-ye_b_811946.htm, accessed on 5 July 2011

[18] Waghorn, D, Tortured Boy becomes face of Syria Uprising, Sky News, 2 June 2011. Available online at http://news.sky.com/home/article/16003801, accessed on 7 July 2011

[19] Abu-Lughod, Lila, Do Muslim women really need saving? Anthropological reflections on cultural relativism and its others, *American Anthropologist*, 2002 p. 783

[20] Williams, M, What's Not To Say About Lara Logan, 15 February. Available online at http://www.salon.com/entertainment/tv/feature/2011/02/15/lara_logan_rape_reaction/index.html, accessed on 10 August 2011

21 Wilson, S, Lara Logan, CBS Reporter and Warzone IT Girl. Available online at http://blogs.laweekly.com/informer/2011/02/lara_logan_raped_egypt_reporte.php, accessed on 10 August 2011

22 Manyon, J, Bribe and Seek, *Spectator*, 3 November 2001. Available online at http://www.spectator.co.uk/spectator/thisweek/9445/part_4/bribe-and-seek.thtml, accessed on 4 July 2011

23 *Daily Mail* Reporter, Ex-GMTV reporter leaves hospital six days after Cairo mob sex-attack, Mail online, 16 February 2011. Available online at http://www.dailymail.co.uk/news/article-1357485/Lara-Logan-assault-Former-GMTV-reporter-suffers-sex-attack-covering-Egypt-uprising.html, accessed on 5 July 2011

24 Bates, D, Find her attackers, White House demands justice, Mail online, 17 February 2011. Available online at http://www.dailymail.co.uk/news/article-1357394/Lara-Logan-attack-CBS-reporter-leaves-hospital-Cairo-mob-sex-assault.html, accessed on 5 July 2011

25 *Daily Mail* Reporter, Stripped, punched and whipped with flag poles, Mail online, 21 February 2011. Available online at http://www.dailymail.co.uk/news/article-1357394/Lara-Logan-attack-CBS-reporter-leaves-hospital-Cairo-mob-sex-assault.html, accessed on 5 July 2011

26 Abdelhadi, M, Eqypt's sexual harassment cancer, BBC News, 18 July 2008. Available online at http://news.bbc.co.uk/1/hi/7514567.stm, accessed on 4 July 2011

27 Miller, J, I want Gaddafi to face street justice, 20 May 2005. Available online at http://www.mirror.co.uk/news/top-stories/2011/05/20/i-want-gaddafi-to-face-street-justice-not-an-international-court-says-iman-al-obeidi-115875-23142229/, accessed on 5 July 2011

28 ibid

29 Tasnim, The Symbol of Eman al-Obeidi, Muslimah Media Watch, 4 April 2011. Available online at http://muslimahmediawatch.org/2011/04/the-symbol-of-eman-al-obeidi/, accessed on July 2011

30 ibid

31 Leigh, K, Exiled and 24: The Young Woman Fighting For Bahrain, *Atlantic*, 29 June 2011. Available online at http://www.theatlantic.com/international/archive/2011/06/exiled-and-24-the-young-woman-fighting-for-bahrain/241190/, accessed on 5 July 2011

32 Abdulaziz Khattack commenting on Leigh, K, Exiled and 24: The Young Woman Fighting For Bahrain, *Atlantic*, 29 June 2011. Available online at http://www.theatlantic.com/international/archive/2011/06/exiled-and-24-the-young-woman-fighting-for-bahrain/241190/#disqus_thread accessed 5 July 2011

33 Sara A Gay, Girl In Damascus Tells It Like It Is, Muslimah Media Watch, 31 May 2011. Available online at http://muslimahmediawatch.org/2011/05/a-gay-girl-in-damascus-tells-it-like-it-is/, accessed 15 August 2011

34 Josephine Tovey, Listen hard for the real heroes in Syria, *Sydney Morning Herald*, 16 August 2011. Available online at http://www.smh.com.au/opinion/society-and-culture/listen-hard-for-the-real-heroes-in-syria-20110614-1g1pp.html#ixzz1V8WZ6PHe, accessed on 10 August 2011

35 Ihsanoglu, E, Islam and/in the West, *Inquirer Opinion*, 11 April 2011. Available online at http://opinion.inquirer.net/4401/islam-andin-the-west, accessed on 5 July 2011

36 Doyle, C, The press, six reasons for failure, Media Credibility Index, 2011, Next Century Foundation. Available online at

http://www.ncfpeace.org/drupal/system/files/Voice_39_complete%5B1%5D.pdf, accessed on 5 July 2011

Note on the author

Jackie Gregory is a Senior Lecturer in journalism at Staffordshire University, having previously worked as a journalist in regional newspapers and the national Catholic print media. She is currently a co-editor for the international online news service Women's Views on News.

Why were Women Correspondents the Face of Coverage of the Libyan Revolution?

Is it patronising, sexist even, to mention the fact that three women reporters were at the forefront of US/UK media coverage of the Libyan revolution? Or is it crucial to any serious discussion about how that revolution was perceived? Glenda Cooper explores the issues

In the end, it came down to a pick-up truck, a laptop and a small satellite dish powered by a car cigarette lighter. And a great degree of bravery: with this, Sky News foreign correspondent Alex Crawford and her crew provided riveting coverage of the rebel advance into Tripoli, scooping her rivals in the background.

Every war has a media "face": Kate Adie in the Gulf conflict of 1991, John Simpson in Afghanistan in 2001, "Scud stud" Rageh Omaar in Iraq in 2003. But the particular media focus for the Libyan revolution was that the first three reporters into Green Square, Tripoli, were all women: Crawford, Sara Sidner of CNN, and Zeina Khodr, of Al Jazeera English – much to their surprise. Says Khodr:

I was really shocked by the focus in Western media on female reporters – there's been nothing like that in the Muslim press. Surely we can both cover wars? – in fact, some women are more brave; some men, some crews were definitely staying away from the front line.

So is it patronising, irrelevant, sexist even to mention Crawford, Sidner and Khodr's gender? Or can the fact that three women were at the forefront of media coverage of a revolution be worthy of discussion about how that revolution was perceived? Executives are quick to say there was no deliberate attempt to foreground women reporting; Jon Williams, World News Editor at the BBC, says: "This wasn't about male or female – it was about showcasing our best people."

Not Just Coincidence
He disputes those on the ground who say it was coincidence. But Khodr, senior correspondent at Al Jazeera English, says she ended up in Tripoli purely because she was assigned on that week's rota. And Crawford says she was sent back to Libya because of her previous experience in Zawiyah earlier in 2011. But she believes there were so many female reporters at the forefront of the reporting in other media organisations because:

> I think they [news desks] did not realise how big a story it was going to be...other organisations sent their big guns miles after the event. When I was leaving Libya and going to Tunisia, [the BBC's] Ben Brown and John Simpson were going in – they are reporters you would expect in the starting line up, but this time in the second line up.

Added to that, up to 35 international journalists from the BBC, CNN, Sky and Reuters were held up in the Rixos hotel, Tripoli, by armed guards loyal to Muammar Gaddafi, before being freed on 24 August, and thus unable to report from outside the hotel's confines.

All three women were television correspondents as well: the domination of the TV image has promoted the idea that Libya was reported by women, adds Lindsay Hilsum, Channel 4 News' International Editor.

> The number of female correspondents reporting wars and other emergencies has been increasing over the years, but I don't really

know why so much fuss about Libya. Maybe because Alex Crawford was so prominent, and the fact that she was doing live rolling TV news meant that people could see her in a dangerous place. No one watched live on TV as Marie Colvin's eye was shot in Sri Lanka. TV somehow makes it more powerfully obvious that the reporters are female.

Hilsum is correct to point out that women war reporters are nothing new: from Clare Hollingworth and Martha Gellhorn in the Second World War to Kate Adie covering the Tripoli bombings of 25 years ago. According to the Freedom Forum in 1998, during the first war in Chechnya nearly half the accredited reporters were women.[1]

And as journalism jobs go, it can be a good one for women: academics Marina Prentoulis, Howard Tumber and Frank Webster, of City University, have argued that women front line correspondents are less subject to gender prejudices than other parts of the profession because they face the same psychological and physical hazards as the men. According to one female national newspaper journalist to whom Prentoulis *et al* spoke for their paper, *Finding Space: Women Reporters at War,* the reality was that:

> Everyone is reduced to an equal and there isn't tension between males or females…no-one would have ever said, for example: "We can't take you because you're a woman"…you were just another reporter.[2]

The difficulty for many women is getting the job in the first place. We have come some way since 1970 when only 6 per cent of foreign correspondents were women.[3] Yet Crawford, a Royal Television Society award winner, who took six years to win a foreign correspondent's role, comments:

> I got turned down continually – it became a running joke in newsroom how many times I got turned down; one friend said to me: "By now most people would have given up – they don't want you." But I kept on going and finally got it.

Very Specialised Group

Those women who succeed in becoming foreign correspondents make up a very specialised group, according to Anthony Feinstein and Mark Sinyor, in a report for the Nieman Foundation for Journalism at Harvard. According to an analysis of more than 200 war reporters, they say:

> The emerging profile of the female war journalist – more likely to be single and better educated than their male colleagues, no more vulnerable to PTSD, depression or overall psychological distress, and keeping up with the men when it comes to drinking – suggests they are a highly select group. It is not by chance that these women have gravitated to the frontlines of war.[4]

Yet those who do succeed in the job still face frequent prurient discussion over their role in a way their male counterparts do not. Underlying the admiration for Crawford *et al* in media commentary of their work in Libya has been an on-going debate about their marital/maternal status; particularly those reporters who are mothers (such as Crawford) and continue to put themselves in danger. In a recent Q&A session at the Edinburgh Television Festival discussing her reporting of Libya, Crawford says of questions over whether she should do this job as a mother of four:

> It's frankly really insulting and very, very sexist…I'm working alongside today the chief correspondent who's a man who's got three children and there will be no one who says what do you think you're doing, how awful, what are you doing to your children? No one, it won't even be raised as an issue and yet the stories that I do, [provoke] quite a lot of comment and a lot of criticism.[5]

Yet women who choose to work as war reporters continually have to justify themselves. In a recent piece for the *Daily Mail*, Janine di Giovanni, who has reported from Bosnia, Chechnya, Somalia, Rwanda, Iraq and Afghanistan, described her decision to step back from war reporting in emotive terms:

> I knew having a child would mean I would miss lots of stories and would never again be the first one inside a city under siege or get the first interview with a dictator. But I would have pages and pages of diaries filled with memories of [her son] Luka's first tooth and

witness the first moment he walked. And no scoop is more satisfying than that.[6]

The Assault on CBS Correspondent Lara Logan

Even Crawford said during her Edinburgh Q&A that her children would prefer her to be a "dinner lady" than a war correspondent putting herself in danger. This debate was thrown into sharp relief following the assault on CBS correspondent Lara Logan while covering the Egyptian revolution in Tahrir Square earlier in 2011.

Logan (a mother of two and, as the *Daily Mail* repeatedly pointed, out a former swimwear model[7]) came in for fevered criticism that she had somehow "deserved" to be assaulted, with the academic Nir Rosen resigning from New York University after he tweeted that she had probably "just been groped".[8] And National Public Radio in the US later had to remove countless offensive messages from their message boards questioning whether Logan should have been reporting from Cairo in the first place.[9]

As a result there were concerns news organisations would be more reluctant to expose female journalists to possible danger by reporting on the "Arab Spring". Such suspicions have made women disinclined to raise the issue in the past: in a piece for the *Columbia Journalism Review* in 2007, Judith Matloff argued that women often failed to report assault in case it stopped them getting future assignments or hindered gender equality[10] – even though a 2005 study for the International News Safety Institute found that of the twenty-nine respondents who took part, more than half reported sexual harassment on the job.[11]

Interviewed after Logan's assault, Jon Williams, International Editor for the BBC, said that it would be naïve to see gender as irrelevant when deploying journalists to hostile environments but that "changing gender of the person doesn't eliminate the risk; it just makes it different…The threat is there and real, how it manifests itself may be different for men and women but it doesn't eliminate the threat".[12] Crawford added:

> After the attack on Lara there wasn't any change; we'd already had a couple of nasty moments of being mobbed outside hotel in Alexandria…The anger seemed very much directed against women broadcasting – they started shouting "bitch bitch bitch", completely

walked past the cameraman who is usually the first one attacked, tried to grab me and the producer.

Yet the women who covered Libya were often keen to play down potential dangers and emphasise the advantages of their gender in covering the story. Crawford said:

> Women are seen as less aggressive…Men find it easier dealing with women and are more likely to take against other men. It doesn't matter what you look like or your age; if you have half an ounce of charm and sociability, you can use that – not in a Machiavellian way but just in getting on with people, making friends…and other females are obviously much more ready to talk to me than a strange foreign bloke.

In fact, Hilsum pointed out that there was a danger that one gender could be discriminated against as a result of difficulty in war reporting:

> Often only women can talk to other women for cultural reasons.…It means women can get 100 per cent of the story and men only part of it. But, as I've said before, I don't think this means men shouldn't be allowed to report wars. I think they have a contribution to make, even if they can't get the whole story.

Yet Khodr's view was that the advantage she had in Libya was not primarily to do with her gender but her particular skills:

> The advantage was that I speak Arabic so you get the story without waiting for the translator, and people tend to be more comfortable as they feel you understand the culture and the situation. Men are very conservative in Libya so they were shocked at me being there but when I approached I felt it was important not to show any weakness.

Women "Often Given the Softer Side of War to Report"
Was the type of coverage in Libya different though because of the numbers of women journalists? The war correspondent Janine di Giovanni, writing in the *Daily Mail*, believes that in war situations the stories women cover mean that they "were not equal to men": "We are often given the softer side of war to report, 'the female angle' so to speak, feeding into the stereotype that women are more 'caring war reporters' than men."[13]

Yet executives and journalists on the ground in Libya disagree with di Giovanni's concerns. Khodr says of the stories she has covered: 'We were covering battles; then we did the makeshift jail where people burned alive. It's going to be a while before we turn to the feature stories," while Hilsum says that she has interviewed far fewer women than usual: "Women in Libya have largely been behind closed doors. They only came out on the streets in the last few days."

Jon Williams points out that while Orla Guerin had covered the plight of families in Misrata and the nurse in a Tripoli hospital, Ian Pannell had done similar stories. Williams goes on to talk of a "humanity and a personalisation of the conflict" in both Guerin and Pannell's reporting; something that is backed up by the academic research. Prentoulis *et al* argue that the shift towards human interest stories, encapsulated in the phrase "the feminisation of news", may be symptomatic of a broader cultural shift, moving towards a "journalism of attachment". They say:

> The latter, favouring more "human" stories of civilian victims and some degree of emotional involvement, may be allowing women reporters more space for approaching war stories in their own way and, at the same time, allowing male correspondents to respond to the intensity of the war, without the "macho" bravado often associated with the war correspondent

Lindsay Hilsum agrees that there is less distinction between male and female reporting in war these days:

> I think you'd be hard-pressed to find a consistent distinction between men's and women's reporting of wars and revolutions. But I would say that when a man does the weepy, human side he is regarded as empathetic and sensitive, but a woman may be perceived as "not coping" if she shows emotion. So women broadcasters have to be very careful not to play into people's stereotypes.

And that perhaps is why the images of female reporters dominated the media agenda; not that there were women correspondents (there have been those for decades) nor that there were so many of them there (unlikely to be statistically greater than normal). But in a world where we are used to a subjective, so-called "feminised" approach to news, seeing Khodr and Crawford in their flak jackets and helmets having to shout their commentary over the sounds of bullets being fired and rebels chanting was to come full circle: just as men can report Williams' "personalisation of the conflict" without it being a shock, Crawford *et al* made clear women can report in the traditional "macho" way – and do it just as effectively, armed only with a car cigarette lighter.

Notes

[1] *Journalists in Danger: Recent Russian Wars*, New York and London, Freedom Forum, 1998 p. 307 quoted in Jean Seaton, *Carnage and the Media*, London: Penguin 2005 p. 178

[2] Marina Prentoulis, Howard Tumber and Frank Webster, Finding Space: Women Reporters at War, *Feminist Media Studies*, Vol. 5, No. 3, 2005 pp 374–377

[3] Annalena McAfee, *Women on the Front Line*, *Guardian*, 16 April 2011. Available online at http://www.guardian.co.uk/books/2011/apr/16/women-war-reporting-annalena-mcafee, accessed on 29 August 2011

[4] Anthony Feinstein and Mark Sinyor, *Women War Correspondents: They Are Different in So Many Ways*, Nieman Reports, Winter 2009. Available online at http://www.nieman.harvard.edu/reports/article/101967/Women-War-Correspondents-They-Are-Different-in-So-Many-Ways.aspx, accessed on 29 August 2011

[5] Alex Crawford in live Q&A at the MediaGuardian Edinburgh International Television Festival, 27 August 2011. Full transcript available online at http://news.sky.com/home/world-news/article/16058071, accessed on 29 August 2011

[6] Janine Di Giovanni, Motherhood and Warfare: The Rise of Women Reporters on the Front Line, *Daily Mail*, 31 August 2011. Available online at http://www.dailymail.co.uk/femail/article-2031387/Motherhood-warfare-The-rise-women-reporters-line.html, accessed on 1 September 2011

[7] See, for example, http://www.dailymail.co.uk/news/article-1357485/Lara-Logan-assault-Former-GMTV-reporter-suffers-sex-attack-covering-Egypt-uprising.html, available online at http://www.dailymail.co.uk/news/article-1357394/Lara-Logan-attack-CBS-reporter-leaves-hospital-Cairo-mob-sex-assault.html; and http://www.dailymail.co.uk/debate/article-1358104/Toe-curling-Richard-Mellor-peaks-Bahrain-Radio-4.html, both accessed on 1 September 2011

[8] *Daily Mail* reporter: No one told her to go there: Now female pundit lays into Egypt sex attack victim Lara Logan and "anima" protestors, 18 February 2011. Available online at http://www.dailymail.co.uk/news/article-1357957/Lara-Logan-attack-Debbie-Schlussel-Nir-Rosen-criticise-CBS-correspondent.html, accessed on 1 September 2011

[9] Mark Memmott, Why have so Many Posts on the Attack on Lara Logan Been Removed, 16 February 2011. Available online at http://www.npr.org/blogs/thetwo-way/2011/02/16/133804167/why-have-many-comments-about-the-attack-on-lara-logan-been-removed, accessed on 1 September 2011

[10] Judith Matloff, Foreign Correspondents and Sexual Abuse: The Case for Restraint, *Columbia Journalism Review*, May/June 2007. Available online at http://www.judithmatloff.com/correspondentsandsexualabuse.pdf, accessed on 1 September 2011

[11] Survey by the International News Safety Institute, *Women Reporting War*, 2005. Available online at ,

http://www.newssafety.org/images/stories/pdf/programme/wrw/wrw_finalreport.pdf, accessed on 1 September 2011

[12] Katie Connolly, Lara Logan attack turns spotlight on female reporters, BBC online, 19 February 2011. Available online at http://www.bbc.co.uk/news/world-us-canada-12510289, accessed on 1 September 2011

[13] Janine Di Giovanni op cit

Note on the author

Glenda Cooper was the 14th Guardian Research Fellow at Nuffield College, Oxford, and former Visiting Fellow at the Reuters Institute for the Study of Journalism. She is currently a PhD student at City University looking at user-generated content and the reporting of disasters. She has worked as a staff correspondent for the BBC, Channel 4 News Radio, the *Independent*, the *Daily Mail*, the *Daily Telegraph* and the *Washington Post*.

When Arab Women Refuse to Fit Western Stereotypes

Julie Tomlin looks at three women who came to the fore during the "Arab Spring" not because they were part of the uprisings on the streets but because of their positions in state-controlled media

What is an "Arab woman" anyway? The question posed by author Joumana Haddad[1] is a challenge to those who are interested in her only because she is an "Arab", "Arab woman" or even an "Arab woman writer".

"The only good reason…I should be interesting to you, the only reason any human being should be interesting to you at all, is because he or she are themselves, not just a flashy, intriguing tag that they are supposed to represent."[2]

This chapter explores the stories of three women who do not fit the new "Arab woman as revolutionary" tag that has captured the imagination of the Western media since the start of the uprisings in January: Shahira Amin, the deputy director and anchor of Egypt's Nile TV, who resigned from her position on 3 February 2011; Reem Haddad, director of Syria's state television network and spokeswoman for the Ministry of

245

Information and Hala Musrati, a Libyan television anchor who became known as "Gaddafi's presenter" during the dying days of his regime.

They are women who captured the media's attention for different reasons, and they are examined in the spirit of Haddad's request that the reader does not "surrender right away to the given image that has been shaped by someone else on your behalf".[3]

"I Am On the People's Side, Not the Regime's"

Egyptian journalist Shahira Amin was hailed as a heroine[4] when she announced on 3 February 2011 that she was resigning from her job at Nile TV. Amin, who was deputy head of the network and a senior anchor and correspondent, said she could no longer work under the "near total blackout"[5] of coverage of the unrest that was sweeping across Egypt.

While the world's media, including Arabic speaking channels Al Jazeera and BBC Arabic, were broadcasting violent clashes in the streets of the capital, Cairo, staff at Nile TV were told they could only report the pro-Mubarak rallies. When protesters took to the streets, buoyed by the success of the revolution in Tunisia, and posted video of their gatherings on YouTube, the state channels were told to say the protests were against high food prices and unemployment. As the calls for Mubarak to step down became louder and more insistent, journalists were only allowed to read press releases sent by the Interior Ministry and the Presidency which portrayed the protesters as part of a conspiracy against Egypt.

It was the first time that there had been direct interference from the regime, said Amin who reached her limit when she was told she could not take a camera crew to Tahrir Square, Cairo. "History is in the making in our country right now and as a journalist I wanted to be part of it," Amin said.[6] Finally, finding herself in Tahrir Square, Amin sent a message to her boss from her phone telling her she would not be returning to the building: "I am on the people's side, not the regime's," she wrote.[7]

Until the uprisings, Amin had felt able to do her job as a journalist with little interference: "Mubarak tried to give this semblance of free speech and democracy so journalists got away with quite a lot," said Amin.[8] Only criticism of Mubarak himself or discussion about religion were off limits. Just three days after Amin's resignation, the powerful edifice of the state-controlled media started "crumbling" as one independent Egyptian journalist Ashraf Khalil described it:[9]

> I was watching television and was shocked to see that on state TV they had brought two protesters into the studio. The protesters were given a free rein to complain about police brutality and the regime, and the interviewer appeared to be earnestly struggling to understand what was happening. I think some of the media simply didn't let themselves see the truth of what was happening and it took a while for them to able to admit the changes to themselves.[10]

In the post-Mubarak era, state media's revisionist attempts to be on the side of the revolution have been viewed with suspicion – and the protesters reserve particular hostility towards executives and managers. "For the lower-level people at *al-Ahram* [the most widely circulating Egyptian daily newspaper, founded in 1875], it was this job or unemployment," said Ashraf Khalil.

> But everyone at a managerial level in any state-run newspaper or television station should be unemployable until they are rehabilitated or work their way up through the ranks again. Their job was to enforce the control of the regime; they weren't journalists.[11]

According to Amin, neither her boss, who "knew nothing about journalism and wanted only to hang on to her chair" nor her "subordinates" were worthy of being called "real" journalists. "They're all there because of their connections and were not hired on their merits," she said.[12]

In Egypt, the media is a field open to women, with many occupying senior roles. But there are clearly challenges ahead if the state media is to progress beyond its mandate to safeguard the interests of a powerful elite. Now working freelance with CNN, *Index on Censorship* and *El Masry el Youm*, Amin has returned to Nile TV to present a talk show, but has not returned to her roles in management or working as an anchor.

Amin, who has already had a run-in with the new military regime over her reporting of virginity tests protesters were made to endure after their arrest in Tahrir Square, is now regarded as a "traitor whistleblower" by former colleagues.[13]

"This is the new Egypt where we were hoping state media would be more open and free. I wanted to be part of the change," said Amin, adding that she considers it her "national duty" to try to reform state TV from within. "Immodest as this may sound, I'm really hoping that the show would be an exemplary model for my colleagues to follow."[14]

Roses in the Desert: Costly PR failures of Syria's Regime

The appointment of Reem Haddad as spokeswoman for the Ministry of Information made formal what was implicit during the unrest in Egypt: that it functions to uphold and support the interests of the regime. Haddad was head of Syria's state-owned TV network which, like all of the country's media, is controlled by the Baath Party through the Ministry of Information. And it was the Information Minister, Mohsen Bilal, who was responsible for appointing her in May 2010. Part of the country's rich and powerful elite, she is the daughter of Sulyman Haddad, a senior military intelligence officer.

Little is known about Haddad's background in journalism, although much has been made of her credentials: she is Oxford educated, speaks impeccable English with a "cut glass" accent and, as the world's media pointed out enthusiastically, she is "pale-skinned", "red-" or "flame-haired" with a remarkable resemblance to either actress Julianne Moore, or Hollywood star Isla Fisher.

If the President Bashar al-Assad's government was trying to capitalise on Hassad's looks to present an "acceptable" face to the world, then it had learnt nothing from the controversial US *Vogue* magazine profile of Asma al-Assad which had caused public outrage. International public-relations firm Brown Lloyd James was given a $5,000-per-month contract to coordinate the profile, published in the magazine's March "power issue".[15]

Titled "Asma al-Assad: Rose in the Desert", the glossy spin was ill-timed, hitting the newsstands just as the Syrian government's crackdown on anti-regime protesters began. The appointment of Haddad handed the Western media a perfect device for reporting the events in a Syria that was closed to its journalists: an attractive woman whose looks could be contrasted with the atrocities carried out by the regime she represented. In a piece titled "Syria hides behind a fair face", James Hider wrote in the *Australian*:

While images seeping out of Syria show scenes of horror and gore, the face that the regime is presenting to the world is that of an attractive woman with an educated British accent, vehemently denying its atrocities.[16]

Haddad came to the fore after she slammed down the telephone on John Humphrys during an interview on BBC Radio 4's *Today* programme on 7 May. Her subsequent denials that the regime was carrying out atrocities against the Syrian people quickly earned her the nickname "Comical Sally", a reference to Saddam Hussein's spokesman Mohammed al - Sahhaf who became known as "Comical Ali" during the 2003 invasion of Iraq for his persistent statement: "We are winning."

Hassad was mocked for suggesting that hundreds of Syrians fleeing the northern town of Jisr al-Shughour to neighbouring Turkey were simply visiting relatives across the frontier. "It's a bit like having a problem in your street and your mum lives in the next street, so you go and visit your mum for a bit," she told the BBC. A friend is reported saying that Haddad probably only believed part of what she was saying but she believed "there's a war here between two ideologies, two groups, and she believes she's on the right side".[17] But the world wasn't "fooled" by her "posh accent and bizarre excuses for atrocities", announced the *Daily Mail.*[18]

Although the regime's PR tactics failed to win over the Western media in the way it had hoped, they perhaps invoked another image of "Arab woman" instead, one that is familiar to "authors and men of letters" in the Arab and Western imagination alike, the genie/woman who, as Nawal El Saadawi explains, is "human on the outside but imbued with the same fundamental nature that leads her to practise deceit, to betray, to conspire against others, and to seduce them into her traps".[19]

To the extent that the portrayal of Haddad became a caricature, there was a failure to reflect upon "complex issues of context, history, gender and international relations".[20] As Susan Slyomovics writes, television creates more powerful caricatures than any cartoon. "Caricatures explicitly reduce the political expression of a country, say Iraq or the United Sates, to a single individual: Saddam Hussein, Bush, or to a woman who symbolises that country."

Women Who Inhibit and Oppress other Women

Little attention has been paid to the women of the privileged elite who, to use Simone de Beauvoir's phrase, maintain a "stubborn reverence" for a leader or regime.[21] And as Nawal El Saadawi observed, the fact that a woman works does not mean they are free unless the work is

> ...linked to, and carried out within the framework of a just society which affords equal opportunities to all, based on their capacities and talents, and not on the class or sex to which they belong.[22]

Nor does the presence of women within a field such as television ensure that women's voices are heard or that their interests are advanced. As "Tasnim" writes on Muslimah Media Watch, it was Hala Musrati, a presenter on state television, who was responsible for "far the most slanderous, recriminating, and misogynistic response" to Iman al-Obeidi's claims that she had been raped by Gadaffi's troops.[23]

> Musrati's words are a particularly virulent example of how women can inhibit and oppress other women. It is not the only example – a woman was the first to shout at al-Obeidi, and another woman attempted to silence her by throwing a dark cloth over her face.[24]

Musrati was also dubbed Libya's new al-Shahhaf for her bizarre mix of traditional thinking about family clan pride, tribe and honour, propaganda and exaggeration. Speaking on *Libya Today*, Musrati called Iman al-Obeidi "a whore" several times and denounced her for speaking out about her rape, claiming that "warm-blooded and honourable" people would "die a thousand deaths" rather than speak about rape and "with time they may even kill the girl herself".[25] Last seen on air brandishing a gun and vowing that she would fight unto death shortly before Libya's state television was forced off air by rebels, Musrati reappeared on a video with anti-Gaddafi fighters, claiming she had not been arrested but had realised that they were "good guys".

Time for the Extraordinary Analysis

Old certainties have been turned upside down in Egypt and Libya and are being shaken in Syria. It is clear, too, that many challenges lie ahead for their political systems and their media if they are to be independent and reflect different voices and groups within the country and not just the rich and the powerful.

But the certainties of the West and its media are also being shaken in many ways, including by the refusal of women in the Arab world to fit its stereotypes. As actor and activist Khalid Abdalla said recently when speaking in London, the West has not realised yet how much it will be changed by the "Arab Spring".

And as Chris Doyle[26] points out, there has been some remarkable reporting of events in the Middle East but this has not been matched by the commentators who are too frequently making their pronouncements from offices in London: "One cannot help feeling that the extraordinary images have yet to be matched by extraordinary analysis."

Notes

[1] Haddad, Jouna, *I Killed Scherherazade: Confessions of an angry Arab woman*, London, San Francisco, Beirut: Saqi Books, 2010 p. 19

[2] ibid

[3] ibid

[4] Kligman, Aimée, The heroine of the day is Egyptian Shahira Amin – she quit Nile TV, *Examiner*, February 2011. Available online at http://www.examiner.com/foreign-policy-in-national/the-heroine-of-the-day-is-egyptian-shahira-amin-she-quit-nile-tv, accessed on 9 September 2011

[5] See Egypt journalist resigns from state TV in protest, Channel 4 News, February, 2011. Available online at http://www.channel4.com/news/egypt-journalist-resigns-from-state-tv-in-protest, accessed on 8 September 2011

[6] ibid

[7] Amin, Shahira, I am on the people's side, not the regime's, Uncut, February 2011. Available online at http://uncut.indexoncensorship.org/2011/02/i-am-on-the-people%E2%80%99s-side-not-the-regimes/, accessed on 3 September 2011

[8] Interview with author

[9] Interview with Ashraf Khalil: Egyptian media facing sea change, Institute of War and Peace Reporting, February 2011. Available online at http://iwpr.net/report-news/egyptian-media-facing-sea-change, accessed on 7 September 2011

[10] ibid

[11] ibid

[12] Interview with author via email 1 September 2011

[13] Interview with author via email 1 September 2011

[14] Interview with author via email 1 September 2011

[15] Bogardus, Kevin, PR firm worked with Syria on controversial photo shoot, the Hill, 3 August, Available online at http://thehill.com/business-a-lobbying/175149-pr-firm-worked-with-syria-on-controversial-photo-shoot, accessed on 6 September 2011

[16] Hider, James, Syria tries to hide behind fair face, *Australian*, 13 June. Available online at http://www.theaustralian.com.au/news/world/syria-tries-to-hide-behind-fair-face/story-e6frg6so-1226073917837, accessed on 7 September, 2011

[17] ibid

[18] Syria sacks "Comical Sally" after her posh accent and bizarre excuses for atrocities fail to fool the world, *Daily Mail*, 17 June. Available online at

http://www.dailymail.co.uk/news/article-2004676/Comical-Sally.html#ixzz1XOlPUoMg, accessed on 7 September, 2011

[19] El Saadawi, Nawal, *The Hidden Face of Eve, Women in the Arab World*, London: Zed Books, 2007 p. 240

[20] Slyomovics, Susan, Sex, Lies and Television: Caricatures of the Gulf War, *Woman and Power in the Middle East*, University or Pennsylvania Press, 2001 p. 97

[21] de Beauvoir, Simone, *The Second Sex*, London: Vintage, 2011 (first published 1949) p. 756

[22] El Saadawi, Nawal, *The Hidden Face of Eve*, London: Zed Books p. 281

[23] Iman el-Obeidi sparked an international controversy when she burst into the lobby at the Rixos Hotel, Tripoli, on 26 March 2011 and claimed to have been gang-raped by Gaddafi's troops

[24] Tasnim, The symbol of Eman al_Obeidi, Muslimah Media Watch, April 2011. Available online at http://muslimahmediawatch.org/2011/04/the-symbol-of-eman-al-obeidi/, accessed on 8 September 2011

[25] Tomlin, Julie Women protest against treatment of rape claim woman, Women's Views on News, March 2011. Available online at http://www.womensviewsonnews.org/2011/03/benghazi-women-protest-against-treatment-of-rape-claim-woman/, accessed on 8 September 2011

[26] Doyle, Chris, The press: Six Reasons for Failure, Media Credibility Index, 2011, Next Century Foundation. Available online at http://www.ncfpeace.org/drupal/system/files/Voice_39_complete%5B1%5D.pdf, accessed on 8 September 2011

Note about the author

Julie Tomlin is a freelance journalist who also works at London's Frontline Club as programme editor and is a co-editor for the international online news service Women's Views on News. She previously worked in local newspapers and was deputy editor of *Press Gazette*.

Section 6. Representing Gaddafi

Richard Lance Keeble

The mainstream media are all too predictable in the coverage of conflict. As George Orwell commented: "Every war when it comes, or before it comes, is represented not as a war but as an act of self-defence against a homicidal maniac." The Nato intervention in the Libyan uprising in 2011 was no exception.

In the opening chapter of this section, John Jewell argues that the propaganda model promoted by the American maverick duo, Edward Herman and Noam Chomsky, can most usefully explain the nature of the media coverage. According to the theory, the media serve largely to promote the interests of the dominant political, financial, cultural and military elites with which they have close economic ties.

So Jewell shows how first the media stressed the moral vacuity of the Libyan leader. Like Stalin and Saddam Hussein before him, Gaddafi was represented as murdering his "own people". The consistent line from the US, UK and France (the leaders in the military intervention against Gaddafi) was humanitarian. On BBC1 on 8 March, British Prime Minister David Cameron said that if Gaddafi "goes on brutalising his own people…in case he does terrible things to his own people…I don't think we can stand aside and let that happen". According to Jewell: "So already the basic elements of war propaganda are established: the enemy is evil and doing nothing in the face of such evil would amount to dereliction of duty."

Jewell also reminds us of Aldous Huxley's words: "the propagandist's purpose is to make one set of people forget that certain other sets of people are human". So it comes as no surprise when Jewell highlights Fleet Street's representation of the President of Libya as a "mad dog", a "monster" and a "rat".

Following 9/11 and Gaddafi's attempts to bring an end to the crippling Western sanctions against his country, many Western leaders travelled to Tripoli to shake hands with the dictator. And suddenly the media consensus shifted: words such as "evil", "murderous, authoritarian strongman", "monster" were marginalised and the tone of coverage shifted to emphasise more Gaddafi's alleged "eccentricities" and "unpredictability".

Next, Andrew Beck argues that the coverage of the Libyan uprising in its early days, showed how the media tend to privilege their own "tribalisms": "both between news organisations (whomsoever is holier than thou) and within news organisations (whomsoever is top dog)":

> Lamenting this latter tendency, the creation of new tribal hierarchies within UK news organisations, veteran BBC war reporter Martin Bell has highlighted both the rise of the anchor and their performative character, whether located in the studio or in the field.

Finally in this section, I focus on the 40-year campaign of the West to eliminate Gaddafi. The American attack on Tripoli in 1986 was the most overt attempt to assassinate the Libyan leader. But there have been many others – mostly conducted in secrecy. Thus the chapter raises a number of issues: To what extent do the mainstream media fail to cover the activities of the secret state and their secret warfare activities – thus giving a completely distorted picture of contemporary conflicts?

In an age of information and news overflow, how useful is it, rather, to consider the silencing function of media? And how important are the close links between the intelligence/security services and Fleet Street in influencing coverage – of both war and peace? Given that the chapter uses a range of sources largely marginalised in the mainstream media, to what extent do journalists' routines need to change radically if they are to cover covert warfare adequately?

How the West Waged the Propaganda War against Gaddafi

John Jewell argues that the mainstream media demonised the "mad dog" President of Libya and his military forces largely in accordance with the predictions of Edward Herman and Noam Chomsky and their propaganda model

Beginnings

After rebel uprisings began in Libya on 15 February 2011, it quickly became apparent that the dictator for more than 41 years, Colonel Muammar Gaddafi, was facing serious challenges to his authority and presidency.

By 23 February, it was becoming clear to audiences in the West that Gaddafi was, in the phrase beloved by politicians and the media, "murdering his own people". The *Daily Telegraph*[1] reported that more than a thousand people had died in the crackdown on protests and that "the UN Human Rights Council will hold a special session on Friday to discuss the crisis". International condemnation followed and a joint statement by Russian prime Minister Vladimir Putin and the European

Union[2] stated: "We highly condemn the violence and the use of force against civilians in Libya, which has resulted in the death of hundreds of people."

It was clear Britain and the USA were aiming for regime change. David Cameron told the House of Commons on 28 February:[3] "We must not tolerate this regime using military force against its own people." Importantly, Cameron added: "We do not in any way rule out the use of military assets."

On 26 February, Al Jazeera[4] reported President Barack Obama stating: "When a leader's only means of staying in power is to use mass violence against his own people, he has lost the legitimacy to rule and needs to do what is right for his country by leaving now."

Then, on 17 March, the United Nations Security Council approved a resolution authorising a no-fly zone and "all military aspects"[5] to enforce it in order to protect civilians under threat of attack from Gaddafi in Libya. Outside Number 10, Cameron stated: "What we are doing is necessary, it is legal and it is right." He continued: "I believe we should not stand aside while this dictator murders his own people. Tonight our thoughts should be with those in our armed services who are putting their lives at risk to save the lives of others. They are the bravest of the brave."[6] So how did the British politicians, with the help of the mainstream media, sell the necessity of intervention in Libya? How did it aim to convince the public, in a time of economic meltdown and uncertainty in Iraq and Afghanistan, that this vast financial expenditure was something that could not be avoided?

Mad Dog

First of all it was necessary to communicate the moral vacuity of the Libyan leader. Like Stalin and Saddam Hussein before him, Gaddafi was murdering his "own people".[7] The consistent line from the US, UK and France (the leaders in the military intervention against Gaddafi) was humanitarian. On BBC1 on 8 March, Cameron said that if Gaddafi "goes on brutalising his own people…in case he does terrible things to his own people…I don't think we can stand aside and let that happen".[8]

So already the basic elements of war propaganda are established: the enemy is evil and doing nothing in the face of such evil would amount to dereliction of duty. Cameron and Obama were startlingly similar in how they saw the situation. In a nationally televised address from the National Defense University in Washington, Obama said: "To brush aside America's responsibility as a leader and – more profoundly – our responsibilities to our fellow human beings under such circumstances would have been a betrayal of who we are...Some nations may be able to turn a blind eye to atrocities in other countries. The United States of America is different."[9] Leaving aside the untruths of this statement, what we can see here is a repetition of themes and ideas which have been the feature of war propaganda for the last hundred years or so: this is the enemy, they do terrible things. We must stop them. If we do not, then we are no better and evil will prosper.

Aldous Huxley wrote that "the propagandist's purpose is to make one set of people forget that certain other sets of people are human".[10] In the media's portrayal of Gaddafi, not only was he dehumanised, he was animalised. Routinely referred to as "mad dog", the *Sun* reported on the 21 March that he was "cowardly" and a "monster".[11] On 24 March the same newspaper asked: "Who let the dog out?" beginning: "MAD dog Colonel Gaddafi made his first public appearance in a week last night – appearing on state television to tell the world: 'I'm staying in my tent.'"[12]

In the broadsheet press the tone was hardly more measured. For Boris Johnson, writing in the *Telegraph*, the demonisation of Gaddafi sat very well with the moral objectives of intervention: "Of course, it is a good idea to try to rid the world of Gaddafi, a crazed dictator who was behind the murder of Yvonne Fletcher, the Lockerbie passengers and many others. We cannot sit idly by, as Hillary Clinton put it, while this lunatic massacres his own people, and, frankly, we can be proud of the way our own government has handled the matter."[13]

Andrew Rawnsley wrote in the *Observer* that "there is a compelling moral case and one of national interest for taking action in Libya".[14]

Such opinions should attract our concern because they illustrate the consensual approach of the British press in its treatment of Gaddafi. In 2004, when Tony Blair was shaking hands with the Libyan leader, speaking of a "new relationship"[15] and urging the British public to "move beyond" the past, the same newspapers and journalists were broadly supportive of bringing Libya back into the international community.

Media Lens website quotes an *Independent* editorial, amongst many other examples, which illustrates this: "Mr Blair is right to argue that there is real cause for rejoicing in a sinner that repenteth. However distasteful to the families of those murdered, an engagement and reconciliation with Libya that leads to the admission of guilt and compensation is better than continued isolation of the North African country."[16]

Rape as a Weapon of War

In 2011, though, Gaddafi was "mad, a tyrant, and capable of any evil-doing" (at least according to the British press). It has long been the practice of British governments and the media to utilise atrocity propaganda to mobilise public support for military action. In the First World War the British press enthusiastically printed many stories of the German army's assault of Belgium. In 1915 the reading public was told of the rape and mutilation of women and children and the bayoneting of babies.[17] At the beginning of the Gulf War in 1991, newspapers reported lies about Iraqi soldiers emptying new-born babies out of incubators in Kuwaiti hospitals and leaving them to die. More recently, in Kosovo in 1999, Tony Blair spoke of hearing "first-hand of women raped, of children watching their fathers dragged away to be shot".[18] In 2003, Prime Minister Tony Blair spoke of Iraqi President Saddam Hussein and "the thousands of children that die needlessly every year under his rule...the torture chambers which if he is left in power, will remain in being".[19]

So what of Gaddafi's army? In late March stories began to appear in the British media which suggested that forces loyal to Gaddafi were using rape as a method of waging war The *Guardian* journalist Ian Black was one of a host of Western journalists who reported on 26 March that a press breakfast being held in the Rixos Al Nasr hotel in Tripoli was interrupted by "a distraught woman accusing Gaddafi's militia of raping her repeatedly". [20] The shocked journalists were powerless to stop the security forces from taking her away and one American reporter stated in Black's report: "We see the fear in people all the time. But this is the most blatant example of the vicious way the regime treats the Libyan people."

The *Sun* was graphic in its reporting of the event. Under the headline, "Gaddafi's henchmen raped me.", the victim, Iman al-Obeidi, was reported saying: "We are supposed to be treated the same but this is what Gaddafi militiamen did to me, they violated my honour. They defecated and urinated on me."[21] We most recently heard of al-Obeidi on July 29th when she arrived in the United States having been granted refugee status. At this point she told a CNN reporter that she was not ready to talk to the media.[22]

By early June, stories of mass rape were circulating with International Criminal Court investigators suggesting that Gaddafi's soldiers were taking Viagra to ensure effectiveness.[23] When Susan Rice, the US ambassador to the UN, actually accused Gaddafi of supplying the Viagra to his troops, it was evident to most, not only seasoned foreign correspondents, that there was simply not the evidence to support such a claim.[24]

The key fact to remember here is that propaganda is not necessarily the dissemination of untruths. No one is denying that these events take place in conflicts nor that rape is despicably used as a weapon of war. My point here is that these types of stories, collectively and individually, fit into an easily understood narrative pattern. The moral authority of the West is reinforced and the righteousness of action against Gaddafi and his evil regime becomes axiomatic. It is also worth noting this incident, strictly speaking, is nothing more than an allegation of rape. Yet it was reported as completely factual. An indication, perhaps, of how such views of "the enemy" become normalised through repetition.

Danger at Home

If one can also illustrate that this far away evil regime constitutes a threat to national security, the danger becomes localised. This tactic was utilised with various degrees of success in the run up to the Iraq invasion of 2003. In January of that year, for example, the press carried reports that the police had foiled a terrorist ring's attempt to launch a chemical attack in Britain using the deadly poison Ricin. Blair stated that the find showed that "this danger is present and real and with us now – and its potential is huge".[25] In March 2011, Justice Secretary Ken Clarke warned of Gaddafi looking for revenge on UK territory: "British people have reason to remember the curse of Gaddafi – Gaddafi back in power, the old Gaddafi looking for revenge, we have a real interest in preventing that."[26]

Oil

What has been less obvious in the media reporting of events is the political and economic necessity of removing Gaddafi from power. Until very recently, many British politicians and business leaders were determined to welcome Gaddafi into the international fold. In 2004, as he was shaking hands with Blair, it was announced that Anglo-Dutch oil giant Shell had signed a deal worth up to £550m for gas exploration rights off the Libyan coast.[27] In 2007, Gaddafi awarded BP onshore and offshore areas equivalent to the size of Belgium and Kuwait[28]. Indeed, the decision to release Abdelbaset Ali Mohamed al-Megrahi, the convicted Lockerbie bomber and return him to Libya, was made in the "overwhelming interests of the United kingdom", according to leaked ministerial letters revealed in *The Times.*[29]. The leaks indicated that Gordon Brown's government made the decision after discussions between Libya and BP over a multi-million-pound oil exploration deal "had hit difficulties".

By 2009, though, due to decreased revenue, Gaddafi was threatening to nationalise the foreign oil companies in Libya[30] and as the insurrection against him gained hold in 2011 he was threatening to expel all Western oil companies in operation in the country.[31] In addition, he invited Chinese, Russian and Indian firms to produce its oil to replace the Western companies.[32] These acts, combined with an incendiary, rambling 90-minute speech to the UN General Assembly in September 2009 during which Gaddafi ripped up the UN charter, suggested to many Western leaders that he was, once again, not to be trusted. The civil protests which began in Libya on 15 February 2011, therefore, enabled Cameron and President Sarkozy of France to begin the process of condemnation. It is certainly in the economic and political interest of the West that Gaddafi be removed from power.

But wars cannot be seen to be waged for these reasons. Since the bombing began it has been necessary to emphasise the liberating nature of the onslaught. Nato states that he purpose of Operation Unified Protector is to protect civilians and civilian-populated areas under threat of attack from Gaddafi[33] and the British media has largely accepted this. The *Sun* reported on the 26 March that Gaddafi's forces had been hit in the city desert of Ajdabiya. One resident is quoted: "Thank you Britain for your bombs, thank you Tornados. You have saved us."[34] For John Simpson of the BBC, there was no evidence, in the early stages of the Nato campaign, of civilian casualties. "Tripoli is hit by coalition bombs and missiles every night, yet there is little reliable evidence of any casualties. The coalition countries know that killing civilians would be disastrous in this war, and they are plainly making big efforts to avoid it."[35] How Simpson could say this with any degree of certainty is unclear: bombs are notoriously indiscriminate in choosing their victims.

Casualties of War
But has the civilian population been affected? According to Mohammed ben Ayad, head of the Libyan telecommunications authority, Nato has destroyed large parts of the country's telecommunications network and damaged hospitals, schools and other civilian enterprises causing $1 billion worth of damage.[36] Even if this, and many more other claims of civilian deaths from a variety of sources, is dismissed as counter propaganda, what is indisputable is the sheer scale and duration of bombardment. Nato, in effect, moved from enforcing a no-fly zone to protect civilians, to bombing Tripoli to effect regime change. On 10 May, Brigadier General Claudio Gabellini (Chief Operations Officer, Operation Unified Protector) told a Nato press briefing:[37] "Since 31 March Nato and partner aircraft have been conducting an average of 150 sorties a day. And since the beginning of the operations more than 10,000 sorties have been conducted."

On 25 May, the *Guardian* reported that Nato had carried out its heaviest air strikes against Tripoli in more than two months of bombing.[38] The same day saw Cameron and President Obama stand to together and declare that they were not about to weaken their resolve in their pursuit of Gaddafi. Cameron said: "The President and I agree that we should be turning up the heat in Libya. I believe the pressure is on that regime."[39] Pressure indeed – while international concern about the Nato campaign deepened,[40] the British public was treated to extended footage of the Downing Street barbecue. Obama and Cameron in shirtsleeves as the "deification" of the American leader in Europe continued its British leg.[41]

In war, what we do not hear about is at least as important in propaganda terms as what we do hear about. With this in mind, what do we know of the rebel forces who oppose Gaddafi? Obama and Cameron speak of freeing Libya from tyranny. At a joint news conference in London on 25 May, Obama stated: "We're mindful that the fate of these regions is going to be determined by the people there themselves, and that we're going to have to work in partnership with them."[42]

Rarely, though, have we heard either leader be any more specific than that. As Julie Lévesque[43] has questioned: who are these rebels? Who arms them? Who finances them? What interests do they have? Do they have ties to foreign countries? Some journalists have made efforts to find out and the revelations of disorganisation are startling. Andrew Harding, the BBC's Africa correspondent, blogged about a meeting in Benghazi[44] "where an official from Libya's rebel administration – a volunteer like so many in this DIY revolution – was trying, with a biro, to explain 'the chain of command that is, or should be, emerging from the chaos'".

What is clear is that the leaders of the National Transitional Council (NTC) are mostly disaffected Gaddafi loyalists. Mustafa Abdul Jalil, a judge from the eastern town of al-Bayida who resigned as justice minister after the uprising began, is seen as the head of the NTC.[45] Ali Aziz al-Eisawi, former Libyan ambassador to India, has travelled extensively to garner world wide support. Worryingly for the West though, other senior figures have links to al Qaeda – Abdel-Hakim al-Hasidi, of the Libyan Islamic Fighting Group, previously recruited men to fight against coalition forces in Iraq.[46]

All this suggests that if Gaddafi is removed from power, a period of great uncertainty and instability is likely to follow. We have seen in Afghanistan and Iraq the terrible consequences of failing to prepare adequately for post-conflict situations. The consistent rhetoric from the world's most powerful man and David Cameron rarely rises above the platitudinous, the binary oppositions of good versus evil and right versus wrong. Beyond regime change, where is the planning?

So the war has been presented as a humanitarian necessity. Gaddafi and his army has been demonised, the righteousness of Nato emphasised. We have heard very little about the economic and political factors involved. Little, too, in this time of recession about the financial cost of British involvement. In May that figure was estimated at around £300 million. Francis Tusa, editor of the Defence Analysis newsletter, stated that operations were costing £38m a week and could cost the UK taxpayer £1bn if the conflict continued into the autumn[47]. In June, Liam Fox, the Defence Secretary, said that costs for the initial operation would be £120m, while the cost of replenishing spent munitions could reach £140m. In an interview with the BBC, he said that in protecting civilian lives, there was a financial price to pay: "We place a higher value on human life than the Gaddafi regime does."[48]

And surely all this would be worth it if lives were saved. Stephen Barnett, Professor of Communications at Westminster University, argues that despite everything, "humanitarianism sometimes trumps all other considerations".[49] Yes, it does – but the idea that lives are being saved in the heat of the Nato onslaught is one increasingly without credence. As Simon Jenkins has argued in the *Guardian*, government offices and police stations are being attacked in residential areas. How that, he writes, "is protecting civilians is not so much unclear as rubbish".[50]

Hypocrisy

The government's humanitarian case for war was undermined further, if not shattered completely, by rank hypocrisy, with events at Downing Street on 19 May. There on the steps, the Prime Minister shook hands and was photographed with the crown prince of Bahrain[51] – a representative of a regime which has consistently killed and tortured peaceful democracy campaigners. As a matter of record, the pro-democracy movement in Bahrain was suppressed with the aid of the Saudi Arabian army. The same Saudi Arabia, as John Pilger points out, that Obama has recently rewarded with a "$60bn arms deal, the biggest in US history".[52]

Since the beginning of June, attacks on Libya intensified. On the 1st of that month, Nato stated that operations had been extended for another ninety days.[53] Secretary General Anders Fogh Rasmussen said: "This decision sends a clear message to the Gaddafi regime: we are determined to continue our operation to protect the people of Libya." On 7 June, the BBC[54] reported that Tripoli saw its "heaviest daytime raids of its nine-week campaign on what it said were command and control centres in and around the capital, with more than 20 air strikes by low-flying jets". By 21 June, Nato was maintaining that continuing civilian casualties in and around Tripoli were "tragic accidents" whilst Moussa Ibrahim, Libyan government spokesman, countered: "Nato is targeting civilians and the object is to intimidate Libyans. They want everyone to give up the fight."[55]

Attacks by Nato intensified into August and on the 8th of that month the allied forces bombed the village of Mahjar south of the city of Zlitan, allowing rebel Libyan forces to enter. In the raid, said the Gaddafi administration, 85 civilians were killed. According to Nato, Mahjar was a legitimate military target. Col. Roland Lavoie said at a press briefing on 9

August: "We do not have evidence of civilian casualties at this stage, although casualties among military personnel, including mercenaries are very likely due to the nature of the target."[56]

Propaganda and counter propaganda and who to believe? What is undeniable, though, is loss of life. Journalist Lizzie Phelan who was at Zlitan and attended the funerals wrote:[57]: "As we captured on film and in history the aftermath of Nato's crimes, person after person came to tell us how Nato was creating a generation of Libyans so filled with rage that they would see no recourse but to send themselves to martyrdom in revenge against the West."

In the UK at least, these events received little if any coverage. Maybe this was because the media was engaged with the process and aftermath of serious public disorder and a preoccupation with tabloid phone hacking. We should note, though, that for the *Sun*, it was business as usual. On the 17 August it reported: "RAF jets have bombed Colonel Gaddafi's propaganda HQ to shut the Mad Dog's mouth." In addition, an unnamed government source warned of Gaddafi using chemical weapons "against his people". This "insider" said: "He still has around ten tonnes of chemical weapons. The last resort of a desperate man is to unleash these."[58] *Plus ça change.*

Since March, Nato forces have bombarded Libya consistently and its warships have enforced an arms embargo. All foreign Libyan financial assets are frozen and the ability of Gaddafi to replenish military stocks has been severely if not totally restricted. Now, in early September we may be reaching the endgame. The Libyan rebels have captured Gaddafi's compound in Tripoli and the tyrant and members of his family have fled the country.[59]

Cameron and Obama have appeared on our screens and in our newspapers as crusaders for democracy. Careful analysis of the reality invites one to arrive different conclusions. And though there are a number of dissenting voices in the British media today, many of them cited in this article, by and large the mainstream press has faithfully reproduced the official line about intervention in Libya. Just as they faithfully reproduced the official line during the Nato attacks on Serbia in 1999 and during the Iraq invasion of 2003.

The Failures of Journalism

We should be concerned at the relationship between media and government. We live in a culture where mainstream media too often simply accepts what it is told. In the case of the run up to the Iraq war in 2003, journalists largely published and broadcast government propaganda over WMDs. *Times* columnist Matthew Paris[60] told the *Independent*: "Mostly on WMD, we believed what we were told. I'm not ashamed about having believed what I was told." Mary Ann Seighart was as revealing in the same article: "If the chairman of the Joint Intelligence Committee produces a dossier saying that they are convinced that there's a very strong case that Saddam has WMD, who are we to question that?"

But governments should be questioned by the "fourth estate" and we should expect our media to question ministerial pronouncements on issues of national security. If they do not, and continue to rely almost exclusively on officials sources of information, then the British public will continue to be misled, or be ill-informed about, serious issues.

It may be the case that the media leaders – the cultural managers such as the editors and prominent columnists whom Chomsky and Herman[61] refer to – share a class interest with the state. So there exists within the news media an institutional bias that guarantees the mobilisation of certain campaigns on the behalf of the elite. Mark Curtis[62], in his excellent work on British foreign policy since 1945, states that the economic structure of the media industry determines our news. He makes the point that these large companies are in the business of making money and ensuring the existence of the status quo. It is not in the interests of the media to antagonise and challenge the system or promote alternatives. In the case made for the removal of Gaddafi, this would appear to be evident.

- This chapter appeared in shorter and original form as Communicating a war in Libya, *International Institute of Communications*, July 2011, Vol. 39, No 3 pp 30-35.

Notes

[1] Libya: More Than a Thousand Dead. *Daily Telegraph*, 22 February, 2011. Available online at
http://www.telegraph.co.uk/news/worldnews/africaandindianocean/libya/8342543/Libya-more-than-1000-dead.html, accessed on 21 April

[2] Speech made by President Barusso following the EU meeting with the Russian government, 24 February 2011. Available online at http://eeas.europa.eu/delegations/russia/press_corner/all_news/news/2011/20110224_01_en.htm, accessed on 21 April.

[3] *Hansard* 28 February 2011. Available online at http://www.publications.parliament.uk/pa/ld201011/ldhansrd/text/110228-0002.htm, accessed on 21 April

[4] Obama: Gaddafi Must Leave Libya Now, Al-Jazeera, 26 February 2011. Available online at http://english.aljazeera.net/news/americas/2011/02/2011226232530835912.html, accessed on 21 April

[5] Nato – Nato and Libya: Operation Unified Protector. Available online at http://www.nato.int/cps/en/SID-05E6D36C-5E477037/natolive/topics_71652.htm?, accessed on 21 April

[6] Prime Minister's Statement on Libya .Number 10.gov.uk. The Official Site of the Prime Minister's Office.. 19 March. Available online at http://www.number10.gov.uk/news/speeches-and-transcripts/2011/03/prime-ministers-statement-on-libya-2-62161, accessed on 15 April

[7] The propaganda campaigns directed at Saddam before the invasion of Iraq in 2003 repeatedly stated that Saddam had murdered "his *own* people". We were meant to infer, of course, that if he could do this to his fellow countrymen, then what horrors could he inflict on us?

[8] BBC 1, 8 March 2011, The One Show. Available online at http://www.bbc.co.uk/news/uk-politics-12683354, accessed on 10 May

[9] President Obama's address to the National Defense University, 28 March 2011. Available online at http://www.youtube.com/user/AlJazeeraEnglish#p/search/0/sdpuHald-5k, accessed on 12 May

[10] Aldous Huxley, '*The Olive Tree and other Essays*, London: Chatto and Windus, 1936 p. 58

[11] *Sun*, 21 March, Where is Gaddafi? Available online at http://www.thesun.co.uk/sol/homepage/news/3480529/Where-is-Colonel-Gaddafi-hiding.html, accessed on 20 April

[12] *Sun*, 24 March, Who let the dog out? Available online at http://143.252.148.160/sol/homepage/news/3485618/Colonel-Gaddafi-breaks-cover-and-appears-on-Libyan-state-television.html, accessed on 24 April

[13] Taking on Gaddafi is a noble cause, but the risks are huge, *Daily Telegraph*, 30 March. Available online at http://www.telegraph.co.uk/comment/columnists/borisjohnson/8394605/Libya-Taking-on-Colonel-Gaddafi-is-a-noble-cause-but-the-risks-are-huge.html, accessed on 20 April

[14] Libya: This is Only the First Step along a Long and Hazardous Road *Observer*, 20 March. Available online at http://www.guardian.co.uk/commentisfree/2011/mar/20/andrew-rawnsley-gaddafi-intervention, accessed on 20 May

[15] Blair hails new Libyan Relationship BBC Online, 24 March 2004. Available online at http://news.bbc.co.uk/1/hi/uk_politics/3566545.stm, accessed on 20 May

[16] Noble war in Libya Media Lens, 28 March Available online at
http://www.medialens.org/index.php?option=com_content&view=article&id=611:nob
le-war-in-libya-part-2&catid=24:alerts-2011&Itemid=68, accessed on 20 May
[17] There is a rich library of texts outlining these atrocities but see for a general overview
of these incidents see Young, P. and Jesser. P. (1997) *The Media and the Military: From the
Crimea to Desert Storm*. Basingstoke: Macmillan. Taylor, P. (2002) *British Propaganda in the
Twentieth Century*, Edinburgh: Edinburgh University Press. Knightley, P. (2003) *The First
Casualty: The War Correspondent as Hero and Myth-Maker from the Crimea to Gulf War II*,
London: Andre Deutsch
[18] BBC Online 14 May 1999. Available online at
http://news.bbc.co.uk/1/hi/uk_politics/343739.stm, accessed on 20 May 2011
[19] *Observer*, 16 February, 2003. Available online at
http://www.guardian.co.uk/politics/2003/feb/16/iraq.foreignpolicy, accessed on 20
May
[20] Libyan Woman is Brutally Silenced after Accusing Gaddafi's Forces of Rape, *Guardian*,
26 March.. Available online at http://www.guardian.co.uk/world/2011/mar/26/libya-
woman-silenced-accusing-gaddafi-forces-rape, accessed on 20 May 20
[21] Kaddafi's Henchmen Raped Me, *Sun*, 28 March.. Available online at
http://www.thesun.co.uk/sol/homepage/news/3494113/Gaddafi-henchmen-gang-
raped-me.html, accessed 28 April
[22] Alleged Libyan Rape Victim Comes to U.S. to Stay, CNN, 29 July. Available online at
http://www.cnn.com/2011/US/07/29/us.libya.al.obeidy.relocates/index.html, accessed
on 4 September
[23] Gaddafi Soldiers Given "Viagra" and Ordered to Rape Hundreds of Women, says
UN, *Daily Mail*, 9 June. Available online at http://www.dailymail.co.uk/news/article-
2001283/Gaddafi-soldiers-WERE-given-Viagra-rape-innocent-women-civilians-says-
UN.html, accessed on 24 June
[24] Gaddafi "Supplies Troops with Viagra to Encourage Mass Rape", Claims Diplomat,
Guardian, 29 April. Available online at
http://www.guardian.co.uk/world/2011/apr/29/diplomat-gaddafi-troops-viagra-mass-
rape, accessed on 18 August
[25] Six Arrested in Poison Terror Alert, *Telegraph*, 8 January 2003. Available online at
http://www.telegraph.co.uk/news/uknews/1418219/Six-arrested-in-poison-terror-
alert.html. accessed on 23 May
[26] He's awake: The Saturday Interview: Ken Clarke, *Guardian*, 25 March. Available online
at http://www.guardian.co.uk/politics/2011/mar/25/ken-clarke-saturday-interview,
accessed 28 April, 2011.
[27] Blair hails new Libyan Relationship, BBC Online, 24 March 2004.. Available online at
http://news.bbc.co.uk/1/hi/uk_politics/3566545.stm, accessed on 20 May
[28] BP Strike it Rich with Libyan Contracts. *Daily Telegraph*, 6 September, 2009. Available
online at
http://www.telegraph.co.uk/finance/newsbysector/energy/oilandgas/6146929/BP-to-
strike-it-rich-with-Libya-contracts.html, accessed on 28 May
[29] Lockerbie Bomber set Free for Oil *Times*, 30 August 2009. Available online at
http://www.timesonline.co.uk/tol/news/politics/article6814939.ece, accessed on 26
May

[30] Why the West is Attacking Kaddafi Information Clearing House, 12 May 2011. Available online at http://www.informationclearinghouse.info/article28079.htm, accessed on 26 May

[31] Kaddafi Offers Oil Production to India, Russia, China, Nogtec Oil and Gas News, 11 March 2011. Available online at
http://webcache.googleusercontent.com/search?q=cache:vxwonejxt1YJ:www.nogtec.co
m/headlines/gaddafi-offers-oil-production-to-india-russia-
china/+Gaddafi+threatens+to+throw+Western+oil+companies+out+of+the+country
.&cd=5&hl=en&ct=clnk&gl=uk&source=www.google.co.uk, accessed on 26 May 2011

[32] Libya: Gaddafi Offers Oil Production to India, China, Russia to Replace Western Companies Energy, Pedia News, 15 March 2011. http://www.energy-
pedia.com/article.aspx?articleid=144557, aqccessed on 26 May

[33] NATO Operation Unified Protector. Available online at
http://www.nato.int/cps/en/SID-A82B1CC5-3BF7F0C4/natolive/71679.htm,
accessed on 25 May

[34] Hit by a Tornado, *Sun*, 26 March. Available online at
http://www.thesun.co.uk/sol/homepage/news/3494133/Gaddafis-tanks-are-hit-by-a-
Tornado.html, accessed on 26 May

[35] Gaddafi Propaganda Fails to Convince, BBC online, 25 March 2011. Available online at http://www.bbc.co.uk/news/world-africa-12867445, accessed on 26 May

[36] Libyan Officials Threaten to Use Human Shields, *New York Times*, 16 May. Available online at http://www.nytimes.com/2011/05/17/world/africa/17libya.html?_r=1, accessed on 25 May

[37] Nato Press Briefing 10 May. Available online at http://www.nato.int/cps/en/SID-
1512A54F-58C67ADE/natolive/opinions_73660.htm?selectedLocale=en, accessed on 26 May

[38] Libyan Capital Hit by Heaviest Nato Strikes in Two Months, *Guardian*, 25 May. Available online at http://www.guardian.co.uk/world/2011/may/25/libya-capital-
heaviest-nato-strikes, accessed on 25 May

[39] PM and President try to Show United Front on Libya, *Independent*, 26 May. Available online at http://www.independent.co.uk/news/world/politics/president-and-pm-try-
to-show-united-front-on-libya-2289134.html, accessed on 26 May

[40] In early May Russian Minister of Foreign Affairs, Sergei Lavrov, expressed concern over civilian casualties of NATO's air campaign among Libya's population. He stated that "the Allies' use of force is disproportionate – violating the UN Security Council's mandate – and killing innocent people". See georgiandaily.com, 5 May. Available online at
http://georgiandaily.com/index.php?option=com_content&task=view&id=21429&Ite
mid=132, accessed on 26 May

[41] President Obama in UK Parliament, BBC Online, 26 May. Available online at
http://www.bbc.co.uk/news/uk-politics-13539137, accessed on 26 May

[42] Full Text of Obama, Cameron News Conference, CNBC, 25 May. Available online at
http://www.cnbc.com/id/43170587, accessed on 26 May

[43] Libya: Media Propaganda and "Humanitarian Imperialism". Global Realm, 10 April. Available online at http://theglobalrealm.com/2011/04/12/libya-media-propaganda-
and-humanitarian-imperialism, accessed on 2 May

44 Who's in Charge? Sorting out Libya's Rebel Armies, BBC Online, 10 May. Available online at http://www.bbc.co.uk/news/mobile/world-africa-13345413, accessed on 17 May

45 Q&A: Who are the Libyan Rebels? *Financial Times*, 20 March 20 Available online at http://www.ft.com/cms/s/0/5bfb98b0-52fd-11e0-86e6-00144feab49a.html#axzz1NT4weQ2p, accessed 26 May

46 Libyan Rebel Commander Admits his Fighters have Al – Qaeda links, *Daily Telegraph*, 25 March. Available online at http://www.telegraph.co.uk/news/worldnews/africaandindianocean/libya/8407047/Libyan-rebel-commander-admits-his-fighters-have-al-Qaeda-links.html, accessed on 26 May

47 Libya Conflict Costs 'Could Top £1bn, Defence Management.com, 23 May. Available online at http://www.defencemanagement.com/news_story.asp?id=16369, accessed on 26 May

48 Libya Mission May Cost UK £260m – Defence Secretary, BBC Online, 23 June. Available online at http://www.bbc.co.uk/news/uk-politics-13882274, accessed on 18 August

49 Why the Libyan No Fly Zone is Good: Juan Cole's Open Letter to the Left. Open Democracy, 28 March. Available online at http://www.opendemocracy.net/anthony-barnett/why-libyan-no-fly-zone-is-good-juan-coles-open-letter-to-left, accessed on 30 March 30

50 Britain has Slipped into Every Interventionist Fallacy In Libya, *Guardian*, 17 May. Available online at http://www.guardian.co.uk/commentisfree/2011/may/17/bombing-libya-gaddafi-exit-strategy, accessed on 25 May 25

51 Anger as Cameron Invites Bahrain Crown Prince to Number 10, *Guardian*, 20 May. Available online at http://www.guardian.co.uk/uk/2011/may/20/cameron-row-bahrain-prince-visit, accessed on 25 May 25

52 Welcome to the Violent World of Mr Hopey Changey, *New Statesman*, 26 May. Available online at http://www.newstatesman.com/international-politics/2011/05/pilger-obama-arab-libya, accessed on 27 May 27

53 Nato Press Briefing 1 June. Available online at http://www.nato.int/cps/en/SID-763B2FC5-5C3BABAA/natolive/news_74977.htm?mode=pressrelease, accessed on 8 June

54 Libya Crisis: Nato Meets to Review Air Campaign, BBC Online. Available online at http://www.bbc.co.uk/news/world-africa-13692885, accessed on 9 June

55 Gaddafi Accuses Nato of New Bomb Blunder, *Daily Telegraph*, 20 June. Available online at http://www.telegraph.co.uk/news/worldnews/africaandindianocean/libya/8588214/Gaddafi-accuses-Nato-of-new-bomb-blunder.html, accessed on 12 August

56 Nato Press Briefing, 9 August. Available online at http://www.nato.int/cps/en/natolive/opinions_77137.htm?selectedLocale=en, accessed on 19 August

57 Waging a Savage War on Libya's People, Information Clearing House, 11 August. Available online at http://www.informationclearinghouse.info/article28812.htm, accessed on 19 August

[58] Gaddafi's Mute Dog, *Sun*, 17 August. Available online at
http://www.thesun.co.uk/sol/homepage/news/campaigns/our_boys/3756200/RAF-
raid-silences-dictator-Colonel-Gaddafis-propaganda-base.html, accessed on 18 August.
[59] Downfall: Gaddafi in Hiding as Rebels Capture his Tripoli Compound. *Independent*, 24
August. Available online at
http://www.independent.co.uk/news/world/africa/downfall-gaddafi-in-hiding-as-
rebels-capture-his-tripoli-compound-2342792.html, accessed on 24 August
[60] Big guns of the press all quiet on the Iraqi front, *Independent*, 16 March 2008. Available
online at http://www.independent.co.uk/news/media/big-guns-of-the-press-all-quiet-
on-the-iraqi-front-796443.html?r=RSS, accessed on 23 March
[61] Edward S. Herman and Noam Chomsky, *Manufacturing Consent: The Political economy of
the Mass Media*, London: Vintage, 1994
[62] Mark Curtis *Web of Deceit: Britain's Real Role in the World*, London: Vintage, 2003 p. 376

Note on the author

John Jewell is Director of Undergraduate Studies at Cardiff University School of
Journalism, Media and Cultural Studies. His research and teaching interests include war,
politics and propaganda and national identities.

The First Casualty of War is Language: How the Libyan Conflict has been Reported in the British Press

Andrew Beck, of Coventry University, undertakes a content analysis of British reporting of the Libyan conflict, focusing particularly on its handling of the "Gaddafi problem".

This chapter focuses on an eight-week period in UK news reporting (27 February to 24 April 2011) about Libya and its President, Colonel Muammar Gaddafi. It moves from the passing of UN Resolution 1973, through the hyperbolic editorials and think-pieces extolling the virtue of rapid, brutal, and short military intervention, and on to the dawning realisation that this could be a long, protracted conflict lacking a "redemptive conclusion" (the religious wording here comes from an 11 April *Guardian* editorial and is not editorialising on my part).

Lacking such a resolution, UK foreign news reporters ended up diverting attention away from those apparently inconclusive struggles and chose to draw attention to themselves as moral arbiters in a moral morass. Vying with each other for readers' and viewers' attention they presented a spectacle of tribal squabbling.

The "Arab Spring" Runs into the Libyan Summer

The UK news media treatment of Libya stands in stark contrast to its earlier coverage of Egyptian "revolution" which led to the toppling of President Mubarak on 12 February 2011. There, Western politicians held off endlessly before tentatively going public with a measured position, delaying public declaration of opinion in the hope that the situation would resolve itself and save them the trouble of adopting a position. With Libya, well before the launch of attacks on Gaddafi forces by the US/UK and French on 19 March 2011, UK journalists, like their political counterparts, knew exactly what the line was: get rid of Gaddafi by all means necessary, and make sure you've got a watertight UN resolution to justify the action and to indemnify you from the consequences of that action.

Let's start by looking at BBC World Affairs Editor John Simpson's various accounts of Colonel Gaddafi. Simpson prides himself on having been in Gaddafi's presence some nine times after first encountering him in 1978. The reason for that odd phrasing is down to his being, as Simpson put it in the *Daily Telegraph* on 27 February 2011: "sometimes a welcome guest, sometimes a pariah to be held in my hotel room for days at a time".[1]

In 1998, when he was invited to Tripoli for an audience with Gaddafi, he made much of the fact that "throughout our 40-minute interview he would lift himself out of his chair and break wind, loudly enough to be heard on the soundtrack".[2] Blaming his failing to secure another audience with Gaddafi on the editor who gave his *Telegraph* article about Gaddafi the Farter the title "Warm Wind of Compromise Blows From Gaddafi", he has, nonetheless, rarely missed an opportunity when subsequently interviewed for radio or television to repeat this vignette of life in Gaddafi's Tripoli tent.

In *Unreliable Sources*, his 2010 book-length consideration of how the Twentieth Century was reported, and how much was lost in that reporting, Simpson makes only one, passing reference to Gaddafi, and then to coral him into a motley group of men he dubs "hostile dictators" irrespective of their ideological or tribal origins. Quoting a *Daily Telegraph* report of 28 October 1908 about Kaiser Wilhelm II, Simpson reflects on one of his speeches: "The tone of all this is somehow familiar, yet it takes the modern reader a little time to recall why. It is very much the way in which hostile dictators have tended to address us in our own time: Ahmadinejad of Iran, Saddam Hussein of Iraq, Colonel Gaddafi of Libya, Robert Mugabe of Zimbabwe, and, further back in time, Idi Amin of Uganda: the half-mocking, half-complaining, self-obsessed tone of a man who has felt himself belittled and now believes he can hit back without any sense of restraint."[3]

It's rather difficult trying to square Simpson's characterisations of Gaddafi the Farter and Gaddafi the Hostile Dictator with his subsequent claim in the closing moments of BBC1's *Andrew Marr Show* on 13 March 2011: "I was always censored by the BBC about Gaddafi." In other words, when it began to look as if Gaddafi was on the way out, the strategy became "escalate the severity of the rhetoric used to characterise him to ensure that the World Affairs Editor continued to occupy both the reporting and the moral high ground".

Facing Both Ways on Libya

UK news reporting about Libya moved on to combine hand-wringing about the difficulty of the Libyan situation with hand-wringing about which course of action, if any, should be taken by the British government. Andrew Rawnsley rehearsed this dilemma of government in the *Observer* on 13 March 2011: "Discussing with me what might be done to stop Colonel Gaddafi slaughtering his people, a minister sighed: 'It is all very difficult.' So it is."[4] But Rawnsley was able to come to this helpful conclusion: "Here is the bottom line: will the West sit on its hands as Gaddafi attempts to extend his tyranny into a fifth decade by massacring those who have risen up for freedom?"[5]

In the same edition of the *Observer*, Chris McGreal, a reporter with over twenty five years' experience living in and reporting on Libya, helped paint the bigger picture explaining why Gaddafi must be toppled. McGreal led his piece with a reminder of the awful role played by Huda Ben Amer, one of the country's most powerful women in Libya past and present. This echoed Nick Meo's 6 March 2011 *Telegraph* piece in which he recounted her role at one of Gaddafi's earliest public hangings: "As the hanged man kicked and writhed on the gallows" she "stepped forward, grabbed him by the legs, and pulled hard on his body until the struggling stopped."[6]

Both McGreal and Meo have little time for her subsequent rise to power as two-time mayor of Benghazi and her becoming one of Libya's richest women. However, whilst Meo did grant that "her enemies believe that Gaddafi may be holding her children hostage – which they claim is a common way for the regime to control its lieutenants", McGreal elects to report on Amer's continuing influence in completely unequivocal terms. He quotes Walid Malak, "an engineer turned revolutionary who has armed himself with a Kalashnikov plundered from a military base abandoned by Gaddafi's forces", as stating the way forward in apocalyptic, tribal terms: "Everyone in Benghazi knows it's them or us."[7]

There were relatively few dissenting voices in UK news media about the supposedly inevitable path to Gaddafi's destruction. Appearing in live debate with *Guardian* columnist George Monbiot and Ken Macdonald QC on BBC2's *The Daily Politics* on 17 March 2011 Matthew Parris, *The Times's* columnist and former Conservative MP, advocated the UK staying out of the Libyan conflict. Despite speculating that there would be "horrendous scenes" in the coming days, he archly satirised the unquestioning support of the Libyan rebels by the British press as: "I think we want the rebels to win. I don't know who the rebels are."

Representing a more reasoned, less emotional, and not at all arch, approach to the Libyan question, the Conservative MP for Penrith and the Borders, Rory Stewart, sat down on 18 March 2011 to write a diary piece for the *London Review of Books*. Published on 31 March and beginning: "Until yesterday, I thought we were at the end of the age of intervention," he ruefully concluded that "[T]oday...it seems as though the real danger remains not despair but our irrepressible, almost hyperactive actions: that sense of moral obligation; those fears about rogue states, failed states, regions and our own credibility, which threatens to make this decade again a decade of over-intervention."[8] Stewart is one of the few writers on the Libyan conflict thus far to observe that, at that time "Libya did [not] appear to meet the criteria for intervention under international law. Gaddafi was the sovereign power, not the rebels, and he was not conducting genocide or ethnic cleansing."[9]

Go to War
Whilst endlessly worrying over the fine points of legal argument is a common British trait in times of conflict, this time around the British press appeared to suffer no agonies of indecision – and immediately

exhorted politicians to go to war. Effortlessly finessing the UK news media's contemporary support for Bush and Blair's war on Iraq into a retrospective lament for the damage done to global humanitarian consensus by that action, an *Independent* leading article of 19 March 2011 congratulated the "international community" on its coming "together over Libya in a way that, even a few days ago, seemed impossible. The adventurism of Bush and Blair in 2003 looked as if it had buried the principle of humanitarian intervention for a generation. It has returned sooner than anyone believed possible."[10]

Despite an emerging tendency supporting an escalating involvement in a Libyan intervention UK news media still sought to promote its objective, non-combatant status. This ranged from the sublime to the ridiculous. Representing the sublime we were presented with the BBC's Head of Foreign News, John Williams, reiterating: "That's why I think it's important that we are always impartial" (BBC *Newswatch*, 28 March). And representing the ridiculous, PR "guru" Mark Borkowski said of the world's media: "The media does what the media does, be it reporting from a war zone or scavenging the celebrity hotspots of the world."[11]

Where were the Politicians?

Whilst the British press maintained its public stance of disinterest, of not taking sides in the Libyan conflict, it was relatively unequivocal where British politicians were still experiencing problems formulating and promoting foreign policy. Interviewed for BBC Radio 4's *Today* programme on 21 March 2011, the UK Secretary of State for Defence, Liam Fox, stated that in respect of Gaddafi being killed: "There is the potential for that to be a possibility." So, notwithstanding UN Resolution 1973, which permitted all action short of landing in Libya and launching land-based attacks on Gaddafi's forces, the Defence Secretary was preparing the rhetorical ground for killing the Libyan President, albeit in a guarded and mystifying manner.

Contrary to the well-known aphorism, the first casualty of war waged by British politicians is not truth but rather the English language. The same day on Radio 4's *Today* programme, John Humphrys' prime objective in engaging UK Foreign Secretary William Hague in the dreary performance of broadcast combat was to get him to admit that troops could land on Libyan soil: a battle albeit a battle of language.

Not only were British newspapers able to support the case for mission creep and the active imprint of British troops' boots on Libyan soil, they were also clearly able to employ an emotionally-charged rhetoric to lead their readers to the inevitable discovery of the moral imperative driving this strategy. Filing another, lengthier piece in the *Observer* magazine on 24 April 2011 under the title: "Go to hell, Gaddafi," the *Guardian's* Chris McGreal helped readers still searching for parallels between Libya in 2011 and other relatively recent conflicts with this incontestable analogy: "Libya's uprising seems to me more akin to South Africa's liberation from apartheid."[12]. In other words: who in their right mind could argue against entry into and intervention in Libya's affairs and still hold high their heads in the global community?

The First Casualty

In the way that war often makes odd bedfellows of ostensibly opposed politicians so war also stimulates public figures to adopt positions at radical odds with their track records. Thus it was that the bald advocacy of killing Gaddafi came from the unusual source of leading human rights lawyer Geoffrey Robertson QC writing in the *Independent* on 1 April 2011: "Since Security Council Resolution 1973 calls for the use of 'all necessary means' to protect the civilian population, it may soon appear that the means most necessary is the forcible removal of Gaddafi."[13]

He managed to justify this by asserting that "Any targeted killing of Gaddafi would discomfort other dictators upon whom the West relies for support and would (in the words of Macbeth) 'scorch the snake not kill it', since vicious London School of Economics-groomed Saif would be waiting in the wings with his even more brutal siblings. But if the Gaddafis refuse a Western ultimatum to fold up their tent and depart, and if the rebel forces (even with new US arms) are on the brink of a bloody defeat, tyrannicide may become Nato's best – or only – option."[14] Robertson has already had his tyrannicidal urgings come true (albeit in the wrong chronological order) in that Saif al-Arab Gaddafi, the President's son, was soon afterwards assassinated in a Nato strike.

But all those hopes and predictions of a quick resolution to the Libyan conflict so quickly led to stalemate. In a world-weary and resigned tone, the *Independent's* leading article of 9 April 2011 concluded: "Three weeks after the first UN-authorised air strikes on Eastern Libya, there is a distinct sense that the conflict is stagnating."[15] And where might this lead as far as the Libyan people were concerned?

> If, as it appears, the conflict is stagnating, with Gaddafi still holding sway in the west with the opposition holding almost uncontested power in the east, the time may be approaching when consideration should be given to an outcome short of a complete opposition victory. It may be premature to talk about the division of Libya, but a *de facto* recognition of two areas under separate control might be the optimum interim solution.[16]

Whilst conflict might have been stagnating in the field there was no lack of it within the UK foreign news reporting community. Broadcast on the evening of 24 April 2011, Channel 4 News Foreign Affairs Correspondent Jonathan Miller hung a background piece to the Libya conflict on the peg of the extent to which some news organisations chose to work within Libyan government restrictions and others didn't. Having rehearsed the problems he had encountered by refusing to accept Libya government restrictions, he stressed that he would not work within such limits whilst walking past BBC News Middle East Editor Jeremy Bowen filing a report to camera. The intention was clear: Channel 4 News stood independent and occupied the moral high ground; the BBC had complied with Gaddafi and was morally deficient.

It is rare for such spats to become public, to be actually broadcast. Nevertheless, it would appear that within the UK foreign news reporting community, it was also a case of them or us. Faced with the prospect of an endlessly protracted struggle and the complete absence of a quick fit solution, redemptive or otherwise, the television news camera ends up being pointed in the wrong direction and the reporter becomes the story. Spurred on by a reliance on the ubiquitous two-way and by the compulsion to perform emotions to camera the news itself becomes sidelined. Budget cuts notwithstanding, anchors are parachuted into a spot somewhere near (cough) the action to deliver their earnest ministrations to camera against the backdrop of the battlefront.

The News is Tribal

Ignoring subtle nuances of family, political, and tribal loyalties and structures UK news media elected to privilege their own tribalisms: both between news organisations (whomsoever is holier than thou) and within news organisations (whomsoever is top dog). Lamenting this latter tendency, the creation of new tribal hierarchies within UK news organisations, veteran BBC war zone reporter Martin Bell has highlighted both the rise of the anchor and their performative character, whether located in the studio or in the field:

> Reporters should also be wary of the creeping symptoms of correspondentitis. This is an affliction of the mind that occurs when they have been around for a while, believe that they have unique insights to offer, and file reports that are chiefly about themselves. The roles of anchor and subanchor play to this weakness with devastating effect. Within the BBC's College of Journalism, there is scope for a School of Humility. Budget cuts may yet deliver it.[17]

Amin.

Notes

[1] John Simpson: Gaddafi was mad, bad and dangerous to know, *Daily Telegraph*, 27 February 2011. Available online at http://www.telegraph.co.uk/news/worldnews/africaandindianocean/libya/8350015/John-Simpson-in-Libya-Gaddafi-was-mad-bad-and-dangerous-to-know.html, accessed on 1 August 2011

[2] ibid

[3] John Simpson: *Unreliable Sources*, London: Macmillan, 2010 p. 77

[4] Andrew Rawnsley: Instead of fearing another Iraq, the West must do right by Libya, *Observer*, 13 March 2011 p. 37. Available online at http://www.guardian.co.uk/commentisfree/2011/mar/13/andrew-rawnsley-west-intervention-libya, accessed on 1 August 2011

[5] ibid

[6] Nick Meo: Huda the executioner – Libya's devil in female form, *Daily Telegraph*, 6 March 2011. Available online at http://www.telegraph.co.uk/news/worldnews/africaandindianocean/libya/8363587/Huda-the-executioner-Libyas-devil-in-female-form.html, accessed on 1 August 2011

[7] Chris McGreal: "It's them or us" as Benghazi's rebels await Gaddafi assault, *Observer*, 13 March 2011 p.6. Available online at http://www.guardian.co.uk/world/2011/mar/12/libya-benghazi-gaddafi-revolution, accessed on 20 August 2011

[8] Rory Stewart: Here we go again, *London Review of Books*, 31 March 2011 p. 21

[9] ibid

[10] Lead editorial: A welcome moment of unity, but there are dangers ahead, *Independent*, 19 March 2011, p.42. Available online at http://www.independent.co.uk/opinion/leading-articles/leading-article-a-welcome-moment-of-unity-but-there-are-dangers-ahead-2246292.html, accessed on 2 August 2011

[11] Mark Borkowski: Are the media fuelling Charlie Sheen's crisis? *The Observer New Review*, p.4. Available online at

http://www.guardian.co.uk/commentisfree/2011/mar/13/charlie-sheen-media-mental-health, accessed on 2 August 2011

[12] Chris McGreal: Go to hell, Gaddafi, *Observer Magazine*, 24 April 2011 p.39. Available online at http://www.guardian.co.uk/world/2011/apr/23/libya-benghazi-gaddafi-revolution, accessed 20 August 2011

[13] Geoffrey Robertson: When tyrannicide is the only option, *Independent Viewspaper*, 1 April 2011 p. 3. Available online at
http://www.independent.co.uk/opinion/commentators/geoffrey-robertson-when-tyrannicide-is-the-only-option-2258671.html, accessed on 2 August 2011

[14] ibid

[15] Leading article: Nato must not be seduced into prolonging the conflict in Libya, *Independent*, 9 April 2011 p. 34. Available online at
http://www.independent.co.uk/opinion/leading-articles/leading-article-nato-must-not-be-seduced-into-prolonging-the-conflict-in-libya-2265467.html, accessed on 2 August 2011

[16] ibid

[17] Martin Bell: Pull up your anchors, *Media Guardian*, 13 June 2011 p. 6. Available online at http://www.guardian.co.uk/media/2011/jun/13/bbc-cuts-anchors, accessed on 3 August 2011

Note on the author

Andrew Beck is Principal Lecturer in Applied Communication at Coventry School of Art and Design, Coventry University, where he also serves as International Development Co-ordinator. He has over thirty five years experience as educator, author, consultant, and curriculum designer. His recent books include *Communication Studies: The Essential Introduction* (2002), *Cultural Work* (2003), *Communication Studies: The Essential Resource* (2004), *Get Set For Communication Studies* (2005), and *Critical Skills in Communication and Social Work* (2012).

Targeting Gaddafi: Secret Warfare and the Media

Richard Lance Keeble highlights the media's coverage – and, more significantly, the non-coverage – of the attempts by the United States and the UK to assassinate Col. Gaddafi, President of Libya, over the last 40 years

On 30 April 2011, Nato bombs killed Saif el-Arab, the 29-year-old son of Libyan President Col. Muammar Gaddafi, and three of his grandchildren who were sheltering in his Tripoli compound. One of the grandchildren, Mastoura, was just four-months-old.[1]

This was not an isolated attempt on Gaddafi's life. Behind a wall of silence, the US and UK conducted over the last four decades a massive, largely secret war against Libya – often using Chad, the country lying on its southern border, as its base – and attempting to assassinate the Libyan leader. Indeed, Nato continued its relentless bombing of the Bab al-Aziziya compound (and assassination attempts) over the months leading up to its seizure by the rebels in August 2011.

Gaddafi Seizes Power – and MI6 Plot to Restore Monarchy Flops

Seizing power in Libya by ousting King Idris in a 1969 coup,[2] Gaddafi (who intriguingly had undertaken a military training course in England in 1966) quickly established close links with the Soviet Union – and so became the target of massive covert operations by the French, US, Israeli and British.[3] Stephen Dorril[4] in his seminal history of MI6, records how in 1971 a British plan to invade the country, release political prisoners and restore the monarchy ended in a complete flop.

Dorril reports: "What became known as the 'Hilton assignment' was one of MI6's last attempts at a major special operation designed to overthrow a regime opposed to British interests." The plan to bring down Gaddafi had originally been a joint MI6/CIA operation but the CIA suddenly withdrew after they concluded that "although Gaddafi was anti-West, he was also anti-Soviet, which meant there could be someone a lot worse running Libya. The British disagreed".[5]

In 1980, according to Richard Deacon, the head of the French secret service, Col. Alain de Gaigneronde de Marolles, resigned after a French-led plan ended in disaster when a rebellion by Libyan troops in Tobruk was rapidly suppressed.[6] But former French intelligence chief Pierre Lethier disputed this claim: "Mr Deacon, I am afraid, has seen fit to spread rumours fabricated by the opposition press in France. Former head of the Action Service and then Deputy Director for Intelligence in 1978, de Marolles fell from grace in 1980 after a sinister conflict within the SDECE (under Count Alexandre de Marenches from 1971 to 1981) following a highly debatable counter-intelligence operation. Unfortunately I cannot say any more about this."[7]

Throughout the early 1980s Gaddafi was demonised in the mainstream US and UK media as a "terrorist warlord" and prime agent of a Soviet-inspired "terror network". According to Noam Chomsky, Reagan's campaign against "international terrorism" was a natural choice for the propaganda system in furtherance of its basic agenda: "expansion of the state sector of the economy; transfer of resources from the poor to the rich and a more 'activist' (i.e. terrorist and aggressive) foreign policy". Such policies needed the public to be frightened into obedience by some "terrible enemy". And Libya fitted the need perfectly.[8]

Easy to Hate

As Chomsky commented: "Gaddafi is easy to hate, particularly against the backdrop of rampant anti-Arab racism in the United States and the deep commitment of the educated classes, with only the rarest of exceptions, to US-Israeli rejectionism and violence. He has created an ugly and repressive society and is, indeed, guilty of retail terrorism, primarily against Libyans."[9]

In July 1981, a CIA plan to overthrow and possibly kill Gaddafi was leaked to the press. At roughly the same time, Libyan hit squads were reported to have entered the United States, though this has since been revealed to have been a piece of Israeli secret service disinformation.[10] Joe Flynn, the infamous con man, was also able to exploit Fleet Street's fascination with the Gaddafi myth. In September 1981, posing as an Athens-based arms dealer he tricked almost £3,000 out of the *News of the World* with his story that the Libyan leader was "masterminding a secret plot to arm black revolutionary murder squads in Britain".[11]

Then in 1982, away from the glare of the media, Hissène Habré, with the backing of the CIA, Egyptian and Israeli troops,[12] overthrew the Chadian government of Goukouni Wedeye. Human Rights Watch records: "Under President Reagan, the United States gave covert CIA paramilitary support to help install Habré in order, according to secretary of state Alexander Haig, to 'bloody Gaddafi's nose'." Bob Woodward, in his semi-official history of the CIA, reveals that the Chad covert operation was the first undertaken by the new CIA chief William Casey and that throughout the decade Libya ranked almost as high as the Soviet Union as the *bête noir* of the administration.[13]

A report from Amnesty, *Chad: The Habré Legacy*,[14] recorded massive military and financial support for Habré by the US Congress. It added: "None of the documents presented to Congress and consulted by Amnesty International covering the period 1984 to 1989 make any reference to human rights violations."

US official records indicate that funding for the Chad-based secret war against Libya also came from Saudi Arabia, Egypt, Morocco, Israel and Iraq.[15] According to John Prades[16], the Saudis, for instance, donated $7m to an opposition group, the National Front for the Salvation of Libya (also backed by French intelligence and the CIA). But a plan to assassinate Gaddafi and take over the government on 8 May 1984 was crushed.[17] One month earlier, an unarmed policewoman, Yvonne Fletcher, was shot while on duty outside the Libyan People's Bureau in St. James' Square, London. And the British accused the Libyan government of being directly responsible.[18]

In the following year, the US asked Egypt to invade Libya and overthrow Gaddafi but President Mubarak refused.[19] By the end of 1985, the *Washington Post* had exposed the plan after congressional leaders opposing it wrote in protest to President Reagan.

Thrilled To Blitz

Frustrated in its covert attempts to topple Gaddafi, the US government's strategy suddenly shifted. In March 1986, US planes patrolling the Gulf of Sidra were reported to have been attacked by Libyan missiles. But Noam Chomsky suggests this incident was a provocation "enabling US forces to sink several Libyan boats, killing more than 50 Libyans and, it was hoped, to incite Gaddafi to acts of terror against Americans, as was subsequently claimed".[20] In the following month, Gaddafi was blamed for organising the bombing of a TWA passenger jet over Greece while President Reagan next claimed to have proof that the Libyan embassy had arranged the bombing of a Berlin discothèque on 5 April 1986 – killing an American serviceman and a Turkish woman and seriously injuring 229 people.[21]

The US responded with a military strike on key Libyan targets. But the attack was widely condemned. James Adams[22] quotes a British intelligence source: "Although we allowed the raid there was a general feeling that America had become uncontrollable and unless we did something Reagan would be even more violent the next time."

Prime Minister Margaret Thatcher was perhaps hoping for an action-replay of the Falklands factor when she gave the US permission to fly 24 F-111 attack jets from the US 48th Tactical Fighter Wing, based at RAF Lakenheath, in East Anglia, to bomb Libyan targets. Also, according to Annie Machon, Mrs Thatcher was "anxious for revenge" after the shooting of P.C. Fletcher.[23] In contrast, Mark Curtis argues that the UK was the only major ally to offer support to President Reagan "partly in return for US intelligence support during the Falklands War [of 1982] which Britain could probably not have undertaken unilaterally".[24]

Dorril reports that the Arab Commando Cell, a front for terrorist Abu Nidal, killed two British hostages, Philip Padfield and Leigh Douglas: "Mrs Thatcher had given the go-ahead for the US bombers to use British bases despite a report which originated with MI6 that the hostages would be killed in retaliation for the raid."[25]

The Libyan attack was an archetypal move of the secret state: only a select few in Thatcher's cabinet were involved in the decision. Yet the bombings appeared to win little support from the public. Harris, Gallup and MORI all showed substantial majorities opposed.

Much of the UK mainstream press, however, responded with jingoistic jubilation. The *Sun*'s front page screamed: "Thrilled to blitz: Bombing Gaddafi was my greatest day, says US airman." The *Mirror* concluded: "What was the alternative? In what other way was Colonel Gaddafi to be forced to understand that he had a price to pay for his terrorism?"; *The Times*: "The greatest threat to Western freedoms may be the Soviet Union but that does not make the USSR the only threat. The growth of terrorist states must be curbed while it can be curbed. The risks of extension of the conflict must be minimised. And in this case it would appear that it has been." The *Star*'s front page proclaimed: "Reagan was right." In the *Sunday Telegraph*, of 1 June, columnist Paul Johnson denounced the "distasteful whiff of pure cowardice in the air" as "the wimps" raised doubts about the US bombing of "terrorist bases" in Libya.

But there was an intriguing mediacentric dimension to the Libyan bombings as the BBC, transformed into the "enemy within" of the vulnerable state, was to come under some considerable attack from the Conservative government over its coverage of the attacks. Though most of the press responded ecstatically to Britain's role in the bombing, all their contrived jingoism could not hide the fact that the raid failed to capture the imagination of important elements of the elite. Opposition even came from cabinet members.

How BBC Became the Perfect Scapegoat

The BBC became the perfect scapegoat. Kate Adie's on-the-spot reports could not fail to mention the casualties.[26] Many of the main targets were missed. Four 2,000lb bombs fell on the suburb of Bin Ghashir, causing far more devastation than any "terrorist" bomb could ever achieve.[27] Even so, Norman Tebbitt, chairman of the Conservative Party, engaged in a highly personalised attack on Adie. Yet there was an air of theatre about the whole event. Adie was one of the most trusted BBC correspondents. And both government and BBC could benefit from the spat. The Tory right, on the ascendancy at the time, and ever hasty to criticise the BBC it so desperately wanted privatised as the "enemy within", was satisfied and the BBC, who stuck by their star reporter throughout the attacks, could appear to be courageously defending media freedom. Amidst the many contradictions and complexities of modern-day politics, mediacentric elements are put to many diverse uses by (usually competing) factions in the ruling elites.

According to US academic Douglas Kellner, the bombing was a manufactured crisis, staged as a media event and co-ordinated to coincide with the beginning of the 7 pm news in the US.[28] Two hours later President Reagan went on network television to justify the raid. Chomsky also argues that the attack was "the first bombing in history staged for prime-time television".[29] Administration press conferences soon after the raid ensured "total domination of the propaganda system during the crucial early hours". Chomsky continues: "One might argue that the administration took a gamble in this transparent public relations operation, since journalists could have asked some difficult questions. But the White House was justly confident that nothing untoward would occur and its faith in the servility of the media proved to be entirely warranted."

Yet the main purpose of the raid was to kill the Libyan President – dubbed a "mad dog" by Reagan. David Yallop quotes "a member of the United States Air Force intelligence unit who took part in the pre-raid briefing": "Nine of F-111s that left from the UK were specifically briefed to bomb Gaddafi's residence inside the barracks where he was living with his family."[30]

In the event, the first bomb to drop on Tripoli hit Gaddafi's home killing Hana, his adopted daughter aged 15 months – while his eight other children and wife Safiya were all hospitalised, some with serious injuries. The president escaped. According to Richard J. Aldrich[31], Gaddafi escaped death by minutes because the Prime Minister of Malta warned him by telephone of the approaching military jets. David Blundy and Andrew Lycett report:

The attack on Gaddafi's Aziziya compound was a military failure. Gaddafi himself was deep underground. The administration building, where he lives, was missed by two bombs which fell thirty yards away, knocking out the windows but doing no structural damage. The tennis courts received two direct hits and a bomb fell outside the front door of the building where Gaddafi's family lives. Blasts tore through the small bedrooms to the right of the living room, injuring two of Gaddafi's sons and killing his fifteen-month old adopted daughter, Hana. Hana was publicly acknowledged only in death. During interviews only a month before Gaddafi had said, sadly, that he had only one daughter, eight-year-old Aisha, and wished that he had more. He did not say that his wife had adopted a baby girl ten months before.[32]

Consider the outrage in the Western media if a relative of Reagan had been killed by a Libyan bomb. There was no such outrage over the Libyan deaths. In November, the UN General Assembly passed a motion condemning the raid. Israel was one of the few countries to back the US over the raid. Yet when the Israeli representative came to justify his country's stance, he used evidence of Gaddafi's alleged commitment to terrorism taken from the German mass-selling newspaper *Bild am Sonntag* and the London-based *Daily Telegraph*.[33]

Intriguingly, in February 2011, the German newspaper *Welt am Sonntag*, the Sunday edition of *Die Welt*, reported that Hana had actually survived, lived in London for a while, trained as a doctor and was currently holding an important position in the Libyan Ministry of Health. The information was apparently gathered from Gadaffi family documents seized in Switzerland. As the rebels advanced on Tripoli in August 2011, this news was covered prominently in most leading Western media. In the *Irish Times*, Mary Fitzgerald located what appeared to be Hana's study in the overrun Bab al-Aziziya compound. But was it all disinformation?[34]

Away from the Media Glare, CIA Aims to Spark Anti-Gaddafi Coup

Following the April 1986 attack, reports of US military action against Libya disappeared from the media. But away from the media glare, the CIA launched by far its most extensive effort yet to spark an anti-Gaddafi coup. A secret army was recruited from among the many Libyans captured in border battles with Chad during the 1980s.[35] In March 1987, the Libyans were defeated at Ouadiddoum in northern Chad, in a major battle involving French and American secret services in league with a number of Arab powers – Egypt and Tunisia, Saudi Arabia, Iraq – and Israel![36]

And, as concern grew in MI6 over Gaddafi's alleged plans to develop chemical weapons, Britain funded various opposition groups in Libya including the London-based Libyan National Movement.

For his part, Gaddafi continued to arm various revolutionary movements including the IRA. In October 1987, French customs seized an Irish-crewed freighter, the Eksund, carrying almost 200 tonnes of arms including Kalashnikov rifles, ground-to-air SAM-7 missiles, a million rounds of ammunition and more than 2 tonnes of Semtex. This was the fifth shipment to Ireland since 1985.[37]

The Libyan leader was also blamed for the bombing of the Pan Am jumbo jet on 21 December 1988 over the Scottish town of Lockerbie in which 270 people died.[38]

Then in 1990, with the crisis in the Gulf developing, French troops helped oust Habré and install Idriss Déby as the new President of Chad in a secret operation. The French government had tired of Habré's genocidal policies while the Bush administration decided not to frustrate France's objectives in exchange for their co-operation in the war against Iraq. Yet even under Déby the abuses of civil rights by government forces have continued.[39]

Attempts to oust Gaddafi also continued. David Shayler, a former MI5 agent, even alleged that MI6 were involved in a plot in March 1996 to assassinate the Libyan leader as he attended the Libyan General People's Congress.[40] His motorcade was attacked by dissidents with Kalashnikovs and rocket grenades but while Gaddafi escaped there were casualties on both sides. Stephen Dorril reports in his seminal history of MI6: "Three fighters were killed but the leader of the hit team, Abd al-Muhaymeen, a veteran of the Afghan resistance who was possibly trained by MI6 or the CIA, 'escaped unhurt'."[41] Shayler claimed MI6 paid the al-Islamiya al-Muqatila, the Islamic Fighting Group, £100,000 to carry out the attack.[42]

Libya Welcomed Back to the "International Community"

Following Libya's decision after the 9/11 US terrorist attacks to build closer ties with the West and renounce all efforts to develop nuclear weapons, UN sanctions against the country were lifted in 2003. To improve the image of Libya in the West, Gaddafi employed the Monitor Group, an American public relations company between 2000 and 2008.[43] The demonisation of Col. Gaddafi predictably declined and members of the political, financial and academic British elite lined up to welcome the Libyan leader back into the "international community".[44]

For instance, on 26 March 2004, an editorial in the *Guardian* commented: "We should congratulate the Foreign Office for its quiet and effective diplomacy...Col. Gaddafi should be encouraged, but not at such a forced pace." An editorial in the *Independent* on the same day described Gaddafi as merely "the Arab world's most eccentric and unpredictable leader", adding: "Mr Blair is right to argue that there is real cause for rejoicing in a sinner that repenteth. However distasteful to the families of those murdered, an engagement and reconciliation with Libya that leads to the admission of guilt and compensation is better than continued isolation of the North African country."[45]

Also during this period, Gaddafi was represented more as an "eccentric and unpredictable leader" rather than an "evil dictator". This picture was reinforced in the coverage of the WikiLeaks revelations on Libya in December 2010. For instance, the cables disclosed that Col. Gaddafi, 68, "suffered from severe phobias, enjoyed flamenco dancing and horse-racing, acted on his whims and irritated friends and enemies alike".[46]

Significantly, the demonisation did not intensify even after Abdurahman Alamoudi was jailed after admitting to participating in a Libyan plot to assassinate Prince Abdullah (now King) of Saudi Arabia. According to court records, Gaddafi wanted Abdullah killed after a 2003 Arab League summit where Gaddafi felt he had been insulted. At one point, Abdullah wagged a finger at Gaddafi and said: "Your lies precede you, while the grave is ahead of you."[47] But Robert Fisk was keen to maintain the demonisation – and emphasise the Blair government's double standards:

> We adore Gaddafi, the crazed dictator of Libya whose werewolves have murdered his opponents abroad, whose plot to murder King Abdullah of Saudi Arabia preceded Tony Blair's recent trip to Tripoli

– Colonel Gaddafi, it should be remembered, was called a "statesman" by Jack Straw for abandoning his non-existent nuclear ambitions – and whose "democracy" is perfectly acceptable to us because he is on our side in the "war on terror".[48]

Return of the "Mad Dog" Demonisation Discourse

The 2003-2011 period can, then, be seen as a significant interregnum in the moves by Western governments to eliminate Col. Gaddafi. Both sides in the conflict cynically decided that some kind of "entente" best served their interests. Gaddafi certainly took the opportunity to secure the lifting of UN sanctions and build up diplomatic and commercial relations with the United States, the European Union and Asian states. The high point of Libya's rapprochement with the West came when Col Gaddafi addressed the United Nations on 23 September 2009.[49] Yet the WikiLeaks cables revealed that Gaddafi flew into a rage after the US refused to let him pitch his Bedouin-style tent in New York. In return, the Libyan leader refused to allow a "hot" shipment of highly enriched uranium to be loaded on a transport plane and shipped to Russia as part of his nuclear-dismantling procedure.[50]

But once the uprising against the regime was launched in Tripoli in February 2011, and Nato began its bombing campaign on 19 March (the anniversary of the attack on Iraq in 2003), the "mad dog", demonisation discourse returned to the media. For instance, on 4 September, *The Sunday Times* headlined a report about the Libyan leader's alleged attempts to escape via the pipes of the $33 billion Great Man-made River Project: "Gaddafi and his sons flee like rats up a waterpipe".[51]

And the Western elites (assisted by a compliant mainstream media) quickly reverted to their previous policy of confrontation with Libya, seizing the new opportunities in their increasingly desperate attempts to eliminate Gaddafi. Immediately after the 25 April attack on Gaddafi, Vladimir Putin, the Russian Prime Minister, significantly accused Nato of aiming to kill the Libyan leader – and going far beyond the remit allowed by the UN resolution 1973 authorising all necessary means "to protect civilians". US defence secretary Robert Gates rejected the claim.[52]

The efforts of MI6 and the SAS in assisting the rebels and capturing Gaddafi once his Tripoli compound was raided on 24 August 2011 were reported prominently throughout the conflict.[53] For instance, *The Times* reported on 25 August 2011 that a 30-strong SAS unit had been working with Qatari special forces along the front line with rebel forces. "The SAS has performed a more discreet role compiling information and co-ordinating with Nato pilots farther back."[54] The SAS was said to be "keen to restore its somewhat battered reputation after an abortive early secret mission to Benghazi when six SAS troopers and two MI6 officers were arrested by Libyan farmers". Reports also emerged of France, Italy and Egypt (in the form of members of Unit 777) sending special forces to support the insurgents.[55]

Indeed, one of the paradoxes of contemporary warfare propaganda is that, at strategic moments such as during the Libyan crisis of 2011, the secret and the invisible are revealed.

Conclusion

This study raises a number of significant questions. To what extent do the mainstream media fail to cover the activities of the secret state and their secret warfare activities – thus giving a completely distorted picture of contemporary conflicts?[56] In an age of information and news overflow, how useful is it, rather, to consider the silencing function of media? And how important are the close links between the intelligence/security services and Fleet Street in influencing coverage – of both war and peace.[57] Given that this study has used a range of sources largely marginalised in the mainstream media, to what extent do journalists' routines need to change radically if they are to cover covert warfare adequately.

And in view of the absence of any media outrage over the many attempts over the last decade to assassinate a head of state (as identified in this study), how important is it for academic analyses of media representations of conflict to consider the selective application of outrage – and the complex factors behind it.

Notes

[1] Milan Rai records dozens of night-time Nato bomb attacks on Tripoli, many of them on or near to the Bab al-Aziziya compound on 24, 25 and 28 May. See Milan Rai: The Coup against Gaddafi, *Peace News*, No 2537, September 2011 p. 6. How many Nato bomb attacks were made on the compound before the rebels took it over at the end of August 2011 we will probably never know

[2] The role of the CIA in the coup is disputed. Blundy, David and Lycett, Andrew (*Qaddafi and the Libyan Revolution*, London: Weidenfeld and Nicolson, 1987: 69) report the

former Libyan Prime Minister, Abdul Hamid Bakoush, saying: "The Americans had contacts with Gaddafi through the embassy in Tripoli. They encouraged him to take over. There were dozens of CIA operatives in Libya at that time and they knew what was going on. The Americans were frightened of the senior officers and the intelligentsia in Libya because they thought that these people were independent and could not be run as puppets." But Blundy and Lycett add (ibid): "Bakoush's refusal to give names that might corroborate his theory does not help his credibility." The comments of David D. Newson, US Ambassador to Libya from 1965 to 1969, suggest that the CIA was taken by surprise. He told the Foreign Affairs Oral History Project: "The agency had reports of a group that was forming, called the Black Boots, probably a group that was centred around an officer by the name of Abdul Azir Shalhi. But that group, if they had any intention of trying to seize power, was pre-empted by the Gaddafi group on which we had no information." See Ronald Bruce St John (2008) *Libya: From Colony to Independence*, Oxford: Oneworld Publications p. 140

[3] Ronald Bruce St John (ibid: 144) reports that the first consignment of Soviet weaponry arrived in Libya in July 1970 being displayed at a parade commemorating the One September revolution. Gaddafi continued to purchase Soviet arms throughout the decade, including a $1 billion package in 1974-1975 "that constituted its largest arms agreement"

[4] See Dorril, Stephen (2000) *MI6: Fifty Years of Special Operations*, London: Fourth Estate

[5] ibid: 736

[6] Deacon, Richard (1990) *The French Secret Service*, Grafton Books: London pp 262-264

[7] In a personal email to the author, 6 May 2011

[8] Chomsky, Noam (1991) *Pirates and Emperors*, Montreal/New York: Black Rose Books p. 120

[9] ibid

[10] Rusbridger, James (1989) *The Intelligence Game: Illusions and Delusions of International Espionage*, London: Bodley Head p. 80

[11] Lycett, Andrew (1995) I study my targets. I find out what makes them tick, *Independent*, 22 June

[12] Cockburn, Alexander and Cockburn, Leslie (1992) *Dangerous Liaison: The Inside Story of US-Israeli Covert Relationship*, London: Bodley Head p. 123; Meredith, Martin (2006) *The State of Africa: A History of Fifty Years of Independence*, London: Free Press pp 352-356

[13] Woodward, Bob (1987) *Veil: The Secret Wars of the CIA*, London: Simon Schuster pp 348, 363, 410-11

[14] See http://www.amnesty.org/fr/library/asset/AFR20/004/2001/fr/2343f1a0-d902-11dd-ad8c-f3d4445c118e/afr200042001en.html, accessed on 1 May 2010

[15] Hunter, Jane (1991) Dismantling the war on Libya, *Covert Action Information Bulletin*, summer pp 47-51

[16] Prades, John (1986) *President's Secret Wars: CIA and Pentagon Covert Operations from World War II through Iranscan*, New York: William Morrow p. 383

[17] Perry, Mark (1992) *Eclipse: The Last Days of the CIA*, New York: William Morrow and Company p. 165

[18] But according to investigative journalist Joe Vialls, Yvonne Fletcher "was assassinated on the direct orders of the American CIA in a coldly calculated 'Psyop' (Psychological Operation) designed to generate intense British hatred against Libya. The operation was a complete success." See http://www.us-uk-interventions.org/, accessed on 18 August 2011. Christopher Hope, in the *Daily Telegraph* of 26 August 2011, reported that the man

seen firing at Pc Fletcher was Abdulmagid Salah Ameri, a junior diplomat working at the Libyan embassy. Hope reported: "Mr Ameri was identified by a witness in a 140-page secret review of evidence conducted at the request of the Metropolitan Police. The report, seen by the *Daily Telegraph*, was written by a senior Canadian prosecutor and addressed to Sue Hemming, the head of counter-terrorism at the Crown Prosecution Service.". See http://www.telegraph.co.uk/news/worldnews/africaandindianocean/libya/8726322/Libya-Man-suspected-of-killing-Pc-Yvonne-Fletcher-identified.html, accessed on 27 August 2011

[19] Martin, David and Walcott, John (1988) *Best Laid Plans: The Inside Story of America's War against Terrorism*, New York: Harper and Row pp 255-256

[20] Chomsky op cit: 124

[21] Files of the former East German secret service, the Stasi, led German prosecutors to the Libyan Musbah Eter, who had worked at the embassy in communist East Berlin. Eter and four other suspects were arrested in 1996 in Lebanon, Italy, Greece and Berlin and put on trial a year later. After a four-year trial, Musbah Eter was finally sentenced to 12 years in prison for aiding and abetting attempted murder. Two other Libyan embassy workers also received convictions for attempted murder: Palestinian Yasser Shraydi, accused of being the ringleader, and the Lebanese-born German, Ali Chanaa, who doubled as a Stasi agent. Chanaa's German wife, Verena, was the only defendant found guilty of murder after the prosecution showed she had planted the bomb. She was sentenced to 14 years' imprisonment. Prosecutors said the three men had assembled the bomb in the Chanaas' flat. The explosive was said to have been brought into West Berlin in a Libyan diplomatic bag. Verena Chanaa and her sister, Andrea Haeusler, carried it into the La Belle in a travel bag and left five minutes before it exploded. Ms Haeusler was acquitted because it could not be proved that she knew a bomb was in the bag. See http://news.bbc.co.uk/1/hi/world/europe/1653848.stm, accessed on 18 August 2011. Intriguingly a documentary broadcast on 25 August 1998 by German public television presented evidence that some of the main suspects in the 1986 Berlin disco bombing worked for American and Israeli intelligence. The report, aired by Zweites Deutsches Fernsehen (ZDF television), claimed Musbah Eter had been working for the CIA over many years. See http://www.wsws.org/news/1998/aug1998/bomb1-a27.shtml, accessed on 18 August 2011

[22] Adams, James (1987) *Secret Armies: The Full Story of SAS, Delta Force and Spetsnaz*, London: Hutchinson p. 372

[23] Machon, Annie (2005) *Spies, Lies and Whistleblowers*, Lewes, East Sussex: The Book Guild p. 104

[24] Curtis, Mark (1998) *The Great Deception: Anglo-American Power and World Order*, London: Pluto Press p. 29

[25] See Stephen Dorril, in *The Silent Conspiracy: Inside the Intelligence Services in the 1990s*, London: Heinemann 1993 p. 289

[26] Sebba, Anna (1994) *Battling for News: The Rise of the Woman Reporter*, London: Hodder and Stoughton pp 266-267

[27] Robert Fisk (2006) *The Great War for Civilisation: The Conquest of the Middle East*, London, New York: Harper Perrenial p. 1093 says one of the F-111s was shot down during the raid and caused civilian deaths when it crashed (as well as the deaths of the two pilots, Captain Ribas-Dominicci and Captain Paul Lorence)

²⁸ Kellner, Douglas (1990) *Television and the Crisis of Democracy*, Boulder, Colorado: Westview Press p. 138

²⁹ Chomsky op cit: 127

³⁰ Yallop, David (1994) *To the Ends of the Earth: The Hunt for the Jackal*, London: Corgi p. 713. Robert Fisk (op cit: 1093) also quotes a US official admitting that Gaddafi was one of the targets of | Operation El Dorado Canyon. A Pentagon official told the *Washington Post* that the F-111s had been included in the raid because their pilots "wanted a piece of the action"

³¹ Aldrich, Richard J. (2010) GCHQ: The Uncensored Story of Britain's Most Secret Intelligence Agency, London: Harper Press p. 457

³² Blundy, David and Lycett, Andrew op cit p. 22

³³ Yallop op cit: p. 695

³⁴ See, for instance, http://www.time.com/time/world/article/0,8599,2088074,00.html, http://www.guardian.co.uk/world/2011/aug/26/hana-gaddafi-daughter-mystery and http://www.guardian.co.uk/world/middle-east-live/2011/aug/26/libya-rebels-hunt-gaddafi-live-updates, http://www.telegraph.co.uk/journalists/martin-evans/8725024/Libya-Hana-Gaddafi-alive-and-well.html, all accessed on 27 August 2011

³⁵ Perry op cit: p. 166

³⁶ In email from Pierre Lethier to the author, 6 May 2011

³⁷ See Stephen Dorril, in *The Silent Conspiracy: Inside the Intelligence Services in the 1990s*, London: Heinemann 1993 p.241-242. In June 1992, Libya agreed to provide information on shipments and IRA contacts to the IRA to Edward Chapman, the British chargé d'affaires at the British mission to the UN in Geneva. "This followed international pressure on Libya to 'contribute to the elimination of international terrorism' following its alleged involvement in the Lockerbie bombing" (ibid)

³⁸ On 31 January 2001, Abdelbaset al-Megrahi, former head of security for Libyan Arab Airlines, had been controversially convicted by a panel of three Scottish judges sitting in a special court at Camp Zeist in the Netherlands, of 270 counts of murder for the bombing of Pan Am Flight 103 over Lockerbie in 1988. Yet evidence emerged following the trial that raised serious questions about the conviction. For instance, Tony Gauci, in whose shop in Malta al-Megrahi allegedly purchased clothes that ended up in the suitcase with the bomb, had expressed interest in receiving an award and following the conviction, Scottish police secretly sought a $2 million payment from the US Department of Justice. As part of the Libyan moves to rejoin the "international community", in 2004 the government formally accepted responsibility for Lockerbie – though it stressed it was only doing so to end the UN sanctions. It also agreed to pay $2.7 billion in compensation to the 270 families of the victims. By 2008, those opposing the conviction included Dr Jim Swire and the Rev. John Mosey, each of whom lost a daughter in the bombing, Archbishop Desmond Tutu and the head of the Catholic Church in Scotland, Cardinal Keith O'Brien. Al-Megrahi was released on compassionate grounds by the Scottish government in August 2009 following doctors' reports that he had terminal prostate cancer and had only a few months to live. Immediately following the fall of Gaddafi's Tripoli compound to the rebels in August 2011, calls to re-arrest al-Megrahi were given prominent coverage in the mainstream media in the UK and US. Stephen Dorril, in *The Silent Conspiracy: Inside the Intelligence Services in the 1990s*, London: Heinemann 1993 p. 288-9 reports Brian Keenan, one of the released Beirut hostage, revealing in 1992 a "strange story connected Lockerbie". Following his release in the

summer of 1990, he was interviewed by Syrian intelligence: "They said the British knew all about Lockerbie. They said the British had all sorts of information prior to the event"

[39] See http://www.amnesty.org/en/region/chad/report-2010, accessed on 1 January 2011

[40] Hunter op cit

[41] Dorril op cit p. 793

[42] ibid: 793-794; Machon op cit: 172; Jaber, Hala (2010) Libyans thwart Fletcher inquiry, *Sunday Times*, 19 September; Thomas, Gordon (2009) *Inside British Intelligence: 100 Years of MI5 and MI6*, London: JR Books p. 235

[43] Mark Allen, the former MI6 officer, who in September 2011 was at the centre of a row over British intelligence links with Libya, later worked as an advisor to BP and with the Monitor Group. He was also involved in the 2009 release of Abdelbaset a-Megrahi and escorted Gaddifi's son said al- islam to meetings in Oxford. See Ian Black, Man in the middle whose WMD triumph may now be overshadowed, *Guardian*, 7 September. Available online at http://www.guardian.co.uk/world/2011/sep/06/libya-mastermind-wmd-triumph-minefield, accessed on 8 September 2011

[44] John Simpson, the BBC's World Affairs Editor, mentions Gaddafi just once in his overview of the reporting of war over the last century (*Unreliable Sources*, London: Macmillan 2010 p 77), demonising him in the process by linking him with Presidents Ahmadinejad of Iran, Saddam Hussein of Iraq, Robert Mugabe of Zimbabwe, and Idi Amin of Uganda. They all, he said, spoke with "the half-mocking, half-complaining, self-obsessed tome of a man who has felt himself belittled and now believes he can hit back without any sense of restraint"

[45] Both editorials cited in Noble war in Libya, Media Lens, 28 March 2011. Available online at http://www.medialens.org/index.php?option=com_content&view=article&id=611:noble-war-in-libya-part-2&catid=24:alerts-2011&Itemid=68, accessed on 26 August 2011

[46] See http://www.telegraph.co.uk/news/worldnews/wikileaks/8188463/What-WikiLeaks-told-us-about-Colonel-Gaddafi-a-profile-of-an-unpredictable-leader.html, accessed on 26 August 2011

[47] In July 2011, US Federal prosecutors asked a judge to reduce the 23-year prison sentence for Alamoudi. Libya TV commented: "The documents explaining why prosecutors want to cut Alamoudi's sentence are under seal, and the U.S. Attorney's Office in Alexandria declined to say how many years they are seeking to cut from Alamoudi's term. But such reductions are allowed only when a defendant provides substantial assistance to the government. It is rare for the government to seek a reduction so many years after the initial sentence was imposed." See http://english.libya.tv/2011/07/09/prosecutors-ask-to-cut-sentence-of-muslim-activist-in-gaddafis-plot-to-assassinate-saudi-king/, accessed on 18 August 2011

[48] See chapter entitled "Gold-plated taps" in *The Age of the Warrior: Selected Writings*, by Robert Fisk, London: Fourth Estate 2008 p. 234. Also available online at http://www.independent.co.uk/opinion/commentators/fisk/robert-fisk-welcome-to-palestine-453319.html, accessed on 18 August 2011

[49] See http://www.guardian.co.uk/world/2009/sep/23/gaddafi-un-speech, accessed on 8 September 2011. Significantly the report on the 100 minute speech says Gaddafi "fully lived up to his reputation for eccentricity, bloody-mindedness and extreme verbiage". Nowhere is he described as a dictator

[50] See Leigh, David and harding, Luke (2011) *WikiLeaks: Julian Assange's War on Secrecy*, London: Guardian Books p. 143

[51] Similar metaphors relating to "rat in the hole" were used when the former President of Iraq, Saddam Hussein, was captured in December 2003. See, for instance, http://news.bbc.co.uk/1/hi/programmes/breakfast/3319491.stm, accessed on 8 September 2011

[52] See Libya: US rejects Putin's claim that coalition wants to assassinate Gaddafi, Ewen MacAskill and Richard Norton-Taylor, *Guardian*, 26 April 2011. Available online at http://www.wsws.org/articles/2011/apr2011/liby-a27.shtml, accessed on I August 2011. By the end of August 2011, Nato jets had flown 20,000 sorties

[53] See, for instance, http://www.telegraph.co.uk/news/worldnews/africaandindianocean/libya/8716758/Libya-secret-role-played-by-Britain-creating-path-to-the-fall-of-Tripoli.html and http://www.dailymail.co.uk/news/article-2029831/Libya--1m-bounty-Gaddafi-MI6-agents-join-hunt.html, both accessed on 27 August 2011

[54] See Hider, James (2011) Eyes peeled for deluded dictator in woman's garb, says ex-aide, *The Times*, 25 August

[55] See *Libya: An Uncertain Future: Reprt of a Fact-Finding Mission to Assess both Sides of Libyan Conflict*, Paris, May 2011, published by International Centre, for the Study and Research into Terrorism and Assistance to the Victims of Terrorism, French Centre for Intelligence Studies and the Mediterranean Peace Forum. Available online at http://www.cf2r.org/images/stories/news/201106/libya-report.pdf, accessed on 8 September 2011. See also Libya: The Other Side of the Story, by Moign Khawaja. Available online at http://outernationalist.net/?p=2559, accessed on 8 September 2011

[56] See Richard Keeble, *Secret State, Silent Press: New Militarism, the Gulf and the Modern Image of Warfare*, Luton: John Libbey, 1997

[57] See Richard Lance Keeble, Hacks and spooks – close encounters of a strange kind: A critical history of the links between mainstream journalists and the intelligence services in the UK, *The Political; Economy of Media and Power*, edited by Jeffery Klaehn, New York: Peter Lang, 2011 pp 87-111

Section 7. Reflections on the Long-Term Effects of the Uprisings

Richard Lance Keeble

In our final section, we look at some of the complex, possible long-term effects of the Arab uprisings. Firstly, Alpaslan Özerdem, from the Coventry University Centre for Peace and Reconciliation Studies, looks at the reaction of the Turkish government to the "Arab Spring" and finds it facing both ways at the same time. Significantly, Turkey, long criticised for its poor human rights record and shaky democracy, has become, according to Özerdem, the beacon of moral guidance in the Middle East.

With the comfort of having considerably improved its own democracy, rule of law and human rights problems domestically, Turkish foreign policy seemed to be wanting to side with the people of Egypt and Tunisia rather than their tyrannical regimes.

On Libya, the response of Turkey, which had developed close ties with Gaddafi, was initially hesitant. However, when Turkey realised that a UN

Security Council Resolution to allow a military intervention became inevitable it switched sides and decided to take part in the Nato-led operation. Özerdem concludes:

> It is ironic that for years, Turkey has criticised the EU and US for being trapped in their double standards between the principles of Western liberal democracies and geopolitical interests in their approach to the MENA region. However, it has unfortunately shown all indicators of a similar entrapment in the "Arab Spring" test. Whether lessons have been learned from this experience will show itself in the future actions of the prospective regional hegemon of the Middle East.

Next, Marwan Darweish examines the impact of the extraordinary events in the Middle East on the Palestinian/Israeli conflict. In the case of Libya, Darweish argues that Nato's military intervention and the removal of Gaddafi from power will hinder the nonviolent mass action demanding social and political change.

> The reliance on Western military intervention will weaken this movement in the Arab countries and the world and reinforce the military doctrine of the West to bring "democracy" through military intervention as has been the case in Iraq and Afghanistan.

Darweish concludes that the Arab revolutions have shown that true change is home-grown, owned and developed by the people today – but tomorrow this could equally be the case for the people of Palestine and Israel.

Finally, Okoth Fred Mudhai, reinforcing the international focus of the text, examines the responses to the Libyan crisis amongst columnists on a leading Nairobi newspaper and finds a number highly critical of the Western media's acceptance of anti-Gaddafi propaganda.

One, for instance, argues that major Western media outlets such as the BBC, Sky and CNN swallowed imperialist propaganda by "spinning the Libyan civil war as a virtuous effort by the West to advance the cause of freedom", and Nato's bombardment as aiming to "protect civilians" when "it is a transparent effort to topple an anti-Western dictator" in an oil-rich country.

Turkey and the "Arab Spring": Principled Politics and *Realpolitik*

Alpaslan Özerdem, from the Coventry University Centre for Peace and Reconciliation Studies, looks at the reaction of the Turkish government to the "Arab Spring" and finds it facing both ways at the same time

A rapid political transformation process, or as it is called in the media, the "Arab Spring", has been re-writing the history of the Middle East and North Africa (MENA) since early 2011. It all started with Tunisia and then moved to Egypt, which seems to be led primarily by youth with the use of new media for mobilisation and resistance. By the time, Colonel Muammar Gaddafi, the long-standing dictator of Libya, appeared on television on 22 February 2011, in order to declare that he was going nowhere, the "Arab Spring" had already removed Zine El Abidine Ben Ali and Hosni Mubarak, the former dictators of Tunisia and Egypt, respectively, from power.

In his speech, Gaddafi claimed that he was a different kind of "leader" and would not leave his country as Ben Ali and Mubarak did in the face of mass demonstrations and public dissent. Gaddafi underlined his defiance by pointing out that he did not really care what the people of Libya wanted for their future and that he was planning to become a martyr in his own country. Subsequently, based on the UN Security Council Resolution (UNSCR) 1973 a Nato-led military intervention in Libya started on 19 March 2011, and appeared to culminate with the flight of Gaddafi at the end of August.

Meanwhile, Bahrain, at the Gulf end of the Middle East went through its own political violence as the result of an uprising of the Shiite majority against the Sunni Royal family rule, which was violently quashed with Saudi Arabia's military assistance. The demonstrations in Yemen against another long-ruling Arab dictator, President Ali Abdullah Saleh, started in early January and the instability in the country continues even after his removal from power on 4 June 2011. Moreover, from Jordan to Morocco and Algeria, a number of other MENA countries have recently experienced some level of dissent too. The Syrian civil resistance against President Bashar al-Assad's regime since late January has been particularly bloody, killing, as of 8 August, more than 2,000 people.[1]

In short, the power of the Kings, military rulers, and leaders of single-party "democracies" in the MENA region has never been so threatened like this since their creations in the post-World War One context by Britain and France. Some of them such as Algeria gained their independence from their French colonisers much later or in some like Iraq and Libya, the Kings were deposed by *coup d'état* regimes, while between some countries such as Syria and Egypt there were attempts to merge states. However, one feature has remained the same for most of them throughout their existence, namely their dependency on external powers for their legitimacy in the eyes of their own people. In other words, not only were most of these regimes in MENA countries created or installed by powerful states but they have also been sustained by them for their strategic and geopolitical importance, no matter how poor their democratic and human rights credentials have been.

A New Era in the Arab World?

It is clear that the political map of these countries is being re-written and in the context of international relations, this new era will mean a major change in the way some of the key international powers such as the United States (US), the European Union (EU), China and Russia approach their foreign policies for MENA. There have already been unusual alliances and responses in the face of this sudden political change in the region. For example, former President Mubarak received direct and indirect political support from Israel and the Palestinian Authority when thousands of Egyptians filled Tahrir Square in Cairo demanding his removal from power.

To a large extent the US and EU response was muted and talked a lot about the need to listen to the demands of people, without taking a clear stance on Mubarak's initial claim that he should remain in power. Another interesting phenomenon in terms of international responses to this political transformation has been the role of Turkey. Over the last decade, Turkey has been showing the signs of its desire of becoming a regional hegemon by playing an increasingly active role in the peace and conflict-related issues of the Middle East. In fact, until very recent times, Turkey followed a defensive foreign policy and there was a deliberate attempt by the state to disown the Ottoman legacy as this was considered a necessary trade-off for the nation-state building project of the Republic.

However, since the end of the Cold War, Turkey has been trying to re-gain its former hegemonic influence in a wide spectrum of places from the Central Asia to the Balkans and Middle East. This policy has become particularly apparent over the last five years, as Turkey has started to become an active actor in international relations. This change in foreign policy has been quite sudden and drastic and is often coined as "neo-Ottomanism" – a term which describes the country's ambitions to expand and revitalise its political influence in large territories once controlled by the Ottoman Empire.

It is probably not surprising to see that Turkey has increased its regional engagement because it occupies a critical geopolitical position between Europe, the Middle East and the Caucasus. It has a burgeoning economy and strong private sector and membership of a wide range of organisations from Nato, G20 and the OECD to the Islamic Conference and a candidacy to the EU. Turkey is a pivotal player in global affairs too, as it is an important peace broker in regional conflicts, a leading country for peacekeeping operations and has been a generous donor for disaster response around the world.

Therefore, the "Arab Spring" has turned out to be a great litmus test for Turkey's ambitions for regional leadership and foreign policy. To investigate Turkey's response to the "Arab Spring" in general, this chapter will focus on Tunisia and Egypt as an example of Turkey's "principled" response based on the values of human rights and good governance; Libya as the type of "we-will-remember-the-principles-when-the-time-is-right" response; and finally, Syria as the response of "it-is-not-easy-to-have-principles".

"Neo-Ottomanism" in Practice?

Until the wave of revolutions started to hit the MENA region, Turkey's popularity in most Middle Eastern countries was at a peak, largely because of its confrontation with Israel under the Premiership of Recep Tayyip Erdoğan over the protracted Palestinian issue. It began with the Israel's military campaign, "Operation Cast Lead", against Gaza in 2008. Before that Turkey was the strongest ally of Israel in the region with strong economic, military and political ties, and even acted as a mediator between Israel and Syria over the Golan Heights. Then, after the Israeli offensive against Gaza, the famous "one-minute" crisis between Erdoğan and Israeli President Shimon Peres took place in Davos on 29 January 2009.

Erdoğan's walkout not only created a public frenzy in Turkey but he has suddenly become one of the most popular politicians in many Middle Eastern countries. There were many tit-for-tat spats between the two countries' foreign ministries before the next crisis took place with the Israel's military intervention on the Blue Marmara ship on 31 May 2010. The ship was part of "the Gaza flotilla", trying to break the Israeli blockade of Gaza by taking humanitarian aid and carrying hundreds of activists. The military attack, which was carried out in international waters and resulted in the death of nine Turkish activists, led to widespread international condemnation and strained the relationship between the two countries further. With this incident, Turkey's popularity among the Arab populations increased tremendously, largely because Erdoğan seemed to be doing what their leaders had always failed to do – to confront Israel by means of effective diplomacy and be a strong voice for the Palestinian cause.

In line with the new foreign policy of "zero-problem with neighbours" by Ahmet Davutoğlu, Minister of Foreign Affairs, Turkey has been deepening its relationships with most MENA countries. For example, with Syria, Lebanon and Jordan it has established a visa-free movement of people and their cabinets hold joint meetings. Turkey was one of the most influential mediators in the latest Lebanese political crisis in January 2010 over a UN investigation of the 2005 assassination of former Lebanese Prime Minister Rafik Hariri. It is able to talk to all sides in the country, including Hezbullah, or in cooperation with Brazil, Turkey, it has managed to make a deal with Iran over its nuclear capabilities. Overall, as pointed out by İhsan Bal from USAK, a think-tank in Ankara: "Erdoğan is trying to win the hearts and minds of the Arab people...Turkey is competing not with the streets but with the administrations that are split from their people."[2]

In short, Turkey was using the soft power of political tools such as diplomacy, trade and cultural ties to become a regional power centre, which has also been perceived as an attempt of "neo-Ottomanism" by some, but doing this the main objective was to maintain the stability in the region. Therefore, it is important to underline that Turkish foreign policy towards the MENA region before the "Arab Spring" was primarily based on the protection of the existing status quo in order to increase its influence through using the means of soft power.

Tunisia, Egypt: Turkey on the Side of Change

In other words, the recent Middle Eastern revolutions have demanded that Turkey re-adjust its foreign policy as the protection of the status quo would also mean continuing to work with "discredited" leaders such as Mubarak, Ben Ali and Gaddafi. In the cases of Tunisia and Egypt, Turkey adopted a "principled" approach in lines with the protection of human rights and people's desires of electing their own leaders in a democratic governance system. Therefore, it has chosen to support the uprisings since it was relatively peaceful. Davutoğlu even thought the political transformation in Tunisia could "be a model for other countries".[3] Turkey was probably the only regional country with a clear stance on the political crisis in Egypt. One week after the mass demonstrations started in the country and while all major international powers were rather timid and quiet about the departure of Mubarak, Erdoğan's speech at the Turkish Parliament, which was a clear message to Mubarak to go, was broadcast live to thousands in Tahrir Square.

It is interesting that Turkey, which was always criticised for its poor human rights record and shaky democracy until very recent times, has now become the beacon of moral guidance on such matters in the Middle East. With the comfort of having considerably improved its own democracy, rule of law and human rights problems domestically, Turkish foreign policy seemed to be wanting to side with the people of Egypt and Tunisia rather than their tyrannical regimes. It is also interesting to note that, as pointed out by Professor Mensur Akgün: "Ankara's early reaction to the developments in Egypt could be in Turkey's interest; the regime change in Egypt would undoubtedly raise Turkey's growing prestige on the Arab streets."[4]

Libya: Turkey Unsure

In the case of Libya on the other hand, Turkey's response was much more hesitant in showing its solidarity to the popular uprising. As peaceful demonstrations in mid-February faced a violent response from the Gaddafi's regime there were indications that the scenario about to unfold in Libya was likely to be different from Tunisia and Egypt. By the time the Transitional National Council (TNC) was established in Benghazi to overthrow the Gaddafi regime, the violence escalated to such an extent that it quickly turned into a civil war. The fighting between the NTC and governmental security forces resulted in high numbers of casualties and displacement. Thousands of foreign nationals who used to work in the oil, gas and construction sectors of the country filled the airports, desperately waiting for evacuation by their respective governments.

It is in such a context Turkey tried to adopt a strategy that can be described as "we-will-remember-the-principles-when-the-time-is-right", as it was largely conciliatory towards the Gaddafi regime and trying to distance itself from the popular uprising and TNC. This was due to its strong economic ties with the Libyan regime and, more significantly, because of a large number of Turkish citizens who live in Libya. In fact, it was the largest evacuation operation Turkey has ever had to undertake – rescuing around 25,000 of its citizens and thousands of other nationals by the deployment of civilian ferries and its navy.[5]

It was only after the completion of this evacuation operation in early March that the Turkish foreign policy response started to side with the rebels. Nevertheless, Turkey continued its attempts as a self-declared peace broker to convince Gaddafi to accept a political solution in early March. After all, Erdoğan was in Tripoli only in November 2010 to receive his Human Rights prize from the hands of the very same Gaddafi. However, when Turkey realised that a UN Security Council Resolution to allow a military intervention became inevitable it switched sides and decided to take part in the Nato-led operation.

After this decision, Turkish foreign policy towards the Libyan civil war became much clearer. Indeed, the way it successfully blocked and changed the French plans on the nature and tactics of the Nato military intervention, insisting that Nato should have the sole control of operations, was a good example of Turkey's newly-gained confidence in international relations. It should be noted that Turkey's emphatic attempt to derail the France's self-appointed leadership plans of the intervention was inspired largely by the desire of settling scores with President Sarkozy's staunch opposition against Turkey's EU ambitions and economic interests in francophone African countries. Going back to its "principled" approach, Turkey attacked France for having a hidden agenda. In a major speech, Erdoğan stressed: "I wish that those who only see oil, gold mines and underground treasures when they look in [Libya's] direction, would see the region through glasses of conscience from now on."[6] Turkey finally recognised the NTC as "the true representative of the Libya's people" on 3 July 2011 and Davutoğlu said "it was time for the Libyan leader Muammar Gaddafi to go".[7]

Turkey and the Syrian Spring/Summer: Too Close for Comfort?

The ongoing Syrian uprising started in late January 2011 with peaceful protests but escalated to political violence by mid-March. To some extent this differs from other MENA uprisings at it has a much stronger Islamist leadership which is challenging the secular state ideology of the Baath regime. Although, the uprising is supported by other groups in the country, the previous dissent in the country by Islamic groups has given them an opportunity to take the lead in the organisation of protests and a sustained campaign of resistance. The security forces seemed to be restrained from using heavy force in controlling protestors at the beginning, but this soon changed and the brutal clampdown on dissent resulted in high death tolls among both civilians and security forces. By April, a refugee crisis had already emerged as many Syrians started to cross the Turkish border to escape from violence. After the siege of Jisr al-Shughur near the Turkish border by the Syrian security forces between

4 and 12 June, the refugee crisis worsened and by mid-June there were over 10,000 Syrian refugees in Turkey.

The Syrian uprising is different for Turkey than others in the MENA region for a number of reasons. First, it is at the other side of their border and Turkey is currently dealing with the uprising's spill-over consequences such as refugees.

Secondly, as is the case with the other regional countries such as Iraq, Iran and Turkey, Syria also has a substantial Kurdish minority. With the changing political realities of the post-2003 Iraq intervention, Turkey has already had to adjust its foreign policy in relation to the Kurdish Autonomous Region in Iraq as it has been trying to deal with its own Kurdish uprising led by Abdullah Öcalan's PKK since the mid-1980s with a death toll to date of more than 30,000 people. Therefore, another cause of instability with the Kurdish population in the region would not be in the interest of Turkey.

Thirdly, under the leadership of President Abdullah Gül as well as Erdoğan and Davutoğlu Turkey has managed to build up a strong and effective bilateral relationships with Syria over the last decade, which resulted in the establishment of the High Level Strategic Council between the two countries. This has been a remarkable achievement considering that only back in 1999 Turkey was prepared to go to war with Syria over the issue of the Baath regime's hospitality to Öcalan.

Fourthly, close relationships with the Assad regime have been an important leverage against Israel and finally, Syria has been the key country in Turkey's new approach to the Arab world because of Syria's special relationships with such countries as Iran and Lebanon. In other words, the pre-"Arab Spring" status quo with Syria was probably the best possible framework for Turkey due to the increasing dependency of the Syrian regime on Turkish support in the international arena, particularly for its mediation efforts for Syria's disputes with Israel and Iraq, and more importantly, its isolation in international relations created by the US.

Consequently, Turkey did all it could to isolate itself from the popular uprising in Syria. The Turkish government's focus has always been on the Libyan civil war, though the political crisis in Syria has been happening only at the other side of the border at the same time. There seemed to be a deliberate attempt to ignore what has been happening in Syria and hope that it would go away without needing to alter the status quo of relationships between the two counties. Hence, the "principled" Turkish foreign policy approach for the uprisings in Tunisia and Egypt did not seem to enter in the picture until mid-June for Syria.

The Turkish government urged the Syrian regime to undertake a comprehensive political transformation to meet the expectations of dissidents, but the criticism was lukewarm and within the basis of good neighbourly relationships. When President Bashar al-Assad announced his political reform package in late March, it was a big relief for Turkey, hoping that this would amount to an effective response to the Syrian uprising.

In other words, Turkey was between a rock and a hard place. On the one hand, the "principled" Turkish foreign policy, connecting with the streets of the Middle East, and on the other hand, the demands of *realpolitik* in the face of losing a loyal ally in regional politics. However, the violent crackdown of protests and dissent by the Syrian security forces reached such a level that the Turkish government started to change its approach reluctantly.

First, it was in terms of press releases from the Ministry of Foreign Affairs, calling on the Syrian regime to act responsibly in quelling popular unrest. Then Erdoğan intervened personally by calling Assad several times and sending special envoys to Damascus. At the same time, the pressure from the US and EU on Turkey to take a more decisive stand against Assad has also increased, which resulted in Erdoğan's warning "that Turkey would not want to see another Hama massacre", referring to the 1982 crackdown in the Syrian city. Noting that Turkey could not remain aloof to developments in Syria, given its proximity, shared border and common history, he called on Assad to act with common sense and prevent the country from "sliding into disintegration". However, all these efforts have seemed to have no impact on Syria. As Kardas pointed out: "The Baath regime continues with mass arrests, storming of cities and shooting of peaceful protesters."[8]

On 9 August 2011, Davutoğlu was in Syria to hold a seven-hour meeting with President al-Assad in Damascus. This visit seemed to have taken place in close cooperation with the US as it was preceded by an intensive communication interaction between Washington DC and Ankara. Turkey urged Syria to take "concrete steps" and Davutoğlu said: "The bloodshed should end and civilian blood should be prevented from being spilled. All the steps needed for the process of reform to start should be taken."[9] This was probably an attempt by the Turkish government to show they were in alliance with the US and EU *vis à vis* the Syrian crisis. It is certainly clear that the bilateral relationships between the two countries have already badly constrained, and ironically, despite the proximity, shared border and common history, Ankara has so far managed to exert only limited influence over Damascus.

Turkish Media over Turkey's Contradictory Realities in MENA

As an influential actor of the political landscape in Turkey, the majority of the Turkish media has seemed to be supporting the government's response to the recent political crises in MENA countries, and even showing similar contradictions. Sevil Çakır Kılınçoğlu's review of some of the most popular Turkish newspapers and media outlets – *Hürriyet*, *Milliyet*, *Zaman*, *Taraf*, *Radikal*, and *Haber Türk* – until May 2011 shows they were generally in full support of Turkish foreign policy in relation to the political transformation in Tunisia and Egypt. For the military intervention in Libya on the other hand, the mainstream media was again in line with the government policy of "non-military" interventionism at the beginning. For example, as pointed out by Kılınçoğlu, when Erdoğan was opposing a military intervention against Libya, "many columnists accused Western powers of acting only according to their strategic and economic interests in Libya, while emphasising that Turkey is backing opposition movements in the Middle East for the sake of democracy and human rights".[10] However, as soon as the Turkish government decided to take part in the Nato-led military intervention, the media also reversed its criticism of such a strategy.

The mainstream media in Turkey also seemed to have a number of contradictions similar to the country's foreign policy. The same columnists who were pro-military intervention over the Libya crisis, according to Kılınçoğlu, "saw nothing wrong with prioritising Turkish economic and strategic interest in Syria, strongly urging against an intervention at any cost". She points out that "the Turkish media are also myopically focused on the economic and political repercussions of a Western intervention with little regard to the human rights abuses that are taking place".[11] However, there were also a number of exceptions from such a contradictory approach to the Arab Spring. For example, Nuray Mert pointed out the way that the Turkish and Western interests have closely overlapped in the MENA region and the Turkish foreign policy was more to do with *realpolitik* than assisting the Arabs in their struggle for freedom. Mert highlights the example of what happened or did not happen in the context of Bahrain: "Both the West and Turkey see no evil, hear no evil, and speak no evil."[12]

So Which Way is Turkey Facing?

As a resourceful partner of the international community in the region and through its political stand on key issues such as the continuing occupation of Palestine by Israel and good governance issues in MENA countries in general, Turkey has raised expectations among the Arab population that it cares about democracy, justice and development in the region. Turkey's response to the "Arab Spring" has shown that, regardless of whether or not there has been a shift in Turkish foreign policy towards "neo-Ottomanism", Turkey has now become a key actor in Middle East and North African politics.

The experience with the "Arab Spring" also shows that with the role that Turkey has been attempting to craft for itself as a regional hegemon it is intending to increase its soft power engagement further. However, for this it would require a high level of political manoeuvring to balance its geopolitical and economic interests with its new "principled" approach in international relations. For the foreign policy of Erdoğan and Davutoğlu, this is the best approach to connect with the ordinary people in the MENA region and encourage these countries in peaceful political transformation and "democratisation". However, such a high moral ground perspective in international politics would also be likely to test the sincerity of Turkey, as there would likely to be variations in its responses according to the type and level of *realpolitik* interests for each country.

In relation to this dilemma it is important to remember that although Turkey is a country with ambitions of becoming a regional hegemonic power, it is also a country trying to merge its Islamic heritage into broader structures and models of western liberal democratic governance. It still needs to address a number of fundamental socio-cultural and development challenges to deal with the legacy of its Ottoman heritage and nation-state building policies of the Republic.

Furthermore, Turkey's internal stability is badly affected by a protracted armed conflict based on Kurdish separatism. Therefore, while attempting to respond to the new political landscape in the region with a creative, ethical and effective foreign policy strategy, Turkey's internal socio-political and economic fault lines are likely to have an impact on its foreign policy successes in the MENA region. For example, without finding a peaceful resolution to its own Kurdish crisis and dealing with its own past on the issue of Armenian genocide, it will be difficult for Turkey to maintain its credibility as a regional hegemon to guide MENA countries in the path of democracy and human rights.

Finally, it is important to bear in mind that in international relations it would be naive to expect a one-size-fits-all type of approach, especially in the context of the MENA countries with hugely varying socio-economic and political characteristics. However, as the leaders of Turkey had supported popular dissent and urged Mubarak to leave power for a peaceful political transformation of Egypt for the principles of democracy and protection of human rights, then they should be held accountable for their actions (or lack of them) on the civilian uprisings in Syria and Libya where Turkey has more significant economic and geopolitical interests.

It is ironic that for years, Turkey has criticised the EU and US for being trapped in their double standards between the principles of Western liberal democracies and geopolitical interests in their approach to the MENA region. However, it has unfortunately shown all indicators of a similar entrapment in the "Arab Spring" test. Whether lessons have been learned from this experience will show itself in the future actions of the prospective regional hegemon of the Middle East.

Notes

[1] Black, Ian. (2011) Syrian Death Toll Rises as Arab States Protest, *Guardian*, 8 August 2011. Available online at http://www.guardian.co.uk/world/2011/aug/08/syria-deaths-arab-states-protest, accessed on 9 August 2011

[2] Özerkan, Fulya. (2011) Turkeys Basks in Prestige from Early Response to Egypt Uprising, *Hürriyet Daily News*, 11 February 2011. Available online at http://www.hurriyetdailynews.com/n.php?n=turkeys-early-challenge-to-egypt-uprising-raise-prestige-say-analysts-2011-02-11, accessed on 1 August 2011

[3] Yavuz, Ercan and Yanatma, Servet (2011) Turkey Says Tunisia Revolt Could Be Model for Others, *Sunday's Zaman*, 22 February 2011. Available online at http://www.todayszaman.com/news-236285-turkey-says-tunisia-revolt-could-be-model-for-others.html, accessed on 1 August 2011

[4] Özerkan op cit

[5]Yanatma, Servet. (2011) Turkey Demonstrates Successful Evacuation Operations in Libya, *Today's Zaman*, 27 February 2011. Available online at http://www.todayszaman.com/newsDetail_getNewsById.action?newsId=236774, accessed on 1 August 2011

[6] Traynor, Ian. (2011) Turkey and France Clash Over Libya Air Campaign, *Guardian*, 24 March 2011. Available online at http://www.guardian.co.uk/world/2011/mar/24/turkey-france-clash-libya-campaign, accessed on 1 August 2011

[7] BBC (2011) Libya: Turkey Recognises Transitional National Council. Available online at http://www.bbc.co.uk/news/world-africa-14009206, accessed on 12 August 2011

[8] Kardas, Saban (2011) Syrian Uprising Tests Turkey's Middle East Policy, Eurasia Daily Monitor, Vol. 8 No. 90, 10 May. Available online at http://www.jamestown.org/programs/edm/single/?tx_ttnews%5Btt_news%5D=3791 0&cHash=4c4d82728f6d28f85a4bb64f1c9764f4, accessed on 1 August 2011

[9] Al Jazeera. (2011) Turkey Raises Pressure on Syria. Available online at http://english.aljazeera.net/news/middleeast/2011/08/20118917850404477.html, accessed on 1 August 2011

[10] Kılınçoğlu, Sevil Çakır (2011) Turkish Media Coverage of the Western Intervention in Libya, Foreign Policy Research Institute. Available online at http://www.fpri.org/enotes/201105.kilincoglu.turkey_libya.html, accessed on 1 August 2011

[11] ibid

[12] ibid

Note on the author

Professor Alpaslan Özerdem is at the Centre for Peace and Reconciliation Studies, Coventry University, UK. With field research experience in Afghanistan, Bosnia-Herzegovina, El Salvador, Kosovo, Lebanon, Liberia, Philippines, Sierra Leone, Sri Lanka and Turkey, he specialises in the politics of humanitarian interventions, disaster response, security sector reform, reintegration of former combatants and post-conflict state building. He has also taken an active role in the initiation and management of several advisory and applied research projects for a wide range of national and international organisations. He has published extensively and is co-author of *Disaster Management and Civil Society: Earthquake Relief in Japan, Turkey and India* (I. B. Tauris, 2006), author of *Post-war Recovery: Disarmament, Demobilisation and Reintegration* (I. B. Tauris, 2008) and co-editor of *Participatory Research Methodologies in Development and Post Disaster/Conflict Reconstruction*, (Ashgate 2010), is co-author of *Managing Emergencies and Crises* (Jones and Bartlett, 2011) and co-editor of *Child Soldiers: From Recruitment to Reintegration* (Palgrave Macmillan, 2011).

Reading Into the Impact of the "Arab Spring"

Marwan Darweish examines the impact of the extraordinary events in the Middle East on the Palestinian/Israeli conflict. He concludes that the Arab revolutions have shown that true change is home-grown, owned and developed by the people today – but tomorrow this could equally be the case for the people of Palestine and Israel

Introduction

The aim of this chapter is to analyse the impact of the Arab revolutions or "Spring" on the region and specifically to highlight the impact on the Palestinian/Israeli conflict. An understanding of the different perceptions of the "Arab Spring" amongst Palestinians and Israelis and the influence it had on their own society and the political leadership will also be explored. I will use interchangeably the term "Arab Spring" and Arab revolutions

The outbreak of the Arab revolutions that swept the Middle East and North African countries from December 2010 came as a surprise to many if not most people including media reporters, researchers and policy makers. It caught diplomats and foreign relation experts on the Middle East affairs unawares and unprepared for the scale and widespread nature of the nonviolent mass demonstrations.

However, civil society organisations in Tunisia and Egypt have argued that this process started a few years ago and that the mass demonstrations of January 2011– in Egypt calling for the removal of President Mubarak, and in Tunisia for the removal of President Bin Ali – and for political freedom was the culmination of long-term work with different sectors in society at grassroots and middle level.

In the last few decades Arab leaders in the Middle East have faced several attempted coups from within the military or attempts by radical Islamist groups to overthrow the regime by force. Al-Qaida and the Muslim Brothers are only two of the organisations that advocated the overthrow of the Arab dictators by military means. However, all these attempts were suppressed and resulted in heavy restrictions and long term imprisonment for those found to be involved. The "Arab Spring", however, was characterised by mass protest and the call for civil and political rights through democratic participation which is in contradiction to the ideology and approach of extremists groups that promote change through violence means. It presented a different strategy based on mass nonviolent participation of the people in contrast to the attempted military coup by Islamist groups or forces within the army. One argument is that the active nonviolent approach adopted by the revolution is the polar opposite and as such has served to undermine the radical Islamist groups of use of violence as a strategy for change.[1]

In both the case of Egypt and of Tunisia the national army refused to use force to maintain presidential power. Analysts argue that the army took a clear position not use force against civilians and prevented a massacre of the demonstrators. Several security sources hinted that the US had direct contact with the military apparatus and demanded they not to use force. Both countries have strategic cooperation with US and Egypt is the second greatest recipient of aid from the US after Israel. This is in contrast to the situation in Syria and Libya where the military played a significant role in the repression of the opposition to the regime. The police and security forces on the other hand conducted a brutal and violent attack against the demonstrators which has caused injury and death for hundreds of civilians. In contrast to the army, the police and security forces lost the trust of the people and much of the anger became directed to them and to the institutions they represent. They employed violence and control tactics aimed at preventing the spread of the demonstrations and to contain the revolution without success.

The Arab revolution in Egypt and Tunisia had two phases. The first phase united all the political, social and religious forces under one slogan "down with the regime" and "go we don't want you". Secular forces, religious groups, trade unions, working and middle classes, young and old men and women went to the streets in Cairo, Tunisia and many other cities and villages to call for the downfall of the regime and for political freedom.

The second phase focused on the civic resistance used to change the structures and the institutions that maintained this regime in power. This required the establishment of transparent and accountable political and judicial structures that would allow the citizens to participate in the decision making and shaping of their society. During this transition phase it will be critical to establish the foundation for free political participation including freedom of organisation, respect of human and civil rights and means to address the social economic root causes of deprivation and marginalisation afflicting the majority of society.

The Main Features of the Arab/Israeli Conflict
This section will present a framework that explores the features characterise of the relationship between Israel and the Arab countries and Israel and the Palestinians. An understanding of the features of this relationship will enable us to recognise the impact and consequences of the Arab Spring on both Israel and the Palestinians.

Denial of Palestinian national and civil rights
Since its establishment in 1948 the state of Israel has based its relations with the Arab countries and the Palestinians on the denial of the Palestinian national rights, the threat of military power and their collaboration with corrupt undemocratic Arab regimes. The Arab revolution sweeping the Middle East and North Africa which started in Tunisia in December 2010, is already impacting on the relationship between Israel and the Palestinians from one hand and Israel and its neighbours on the other.

Since its foundation the Zionist movement has perceived the Arab indigenous population of Palestine as aliens and primitives proposing that the Jews from Europe will bring modernisation and technology to develop the country and "turn the desert to bloom". The Zionist movement portrayed the Palestinians as an obstacle in the way of achieving a Jewish state. Therefore, it was necessary to diminish the number of the Palestinian population to ensure a Jewish majority in the newly established state of Israel.

Ben Gurion, leader of the Zionist Movement and the first Prime Minister of Israel, declared as early as 1920 that the "Arabs of Palestine did not constitute a separate national entity but where part of the Arab nation"[2] and ideally it would be better to have Palestine empty of its Arab Palestinian inhabitants. It is clear that there was a clash between the fulfilment of the Jewish aspiration for a homeland in Palestine and the rights of the Palestinians over their land and sovereignty. Later on the Israeli Prime Minister from 1969 to 1974, Golda Meir, took the preposterous position of publicly denying the existence of the Palestinian people.

Military power

The use of military force by Israel towards the Arab countries and Palestine was one of the features of this relationship. Israel is the strongest military power in the Middle East and one of the top ten military capabilities in the world. It has had a nuclear capability since late 1960, remaining the only one in the Middle East yet has continued to refuse until now to sign the nuclear proliferation treaty.

Jabotinsky, founder of Revisionist Zionism and father of the Israeli right, argued that it is only through the establishment of military force impervious to Arab pressure that the Jewish homeland can be secured. Ben Gurion voiced the same conclusion after the outbreak of the Arab Revolt in 1936 and advocated a gradualist strategy combined with the use of military power to force the Arab neighbours and the Palestinian inhabitants to be unable to resist the establish Jewish state in the "Land of Israel". To implement such a dream ultimately Israel has had to base its approach on the use of force as it would not be by free choice that the Palestinians would give up their national rights. Israel believed that only through suppression would it impose on the Palestinians and Arabs to negotiate from a weak position.[3]

Examination of the history of the Israeli/Arab conflict since 1948 shows clearly the success of this policy. Israel first signed a peace agreement with President Sadat of Egypt, Israel then signed the Oslo agreement with the PLO and immediately after that the peace agreement with Jordan. In all of them Israel was the powerful party and the Arabs were the weak side.

There is close military and political cooperation between the US and Israel and since the signing of peace agreement between Israel and Egypt in 1979 Egypt has become a strategic ally to the US and leader of the moderate Arab camp. However, Syria continues to be seen as leading the more radical and anti-American camp.[4]

Corrupt Arab Regimes

Most of the Arab alliances of Israel and the US in the Middle East are characterised by their corruption and undemocratic regimes such as Mubarak, Bin Ali, Saudi Arabia and the rest of the Gulf States. The people of these Arab countries have experienced political and economic corruption, grinding poverty and frequent violation of their human rights.

The Middle East countries and North Africa have about two thirds of the known world reserve of oil and natural gas. However, this wealth has been unable to fulfil the political and economic aspirations of the people in the region. The standard of living is still poor and most of the wealth of these countries is in the hands of small, exceptionally rich minority. This failure to benefit the population from the wealth of the country has caused political tension, frustration and alienation from the political leadership and state. In 1960, Egypt and South Korea, for example, had the same income per capita yet by 1992 Korea was 10 times that of Egypt. Therefore, this economic impoverishment of the majority of population has been open to exploitation by radical secular and Islamic groups in the region as they provide fertile ground for recruitment to political and military opposition aimed at the overthrow of the regimes.[5]

Most of the Arab leaders have been in power for decades since the struggle for national liberation in the 1940s and 50s against the French and the British colonialism of the Middle East and North Africa. The President of Syria, Bashar Assad, King Abdullah the second of Jordan and the King Mohamed the fifth of Morocco all inherited political power through their fathers. In the last few years Mubarak was preparing the ground for his son Gamal to take power, had he been able to pass it on.

Imbalance of power between the Palestinians and Israel

Israel imposed military rule on the Palestinians who remained within the borders of the newly created state of Israel in 1948 and have imposed complex dual legal systems and policies on the Palestinians in the West Bank and Gaza Strip since 1967; one for the Jewish settlers and another for the Palestinians. The settlers enjoy civil and political rights as the state's Jewish citizens while on the other hand the Palestinians have been denied civil and human rights. "A prolonged system and structure of discrimination has led to severe economic deprivation, exhaustion, despair and denial of the national rights of the Palestinians."[6]

Israel has total military control over the Palestinian territories including entry and exit from the territories and it has imposed a restriction on the movement of the Palestinians within the territories through hundreds of checkpoints and travel orders. It also has control over resources such as water and land, planning and building permissions.

Reflections on the Impact of the Arab Revolution on Palestinians

This section will discuss the influence of the Arab revolutions on Palestinian society and politics; it will argue that the political changes in Egypt, Tunisia and Syria provided opportunities and possible new directions for the Palestinian struggle for independence.

Reconciliation between Hamas and Fatah

Since the election of Hamas in 2006 and the military takeover of Gaza Strip the conflict between Hamas and Fatah intensified. Hamas controlled the Gaza Strip and Fatah the West Bank. This division reflected on the daily life of the Palestinians and fostered alienation between sections of the Palestinian population.

The Arab revolutions provided motivation and justification for Palestinian youth in the West Bank and Gaza Strip to take to the street to demand dialogue and unity between Hamas and Fatah and call for the formation of new unity government. They were critical of both parties because they represented their own parochial interests rather than the popular aspirations of the Palestinians. Palestinians are aware that to face Israel they have to find a way to unite and hold a clear strategy. The leadership of Hamas and Fatah become more sensitive to public opinion and demands for unity but not without demonstrators having to face violence by the Palestinian security forces.

Egypt played a leading mediation role since 2007 between the two parties. However, all the attempts failed. There were different factors that contributed to the failure of dialogue and reconciliation efforts. An important factor is that any agreement between Hamas and Fatah needed the Israeli government and US approval. Both had the leverage over Mubarak not to support any agreement that might strengthen Hamas's and its allies' influence.

The strategic changes produced by the Arab revolutions presented new opportunities and space to restart the dialogue on new ground. The removal of Mubarak, an ally of Fatah and an acknowledged disenchantment with the US permitted a reorientation amongst the factions. The split between Hamas and Fatah has been reflected through regional powers in the Middle East; Egypt and US as supporters of the Palestinian National Authority (PNA) and Fatah while Hamas has been aligned with Syria and Iran.

The fall of the Mubarak regime and the unstable Assad regime in Syria, where Hamas has its headquarters has created new dynamics that lean towards Cairo. This situation has been further enhanced by the "likely improvement in the bilateral relations; the prospect that the Muslim Brotherhood (Hamas's parent organisation) would play increasingly central role in the Egyptian politics".[7] The geographical proximity and the historical ties with Egypt further motivated Hamas to sign the agreement on 4 May 2011. According to the agreement a unity government will be formed mostly from technocrats and independents in preparation for Presidential, legislative council, and Palestinian National council election within a year. The control of the security forces is to be delayed until the election. However, new mechanisms were put in place for the start of reconciliation at the grassroots level.

A short time after the fall of Mubarak's regime the military council met with the Hamas leadership and introduced new arrangements for the Rafah crossing, which had been under Egyptian control. This new arrangement allowed more people especially those in need of medical treatment to leave the Gaza Strip.

Nonviolent marches back to Palestine
The "Arab Spring" highlighted the significance of nonviolent strategies in the Palestinian struggle and encouraged people to use nonviolent tactics

to achieve their national and civil rights. In an act of remarkable courage thousands of Palestinian refugees from Syria crossed the heavily protected border with Israel on 15 May 2011, to commemorate Nakba day (Catastrophe day). This action highlighted the plight of the refugees and showed that the Arab regimes do not have the legitimacy and the authority to decide their fate.

This nonviolent protest, inspired by the Arab revolutions and the mass actions in Tahrir Square, the streets of Tunisia and Yemen, was enacted simultaneously in the West Bank, on the borders of Lebanon, Syria, Jordan and Gaza with Israel. Israel cracked down heavily on the protesters and it was reported that more than twenty demonstrators been killed over the different locations. However, Israel's use of military power to suppress nonviolent civil resistance failed and made clear that highly sophisticated aircraft and missiles cannot prevent such an action. Ehud Barak, Israeli defence minister warned that "we are just at the start of this matter and it could be that we'll face far more complex challenges".[8]

In 1948 thousands of Palestinians were forced out of their homes to the neighbouring Arab countries. The recent nonviolent action provided hope for them in their demand for participation in the peace process and the right to return. These marches were organised by young people through social networks media such as Facebook and YouTube.

The Arab revolutions highlighted the demands of millions of people in the Arab world for freedom and democracy, participation, social justice and an end to corruption. These calls gave the Palestinian leadership cause for concern given that the PNA had been frequently accused of mismanagement and corruption. It is not by accident that one of Fatah's executive committee members was expelled on corruption charges and now faces legal prosecution.

This also accelerated the call to replace the PLO old guard and give the young generation a chance to play a role in shaping the future of the Palestinian society and polity. For some years the young generation who were born and have lived under Israeli occupation since 1967 have been demanding participation in a greater role in politics.

The Palestinian Israeli conflict is at the core of the conflict in the Middle East. For many years the Palestinian resistance was a source of pride and admiration from neighbouring Arab countries and over the years they have made a great show of their support for their follow Arabs in Palestine. Now it is the Palestinians turn to look to the revolutions in Egypt, Tunisia and Yemen as a source of inspiration and model for progressive change. This has changed the image of Arab citizens in the eyes of the Palestinians.

The "Arab Spring" instilled a new sense of possibilities amongst Palestinians and the plan to seek UN recognition of the state in the areas occupied since 1967 might be a turning point in the nonviolence resistance

Consequences of Arab revolution on Israel:

Fear from democracy in the Arab world

The corrupt and undemocratic regimes in the Middle East suited Israel's interests and image. Israel revelled in the claim to be the sole democracy in the Middle East. The Arab leaders lacked credibility and support amongst their people given that they violate their basic human and political rights. Therefore the Arab dictators had no moral legitimacy to criticise Israel about its violation of human rights in the Palestinian occupied territories or to make a credible demand for statehood for the Palestinians.

The first response to the Arab revolutions, by both the Israeli public and the politicians, was of complete surprise and denial portraying it as unauthentic and short-lived. Their propaganda focused on the "danger to Israel" and the risk that the "Muslim Brothers" would gain power. The Israeli image of the Arabs is one of being "anti-Semitic" and "Islamist in nature". Arabs are perceived as undemocratic, fundamentalist, accepting of oppression and hierarchical authority so it does not fit with this belief that they will call for social justice, freedom and democracy. Israel wants to maintain it's image as the "only democracy in the Middle East" and as the "shining star" in the Arab darkness of the Middle East.[9] Essentially Israel generally does not associate itself culturally, politically or economically as part of the Middle East but part of the West.

However, by mid-March this tone had changed and the Israeli public become more aware that this is a historical change sweeping the region and the main concern of the military and the government is to assess the impact of the Arab revolution on the relationship with their peace partners: Egypt and Jordan.

Israel has never supported democratic change in the Arab world nor stood up against the violation of human rights in the Arab countries nor encouraged the work of civil society organisations there. The Israeli immediate response has been insular; that "we are not part of it" and they have advocated that more resources should be allocated to complete the building of the wall between Gaza and Egypt.

The Arab/Israeli relations have been characterised by Israel's military superiority and the use of military power to maintain its control of the region. The unarmed civil resistance in the Middle East has undermined Israel's doctrine of military force. It is possible that Israel is now aware that military might will not be able to deal with a determined popular nonviolent movement. As the Israeli Defence Minister said to the *Haaretz* newspaper: "The Palestinians transition from terrorism and suicide bombings to deliberately unarmed mass demonstrations is transition that will present us with difficult challenges."[10]

The wind of change in the Middle East also inspired thousands of Israelis this summer. It is estimated that more than 300,000 demonstrators took to the streets of Tel Aviv on 6 August 2011 and more in other cities to press their demands for social justice and to protest over the lack of housing, expensive rents and the high cost of living that has hit mainly the poor but also the middle income bracket in Israel. The campaign started with a handful of tents erected in the centre of Tel Aviv to highlight the social and economic injustice in Israel and the movement rapidly mushroomed into more than fifty Arab and Jewish localities in Israel benefitting from wide public acclaim and enthusiastic support.

This movement was exceptional for Israel and managed to bring under one umbrella political and social groups from the entire political spectrum; right and left, secular and religious, Jews and Arabs. It even included settlers from the occupied territories which caused intense controversy. Netanyahu, the Israeli Prime Minister, could not ignore this movement and immediately set up a committee to meet with the protesters and suggest recommendations.

These protests along with earlier demonstrations organised by the Israeli left to highlight 44 years of Israeli occupation of the West Bank and Gaza, which attracted a significant participation of more than 20 000 people, were inspired by the "Arab Spring".

Conclusion

The Arab Spring or revolutions inspired both Palestinians and Israelis to take nonviolent direct actions to address social and political issues. The use of nonviolence for social and political change has questioned Israel's military doctrine and highlighted the human security aspects of the citizens and inspired many people struggling for peace and justice including the Palestinians. The widespread demand for democratic changes and respect for human rights has delegitimised the Arab regimes and its dictatorships and opened the door to a new era of self determination and change.

In the case of Libya the military intervention and the removal of Gaddafi from power will without a doubt hinder the nonviolent mass action demanding social and political change. The reliance on Western military intervention will weaken this movement in the Arab countries and the world and reinforce the military doctrine of the West to bring "democracy" through military intervention as has been the case in Iraq and Afghanistan.

The "Arab Spring" with its mass participation of ordinary citizens from all walks of life has challenged the West and the US philosophy that they can bring democracy to the Middle East through "regime change". The invasion of Iraq and Afghanistan aimed to topple the regime and establish Western-style democracy in the region. The Arab revolutions countered this new colonial ideology of imposing liberal type democracy showing that true change is home grown, owned and developed by the people in this case the people of Egypt, Tunisia and Libya today – but tomorrow this could equally be the case for the people of Palestine and Israel.

Notes
[1] Michael Theodoulu, the *National*, 27 July 2011
[2] Avi Shlaim, *The Iron Wall: Israel and the Arab World*, London: Penguin Books, 2000 p. 17
[3] Avi Shlaim, *Israel and Palestine: Reappraisals, Revisions, Reflections.* London: Verso, 2009, part 1. See also ibid pp 11-22
[4] Noam Chomsky, *Hopes and Prospects*, London, Penguin Books, 2010. For more details see chapter ten pp 251-258.

[5] Heather Deegan, *Third Worlds: The Politics of the Middle East and Africa*, London: Routledge, 1996 pp 154-156. For more details see the web site and reports of Transparency International

[6] Marwan Darweish, Human Rights and the Imbalance of Power: The Palestinian-Israeli Conflict, Veronique Dudouet and B. Schmelzle (eds) *Human Rights and Conflict Transformation: The Challenge for Just Peace*, Germany: Berghof Handbook Dialogue Series 9, 2010 p. 88

[7] Crisis Group International, *Palestinian Reconciliation: Plus Ça Change*, Middle East Report No. 10, July 2011 p. 1

[8] Jonathan Cook, On an old anniversary, a new sense that change is possible, the National, 17 May 2011. See also www.economist.com/blogs/democracyinamerica/2011/05/israel_and_palestine_0, accessed on 16 August 2011

[9] Interview conducted with Israeli Jewish academic on 15 June 2011

[10] *Haaretz* Hebrew newspaper, 15 May 2011

Note on the author

Dr Marwan Darweish is a Senior Lecturer at the Centre for Peace and Reconciliation Studies (CPRS) at Coventry University and an expert in peace processes and conflict transformation. He has extensive experience across the Middle East region and a special interest in the Israeli/Palestinian conflict and ongoing peace negotiations. He has wide-ranging experience in leading and facilitating training courses and undertaking consultancies associated with conflict transformation and peace processes. He has also led conflict management and transformation programmes in East and Central Africa. Before joining Coventry University, Dr Darweish worked as Peace and Conflict advisor at Responding to Conflict (RTC). Email contact: m.darweish@coventry.ac.uk

Africa and the "Arab Spring": Analysis of Selected *Nation* (Nairobi) Commentaries

Too many Western media outlets promoted anti-Gaddafi propaganda uncritically. At least that is the view of commentators in a leading Nairobi newspaper examined here by Okoth Fred Mudhai

Introduction

The uprisings in the Arab world during 2010/11 have been viewed as manifestations of the public sphere theory[1] – especially the digital public sphere variant[2] – with the expansion of spaces for dissent in a wave of protests. As Seyla Benhabib commented:

> The transnational media revealed the lies that the state-owned televisions and some newspapers in these countries had been spewing for years. Much has been made of the force of the new media such as Facebook and Twitter in these revolutions, and this is undoubtedly true.[3]

Yet this assertion is contentious, going by some of the papers at a September 2011 Copenhagen conference, themed "Covering the 'Arab Spring': Middle East in the Media – Media in the Middle East",[4] and debates at a London conference I attended in March 2011 on "Children and Young People's Media in Africa: Evolving Markets, Producers and Audiences".[5]

Using basic thematic analysis,[6] this chapter examines five commentaries – by Kituyi,[7] Mutiga,[8] Onyango-Obbo,[9] Samora,[10] and Sigei[11] – sampled mainly[12] from a database search covering 1 June 2011 to 9 September 2011 using the term "Libya" for "Op-Ed" category allowing "all words" and "text only" on the website of the *Nation* (www.nation.co.ke). The aim of this limited study is to gain an insight into some of the recurring themes in one of Africa's top national newspapers published by an "independent"[13] regional multimedia conglomerate, the Nation Media Group (www.nationmedia.com).

Libya is chosen as it is the latest "Arab Spring" uprising, while the period is chosen to allow the latest insights as well as capture speculation about long-term impacts, while opinion articles are chosen due to very limited original sourcing-reporting of the North African crises by African media. These have relied mainly on agency copy and Western broadcasters with better resources and comparatively lower risks. Four forward-looking themes emerge from the small sample – media bias, contagion, reconstruction, and the pan-African project.

Common Themes

Mutiga argues that major Western media outlets such as the BBC, Sky and CNN swallowed imperialist propaganda by "spinning the Libyan civil war as a virtuous effort by the West to advance the cause of freedom", and Nato's bombardment as aiming to "protect civilians" when "it is a transparent effort to topple an anti-Western dictator" in an oil-rich country.

Examples he gives includes the *Daily Mail* story on a charity's report that Gaddafi fighters were "fuelled by Viagra" to use rape as a weapon[14] and stories "that the Gaddafi side has only been surviving with the help of black African mercenaries", thus greatly endangering the lives of many of the migrant workers, in order to "portray Gaddafi as a hopelessly unpopular tyrant" for whom Libyans would not fight voluntarily.

Mutiga continues: "The performance of the BBC throughout the conflict has been particularly disappointing (p. 1)...The BBC even went to the extent of showing Indians rallying in support of an anti-graft crusader and said those were pictures of Libyans celebrating a taste of freedom in Tripoli" (p. 2). Mutiga does not condemn all Western media, as he singles out the *Independent* for highlighting the other side of the story, such as "one where 30 black men were shot at close range". Indeed Patrick Cockburn[15] reported at length the results of an Amnesty International (AI) investigation that found no evidence of systematic rape, use of mercenaries or use of heavy weapons against civilian crowds by Gaddafi's side. Cockburn (2011) generously quotes a crucial part of the report by the AI[16] (which during the run-up to the Iraq conflict of 1991 accepted uncritically the misinformation about Iraqi troops seizing babies from incubators in Kuwait) on Libya:

> Much Western media coverage has from the outset presented a very one-sided view of the logic of events, portraying the protest movement as entirely peaceful and repeatedly suggesting that the regime's security forces were unaccountably massacring unarmed demonstrators who presented no security challenge.

Mutiga calls for "serious pan-African media houses that tell their own story rather than hoping self-interested Westerners can somehow do the job". Of course, as he acknowledges in his article, African media – including his newspaper – relied heavily on Western media and news agencies for continuous coverage of such major events.

Onyango-Obbo points out that "one issue that has been discussed more than the rest is whether the North African uprisings can happen with the same result in sub-Sahara Africa". To Samora, the "Arab Spring" – especially the defeat of Gaddafi – "has inspired down-trodden people across Africa" although, tellingly, he notes "few Zimbabweans had the courage to celebrate publicly, preferring to exchange messages via social networks and other discreet platforms" (p. 1). He cites recent events in Senegal and Ivory Coast as harbingers and suggests Uganda and Zimbabwe are at risk. Small windows of freedom make contagion difficult but major reform battles cannot be ruled out long-term.

One of Kenya's top civil society leaders is reported to have sent "Arab Spring"-related warning signals to sub-Saharan African (SSA) countries eager to share in China's US $80 billion turn-a-blind-eye foreign direct investment and trade deals with the continent.[17] Sigei notes that the National Council of NGOs' chairman Ken Wafula cautioned at a China-Africa forum in Nairobi that "… it was becoming increasingly clear economies that grow without corresponding expansion in democracy will sooner or later collapse…Libya is a good example in Africa".

Onyango-Obbo thinks analysts have phrased this question of contagion wrongly. "I was one of those who early in the year asked whether the Arab revolt could spread to the rest of Africa. I was mistaken. I asked the wrong question." He appears to suggest that it is the Arab North that is catching up with the struggles for freedom and democracy that have been going on for decades in SSA.

Reconstruction is key to the long-term impact of the "Arab Spring". Recent moves include a pledge of US $38 billion by a global partnership, of eight governments and about the same number of international lenders, to facilitate democratic and economic reforms in "Arab Spring" countries – Tunisia, Egypt, Morocco and Jordan.[18]

Former Kenyan Trade Industry Minister Kituyi argues that SSA countries which "benefitted immensely from the largesse of the Gaddafi regime" who "pretend away the reality that the gravy train is gone" are ruling themselves out of Libya's reconstruction holding on to "their sense of being orphaned by Gaddafi". Dr Kituyi, a director of the Kenya Institute of Governance, warns that Africa's absence from post-Gaddafi deliberations "has reduced Africa's role in the shaping of one of the most important governments on the African continent in the coming days". If this reconstruction works positively, then Onyango-Obbo envisages:

> …a possible new pattern…in which the most democratic and wealthy nations in Africa are the bottom of the continent (South Africa, Botswana, Mauritius, Cape Verde, Zambia), and its tip (Tunisia, Egypt. Libya). The poor and repressive ones will be clustered in the middle. Sub-Sahara Africa as a political and economic concept will make less sense.

One other theme has been the fate of Gaddafi's United States of Africa project, as Onyango-Obbo comments:

> Now that he is about to be history, questions are being asked whether the new Libyan government will keep up his big pan-African project. Indeed, ever since the wave of "Arab Uprising" revolts ousted Tunisia's Zine al-Abidine Ben Ali in January and Egypt's Mubarak a month later, the relationship between the mainly Arab North of Africa and its "sub-Sahara" south part have gained prominence.

The writer's prediction is that "it is impossible to see the government that succeeds him investing as much money and time into it as the colonel did". He thinks this will be "a good thing", as pushing the idea more gently would make it more palatable and thus massage the egos of the more stubborn leaders. "Gaddafi's departure could be a boon for African unity," the writer predicts, adding that failing that, the "Arab Spring" will still have "shifted the narrative of African politics in a progressive direction" going by the perceived unity in favour of Gaddafi – ignoring the increasing number of countries, such as Nigeria and Ghana, recognising the rebel's National Transitional Council.

Conclusion

Of the recent "Arab Spring" uprisings that felled strongmen in Tunisia and Egypt, the one most painful for SSA presidents, prime ministers and their cronies is the fall of Libya's Gaddafi. He had used his oil resources to play patron to many of them – financing elections, entering into business deals and providing hope for a more powerful united Africa.

The Gaddafi regime's assistance with freedom struggles in South Africa and in Zimbabwe perhaps accounts for Mugabe's expulsion of Libyan diplomats from Harare for acknowledging the NTC. And they partly help explain the Africa Union's attempts to promote a negotiated end to the conflict in Libya. These together with the increasing dangers to black Africans – including journalists – perceived as mainly mercenaries in Libya, provide the context for African media commentators' views on the "Arab Spring".

Notes

[1] Benhabib, Seyla (2011) Arab Spring: Religion, Revolution and the Public Sphere, Social Science Research Council. Available online at http://publicsphere.ssrc.org/benhabib-the-arab-spring-religion-revolution-and-the-public-square/, accessed on 9 September 2011. Also *Eurozine*. Available online at http://www.eurozine.com/articles/2011-05-10-benhabib-en.html, accessed on 9 September 2011

[2] Zuckerman, Ethan (2011) Arab Spring and the Digital Public Sphere. Available online at MIT,cfp.mit.edu/events/11May/CFP%20Spring%202011%20PDFs/Zuckerman-CFP-Spring-2011.pdf, accessed on 9 September 2011

[3] Benhabib, Seyla op cit

[4] See http://www.i-m-s.dk/page/covering-arab-spring#abstracts, accessed on 9 September 2011

[5] See http://www.westminster.ac.uk/schools/media/camri/events/camri-events-calendar/2010/childrens-and-young-peoples-media-in-africa-evolving-markets,-producers-and-audiences, accessed on 9 September 2011

[6] Boyatzis, Richard E. (1998) *Transforming Qualitative Information*, London: Sage.

[7] Kituyi, Mukhisa (2011) Africa must come to terms with change of guard in Tripoli', *Sunday Nation* 3 September 2011, Available online at http://www.nation.co.ke/oped/Opinion/Africa+must+come+to+terms+with+change+of+guard+in+Tripoli+/-/440808/1229770/-/item/0/-/bmm59l/-/index.html, accessed on 9 September 2011

[8] Mutiga, Muriithi (2011) BBC's wartime propaganda in Libya illustrates need for pan-African media, *Sunday Nation*, 3 September 2011. Available online at http://www.nation.co.ke/oped/Opinion/-/440808/1229710/-/item/0/-/s436yez/-/index.html, accessed on 10 September 2011

[9] Onyango-Obbo, Charles (2011) Why we were wrong about Gaddafi, Ben Ali and Egypt's Hosni Mubarak, *Sunday Nation*, 24 August 2011. Available online at http://www.nation.co.ke/oped/Opinion/-/440808/1224602/-/mu51joz/-/index.html, accessed on 9 September 2011

[10] Samora, Mwaura (2011) Will the Arab uprising spread to sub-Saharan Africa? *Daily Nation*, 8 September 2011. Available online at http://www.nation.co.ke/Features/DN2/Will+the+Arab+uprising+spread+to+Sub+Saharan+Africa/-/957860/1232568/-/nfbwby/-/index.html, accessed on 9 September 2011

[11] Sigei, Julius (2011) China targets civil society in final onslaught on West's hold in Africa', *Saturday Nation*, 9 September 2011. Available online at http://www.nation.co.ke/News/-/1056/1233468/-/10fxwt7z/-/index.html, accessed on 9 September 2011

[12] Two of the relevant articles examined, falling in this period, did not come up in the stated research results so they were selected purely on a combination of headline words and prominence of their headline link on the home page

[13] The firm is associated with founder and key shareholder, the Aga Khan – worldwide leader of Ismaili Muslims numbering more than 20 million – who has business and charity interests in Kenya and makes a point of meeting the President at State House whenever he visits the country

[14] 27 April 2011. Available online at http://www.dailymail.co.uk/news/article-1380364/Libya-Gaddafis-troops-rape-children-young-eight.html, accessed on 10 September 2011). The UK paper is considered to have "outdone itself" by DisInfo

watch website. See online at http://www.disinfo.com/2011/04/british-newspaper-claims-gaddafis-viagra-fueled-troops-raping-children/, accessed on 10 September 2011, with one commentator likening this to the "incubator babies" propaganda during the lead-up to the Iraq conflict of 1991

[15] Cockburn, Patrick (2011) Amnesty questions claim that Gaddafi ordered rape as weapon of war, *Independent* , 24 June 2011. Available online at http://www.independent.co.uk/news/world/africa/amnesty-questions-claim-that-gaddafi-ordered-rape-as-weapon-of-war-2302037.html, accessed on 9 September 2011

[16] AI appears to have learnt from its previous mistakes as it was one of those who fell for the now familiar Kuwaiti incubator babies hoax, which influenced the Iraq Operation Desert Storm in 1991, though they later announced they had found no evidence of the claim

[17] Sigei, Julius op cit

[18] Viscusi, Gregory (2011) G8: Lenders mobilise $38b for "Arab Spring", Bloomberg, 10 September 2011. Available online at http://www.bloomberg.com/news/2011-09-10/g-8-aid-to-arab-spring-nations-to-be-boosted-to-38-billion-baroin-says.html, accessed on 9 September 2011

Note on the author

Dr Mudhai is a Senior Lecturer in Journalism and Global Media-Communication at Coventry University, UK. His publications include a chapter on internet and journalism in *Beyond Boundaries: Cyberspace in Africa* (2002), a chapter on civic use of mobile phones in *Reformatting Politics: Information Technology and Global Civil Society* (2006), a chapter on radio culture in *Popular Media, Democracy and Citizenship in Africa* (2010) and a number of journal articles. He is co-editor of *African Media and the Digital Public Sphere* (2009) and was part of IT and Civil Society Network at the US Social Science Research Council (2003-2005). His journalism awards include two on ICT at global level. He was a full-time journalist at the Standard Group (Nairobi) in the 1990s, also contributing to outlets in Africa, the UK and the USA.

Afterword

"A Radical New Approach to Academic Publishing"

Tim Luckhurst, Professor of Journalism at the University of Kent, highlights the way in which this text draws together the work of academics and practising journalists in a unique and fully up-to-date exploration of the "Arab Spring" coverage. He concludes: "It makes real a commitment to engagement and relevance that is a credit to the academy and evidence of its social and democratic value"

Since the Gavrilo Princip of the "Arab Spring", Mohammed Bouazizi, set himself alight in the Tunisian town of Sidi Bouzid, on 17 December 2010, the forces he unleashed have been gathering momentum. Within weeks, the Tunisian President, Zine El Abidine Ben Ali, was in exile. Rolling on, the wave reached Bahrain, Egypt, Jordan, Libya, Syria and Yemen. Hosni Mubarak has appeared in an Egyptian court of law. Bashar al-Assad has confronted the inspiring courage of unarmed Syrians yearning to be free.

As I write Emirs, Kings and Presidents for Life are still reaching for mechanisms of oppression as fury expresses the boiling frustration of peoples denied freedom, prosperity and fundamental rights. Lazy characterisations of peoples and traditions as uniquely accepting of totalitarian government are falling apart beneath a torrent of evidence.

Governments in Europe, North America, the Middle East and Africa have agonised about how to balance economic self-interest, strategic priorities and ideological principles. Indecision gave way to a decisive UN resolution and robust intervention in Libya, but protesters in Bahrain and Syria died unaided. Liberal interventionists discovered relativism, isolationists flirted with principle and the voice of the people was heard in streets and squares on which it had long been silenced by intimidation or force.

Exiled idealists returned to campaign and sometimes to fight for freedom in their homelands. Electorates in wealthy democracies saw their armed forces deployed in conflicts they struggled to comprehend. Electorates battered by recession saw military and overseas aid spending rise when domestic expenditure would not. Revolutionaries who believed they had won feared for their dreams as transitional governments adopted their own versions of repression and political engagement posed new challenges.

Whether seeking to influence or organise, to participate or merely to understand, citizens sought information and clarity. News organisations, many of them impoverished by the economic impact of the internet, rushed to respond with sparkling new technology and often limited expertise. User-generated content offered some answers, but the burden of depicting and explaining dramatic and baffling events to the watching world was born by professional journalists.

Reporting Compounded by New Complexities
For these reporters and their editors, the challenge of a fast-moving and immensely significant story has been compounded by new complexities. Modern lightweight digital technology offers unique opportunities to cover protests, battles and humanitarian consequences in real time. But while the kit can deliver images, sounds and text with ease, and at unprecedented speed, the risks and ethics involved in using it are more complicated than ever.

Plugging a miniature satellite dish into a truck's cigarette lighter is the work of seconds. Deciding where to point the camera it supports is harder. Which pictures, words and sounds best convey the reality of events and emotions in that place at that moment? Truly difficult is blending these fragmentary reports with the explanation and analysis needed to convert impression into understanding. Modern editors struggle incessantly to make sense of the events they convey. Their task is complicated by a stream of user-generated content, much of it deliberately misleading, some of it clearly and intensely revealing.

To these challenges must be added old constants of international conflict and unrest reporting; language barriers, absence of authoritative sources and torrents of rumour and hyperbole, each passionately believed by the crowd until a better one replaces it. Wars and revolutions change but the fog they create is still as thick. And then there are the deadlines; more pressing than ever as rolling broadcast news competes with instantly updatable newspaper websites and amateur blogs that range from the intriguing to the overtly deranged. Professional newsrooms had only begun to understand these products of a horizontally connected world when an old enemy, fantasy masquerading as insight, emerged in the form of that lesbian who never was, the "Gay Girl in Damascus".

The First News-Worthy Events of the Multimedia Era

Granted, the phenomenon called the "Arab Spring" has not produced the first newsworthy events of the multimedia era. Much of the technology deployed to cover these events has been used before in Afghanistan, Iraq and the Gaza Strip. Some of the problems have been encountered too and professional newsrooms are accustomed to learning fast. But in locations including Tunisia, Egypt and Libya the revolutionary uprisings of 2011 have produced opportunities for reporting without restriction, censorship and embedding that are comparable to those that existed in Barcelona in the first months of the Spanish Civil War in 1936. Reporters willing to take personal risks have experienced freedom to investigate and explore of a type experienced by George Orwell, Martha Gellhorn and the *Chicago Tribune* correspondent, Jay Allen.

The range of potential subject matter is vast: fighting, non-violent protests and brutal repression have vied for attention with political ideologies, humanitarian concerns and international diplomacy. Corruption, development and injustice are in the editorial mix, so too propaganda, constitution building, horizontal communication and myth-making. The representation of women in leadership roles and of events by women journalists has received attention, but, like other important topics, these issues have struggled to beat the instant attention-grabbing power of bombs and bullets and the sophisticated spin machines deployed by Western governments.

So how well or badly have journalists performed? Have professional, top-down big-media organisations deployed their resources to good effect? Have they been effectively challenged by alternative journalism's occasionally valuable ability to challenge mainstream story-telling and shine a spotlight on its flaws? Has peer-to-peer communication between citizens on social networks challenged the authority of professional reporting? Has journalism as a profession demonstrated new confidence and sensitivity as the curator of accurate, fact-based reporting firmly located in appropriate context? Has awareness of human suffering at last taken its rightful place alongside the kinetic drama of conflict?

Has Journalism Performed its Fourth Estate Functions?

There has been plurality in the supply of news, but has it delivered the diversity convinced liberals know is essential if good is to drive out bad in the market for ideas? Has journalism produced during the "Arab Spring" performed its fourth estate duties by informing and investigating, promoting empathy and delivering a balanced and comprehensive first draft of history? Or has it confirmed the ideological prejudices of critics who believe big media exists for no more noble purpose than to sell a product called news as Mohammed Bouazizi tried to sell fruit and vegetables?

Academics who purport to study and understand journalism have scant purpose if they cannot attempt to answer such questions meaningfully and at a speed that renders their conclusions relevant. In the past, academic study of journalism has declined to meet such challenges. Influenced by the culture of less urgent disciplines and persuaded by the bizarrely counter-intuitive notion that a job worth doing well must be done slowly, they have procrastinated beyond the point of relevance.

This is among the reasons that few good journalists have taken the academic study of their profession seriously. Certain, as they must be, that important work must be done fast, and that quality and speed are partners, not antagonists, journalists have tended to ridicule the cautious, plodding pace of academic endeavour if they have noticed it at all.

Further limiting the academy's speed of response and its ability to sponsor public exchange of ideas has been the traditionally glacial pace of academic publishing. It is sad but true that many academics take months to review an article and much longer to write one. Important academic books are published less rapidly than ships are built.

But, in the last few years, a developing partnership between academics, professional journalists and the news industry has started to challenge the atmosphere of complacency and the slothful approach to publishing. At its heart are two people and one excellent idea made possible by new technology and hard work. The people are the editors of this book John Mair, of Coventry University, and Richard Lance Keeble, of the University of Lincoln.

Pioneering a New Model
Determined that debate about current controversies in journalism should be informed by academic analysis, and that it should make real impact, they have pioneered a new model in academic publishing. Keeble and Mair use digital communications, electronic editing and on-demand printing to take academic books from conception to publication in six months.

They start with a conference, sponsored and reported by the BBC College of Journalism, at which leading academics, top journalists and interested students gather to discuss and debate. These Coventry Conversations attract stellar casts from newsrooms, universities and the cyber sphere. Those who cannot be physically present contribute via webcast.

From this excellent starting point, the editors proceed to commission a blend of fully referenced and tightly reviewed chapters by academics and contributions by working journalists who are intimately familiar with the issues. The finished volumes are launched in locations where journalists and their critics gather. London's Frontline Club has been a popular venue. It is always packed, with standing room only available as discussion ranges widely over topics raised in the most recent volume.

335

This book is the latest in a pioneering and brilliantly successful series that has taken huge steps to connect and stimulate readers within and beyond the academy with practitioners in journalism. By beating the lethargic publishing schedules that so often restrict academia's ability to achieve impact it narrows the gulf between journalism theory and journalism practice. By abandoning the idle pretence that excellence and speed are incompatible with rigour it allows academic talent to engage actively with the world.

Academic study of journalism has a long way to go before it will be taken entirely seriously. Too little of it reaches the standards of accuracy, fairness and relevance attained daily by serious newspapers, broadcasters and websites. Like its predecessors, this book achieves those standards and applies to them the critical and theoretical perspectives universities know best how to teach and research.

Have Al Jazeera's journalists and citizen contributors approached the "Arab Spring" as observers or participants? How vital was Nato intervention in preventing a massacre in Benghazi as Colonel Gaddafi's regime fought back? Is 2011 in North Africa and the Middle East a delayed continuation of the events that changed Europe in 1989 or 1789? What has been the role of Twitter and other social networks in spreading revolutionary ideals? Have such mechanisms performed as their enthusiasts believe they should, giving voices to the powerless and permitting freedom of expression that is truly beyond the reach of censorship? Have they also exacerbated and accelerated the spread of rumour and conspiracy?

Have journalists tried to convey the full human and political reality of these dramatic events, or have new technologies proven as conducive to herd-mentalities and pre-conceived narratives as any that went before? Has context been absent or ignored? Have Western news media reinforced misleading pre-conceptions about the Arab and Muslim world? Did casualties of the fighting such as Tim Hetherington, the brilliant photojournalist killed in Misrata, Libya, die trying to supply crucial bits of the jigsaw others chose to ignore? Can we even be sure that representative people and forces are replacing discredited regimes or that groups depicted by Western governments as sympathetic to liberal ideals are really so inclined?

Historians will debate these issues at length. Their role will be crucial. But if an essential duty of journalism and journalism academia is to attempt an informed first draft from which citizens can extract value and historians useful evidence, then this book is an unalloyed triumph. It is to be commended not simply because of the energy, effort and excellence it has united, but because it makes real a commitment to engagement and relevance that is a credit to the academy and evidence of its social and democratic value.

Note on the author

Tim Luckhurst is Professor of Journalism at the University of Kent and the founding head of the university's Centre for Journalism. He is best known as a former editor of the *Scotsman*, Scotland's national newspaper. He began his career in journalism on BBC Radio 4's *Today* programme for which he produced, edited and reported from the UK and abroad. For BBC Radio he covered the Romanian Revolution of 1989, reported from Iraq, Israel, Jordan and Kuwait during the first Gulf War and reported the Waco Siege. He reported conflict in Former Yugoslavia from Kosovo, Macedonia and Serbia for the *Scotsman*. He was co-editor of *Today*'s coverage of the 1992 General Election and worked as the BBC's Washington Producer during the first year of the Clinton presidency. He returned to the UK to become a senior member of the team that designed, launched and edited BBC Radio Five Live. From 1995 to 1997 he was Editor of News Programmes at BBC Scotland. He joined the *Scotsman* in 1997 as Assistant Editor and was appointed Deputy Editor in 2008 and editor in January 2000. He has won two Sony Radio Academy Gold Awards for news broadcasting (*The Romanian Revolution 1989* for Radio 4's *Today* programme and the *IRA Ceasefire of 1995* for Radio Five Live). His publications include *This is Today: A Biography of the Today Programme*; It is thrown against me that I have a castle: A portrait of newspaper coverage of the Central Southwark by-election, February 1940, *Journalism Studies*, April 2011; Bias Bunkum and Capital It Is, *British Journalism Review*, June 2011; Dr Hack, I presume: Liberal Journalism in the Multimeida Age, in *Face the Future*, edited by John Mair and Richard Lance Keeble, Arima 2011, and Compromising the First Draft, in *Afghanistan War and the Media*, edited by John Mair and Richard Lance Keeble, Arima 2011 as well as contributions to *What a State: Is Devolution for Scotland the End of Britain?* He writes for publications including the *Guardian* and the *Independent* and is a frequent contributor to programmes on BBC Radio and Television, Sky News, LBC and TalkSport.

Lightning Source UK Ltd.
Milton Keynes UK
UKOW021448071111

181629UK00001B/94/P